AF798912

India Labour and Employment Report 2014

INSTITUTE FOR HUMAN DEVELOPMENT

www.ihdindia.org

The Institute for Human Development (IHD), a leading centre for studies on labour markets, livelihoods and human development, aims to contribute to the building of a society that fosters and values and inclusive social, economic and political system, free from poverty and deprivations. Towards achieving its goal, it engages in analytical and policy research, teaching and training, academic and policy debates, networking with other institutions and stakeholders, and publication and dissemination of the results of its activities. The major themes of current work of IHD are: growth and employment; education and capabilities; health and nutrition; gender and development; security and vulnerability; governance and institutions.

INDIAN SOCIETY OF LABOUR ECONOMICS

www.isleijle.org

The Indian Society of Labour Economics (ISLE) is a broad-based professional association of researchers, scholars and other stakeholders interested in the areas of labour and development issues. The Society promotes scientific studies of labour markets, industrial relations and related issues and provides a forum for exchange of ideas and dissemination of knowledge. The Indian Journal of Labour Economics, a quarterly Journal of the Society, now in its 56th year of publication, is peer reviewed and widely-circulated, promoting and featuring scientific studies on labour issues.

India Labour and Employment Report 2014

Workers in the Era of Globalization

ACADEMIC FOUNDATION
NEW DELHI
www.academicfoundation.com

INSTITUTE FOR HUMAN DEVELOPMENT
NEW DELHI
www.ihdindia.org

First published in 2014
by

ACADEMIC FOUNDATION
4772-73 / 23 Bharat Ram Road, (23 Ansari Road),
Darya Ganj, New Delhi - 110 002 (India).
Phones : 23245001 / 02 / 03 / 04.
Fax : +91-11-23245005.
E-mail : books@academicfoundation.com
www.academicfoundation.com

and

INSTITUTE FOR HUMAN DEVELOPMENT
NIDM Building, IIPA Campus
Indraprastha Estate, New Delhi -110002
Phone: + 91 11 2335 8166/2332 1610
Fax: +91 11 2376 5410
E-mail : mail@ihdindia.org
www.ihdindia.org

Cataloging in Publication Data--DK
Courtesy: D.K. Agencies (P) Ltd. <docinfo@dkagencies.com>

India labour and employment report, 2014.
p. cm.
Includes bibliographical references (p.).
ISBN 9789332701205

1. Labor market–India. 2. Manpower policy–India. 3. Globalization–Economic aspects–India. 4. Economic development–India. I. Institute for Human Development (New Delhi, India)

DDC 331.0954 23

Typeset by Italics India, New Delhi.

Printed and bound by The Book Mint, New Delhi.
www.thebookmint.in

Contents

ILER 2014 Team

Principal Author and General Editor

Alakh N. Sharma, Director, Institute for Human Development (IHD) and Editor, *Indian Journal of Labour Economics*

Principal Contributors and Senior Editors

T.S. Papola, Honorary Professor, Institute for Studies in Industrial Development and President, Indian Society of Labour Economics Research and Development Trust

D.N. Reddy, Professor, S.R. Sankaran Chair and Visiting Professor, IHD

Background Paper Writers

Sant Lal Arora, Visiting Fellow, IHD

K.P. Kannan, Chairman, Laurie Baker Centre for Habitat Studies, Thiruvananthapuram and Visiting Professor, IHD

R.P. Mamgain, Professor, Giri Institute of Development Studies, Lucknow; Formerly Senior Fellow, IHD

Balwant Singh Mehta, Associate Fellow, IHD

Dev Nathan, Professor, IHD

Gerry Rodgers, Visiting Professor, IHD and Former Director, International Institute for Labour Studies, Geneva

Sandip Sarkar, Professor, IHD

K.R. Shyam Sundar, Professor, XLRI Xavier School of Management, Jamshedpur

IHD Research and Data Processing Team

Sant Lal Arora, Visiting Fellow, IHD

Abhishek Kumar, Research Associate, IHD

Balwant Singh Mehta, Associate Fellow, IHD

Overall Reviewers

Ajit Ghose, Honorary Professor, IHD; Formerly Senior Economist, ILO

J. Krishnamurty, Visiting Professor, IHD; Former Professor, Delhi School of Economics

Gerry Rodgers, Visiting Professor, IHD and Former Director, International Institute for Labour Studies, Geneva

Preface

The eradication of poverty and expansion of productive employment to ensure work for all have been important concerns of development policy throughout the past six decades of development planning in India. However, while the country has taken several strides after Independence, the problem of widespread poverty and unemployment/underemployment still persists. The process of globalization initiated since the early 1990s has also resulted in certain trends in labour markets, which have put the employment issue centrestage. While the economy has grown at an average rate of around 6 per cent since the early 1990s and new avenues of employment opportunities have been opened, there are also large employment deficits. Most of the employment created is informal in nature and of poor quality with low productivity. The benefits of high growth have largely accrued to the better-off sections with higher educational and skill endowments. Consequently, inequalities have widened and vulnerabilities have grown and as such, the insecurities of livelihoods are widespread with a very small percentage of workers having social protection. Paradoxically, there is also evidence of tightening of the labour market as revealed by an increase in real wages at the macro level, notwithstanding a decline in some occupations at micro levels.

The industrial relations system is also undergoing significant changes in the wake of changes in the labour market. There has been an increasing trend of labour market flexibility with the expansion of flexible categories of workers such as temporary, contract and casual. There is clearly a weakening of the trade union movement and collective bargaining mechanism along with erosion of workers' rights.

Thus, the processes of liberalization and globalization have led to a significant churning in the Indian labour market, many a times leading to contradictory trends and patterns. This has also resulted in a great deal of ambiguity in policy discourse relating to labour markets and employment in the country, sometimes also leading to a hardening of positions by the stakeholders concerned such as trade unions and employers. There is also confusion among the policy-makers with regard to the employment policy because of the contradictory trends witnessed and variant arguments of the contending interest groups. While many studies have been undertaken on labour markets and employment, at both the macro and micro levels, there is lack of analytical documentation on these issues and hence ambiguities characterize the discourse on labour and employment issues in the country. There is thus a clear need for a coherent and clear picture of the emerging labour market and employment scenario to facilitate a systematic understanding of the same.

The India Labour and Employment Report (ILER) aims at bridging this gap by amalgamating information and insights from the available data and research, which is presently available only in a fragmented manner. It also attempts to bring about a better understanding regarding the status, trends and emerging perspectives pertaining to labour markets and employment. Planned as a bi-annual publication to be brought out by the Institute for Human Development (IHD) and the Indian Society of Labour Economics (ISLE), the first Report provides an overview of the labour market and employment outcomes that the Indian economy has delivered during the process of globalization. The Report assesses the gains and losses for labour in the first round of globalization. It reveals many markers of change as well as deep challenges.

The central message of this report is that it is vital to ensure an effective, responsive, fair and comprehensive labour and employment policy for achieving sustainable and inclusive development. It is hoped that the Report would contribute to a better understanding of labour markets and employment issues in India and propel them into the centre of the policy debate.

New Delhi
December 2013

Alakh N. Sharma

Director, Institute for Human Development
and Editor, *Indian Journal of Labour Economics*

Acknowledgements

This report is the outcome of the joint efforts of a team of researchers at the Institute for Human Development (IHD). Alakh N. Sharma, the principal author and general editor of the Report, coordinated the entire endeavour at IHD, and T.S. Papola (Institute for Studies in Industrial Development) and D.N. Reddy (IHD and S.R. Sankaran Chair, National Institute of Rural Development) were the principal contributors and senior editors. A number of people contributed background papers which provided the main inputs for this Report. They were: Sant Lal Arora (IHD), K.P. Kannan (Laurie Baker Centre for Habitat Studies, Thiruvananthapuram, and IHD), R.P. Mamgain (Giri Institute of Development Studies, Lucknow, and formerly at IHD), Late Ashok K. Mathur (IHD), Balwant Singh Mehta (IHD), Dev Nathan (IHD), Gerry Rodgers (IHD, and formally at the International Institute for Labour Studies), Shreya Sarawgi (IHD), Sandip Sarkar (IHD), and K.R. Shyam Sundar (XLRI Xavier School of Management). Thanks are due to all the background paper writers for their valuable contributions.

Several scholars commented on the background papers and various chapters of the Report. In particular, very useful comments were received in a workshop on the Report organized at IHD. The commentators included R. Radhakrishna (Centre for Economic and Social Studies, Hyderabad, and formerly at the National Statistical Commission), Sudipto Mundle (14th Finance Commission and National Institute of Public Finance and Policy), C.P. Chandrasekhar (Jawaharlal Nehru University), Abhijit Sen (Planning Commission), Praveen Jha (Jawaharlal Nehru University), Shailaja Fennel (Cambridge University), K. Sundaram (Delhi School of Economics), S.S. Suryanarayanan (formerly at Planning Commission) B.N. Goldar (Institute of Economic Growth), K.L. Krishna (Madras Institute of Development Studies and Delhi School of Economics), Kunal Sen (University of Manchester), Arup Mitra (Institute of Economic Growth), Himanshu (Jawaharlal Nehru University), Rohini Nayyar (Formerly at Planning Commission), K.L. Datta (Formerly in the Union Ministry of Rural Development), Ravi S. Srivastava (Jawaharlal Nehru University), S. Mahendra Dev (Indira Gandhi Institute of Development Research), Late C.S. Venkata Ratnam (International Management Institute), Kamala Sankaran (University of Delhi), Jayati Ghosh (Jawaharlal Nehru University), Navin Chandra (IHD), Late Arjun Sengupta (National Commission for Enterprises in the Unorganized Sector), Amitabh Kundu (Jawaharlal Nehru University), and T.C.A. Anant (Ministry of Statistics and Planning, and Delhi School of Economics). Immense thanks are due to all of them.

Sant Lal Arora, Abhishek Kumar and Balwant S. Mehta at IHD not only prepared the Statistical Appendices, but along with Sandip Sarkar, also helped considerably in enriching the statistical information of other chapters. The report was reviewed overall by Ajit Ghose, J. Krishnamurty and Gerry Rodgers. Their comments contributed a lot towards improving the Report. In particular, the critical suggestions of Ajit Ghose and Gerry Rodgers at various stages were immensely helpful.

The partial financial support of International Development Research Centre (IDRC), Canada, considerably facilitated the preparation of this Report. In particular, the constant encouragement and persuasion of Edgard Rodriguez expedited the process of its preparation. The contributions of IDRC and Edgard are gratefully acknowledged. The International Labour Office (ILO) also provided a small financial support at the beginning of this exercise and thanks are due to it.

Shreemoyee and Anupma Mehta ably copyedited the manuscript. Their contribution is duly acknowledged. Finally, Jyoti Girish and Priyanka Tyagi, colleagues at IHD, helped in coordinating the whole exercise of preparing and bringing out the Report. Immense thanks are due to all of them.

List of Abbreviations

AABY	Aam Aadmi Bima Yojana
AIADMK	All India Anna Dravida Munnetra Kazhagam
AITUC	All India Trade Union Congress
ASI	Annual Survey of Industries
BEWU	Bombay Electric Workers Union
BJP	Bharatiya Janata Party
BMS	Bharatiya Mazdoor Sangh
BPL	Below the Poverty Line
BPO	Business Process Outsourcing
BSS	Basic Social Security
CAGR	Compound Annual Growth Rate
CBGA	Centre for Budget and Governance Accountability
CDS	Current Daily Status
CEC	Consumption Expenditure Class
CITU	Centre of Indian Trade Unions
CLA	Contract Labour Act
CLRA	Contract Labour (Regulation & Abolition) Act
CPSE	Central Public Sector Enterprises
CSS	Contingent Social Security
CTUO	Central Trade Union Organization
CV	Coefficient of Variation
CWS	Current Weekly Status
DGE&T	Directorate General of Employment & Training
DHDR	Delhi Human Development Report
DMK	Dravida Munnetra Kazhagam
DWCRA	Development of Women and Children in Rural Areas
EAS	Employment Assurance Scheme
EMI	Employment Marketing Information
EPFO	Employees Provident Fund Organization
EPS	Employees's Pension Scheme
ESI	Employment Situation Index
ESIC	Employees' State Insurance Corporation
ESIS	Employees State Insurance Scheme
FDI	Foreign Direct Investment
FICCI	Federation of International Chambers of Commerce and Industry
FPS	Fair Price Shop
GDP	Gross Domestic Product
GE	Generalized Entropy
GER	Gross Enrolment Ratio
HMSI	Honda Motorcycles and Scooters India
IAMR	Institute of Applied Manpower Research
IAY	Indira Awas Yojana
ICFTU	International Confederation of Free Trade Unions
ICRIER	Indian Council for Research on International Economic Relations
IDA	Industrial Disputes Act
IFCEMGWU	International Federation of Chemical, Energy, Mine and General Workers' Union
IHD	Institute for Human Development
IIPA	Indian Institute of Public Administration
IIT	Indian Institute of Technology
IKP	Indira Kranthi Patham
ILC	Indian Labour Conference
ILO	International Labour Organization
INTUC	Indian National Trade Union Congress
IRDP	Integrated Rural Development Programme
IRMA	Institute for Rural Management Anand
IRS	Industrial Relations System
IT	Information Technology
ITC	Industrial Training Centre

ITES	IT-Enabled Services
ITGLWF	International Textile Garment and Leather Workers' Federation
ITI	Industrial Training Institute
ITUC	International Trade Unions Congress
IUF	International Union Federation
JGRY	Jawahar Grameen Rozgar Yojana
JMC	Joint Management Councils
JRY	Jawahar Rozgar Yojana
JSS	Jan Shikshan Sansthans
LFPR	Labour Force Participation Rate
LIC	Life Insurance Corporation
MEEU	Mumbai Electric Employees Union
MEGS	Maharashtra Employment Guarantee Scheme
MGNREGS	Mahatma Gandhi National Rural Employment Guarantee Scheme
MHRD	Ministry of Human Resource Development
MNC	Multinational Corporation
MoF	Ministry of Finance
MoLE	Ministry of Labour and Employment
MoMSME	Ministry of Micro, Small and Medium Enterprises
MoRD	Ministry of Rural Development
MRTP Act	Monopolies and Restrictive Trade Practices Act
MSE	Micro and Small Enterprises
MSMED Act	Micro, Small and Medium Enterprises Development Act
MSMEs	Micro, Small and Medium Enterprises
NASSCOM	National Association of Software and Services Companies
NASVI	National Alliance of Street Vendors of India
NCEUS	National Commission for Enterprises in the Unorganized Sector
NCHM&CT	National Council for Hotel Management & Catering Technology
NCL	National Centre for Labour
NCSD	National Council for Skill Development
NES	National Employment Service
NGO	Non-Government Organization
NLM	National Livelihoods Mission
NMSS	National Minimum Social Security
NPAs	Non-Performing Assets
NPMO	National Platform of Mass Organizations
NPS	New Pension Scheme
NPSD	National Policy on Skill Development
NREGS	National Rural Employment Guarantee Scheme
NREP	National Rural Employment Programme
NRF	National Renewal Fund
NRY	Nehru Rozgar Yojana
NSAP	National Social Assistance Programme
NSDC	National Skill Development Corporation
NSDM	National Skill Development Mission
NSS	National Sample Survey
NSSO	National Sample Survey Organization
OBCs	Other Backward Classes
PDS	Public Distribution System
PMEGP	Prime Minister's Employment Generation Programme
PMIUPEP	Prime Minister's Integrated Urban Poverty Eradication Programme
PMRY	Prime Minister's Rozgar Yojana
PPP	Purchasing Power Parity
PRIs	Panchayati Raj Institutions
RBI	Reserve Bank of India
RC	Rural Casual
REGF	Rural Employment Generation Fund
REGP	Rural Employment Guarantee Programme
REL	Reliance Energy Limited

RG&CCI	Registrar General & Census Commissioner of India
RLEGP	Rural Labour Employment Guarantee Programme
RR	Rural Regular
RSBY	Rashtriya Swasthya Bima Yojana
RUDSETIS	Rural Development and Self Employment Training Institutes
SC	Scheduled Caste
SDI	Skill Development Initiative
SEWA	Self Employed Women's Association
SEZ	Special Economic Zone
SGRY	Sampoorna Gram Rozgar Yojana
SGSY	Swarnajayanti Gram Swarozgar Yojana
SHGs	Self Help Groups
SIMA	Southern India Mills Association
SJSRY	Swarna Jayanti Shahari Rozgar Yojana
SLC	Standing Labour Committee
SME	Small and Medium Enterprises
SNCL	Second National Commission on Labour
SPF	Social Protection Floor
SSA	Sarva Shiksha Abhiyan
SSC	Sectoral Skill Council
SSIs	Small Scale Industries
ST	Scheduled Tribe
TLA	Textile Labour Association
TPDS	Targeted Public Distribution System
TRYSEM	Training of Rural Youth for Self Employment
TUFS	Technology Upgradation Fund Scheme
UBSP	Urban Basic Services for the Poor
UC	Urban Casual
UFW	Unpaid Family Worker
UNCTAD	United Nations Conference on Trade and Development
UNICEF	United Nations Children's Fund
UPA	United Progressive Alliance
UPR	Usual Place of Residence
UPS	Usual Principal Status
UPSS	Usual Principal and Subsidiary Status
UR	Urban Regular
US	Usual Status
USEP	Urban Self Employment Programme
UWEP	Urban Wage Employment Programme
UWSSA	Unorganized Workers Social Security Act
VRS	Voluntary Retirement Scheme
WCSDG	World Commission on the Social Dimension of Globalization
WDL/N	Workdays Lost in Work Stoppages per one Thousand Employees
WDL/WI	Workdays Lost per Worker Involved (Average Duration)
WDL/WS	Workdays lost per Work Stoppage (Average Volume Lost)
WI/N	Number of Workers Involved in Work Stoppages per one Thousand Employees
WI/WS	Workers involved per Work Stoppage (Average Size)
WPR	Workforce Participation Rate
WS/N	Work Stoppages per one lakh employees in the Organized Sector

Glossary

Aajeevika:	National Rural Livelihoods Mission (NRRM) – a scheme launched by Ministry of Rural Development (MoRD), Government of India in 2011, which aims at creating efficient and effective institutional platforms of the rural poor enabling them to increase household income through sustainable livelihood enhancements and improved access to financial services.
Aam Aadmi Bima Yojana:	Insurance scheme for common people (implemented by the Government of India).
Activity Status:	It is the activity situation in which a person is found during the reference period. According to this, a person could be in one or a combination of the three broad activity statuses during the reference period *viz.*, (i) working or being engaged in economic activity (work), (ii) being not engaged in economic activity (work) but either making tangible efforts to seek work or being available for work if work is available, and (iii) being not engaged in economic activity (work) and also not available for work.
Casual Employment:	All those who do not have any tenure and are mostly employed on daily wage basis are casual workers.
Coolie:	A historical term for manual labourers and a contemporary social slur.
Crore:	It is equal to ten million.
Economic Activity:	Any activity resulting in the production of goods and services that add value to the national product is considered as an economic activity for the employment and unemployment surveys conducted by NSSO.
Employment by Current Daily Status (CDS):	All those who have performed at least four hours of work on any one day of the preceding reference week of the survey are considered as working for a full day and are considered as working for half day if they pursue at least one hour in a day. Employment by CDS refers to person-days of employment, not number of persons employed.
Employment by Current Weekly Status (CWS):	All those who have performed any economic activity at least for one hour on any day of the reference week of the preceding seven days are included under CWS employment.
Employment by Usual Principal Status (UPS):	Usual principal status refers to the activity in which the worker was engaged most of the time during the reference period of last 365 days preceding the date of the survey. All those engaged in a principal activity for most of the period are covered under UPS employment.
Employment by Usual Principal and Subsidiary Status (UPSS):	Subsidiary status workers are those who are engaged in an economic activity for a smaller duration in the reference period. All those engaged in principal activity (UPS) and subsidiary activity are included in UPSS employment.
Employment Elasticity (w.r.t. growth):	Employment elasticity with respect to GDP during a period is the ratio of the average annual growth of employment to average annual growth of GDP during that period.

Employment Status:	Employment status is classified into three categories, *viz.*, self-employment, regular employment and casual employment.
Formal Workers (or Formal Employment):	Formal workers consist of those working in the unorganized/informal sector, who are regular workers with social security benefits provided by the employers and the workers in the formal sector with any employment and social security benefits provided by the employers.
Indira Awas Yojana:	A scheme of housing for the poor implemented by the Government of India.
Indira Kranthi Patham:	A state-wide poverty reduction project started by the Andhra Pradesh Government to enable the rural poor to improve their livelihoods and quality of life by setting up their own organizations.
Informal Workers (or Informal Employment):	Informal workers consist of those working in the unorganized/informal sector enterprises or households, excluding regular workers with social security benefits provided by the employers and the workers in the formal sector without any employment and social security benefits provided by the employers.
Jan Shikshan Sansthan:	A scheme of National Literacy Mission , set up by the Government of India, which aims at providing vocational skills to non-literate, neo-literates as well as school dropouts by identifying skills that have a market in the region of their establishment.
Janani Suraksha Yojana:	National Maternity Benefit Scheme.
Janashree Bima Yojana:	A special scheme for women self-help group members for insurance and education of children.
Jawahar Rozgar Yojana:	A wage employment scheme launched by the Government of India on April 1, 1989 by merging National Rural Employment Programme (NREP) and Rural Landless Employment Gaurantee Programme (RLEGP). It is not in operation now.
Kudumbashree:	A scheme launched by the Government of Kerala in 1998 for wiping out absolute poverty from the state through concerted community action under the leadership of local self governments. It is one of the largest women's empowering projects in the country.
Labour Force (LF):	Labour force constitutes all the persons who are working, seeking work and unemployed or available for work.
Labour Force Participation Rate (LFPR):	LFPR is the proportion of the country's population actively engaged in the labour market either by working or seeking work. It is an indication of the total supply of labour.
Lakh:	It is equal to one hundred thousand.
Mathadi Workers:	Headload workers.
Organized/Formal Sector:	It consists of the government/public departments and public/private enterprises plus the private enterprises which employ 10 or more workers.
Panchayati Raj Institutions:	Local governance institutions.

Rashtriya Swasthya Bima Yojana:	National Health Insurance Scheme. (A scheme implemented by the Government of India).
Regular Employment:	All those wage/salary workers who are on relatively longer tenure of works and who are usually paid wages/salary on a weekly or monthly basis.
Sampoorna Grameen Rozgar Yojana:	Universal Rural Employment Programme – a scheme launched by the Government of India to attain the objective of providing gainful employment for the rural poor in 1999.
Sarva Shiksha Abhiyan:	The Government of India's flagship programme for achievement of Universalization of Elementary Education (UEE) in a time-bound manner, as mandated by the 86th amendment to the Constitution of India providing free and compulsory education to the children in the 6-14 years age group.
Self-employment:	All those who are 'own account workers', working employers, unpaid family workers and home-based workers are included under self-employment.
Swarna Jayanti Shahari Rozgar Yojana:	A Government of India-sponsored urban employment scheme which came into effect on December 1, 1997. It provides gainful employment to urban unemployed and underemployed poor, through encouraging the setting up of self-employment ventures by the urban poor living below the poverty line
Swarozgaris:	Self-employed people.
Unemployment Rate:	Unemployment rate is the proportion of the labour force that does not have employment and is seeking and/or available for work. Unemployment rate is also expressed in terms of employment status *viz.*, Unemployment (UPS), which includes all those who did not find work during the major part of the reference period (365 days); Unemployment (UPSS): those who did not find work during the major or minor part of the year; Unemployment (CWS): those who did not find work at least for one hour in any day in the preceding week; and Unemployment (CDS): days during which the concerned persons were not in employment at least for four hours. It is expressed in person-days of unemployment.
Unorganized/Informal Sector:	Enterprises that employ less than 10 workers and are not government/ public and public/private limited are in the unorganized/informal sector. These enterprises can belong to any of the following five categories: (i) proprietary, (ii) partnership, (iii) co-operative societies/trusts/other non-profit organizations, (iv) employer's households (private households employing maid servants, watchmen, cooks, etc.), and (v) others.
Work Participation Rate (WPR):	WPR is the proportion of the country's labour force who are engaged in work.
Varishtha Pension Bima:	Old Age Pension Scheme (A scheme implemented by the Government of India).

List of Tables, Figures and Boxes

Tables

Figures

Boxes

Executive Summary

I. The Context

- India has witnessed an impressive GDP growth rate of over 6 per cent since the 1980s. Growth has been particularly rapid since the post-reform period of the 1990s. This high growth has contributed to a sustained increase in per capita income and a decline in absolute poverty, as well as modest improvement in standards of living. It has also brought important changes in employment conditions in the country.
- The structure of the labour market, patterns of employment growth, and labour-market institutions play an important role in shaping development patterns and outcomes. However, there is a lack of analytical documentation on these issues. The India Labour and Employment Report, planned as the first of a series of periodic publications by the Institute for Human Development (IHD), aims to fill the gap.
- The first report—**India Labour and Employment Report 2014**—provides analyses of the changes in the labour market and employment since the inception of economic reforms. It explores the dynamics of these changes, by looking at labour market institutions and different types of employment, and labour market policies. It also outlines the emerging agenda for policies and measures that emerge from such analyses.

II. Labour Market and Employment Conditions in India

- Today, India is counted among the most important emerging economies of the world but employment conditions in the country still remain poor.
- Overall, the labour-force to population ratio (for the age group 15 years and above) of 56 per cent is low in India as compared to nearly 64 per cent for the rest of the world. The low overall participation in India is largely because the female labour force participation rate (LFPR) is dismally low at 31 per cent, though official figures are clearly underestimated. This is amongst the lowest in the world and the second lowest in South Asia after Pakistan.
- Even today the large proportion of workers engaged in agriculture (about 49 per cent) contribute a mere 14 per cent to the GDP. In contrast, the service sector, which contributes 58 per cent of the GDP, barely generates 27 per cent of the employment, and the share of manufacturing in both employment (13 per cent) and GDP (16 per cent) is much lower than in East Asian and South-east Asian countries. This unbalanced pattern of growth is at variance with not just the experience of the fast-growing economies of East and South-east Asia but also the historical experience of the present-day developed countries of the West.
- An overwhelmingly large percentage of workers (about 92 per cent) are engaged in informal employment and a large majority of them have low earnings with limited or no social protection. This is true for a substantial proportion of workers in the organized sector as well. Over half the workers are self-employed, largely with a poor asset-base, and around 30 per cent are casual labourers seeking employment on a daily basis. About 18 per cent of those employed are regular workers, and amongst them less than 8 per cent have regular, full-time employment with social protection and the remaining 12 per cent are informal workers with no social protection.
- The levels of education and professional and vocational skills are extremely low. Less than 30 per cent of the workforce has completed secondary education or higher, and less than one-tenth has had vocational training, either formal or informal. Although these figures, based on National sample Survey Organization (NSSO) surveys, do not capture many types of skills that are informally acquired, they still suggest that skill-acquisition is generally very low.
- Since good quality 'formal' employment is rare, access to it is extremely unequal. Disadvantaged social groups such as Scheduled Castes (SCs), Scheduled Tribes (STs), and large sections of the Other Backward Classes (OBCs) are mostly concentrated in low-productivity sectors such as agriculture and construction and in low-paying jobs as casual labourers, while Muslims are concentrated in low productivity self-employment. On the other hand, upper-caste Hindus and 'others' (comprising minorities such as Jains, Sikhs and Christians), have a disproportionate share of good jobs and higher educational attainments. There is an overlap between poverty and poor quality of employment as well.
- There is considerable regional differentiation in access to good quality employment. A preliminary Employment Situation Index (ESI) prepared for this Report shows that generally workers in the southern and western states of India have much better access to good quality employment than do workers in states in the central and eastern regions. Himachal Pradesh ranks number one, in particular because of a

good performance with respect to women's employment, while Bihar ranks last.

- There is considerable segmentation in the labour market in terms of forms of employment, sector, location, region, gender, caste, religion, tribe, etc. In spite of increased mobility over the years, acute dualism and sometimes fragmentation persists in the labour market. There is a great deal of movement between places of residence and work, and rural-to-rural and rural-to-urban migration is substantial, especially in terms of circular and temporary migration.
- Women, in general, are disadvantaged in the labour market. In addition to their low share in overall employment, greater proportions of them are engaged in low-productivity, low-income, insecure jobs in farms, and in the unorganized and informal sectors as compared to men.
- As is typical for a poor and developing economy, most workers in India cannot afford to be unemployed, and hence the level of open unemployment is quite low at 2.7 per cent. Even the more comprehensive current daily status (CDS) measure of unemployment is only 5.6 per cent. In reality, the problem is not primarily one of unemployment but lack of productive employment.

III. Labour Market Performance and Employment Outcomes in the Last Three Decades

Labour markets have witnessed significant changes in two decades since the economic reforms, which started in the 1990s. There are both negative and positive aspects to these changes.

Some major concerns that have emerged from the analyses are as follows:

- There has been increasing informalization of the workforce. The transfer of workers from agriculture to non-agriculture has been slow, with some acceleration in recent years, but most of the employment generated has been informal and insecure. To illustrate, the percentage share of contract workers in the organized manufacturing sector has increased from 13 per cent in 1995 to 34 per cent in 2011. The growth of regular, protected jobs is also slow.
- A noteworthy trend has been the decline in the work participation of females during 2005-12. Taking all age groups into account, it stood at 29 per cent in 2004-05, decreasing to 22 per cent in 2011-12. Discounting for enrolment in educational institutions and the so-called income effect, this substantial decline has much to do with lack of appropriate employment opportunities for females. This is evident from the very high levels of young female unemployment. The employment of women remains 20 to 40 per cent below that of men.
- Labour market inequalities are large and disparities and inequalities have generally increased. The most striking is the disparity between the regular and casual and organized and unorganized sector workers: the average daily earnings of a casual worker stood at ₹ 138 in rural areas and ₹ 173 in urban areas in 2011-12, and that of a regular worker at ₹ 298 in rural areas and ₹ 445 in urban areas, while that of a central public sector enterprise employee was ₹ 2,005 per day. And, of course, the public sector employee has many other benefits as well as a secure job. Thus, a rural casual worker earned less than 7 per cent of the salary of a public sector employee.
- The gap between per-worker earnings in agriculture and non-agriculture has considerably widened and now stands at a ratio of 1: 6. The share of wages in total value-added in manufacturing has been declining consistently. From around 0.45 in the 1980s, it fell to around 0.25 in 2009-10. The shift from wages to profits is large, and is closely connected with acceleration of growth in recent years. Thus, there is a substantial shift towards income from capital, contributing to the overall increase in income inequality.
- The increasing 'informalization' of employment has gradually eroded the strength of trade unions. It is also evident from the sharp decline in the percentage of work-days lost due to strikes, alongside a considerable increase in the incidence of closures. As such, the space for collective bargaining has been shrinking. Recent years have witnessed a significant rise in industrial unrest in several new manufacturing units, which poses a challenge for industrial peace, and is detrimental to the growth of the manufacturing sector.

But the story is by no means entirely negative.

- Notwithstanding disparities, there has been a significant increase in real wages at the rate of over 3 per cent per year, on average, during the three decades between 1983 and 2011-12.

Labour productivity has also shown an increase, although it remains low in comparison to global figures.

- The process of informalization of the workforce seems to have halted since 2004-05. In fact, the growth of organized sector employment has been high after this period and the share increased from 11.8 per cent in 2004-05 to 17.0 per cent in 2011-12. Although the majority of this growth was still informal in nature, for the first time the share of regular formal employment increased from 6.6 to 7.5 per cent.
- The process of diversification of employment away from agriculture has also accelerated. Although the large share has gone to services and construction, and only marginally to manufacturing, the process has led to an acceleration in labour productivity. The level of per worker productivity has increased three times during the period 1993-94 to 2011-12. The wage share in the organized manufacturing sector, after declining steadily until 2007-08, started recovering to some extent in the last few years.
- The rise in wages has led to a decline in absolute poverty. Importantly, although the decline in poverty has been across all socio-religious groups, the largest decline has been observed among the SCs, STs and OBCs as well as among upper Muslims. Thanks to the reservation policy, the proportion of SCs, and to a very small extent STs, in the public sector, has increased between 1999-2000 and 2011-12, although their access to the private sector has declined. The proportion of Muslims employed in both private and public sectors has also declined. The most noticeable trend is the significant increase in the proportion of OBCs employed in both private and public sectors, and a significant decline in the proportion of upper-caste Hindus as well as 'others' in both categories. Thus it seems that access to quality employment of the deprived groups has increased at the expense of the upper strata, although access to the private sector of some groups (STs and Muslims), remains a matter of concern.
- There is a rising middle class, which includes better-educated and skilled workers with rising incomes and high levels of consumption. This may give some sustainability to the growth process.
- There has been significant growth in some advanced sectors of the economy such as information technology, automobiles, pharmaceuticals, etc., which has had a spillover effect on other sectors. Productivity in several industries has increased.
- Recent years have also witnessed a rise in the unionization of informal sector workers. The popular movements about the right to work and its implementation (in the form of the Mahatma Gandhi National Rural Employment Guarantee Act or MGNREGA), have contributed to worker awareness and improved their bargaining power. This is indeed good for democracy and workers' rights. Persistent structural inequalities by caste and gender are likewise being recognized and tackled by popular movements.

To summarize, while the three decades of rapid growth have not radically transformed the labour market and employment conditions in the country, it has brought fairly substantial improvements. Nevertheless, low productivity employment in both agriculture and other sectors continues to dominate the labour market, and the disparities and inequalities across groups and regions remain large.

IV. Employment Challenges

The challenges of employment in India are complex, which are not reflected in the low levels of open unemployment.

- The most important challenge is the large number of 'working poor' and under-employed engaged in low-productivity activities in the unorganized sectors. By the current poverty line (equivalent to about US$ 1.25 per day in terms of purchasing power parity or PPP), one-fourth of all workers—about 118 million—are poor. They are largely either casual workers or own-account workers. If the current poverty line is raised to about US$ 2 per day (in terms of PPP), the percentage of working poor will increase to nearly 58 per cent and the number of such workers would be around 276 million. Overcoming the low productivity and poor income streams of this large group is indeed a gigantic task.
- Furthermore, these figures do not fully capture the vulnerability of the working poor. The low earnings are compounded by deplorable conditions of work in many informal sector enterprises, as well as in the work premises of self-employed workers engaged in petty activities either at home or on the streets. They suffer from high health risks as well as lack of safety standards.

- Although, overall, open unemployment is low, the problem of youth unemployment, particularly that of educated youth, is gradually becoming a major concern. About 30 per cent of the total unemployed in the year 2011-12 were graduates and above, up from 21 per cent in 2004-05. Differently put, the rate of unemployment among graduates (including technically trained), and diploma holders was around 18 per cent.

- Then there will be many new entrants to the labour force and there is potential 'demographic dividend'. India's labour force is growing at a brisk rate despite the fact that more young people are increasingly opting to prolong their years of education. By 2030, India's workforce will be larger than that of China. Most of the new entrants will be in the urban areas. Providing education and skills to the growing young population and meeting their job aspirations pose a huge challenge. As the pace of migration and urbanization is likely to accelerate in the future, there will be the huge task of planning urban growth and formulating effective labour market policies. Failure to do so can be disastrous.

- The unequal access of women to employment, and discrimination in the labour market, poses yet another challenge. An important reason for the declining participation of women in work is the lack of appropriate employment opportunities. In the wake of rising educational levels, the future will witness a surge in the number of educated women; many of them will be graduates or more. At present, qualified women have much higher labour force participation than average. The country has unfortunately not been able to create enough jobs even for the limited number of educated females in the labour force. This is reflected in the very high rates of unemployment of young women—around 23 per cent among 15 to 29 year-old women, which is double that of their male counterparts. So the challenge for creating suitable employment opportunities for the youth bulge is particularly acute with regard to young women.

- The inequalities and disparities that exist in access to employment across regions and social groups remain a huge challenge in India. This is particularly evident in the distribution of formal regular jobs and employment in productive sectors, which is skewed in favour of dominant groups and certain regions. Not surprisingly, states like Bihar, Odisha, Uttar Pradesh, and Madhya Pradesh, which carry the tag of 'backward' states, fare the worst on all indicators of good quality employment and the historically deprived groups like the SCs and STs resident in these states thus face a double disadvantage in access to decent employment opportunities.

V. Policy Agenda

- A medium- to long-term employment strategy should be envisaged to deal with the challenges highlighted above. It should ensure that the organized sector, particularly manufacturing, grows much more rapidly than in the past and leads to a process of economy-wide productivity growth, along with employment expansion and rising wages. Even in the organized sector, informal employment should not grow at the cost of formal jobs.

- Regulatory interventions in informal enterprises should ensure that a minimum quality of employment is maintained and the basic rights of workers are respected. The recent growth in the productivity and wages of workers in the unorganized sector is an important and welcome development. Although small, it has important implications for employment and development policies of the country. The need is to sustain and accelerate this process.

- Appropriate policies and measures to address the issue of education and skills acquisition, and of skills mismatches need to be urgently put in place. The rising aspirations of the youth have to be met and the ongoing 'youth bulge' is likely to exacerbate this challenge. The challenge pertains not only to the achievement of a major quantitative expansion of the facilities for education and skill-training, but also to the equally important task of raising their quality. If it is to compete globally, India has to invest heavily in its National Skill Development Mission.

- There are significant differences in access to quality employment across different social groups and regions. While economic growth in India has led to an increase in the quantity of employment, the access to quality jobs is still very low. Policy also needs to take into account the social and regional dimensions of access to employment. Affirmative action policies have played a role, but some states and regions, and certain deprived sections among the social groups need special attention. There is also a need to examine whether only sub-groups within the reserved groups, the poorest amongst the upper groups, and certain sections of minorities need to be included in the gamut of affirmative action policies.

- Macroeconomic policies have been pursued independently from the employment goals of the country. There is a need for restructuring these policies to make them supportive of an appropriate employment strategy. Some of the strategies are: tax incentives for particular types of investment or economic activity, public sector investment in infrastructure or institutional support which promotes enterprise development, research and development which aims to open up new production methods which are more labour-intensive, training and skill systems which make labour more productive, labour codes which encourage hiring, promotion of small and medium enterprises that are known to be more labour-intensive and so on.
- Despite an improvement in management levels over the years, direct employment-generation programmes, with the possible exception of MGNREGA, have not had the desired impact in large parts of the country. Apart from the need for their restructuring, several of them also need to be more focused in the deprived regions. These regions include areas dominated by the tribal and backward populations, as also remote regions of the country, in order to unpack the full potential of both programmes and regions.
- Debates on labour market flexibility must be resolved in a way that meets the needs of both workers and enterprises. The question is how to ensure flexibility for market adjustments without compromising the basic interests of labour. Trade unions may agree to a job security trade-off in return for adequate separation benefits, say 45 days wages for every completed year of service as suggested by the Second National Commission on Labour, and adequate income security for all workers—employed or unemployed. It is necessary to ensure equal pay for all types of workers—regular, casual, contract, and temporary, to strictly enforce the payment of minimum wages and to provide social security to all workers. Simplification and modernization of labour laws, the necessity of which is widely felt, has to be on the agenda.
- Given the widespread insecurity of livelihoods, it is extremely important to provide a minimum level of social security to all workers, which will certainly promote flexibility. Of course, the major role in this has to be played by the government and it is now widely believed that at the present juncture of development, it is possible for the country to do this. What is needed is political will to make universal social security a reality. However, this political will also needs to be backed by an appropriate design so that social security can achieve both the goals of providing a Social Protection Floor (SPF) and contributing to the development process. Combined with better public provision of educational and medical services, a universal and portable social protection floor could function as an important instrument in pushing the economy on to the high road of not only rapid but also more inclusive and sustainable growth.
- Effective policy requires a greater effort at mapping and documenting today's principal labour and employment developments. Economic growth is creating new employment patterns and new labour market issues, new income opportunities and new forms of exploitation, new institutions and forms of organization, new linkages between work and poverty. The diverse and complex character of work and employment in India needs in-depth analyses. These aspects need to be better specified, measured and understood if more effective and equitable employment and labour policies are to be put in place. This Report provides an overview of several facets of labour and employment in India and opens the door for more in-depth research, and this will be undertaken in subsequent reports. The general statistical system of the country should proactively fill the gaps that exist in our understanding of some of these aspects of the labour market borne out of data limitations.
- Thus, this Report reveals many markers of progress as well as challenges posed by changes in the labour market in India in the last three decades. The fact that comprehensive, responsive and effective labour and employment policies remain central to sustainable and inclusive development lies at the crux of this Report.

1

Labour in Globalizing India: An Overview

1.1 Introduction

India's nearly 470 million workers account for 15 per cent of the world's workforce. As in many other parts of the world, women are under-represented in the labour market and their participation in work is also much lower in India than in many other countries. The conventional measure of overall labour force to population ratio (in the age group of 15 years and above) in India (56 per cent) is much lower than that of the world (64 per cent). The low participation in India is largely because the female labour force participation rate (LFPR) is dismally low at 31 per cent. About one half of India's workforce is employed in the agriculture sector as compared to a world average of one-third. Similarly, the self-employed constitute about 40 per cent of non-agricultural employment in India while globally, the proportion of self-employed in non-agriculture is only 30 per cent (ILO, 2012).

So the structure of India's workforce differs in important respects from the global structure. There are several other characteristics of the Indian labour force which, to say the least, are intriguing even to an Indian, particularly when seen in the current context of India's rising economic stature in the globalizing world. While the skills and salaries of the upwardly mobile Indian workers have contributed handsomely to India's prospects of emerging as an economic power, at the same time it is true that the percentage of workers who are earning less than US $1.25 per day (PPP) is about one-fourth as compared to one-eighth in the world. If we compare the workers who are earning less than US $ 2 per day (PPP) it is about 59 per cent in India as compared to only 28 per cent in the world. (ILO, 2012; Govt. of India, Planning Commission, 2012). The primary cause of poverty is not unemployment. The unemployed comprise only about 2 to 3 per cent of those in the labour force; even when the concept of unemployment is stretched to include under-employment, it only reaches about 6 to 7 per cent. Poverty among the employed is extensive; many of the openly unemployed are not poor.

> Low earnings from employment, rather than unemployment, constitute the main source of poverty

There are many such puzzles in the pattern of work and employment in India. Conventional models of economic development foresee an increase in the proportion of wage and salary earners and a decline in that of the self-employed over time. This has happened in India but rather slowly. According to the data from NSSO, even today over half of those working are self-employed who are working on their own farm or business and not for wages or salary. And their proportion has declined from 61 per cent in 1972-73 to 52 per cent in 2011-12—a decline of merely 9 percentage points over nearly four decades. There are certainly more self-employed people in rural areas (56 per cent) and this is not surprising given the number of self-employed cultivators. Nevertheless, even in urban areas the proportion is quite high at 42 per cent.

> Among the wage workers, the proportion of non-permanent, casual and contract workers has increased in the organized sector

Meanwhile, the proportion of workers in the category of regular wage/salary earners has marginally increased over several decades. It was 15.4 per cent in 1972-73, dropped to 13.2 per cent in 1993-94, has risen since then, albeit slowly, reaching a figure of 17.9 per cent in 2011-12. About 64.9 per cent of those employed on a regular basis, are in the organized sector. As per DGE&T, organized sector employment, which covers only secondary and tertiary units in the private sector employing 10 or more persons and all public sector units, after increasing during the 1980s and 1990s, continuously declined during 1997-2005 before witnessing some growth. Public sector employment has shown continuous decline since 1997, while employment in the organized private sector has shown an upturn in recent years.

It is, however, observed that as per NSSO, among wage workers, the proportion of non-permanent, casual and contract workers has increased in the organized sector. Informal workers, that is, those without employment stability and social security, constituted 41 per cent of those employed in the organized sector in 1999-2000, and their share increased to 48 per cent by 2004-05, which went up to 58 per cent by 2011-12. According to NSSO data, the proportion of casual workers in the total workforce as a whole has been increasing over the years, from 23 per cent in 1972-73 to 30 per cent in 2011-12. Overall unemployment rates have varied very little, over the years.

How do we interpret these trends? India is vast and diverse. The overall trend may be the average of very different patterns in different parts of the country. Furthermore, robust national employment data is only available at five year intervals, and even then there are questions about the consistency between one round and another.

In this report we look at the longer term picture, while trying to understand the patterns and trends. An important point of inflexion in Indian economic history was introduced with the economic reforms at the end of the 1980s and the early 1990s. These reforms are widely seen to have set India on its path of accelerated growth. We can use National Sample Survey data on employment for 1983, 1993-94 and 2011-12 for assessing the post-reforms performance in respect of employment and other labour market indicators in comparison to the pre-reforms period. Changes during 1983/1993-94 should mainly reflect the period before economic reform, especially since the impact of reform on the labour market is not immediate. Changes during the period 1993-94/2011-12 should reflect the impact after economic reforms.

1.2 Employment, Unemployment and Labour Force Dynamics

No doubt, employment has been continuously increasing, but so has unemployment, at least in absolute terms, if not as a percentage of labour force. Employment has grown at a rate of 2.4 per cent during 1972-73 to 1983, 2 per cent during the next ten years and at 1.8 per cent during 1993-94 to 2004-05. Employment growth of merely 0.5 per cent per annum was recorded during 2004-05 to 2011-12, the period that saw the highest growth of the Gross Domestic Product (GDP) by 8.5 per cent per annum. During the entire 18-year post-reforms period (1994-2012), employment growth is estimated to be about 1.5 per cent. Unemployment rates have fluctuated with a marginally increasing trend.

An increase in employment with no decline in the unemployment rate is obviously explained by faster expansion in labour force than in employment. The increase in the labour force was no doubt a result of the increase in population. But the former is not a fixed proportion of the latter; the rate of participation of population in labour force (LFPR) changes over time. Persons with similar age and sex attributes become a part of the labour force at one time and withdraw from it at another time. This is particularly true of women and children. Most women from poor households participate in the labour force, but they may withdraw from it with an increase in household income and then join again at much higher level of incomes and also when they have acquired a certain level of education. So, the female labour force participation rate is observed to have a U-shaped relationship with the per capita income level. Children of poor families very often work to supplement household income, but an increase in household income enables them to go to school and thus withdraw from the labour force. Then, there are children who, at any point of time, are neither in school nor at work—the 'nowhere' children who may alternate among different kinds of status—student, working and nowhere—from time to time (Chaudhuri, 1997). Worker or non-worker is thus not always the permanent status of a person. Fluctuations rather than any secular trend in labour force participation rates over time indicate such movements of persons in and out of the labour force. For example, using the Usual Principal and Subsidiary Status (UPSS), the LFPR was recorded to be 43 per cent in 1983, it declined to 42.3 per cent in 1993-94 and further to 40.5 per cent in 1999-2000, but increased to 43 per cent in 2004-05 only to decline again to 39.5 per cent in 2011-12. Among women, LFPR rates are lower and were found to have significantly declined from 30 per cent in 1983 to 29 per cent in 1993-94, 26 per cent in 1999-2000 and 22.5 in 2011-12. By the Usual Principal Status (UPS) criterion, overall participation rates were lower: 38.4 per cent in 1993-94, 39 per cent in 2004-05 per cent and 36.4 per cent in 2011-12. For women, LFPR by UPS criterion was much lower at 21.1 per cent in 1993-94, 22.4 per cent in 2004-05 and 16.8 per cent in 2011-12. Women are more often subsidiary workers than men: in 2011-12 for male UPS participation rate was 55 and UPSS rate was 55.6 with a difference of only 0.6 per cent; corresponding rates for women were 16.8 and 22.5 per cent, respectively with a difference of 5.7 per cent.

The female labour force participation rate is observed to have a U-shaped relationship with the per capita income level.

1.3 Structural Changes in the Economy and Employment: Growing Asymmetry

conventional wisdom and historical experience most of the 'pre-modern' features characterizing the labour markets of a developing economy are expected, to give way to more rational, clearer and less inequitable attributes of a 'modern' labour market in the process of economic development. This is also expected to be accompanied by a gradual replacement of 'traditional' institutions and practices by modern ones. As a result, identification, description and analysis of concepts and categories are also expected to get crystallized and become easier and less ambiguous. Thus transformation of an economy from a dominance of subsistence-oriented economic activities, agriculture and informal modes of work and production organizations to one with its major part in the capitalist, industrial and formal sectors is likely to lead to a change in labour categories and employment structure. In this process, there are changes not only in the shares of different sectors in employment, but also in the modes of work and employment status of workers. Certain pre-modern forms of employment such as child and bonded labour are also expected to disappear with the emergence of a modern industrial society.

Thus workers would increasingly become either fully employed or fully unemployed, and the extent of under-employment would decline as the economy develops (Raj, 1977; Papola, 1992). More and more workers would work as wage and salary earners, the proportion of the self employed would decline. Most workers would be employed on a formal basis; informal enterprises would increasingly become formal and formal enterprises would employ most workers as regular employees. Thus most workers would have formal time-based contracts, clear rules and procedures to govern conditions of work and employment tenure. Employer and employee identification would be unambiguous and employer–employee relationships well-defined. One would also expect an increase in the degree of unionization and greater role of unions and collective bargaining in industrial relations. In other words, labour markets are expected to become more rule-based and labour institutions more visible and effective as the economy makes a transition from the subsistence, agriculture–dominated and informal character to the capitalist, industrial and formal status.

What has been the Indian experience in these respects over the past decades? While some expected trends have been revealed, labour market behaviour that has accompanied economic development in India over the past five to six decades has also displayed certain unique and intriguing features. With the share of GDP from agriculture declining, there has been a decline in its share in employment as well; but the two rates of decline are very dissimilar. Where the share of agriculture in GDP has declined from 59 per cent in 1950 to 14 per cent in 2011-12 (decrease of 45 percentage points), its share in employment has shrunk from 73 per cent in 1950 to about 49 per cent in 2011-12 (decline of only 24 percentage points). Industry contributed 16 per cent to GDP and employed 12 per cent of workforce in 1950. In 2011-12 the respective figures were 27 and 24 per cent. Share of services in GDP has increased sharply from 25 per cent to 58 per cent, its share in employment has increased but to a much smaller extent, from 21 per cent in 1950 to 27 per cent in 2011-12. While the decline in agriculture's share in GDP, and to a lesser extent employment, is indicative of structural transformation, it has led to a sharp difference between output per worker in agriculture and non-agriculture. This disparity increased from 1:3 in 1950 to 1:6 at present.

The services sector has increased its share in GDP sharply but its share in employment has only marginally increased over the years. The share of industry, both in GDP and employment, has increased almost equally. Thus the increase in disparity between agriculture and non-agricultural sectors has primarily been a result of relatively slow growth of employment in the services sector in spite of a relatively high GDP growth. Employment elasticity in this sector declined from 0.77 in 1972-73/1983 to 0.57 during 1983/1993-94 and further to 0.43 during 1993-94/2004-05. During 2004-05/2011-12, it is estimated to have been still lower at 0.17. Agricultural GDP grew relatively slowly, thus experiencing a decline in its share from 41 per cent in 1972-73, to 14 per cent in 2011-12, but it also registered an even lower rate of employment growth. Employment elasticity in agriculture declined from 0.46 during 1972-73/1983 to 0.35 during 1978/1993-04 to 0.26 during 1993-94/2004-05. During 2004-05/2011-12, it turned out to be negative (–0.42). Industry, particularly manufacturing, on the other hand, continued to have relatively high employment elasticity till the recent past. There had been an increase from 0.53 during 1983/1993-94 to 0.59 during 1993-94/2004-05 but it has declined to 0.48 during 2004-05/2011-12. In manufacturing the estimates are 0.41 and 0.47 for 1983-94 and 1994-2005 respectively, though it declined to 0.13 during 2005-

Economic development is now characterized by structural changes away from agriculture towards industry and subsequently towards services

12. Since GDP growth in industry has been relatively low, in spite of higher employment elasticity, its employment growth is not very high (Papola, 2007 and 2009; Papola and Sahu, 2008).

Structural changes in employment have thus not been in line with either that postulated by the conventional theory of development or experienced historically by developed countries of today. It is different also from the pattern of changes taking place in most other developing countries, particularly in South East and East Asia (Papola, 2006). Historically, economic development has been characterized by structural changes away from agriculture, first to industry and subsequently to services, after industry had attained a share of 50 per cent in output. Changes in output structure have been accompanied by a corresponding shift of workforce first to industry and then to services. As a result, today, developed countries have a product structure similar to their employment structure—in each of them agriculture accounts for less than 5 per cent, both in GDP and employment and services contribute 70 to 75 per cent and industry 25 to 30 per cent, both in GDP and employment. Inter-sectoral productivity differences are thus rather insignificant. Countries of South East and East Asia, such as China, Korea, Indonesia, Thailand and Malaysia, have large industrial sectors with a 40 to 50 per cent share in GDP and a significant share in employment.

India, thus, stands apart from the development experiences not only of the developed countries but also of these developing countries of Asia. It seems to have jumped from the first stage (agricultural) to the third stage of a service-dominated economy without an intermediate industrial phase. This has been accompanied by large asymmetries between GDP and employment shares in the agricultural and services sectors resulting in large and increasing productivity variation between the two. It is, therefore, often asked if India is pioneering a new, service-led model of development and if this model is sustainable in the long run, particularly in respect of meeting the tests of macroeconomic balances, employment generation and equity (Papola, 2006).

1.4 Persistent Dominance of the Unorganized Sector

One of the peculiarities of Indian labour is the wide prevalence of the subsistence mode and unorganized nature of production of goods and services. Out of the 472 million workers in 2011-12, about 392 million or 83 per cent were estimated to be working in the unorganized or informal sector defined to comprise all privately-owned unincorporated enterprises employing less than 10 workers. Out of 392 million workers in the unorganized sector only about 2 million workers had formal employment. Even the organized sector which comprises 80 million workers had 46 million workers (58 per cent) in the informal category of employment. In this way informal workers account for about 92 per cent of the total workers. Agriculture is predominantly unorganized and all but 0.4 per cent of workers in agriculture are in its unorganized segment. Even in non-agricultural activities, 68.2 per cent workers are informal, ranging from owners of highly profitable, though small, enterprises, large farmers and high-income professionals to casual workers at below subsistence level wages, marginal farmers and those eking out their livelihood from tiny businesses and street vending. Of those working in the unorganized sector about 38 per cent (7 per cent regular and 31 per cent casual) were estimated to be wage workers and the rest self-employed (62 per cent). The largest group among the unorganized sector workers was that of the self-employed in agriculture (38 per cent), followed by self-employed in non-agriculture (24 per cent) and casual workers in agriculture (20 per cent). Most self-employed earn what is primarily a return on their labour, as there is very little or no capital involved in their production or business. Yet they may not be interested in or seeking wage-earning jobs. Even when many of them are close to being in wage employment in putting-out and outsourcing systems, they are not strictly in an employer–employee relationship.

Even within the organized sector, about 58 per cent of the workforce is engaged in informal employment.

The most important feature of the Indian employment scenario is, no doubt, the predominance of the informal economy. Employment in the informal sector and informal employment within the formal sector are characterized by insecure jobs, unstable employment, low earnings and no social security. Employment therefore, is of low quality, devoid of the characteristics of decent employment. Practically all new employment in the post-reform period, particularly from the late 1990s till 2004-05, has been either in the unorganized sector or in the form of informal jobs in the organized sector. Thus, there has been a continuous deterioration in the overall quality of employment. As per the DGE&T reports, which have a limited coverage of secondary and tertiay units, organized sector employment has, in any case, seen a continuous decline, particularly in the public sector, since 1997. It is against this background that an increase of about 2.5 million jobs in the organized sector during 2005-11 (as against a decline of 1.7 million during 1997-2005) is seen as a significant development. Employment in the private organized sector has, in fact, increased by about 3 million. The aggregate increase is diminished due to continuing decline in the public sector employment. The NSSO data also shows an increase in organized sector employment, and more importantly formal employment, between 2004-05 and 2011-12. This recent increase, although small, is an important development and needs to be examined in depth.

> Practically all new employment in the post-reform period, particularly from the late 1990s till 2004-05, has been either in the unorganized sector or in the form of informal jobs in the organized sector.

1.5 Multiple Bases of Labour Market Segmentation

Several diverse and often contradictory trends are seen to be playing out in the Indian labour market. Its structure, processes and outcomes often defy logic. Not only do shortages and surpluses co-exist, wage differentials that cannot be explained by economic factors persist and even increase despite increasing occupational and geographical mobility. Again sometimes people do not move despite the attraction of higher earnings. There is no doubt that supply responses to earnings have improved in recent years, but lack of information and increasing occupational segmentation prevent movement towards 'market clearing' of any sort. At the same time, there is evidence to suggest that market forces have considerable impact on labour market outcomes, but mostly within segments: occupational, industrial and geographical.

In any labour market, segmentation based on occupational skills and consequently industry and sectors is quite common. These, however, do not exhaust the bases of segmentation in the Indian labour market. Constraints on geographical mobility due to distances and language and cultural differences are obvious obstacles in the evolution of a common nationwide labour market. Caste and community is often another basis for segmentation. The large mass of poor households and those belonging to socially marginalized groups supply unskilled manual labour for menial and shop floor work while skilled, supervisory and managerial workers mainly come from higher socioeconomic classes. Mobility from the former to the latter is limited by differential access to education and training facilities and the schism between training for primary and advanced skills in the system, besides discrimination in hiring often practised by employers (Papola, 2005; Madheswaran and Attewell, 2009). So, Industrial Training Institutes (ITIs) which train craftsmen, draw their trainees from the poorer sections and Indian Institutes of Technology (IITs) and Indian Institutes of Management (IIMs), which train engineers and managers, mostly from the richer groups. There are no clear mechanisms to upgrade from the former to the latter during one's working life. Thus there is one labour market for the poor and another for the better-off and there is little traffic between the two.

There is, of course, gender discrimination both in supply and demand for labour which tends to segregate the female labour market from the male labour market. While women constitute a much smaller proportion of both the labour force and workforce, there are distinct conventionally earmarked spheres of work for women and the entry of women into most 'male-dominated' occupations is severely constrained. Conventional 'women's work' is characterized by lower earnings and limited upward mobility. Thus a smaller proportion of women enter the labour market and a still lower percentage of them as compared to men succeed in getting jobs; and, the jobs they get carry lower earnings and lower opportunities for upward mobility than men. Women are more often self-employed and subsidiary workers and a large majority of the self-employed women in the non-agricultural work are home-based. While there has been an increase in the number of job opportunities for women in certain fast-growing export-oriented sectors like garments and IT-BPO, most jobs that women have got in these activities also happen to be low-end and precarious.

> Women's work is characterized by lower earnings and limited upward mobility.

Widespread prevalence of child labour has been a well known feature of the employment situation in India. Law prohibits the employment of child labour in 'hazardous' activities and regulates its use in others. Yet it is widely prevalent in the former and is used in the latter with rampant violation of regulatory provisions. With stricter implementation of the law and pressure from buyers (importers) and civil society, the incidence of child labour is reported to be on the decline. The 2001 Census reported about 10 million children working; NSSO reported their number to be 9 million in 2004-05 which fell to 4 million in 2011-12. It is hoped that with the enactment of the Right to Education Act (2009), the situation will improve significantly.

Bonded labour, the worst form of vulnerable employment, is also evident, particularly in agriculture in parts of which remnants of feudalism are still visible. Debt bondage, of course, is the most prevalent form of the new bondage. With difficulties in defining bondage and identifying bonded labour, estimates of incidence of bonded labour vary widely: from a figure of 343,000 by NSSO (1977-78) to 2.62 million (1978) by the Gandhi Peace Foundation. The Ministry of Labour identified 288,098 bonded labourers for rehabilitation in different states in 2007-08. Bonded labour is found to be concentrated in brick kilns, construction, stone quarries and gem processing and other activities in which a large number of seasonal migrants are employed. It appears that the Bonded Labour Act (1976) has been ineffective and other, particularly sector-based, action may be necessary to tackle the problem of bonded labour.

Migrant workers constitute another vulnerable group that is often subject to exploitative employment relations and poor living conditions. Historically most migration for work was from rural to urban areas for lifetime employment in the organized industry and for government jobs.

In recent decades, new features of migratory employment have emerged. Among these, the four major features are:

- First, overall lifetime rural–urban migration has shown a declining trend; lifetime migrants, who constituted 45 per cent of the urban population in 1961, declined to 38 per cent in 1981, and further to 36 per cent in 2001.
- Second, most new migrants to urban areas now seek work in the unorganized sector as organized sector employment has not been growing.
- Third, rural to rural migration for work, particularly from poor states to agriculturally better developed states, now constitutes a significant migration stream.
- Fourth, short-term seasonal migration has emerged as an important stream; all rural to rural migration for agricultural work falls in this category, as also migration for work in activities such as construction, brick kilns and cotton seed production, which mostly operate on a seasonal basis.

> Migrant workers suffer from low earnings and exploitative conditions of work, and are denied basic welfare benefits

Lifetime rural to urban migrants are not necessarily worse off than non-migrants: they, in fact, have lower poverty and unemployment rates than the non-migrants. But most migrant workers in the unorganized sector and seasonal activities suffer from low earnings, exploitative employment relations and poor working and living conditions. In addition they, particularly if they have migrated from other states, are sometimes denied some basic welfare benefits that require domicile status. The Inter State Migrant Workers Act (1979) that was expected to look after their interests has proved to be a non-starter.

1.6 Wage Increase, Wage Differentials and Minimum Wages

The labour market implications of the prevailing pattern of growth are not very clear. As pointed out earlier, employment growth has not only been lower than the growth of the labour force but also far lower than what could be seen as commensurate with the rate of economic growth. Sectors and sub-sectors of the economy which have grown fast and made major contribution to the recent economic growth have shown a steep decline in employment elasticities. And sectors that have shown higher and even rising elasticities have not grown fast enough to produce a

Sectors and sub-sectors of the economy which have grown fast and made a major contribution to the recent economic growth have shown a steep decline in employment elasticities.

significant employment impact. Yet, the average daily wages of the workers, as recorded by NSSO surveys, have registered a significant increase: those of regular workers have risen at an average rate of 3.0 per cent per annum in rural and 2.8 per cent in urban areas; and those of casual workers at 3.4 per cent in rural and 2.6 per cent in urban areas in real terms during 1983/2011-12. The rate of increase was much lower during 1983/1993-94 than during 1993-94/2004-05 in the case of casual workers, while it was the same for regular workers. Overall, the wages of regular workers grew by 3.0 per cent and those of casual workers by 3.2 per cent per annum during 1983-2012. The overall trend in agricultural wages has been similar to that of rural wages. However, casual agricultural workers saw a higher growth in their wages as compared to regular wages. In urban areas, regular workers in services and casual workers in industry have gained the largest increase in wages.

Wage disparities have changed very little between rural and urban areas and between male and female workers. Wages of casual workers were 35 per cent lower in rural than in urban areas in 1983; in 2004-05 they were 25 per cent lower and in 2011-12, they were lower by 20 per cent. Women casual workers in rural areas received 37 per cent lower wages than their male counterparts in 1983; the ratio was the same in 2004-05. The situation has hardly changed in 2011-12. Disparity between labour and non-labour incomes, however, has significantly increased as indicated by changes in the shares of factor incomes in value added. For example, wages constituted 47 per cent of value added in organized manufacturing in 1981-82; the share declined to 32 per cent in 1993-94 and further to 25 per cent in 2010-11. Profits, on the other hand, increased their share from 23 per cent in 1981-82, to 32 per cent in 1993-94 and to 58 per cent in 2010-11.

Large variations exist in the wage rates across states. In 2011-12, the average daily wages of casual workers in rural areas ranged from ₹ 87 in Chhatisgarh and ₹ 107 in Madhya Pradesh to ₹ 309 in Kerala and ₹ 211 in Jammu & Kashmir. In urban areas, they varied between ₹ 112 in Chhattisgarh to ₹ 315 in Kerala. Growth in wages has also varied widely: during 2005-12, Karnataka and Andhra Pradesh had the highest increase in wages of casual workers in rural areas (about 9% per annum); the increase was low in Himachal Pradesh and Jammu & Kashmir (less than 3% per annum).

A large number of workers fail to receive minimum wages that are fixed for them. As per data from the NSSO survey for 2009-10, 73 per cent of the rural-farm, 37 per cent of rural non-farm and 54 per cent of urban non-farm casual workers received wages that are less than the statutorily fixed minimum wages. The proportion of such workers was much higher among women workers: 87 per cent and 65 per cent in rural and 82 per cent in urban areas, respectively.

1.7 Large Number of 'Working Poor': The Disconnect between Work and Income

In all, 25 per cent of those working had an income which was less than the officially fixed poverty line. Casual workers, no doubt, have the highest incidence of poverty: 36 per cent among them were recorded to be poor in 2011-12. But 24 per cent of the self-employed were also poor and even among regular workers, 9 per cent were poor. The incidence of poverty in all categories of workers has certainly declined, as has the overall poverty ratio in the population. Overall, the incidence of poverty among the workers has come down from 48.8 per cent in 1993-94 to 25 per cent in 2011-12; that among the self-employed from 44.8 per cent to 24.1 per cent, and among casual workers from 66.5 per cent to 36 per cent over the same period. The point remains that low earnings from employment, rather than open unemployment, is the main source of poverty. Ninety per cent of the poor are 'employed'. The Incidence of poverty among the employed is higher than among the unemployed; and, counter intuitively, over the years, the decline in the incidence of poverty has been higher among the unemployed than among the employed. In 2004-05, about 21 per cent of the unemployed were poor, while among the employed,

Informal employment has given rise to a disconnect between work and income and between employment and poverty status.

26 per cent were poor. Over the period 1993-94/2011-12, the incidence of poverty among the employed declined from 48.8 per cent to 25 per cent but that among the unemployed also it declined from 32.4 per cent to 21 per cent.

This disconnect between work and income as also between employment and poverty status is primarily caused by the predominance of informal employment. Informal employment has always accounted for a major part of employment in India, and its share till 2004-05 increased, rather than declined over the past three decades—contrary to the expected trend. It appears that the organized sector contributed a significant and increasing share of the GDP as well as employment till the mid-1970s when it was estimated to account for 17 per cent of the total employment. By the early 1990s, its employment share had come down to about 15 per cent. With the introduction of economic reforms linked to globalization, it was expected that the organized sector would grow in importance. Instead, its share in employment is estimated to have come down to about 12 per cent by 2004-05. For 2011-12, it is estimated to be slightly higher at 17 per cent. Further, the proportion of 'informal employment' has significantly increased in the organized sector. It was 41 per cent in 1999-2000 but increased to 58 per cent in 2011-12. Workers in such informal arrangements not only draw lower earnings than regular workers, but also get work only off and on depending on market needs. They remain outside the purview of various social protection schemes floated by the state.

Economic development, modernization, fast growth and globalization have not led to a significant increase in the proportion of workers employed on a regular wage and salary basis. Regular workers have constituted a small and stagnant share of the total workforce. They constituted 15.4 per cent of the total workers in 1972-73; by 1983 their proportion declined to 13.5 per cent. The share further declined to 13.2 per cent in 1993-94 but has shown a marginal increase since then, reaching 17.9 per cent in 2011-12. The share of those employed casually, on the other hand, has increased from 23.3 per cent in 1972-73 to 33.2 per cent in 1999-2000, though the next five years till 2004-05 saw a decline to 28.9 per cent but again witnessed a marginal increase and stood at 29.9 per cent in 2011-12, which is over 6 percentage points higher than in 1972-73. The self-employed category was expected to and did, in fact, experience a decline from 61.4 per cent in 1972-73 to 52.8 per cent in 1999-2000. It increased to 56.9 per cent in 2004-05, but resumed the declining trend during 2005-12, reaching 52.2 per cent in 2011-12. The long-term trend is thus one of an increase in the share of casual workers and a decline in that of the self-employed workers with only a small increase in the proportion of regular workers.

1.8 Underemployment: A Continuing Characteristic of Employment

In an economy characterized by large numbers of the working poor, massive informal employment and a dominance of casual workers and self-employment, the relationship between work and income has been blurred. Furthermore, the distinction between the employed and the unemployed is also often unclear as a large number of Indian workers cannot really be classified exclusively in either of the two categories. Many of them are employed for part of the year and unemployed for another. The phenomenon of under-employment (individuals being engaged in part-time employment or in full-time employment but only for some time in the year, despite being willing to and capable of working full-time all the year round) widely prevails; certainly to a much greater extent than what is estimated as 'open' or 'chronic' unemployment. That underemployment is a much larger problem than unemployment in developing countries like India has been widely recognized by economists in India and abroad as well as by international organizations and Indian policy-makers. It was, however, postulated to decline with economic development. Development with the concomitant changes in technology and organization of production was expected to lead to employment of most people on a full-time basis, thus leading to a situation where those working would be fully employed and those not working also fully unemployed.

Distinction between the employed and the unemployed is also often unclear as a large number of Indian workers cannot really be classified exclusively in either of the two categories.

Such change does not seem to have taken place. As is typical in poor, agrarian, developing economies, open unemployment rates in India are low, irrespective of the methodology used to measure it. In 2011-12, these rates varied between 2.2 per cent on UPSS basis to 5.6

per cent on Current Daily Status (CDS) basis; other rates being 2.7 per cent as per Usual Principal Status (UPS) and 3.7 on Current Weekly Status (CWS) criteria.

If we take UPS rates, which measures unemployment as lack of work for major part of the year among persons who have work as their principal activity, then the unemployment rate has fluctuated around 3 per cent in different periods of NSS rounds; the highest being 4.3 per cent in 1977-78 and lowest at 2.5 in 2009-10.

Unemployment measured by CDS includes all person-days of unemployment of both the employed and the unemployed and was estimated to be around 8 per cent in 1972-73, 1977-78 and 1983, 6 per cent in 1987-88 and 1993-94, 7 per cent in 1999-2000, again 8 per cent in 2004-05. It declined to 5.6 per cent in 2011-12.

The difference between these two rates could be taken as the measure of underemployment which was high at about 5 per cent during the first three NSS rounds, declined to 2.5 to 3 per cent in the next two reference years, but increased to around 5 per cent in 1999-2000 and 2004-05. In 2011-12, it is lower at around 3 per cent. Thus , on the one hand, there are a large number of employed who earn very low incomes, and on the other, a significant proportion have work only for part of the time they could work.

1.9 Labour Market Flexibility: The Noise and the Reality

Liberalization of trade and industrial policies has led to fierce competition among producers across as well as within the national economies, and they have found reduction in labour costs as the easiest way of facing it. Besides lowering wage rates and employment wherever possible, flexible labour contracts that do not necessitate payment of social security and separation costs are being used on an increasingly large scale. Besides, the use of global production networks and decentralized technologies have facilitated, and production on the outsourced and order-based supply basis, has necessitated, greater use of temporary, casual and contract labour. This has been observed both in the organized and unorganized sectors in India, despite the legal framework to regulate such employment in industry.

A comprehensive legislative framework has been in existence in India for regulating various aspects of employment, especially in the organized industrial sector. The numerous labour laws and the aspects and details of employment that they cover have sometimes prompted some observers to remark that the regulatory framework is too 'restrictive' and had come into existence even before the emergence of a sizeable class of industrial labour to which it is meant to apply. But the regulatory framework has been accepted as a part of the social contract between industry and labour, with the state acting as the watchdog and referee. This social contract seems to have come under serious stress over the past few decades, particularly with the introduction of economic reforms and India's initiative to globalize in the early 1990s. Areas of disagreement seem to have widened as well as got sharpened. Industry now finds several regulatory provisions highly restrictive, adversely affecting growth of industry and employment in a globally competitive environment; and demands changes in laws enabling more flexible arrangements in employment and other conditions of work. Unions have resisted any such move and in fact, protested against non-regulation of the increasing use of flexible labour.

> Labour regulations have been questioned both for their rationale and their effectiveness

Though the debate has raised larger issues of the cost and benefits of labour regulation in general, the focus has been only on a few regulatory provisions. Regulation of minimum wages under the Minimum Wages Act and conditions of work under the Factories Act have often been questioned both for their rationale and effectiveness, but the major bones of contention have been the issue of job security under the Industrial Disputes Act (1947) and of restrictions on the use of short-term indirect labour under the Contract Labour (Regulation and Abolition) Act (CLA) (1970). The Industrial Disputes Act (IDA) 1947 stipulates conditions for lay off and retrenchment of labour and closure of enterprises. It provides a procedure, notice period and compensation to the workers and also for prior government permission if the enterprise employs 100 or more workers. It is, in fact, this last provision that has been the centre of controversy most of the time. The CLA prohibits use of contract labour in the 'core' or 'perennial' activities of an enterprise, warranting use of labour on a regular basis and regulates conditions of work where contract labour is permitted. Industry regards it as an obstacle in expanding production and employment particularly in lines where production is primarily dependent on fluctuating demand.

> The 'relaxed' attitude of the government with regard to compliance of labour laws has rendered them ineffective.

There have been no changes in either of these laws, yet in recent years, it has been possible for the enterprises employing 100 workers or more to reduce their workforce or close down. The extent of use of contract labour is found to have significantly increased: percentage of such labour from 10 per cent in 1992-93 to 23 per cent in 2000-01, and further to over 27 per cent in 2004-05 and 34 per cent in 2011-12 in the organized manufacturing sector. This is partly a result of the 'relaxed' attitude that the governments have tended to adopt in respect of compliance of labour laws. Thus, the state governments, in many cases, on the advice of the central government, have done away with the requirements of regular inspection of factories by labour inspectors. In several cases, the state governments have also made changes in the rules and amended the provisions of labour laws to allow exemption to various categories of enterprises from adherence of certain provisions of labour laws (such as CLA). In some cases (for instance in Andhra Pradesh), coverage of the provisions of CLA has been reduced by making the Act inapplicable to certain categories of enterprises and by so defining non-core activities, that the 'core' activity gets reduced to a narrower definition. Also the permissions to retrench and close down (under the IDA Chapter VB) have been granted more freely by the state governments in recent years (Reddy, 2008; Shyam Sundar 2008a).

1.10 Increasing Informalization of Employment: Challenge of Social Security

The emerging production pattern characterized by processes like global value chains, and technological developments facilitating decomposition and decentralization of production have already set a trend towards employment of labour increasingly on an informal basis, either by outsourcing work to enterprises in the unorganized sector or hiring workers on a non-regular basis in the organized sector. The relaxed attitude towards implementation of labour laws, as described above, have further accentuated this trend. As a result, the proportion of workers, who are in non-regular employment or in units outside the coverage of job and social security provisions, has significantly increased. In other words, the percentage of workers with some kind of protection against loss of job or risks of work and life, which was already very small, has further shrunk and the proportion of those without any social security or protection has increased at least till 2004-05.

> The proportion of workers who are in non-regular employment or in units outside the coverage of job and social security provisions, has significantly increased.

Thus a major challenge seems to be emerging in the field of social security for Indian workers. The numbers and proportion of workers without any social safety net is increasing. All workers with formal employment have, in principle, some social security coverage but, all of the workers in informal employment that accounts for about 92 per cent of the total workers, are not covered by social security. If we look at their distribution by unorganized and organized sectors, the unorganized sector has 99.5 per cent and organized sector has 58 per cent informal workers without social security. Most of them are not able to make a significant contribution to any fund or scheme that can give them social security benefits. Most of them are also self-employed or have no fixed or easily identifiable employer who can be asked to contribute to such a fund. Furthermore, the majority are spatially and occupationally highly dispersed. As a result, implementation of any contributory, insurance-based scheme becomes financially and organizationally very difficult. The capacity and willingness of the state to fund a social security scheme covering minimum benefits to all workers are also becoming increasingly doubtful.

In the globalization–induced liberal economic policy regime a shift from social assistance to social insurance, rather than the reverse, is more likely as the mode for funding social security for workers. NCEUS had worked out a comprehensive scheme for providing minimum social security benefits to all informal workers, combining social insurance and social assistance modes. Part of the scheme has found favour with the government in the enactment of the Unorganized Workers' Social Security Act, 2008, but much more needs to be done to provide an adequate social protection to all workers. This poses a serious challenge to economists, government and civil society in terms of devising, examining, proposing and implementing different models of social security.

1.11 Labour Organizations and Labour Rights: Some Disconcerting Signals

In India, trade union presence has been limited: only 2 per cent of all workers, 5 per cent of non-agricultural workers and 35 per cent of organized sector workers are unionized. Yet unions had a much larger impact than reflected in their membership due to their link with major political parties and social recognition of their role as institutions for democratic development and social justice and not mere partisan organizations protecting some groups. In recent years, trade unions have been on the defensive in India, as everywhere else, with the ascendancy of globalization. As a result, there appears to have been serious erosion in the worker's rights. And this has happened despite the labour laws which are often claimed to be highly prejudiced in favour of labour providing it 'excessive' protection. 'Labour militancy' seems to have given way to 'employer militancy', as is reflected in the increasing importance of lockouts and declining contribution of strikes in the incidence of industrial disputes (Shyam Sunder, 2008a). There seems to be a decline in the importance of central trade union organizations and increase in the 'autonomy' of local and enterprise unions. This trend has been further strengthened by the emergence of 'independent' trade unions and of a large number of non-trade union, non-government organizations, particularly in the unorganized sector where national trade union organizations have not been able to make much headway (Shyam Sundar, 2008b). The overall decline in the sphere of union activity and influence has been accentuated by an increase in informalization of workforce and decrease in the proportion of regular workers in the organized sector.

> The overall decline in the sphere of union activity and influence has been accentuated by an increase in informalization of workforce and decrease in the proportion of regular workers in the organized sector.

> There has been decline in the importance of central trade union organizations and increase in the 'autonomy' of local and enterprise unions.

There has been a change in the public perception of labour and trade unions as reflected in the change in the attitude and behaviour of the government, judiciary, public and media towards labour. Governments no longer seem to find themselves obliged to treat labour as a weaker party and, therefore, favour it in disputes. At best, employer and employees are treated as equal, but quite often industry is looked at with a positive and labour with a negative prism—the former contributing while the latter obstructing economic growth and national development. This attitude has also often got reflected in public perception and media. The judiciary has, of late, given judgements (for example, in the Tamil Nadu government employees' strike and some cases involving regularization of long-term casual workers) which support similar views (Papola and Sharma, 2004). Thus the sources to which labour in India has in the past looked for support for their rights seem to be drying up. Implications of such attitudinal changes need to be analysed in terms of their impact not only on trade unions and the working class, but also for the society and polity at large.

1.12 Globalization and Indian Labour: A Recapitulation

Since the beginning of 1980s when India initiated the process of liberalization of its economy and particularly since 1991 when major economic reforms were introduced, the Indian economy has seen spectacular changes. Not only has economic growth rate more than doubled than in the earlier decades, but the structure of the Indian economy has undergone major change, particularly in respect of the importance of the external sector—foreign trade and investment. Foreign trade, imports and exports together, made up 15 per cent of India's GDP in 1990-2001, by 2010-11 it rose to 43 per cent. Foreign investment—both direct and portfolio—increased from $103 million in 1990-2000 to $ 42 billion in 2010-11 (GoI, *Economic Survey*, various years). Going by these indicators, India has made a rapid march towards globalization during this period.

As everywhere else, there were both expectations and apprehensions about the impact of globalization on labour in India. Faster economic growth following liberalization was expected to lead to increase in employment opportunities and increasing demand for labour was expected to tighten the labour market and lead to improvement in wages and conditions of work. Competition unleashed by trade liberalization and domestic reforms, on the other hand, could, it was apprehended, force employers to cut labour, particularly, non-wage costs, thus resulting in a decline in the extent of job security and social protection. Experience elsewhere during the 1990s provided rather mixed signals with sharply contrasting impact of trade liberalization on employment and wages (WCSDG, 2004). Employment grew in some countries, but unemployment rose in many others. More importantly, gains and losses were unequally shared: mostly the skilled and better-endowed gained and the unskilled and the poor lost. Pressures to increase 'labour market flexibility' due to increasing competition increased, resulting in a rise in the extent of informal employment; and, increased international mobility of capital without similar movements of labour reduced the bargaining power of labour.

> The rapid growth of exports that took place was not accompanied by a similar growth in employment.

The Indian experience of globalization for over one and a half decades since 1991 a suggests a similar impact on labour as elsewhere. There have been job losses in sectors, but overall, these have been offset by increase in job opportunities in others. Employment growth, however, slowed down in the post-liberalization period, as compared to the earlier decade, despite an acceleration in the rate of economic growth. The employment content of growth declined. In fact, the employment content of exports also, strangely enough, declined with trade liberalization which was expected to encourage the exports of labour-intensive products. Following liberalization, the export of skill and technology-intensive products increased faster and the share of labour-intensive products in exports declined. Thus the rapid growth of exports that took place during this period was not accompanied by a similar growth in employment. Yet, when there was a downturn in the growth of exports following the global meltdown in 2008-09, the labour-intensive exports seemed to have been worst affected as most job losses were witnessed in these sectors. Thus the positive employment effects of booming exports following liberalization were only moderate; the adverse effects of the slowdown in exports due to the global crisis seem to be rather sharp.

The Impact of globalization has evidently been adverse on the overall quality of employment. The share of jobs with employment security and social protection has declined and of those with no social security has increased (at least till 2004-05). First, jobs that have been lost were more often of the regular and protected category. Second, new jobs that have been created are most often in the unorganized sector or of the informal nature in the organized sector. Third, in line with the neo-liberal economic thinking characterizing policies of liberalization and globalization, governments have developed a rather relaxed attitude towards enforcement of labour laws on job security and condition of work, thus encouraging employment on a non-regular basis even where workers could have been employed on a more regular basis. Deterioration in the quality of employment by way of decline in the extent of job and social security, however, seems to have been mitigated to a certain extent by a significant rise in real wages.

> The problem of globalization is not of a decrease in employment generation, but that of low-quality jobs.

What have been the gains and losses of Indian labour in the first round of globalization? No doubt, there has been a net increase in the quantity of employment, though not commensurate with the accelerated growth of the economy. Some new jobs have also been of high quality, in respect of earnings and upward mobility, mostly in the fast-growing globally connected segments of the services sector. But most new jobs are of poor quality in respect of stability and security, if not earnings. The major losers have been in the intangible aspects—rights, public perceptions and political power. Labour has lost the pride of place it occupied in social and political space in the country earlier. The ascendancy of capital had already relegated labour to a defensive position. Change in public perception of labour and their organizations and influence of neo-liberal economic thinking on public policy and action has resulted in an erosion of the socio-political status of labour as a class. These changes are likely to have an adverse impact on the rights of labour. And this is a more serious challenge for labour organizations than the labour market outcomes of globalization, which, in fact, are expected to show reasonable improvements as a result of reasonably faster growth of employment and increase in wages resulting from a sustained high rate of economic growth.

2

Economic Growth and Employment: Performance and Emerging Challenges

2.1 Introduction: Growth and Employment

India has witnessed rapid growth in gross domestic product (GDP) during the last three decades, a trend that first manifested in the 1980s and picked up pace in the 1990s when domestic and external sector economic reforms were first introduced. During the three decades preceding the high growth period, India had grown at around 3 per cent per annum and with a population growth rate of about 2.5 per cent, there was only a very small increase in per capita income during this period. On the other hand, during the three decades of high growth, the average rate of GDP growth has been close to 6 per cent and during the two decades since early 1990s, it has been above 6.5 per cent. With a population growth rate below 2 per cent per annum, it has resulted in a substantial rise in per capita income. Following the slowdown induced by the global financial crisis in 2008-09, the Indian economy responded strongly to fiscal and monetary stimulus and achieved a growth rate of 8.6 per cent and 9.3 per cent respectively in 2009-10 and 2010-11. However, due to factors such as high fiscal deficits and slowing down of saving and investment rates, including foreign investment in the subsequent two years, 2011-12 and 2012-13, the growth rates slowed to 6.2 per cent and 5.0 per cent respectively. Notwithstanding this slowdown, during the 10 years between 2001-02 and 2011-12, the growth rate was 7.8 per cent per annum with per capita income growing at around 6.3 per cent per annum (*Economic Survey, 2012-13*, Government of India, 2013). The slowdown in growth rates has been experienced by countries worldwide, including China and Brazil, although the Chinese growth rate is still above 7 per cent. India continues to be one of the fastest growing economies of the world, next only to China.

> GDP growth has been close to 7 per cent since the 1990s, and with a population growth rate below 2 per cent, it has resulted in substantial rise in per capita income.

Along with the high GDP growth rate, the Indian economy has been more and more globally integrated during the past three decades. India's external trade, that is, exports plus imports, as a proportion of GDP has vastly increased, from less than 19 per cent in 1997-98 to around 43 per cent in 2010-11. Global financial integration and trade globalization has been rapid for India. There has been a significant increase in the country's foreign exchange reserves to over US$ 300 billion in 2011 (Ibid). It is widely believed that the high growth in India has been largely due to the process of economic reforms in which entrepreneur class has played a crucial role, propelled by rising labour productivity.

> A remarkable feature of the Indian growth story has been its resilience to a number of external and internal shocks.

A remarkable feature of the Indian growth story is its resilience. It has been able to withstand both internal and external shocks to a large extent. The country has been witnessing at regular intervals calamities like droughts and floods. Earlier such events used to have significant macro-economic impact on GDP leading to inflationary trend. However, over the years their impact has been reduced. In the same way, although the global financial crisis of 2008 had an adverse impact on the Indian economy as well, the country was able to absorb the shock significantly. With several fiscal measures and stimulus packages, no significant adverse effect was witnessed in livelihoods. In fact, the second global financial crisis—the euro zone crisis—in combination with the several domestic constraints, both economic and non-economic, has impacted the Indian economy more severely than the first one. As in most parts of the world, this second slowdown has come so quick on the heels of the previous one that the latitude that the country has in terms of fiscal and monetary policy is severely curtailed. There is a need for innovative approaches to policy-making and implementation to put India on the path of recovery (*Economic Survey, 2011-12*, Government of India, 2012). At the same time, it is widely believed that the current economic situation (brought on by global factors as well as constraints imposed by fractured politics in decision-making) is likely to bottom out and the country would tide over it in the near future. Of course, it depends to a large extent on the politics and policies and their efficacy and implementation.

India's growth potential is great, given the youth bulge of the next few decades and the fact that large parts of both rural and urban India are still economically backward and have a great scope of development. If appropriate policies, with emphasis on domestic demand are adopted, India can have sustained growth over next two decades, although the rates may be lower than the historical growth rate achieved by China during the last four decades.

> Rapid economic growth has not significantly transformed the labour market and employment conditions in India resulting in a non-inclusive growth process.

The high growth phase in India has been accompanied by improvements in standards of living and other social indicators as well as significant reduction in poverty from 45.3 per cent in 1993-94 to 37.2 per cent in 2004-05 and further to 21.9 per cent in 2011-12 (25.7 per cent in rural and 13.7 per cent in urban areas). During the 11-year period between 1993-94 and 2004-05, the average decline in the poverty ratio was 0.74 percentage points per year which accelerated to 2.18 percentage points per year during the period 2004-05 to 2011-12, the rate of decline being about three times that experienced in the 11-year period, 1993-94 to 2004-05 Planning Commission, 2013a. Although this official poverty line probably underestimates the level and depth of deprivation and vulnerability, there is no doubt that absolute poverty has been declining. Of course, all the decline in absolute poverty is not only because of growth but other factors have played their roles. However, it needs to be noted that the current poverty line is estimated approximately at purchasing power parity (PPP) of US$ 1.25 per day and if the rate is enhanced to US$ 2.0 per day PPP which is internationally widely accepted, the level of poverty in India will be around 55 per cent (see Appendix Table 9.3).

Three decades of rapid growth have not significantly transformed the labour market and employment conditions in the country. The improvements in employment conditions have been rather modest and the traditional low productive employment remains dominant in the economy. The disparities and inequalities, both across regions and groups, have generally widened over the years. The growth process has not been inclusive and a significant proportion of the population has not benefited as much from it as the rich and upper middle income groups. Thus, a disconnect between growth on the one hand and labour markets and employment on the other has manifested.

The subsequent sections explore the trend, nature and pattern of employment in India, particularly during the three decades after the initiation of the process of liberalization and globalization of the economy. They also assess the employment and labour market performances including the extent of unemployment, migration of workers and gender discrimination. The final section presents the key features and challenges of the employment situation.

The analysis in this chapter is largely based on the quinquennial rounds of data from the National Sample Survey Organization (NSSO) which is available since 1972-73. The NSSO rounds pertaining to the years 1983, 1993-94, 2004-05 and 2011-12 have been mostly used in this chapter as well as in the next two chapters. Apart from NSSO, data from sources such as Registrar General & Census Commissioner of India, Annual Survey of Industry (ASI) for the organized manufacturing sector and Directorate General of Employment and Training (DGE&T) have also been used.

2.2 Characteristics and Structure of the Indian Labour Market

India's labour market is characterized by a low female participation rate, visible in its poor labour sex ratio and also low worker-total population ratio. The overall labour force participation rate (LFPR) stands at around 40 per cent which for women is 23 per cent. While the male LFPR has been stable at 55-56 per cent during three decades from 1983 to 2011-12, the female LFPR has shown a decline from around 30 per cent in 1983 to 23 per cent in 2011-12 (Table 2.1). The female LFPR, a matter of vigorous debate, has been discussed in greater detail in the next section.

Table 2.1

Labour Force Participation Rate and Workforce Participation Rate (UPSS) by Gender (All Ages): 1983 to 2011-12

Year	*LFPR*			*WFPR*		
	M	*F*	*P*	*M*	*F*	*P*
1983	55.1	30.0	42.9	53.9	29.6	42.0
1993-94	55.6	29.0	42.8	54.5	28.6	42.0
2004-05	55.9	29.4	43.0	54.7	28.7	42.0
2011-12	55.6	22.5	39.5	54.4	21.9	38.6

Note: M: Male; F: Female; P: Persons; UPSS: Usual Principal and Subsidiary Status; LFPR: Labour Force Participation Rate and WFPR: Workforce Participation Rate.

Source: Computed from unit level data of various NSSO rounds.

Box 2.1

Employment and Unemployment Measurement in India

The National Sample Survey Organization (NSSO) has been conducting quinquennial surveys on a regular basis since 1972-73 to generate national level data on employment and unemployment in India. The NSSO has, over time, developed and standardized measures of employment and unemployment. The NSSO collects data on employment and unemployment using three broad measures or approaches: 1. Usual Status (US), 2. Current Weekly Status (CWS), and 3. Current Daily Status (CDS). The Usual Status is further categorized at two levels: (i) Usual Principal Status (UPS) and (ii) Usual Principal and Subsidiary Status (UPSS).

Usual status relates to the activity status of a person during the reference period of last 365 days preceding the date of the survey. The activity status in which a person spent a relatively longer time (major time criterion) is considered as the UPS. To decide the usual principal activity status of a person, a two-stage classification is used to determine the broad activity status, namely, labour force (employed and unemployed) and out of labour force within which the detailed activity status is determined depending on the relatively longer time spent in the activity. Besides the usual principal activity status, a person could have pursued some economic activity which is the subsidiary economic activity status of that person. If these two are taken together, the measure of UPSS is obtained.

CWS of a person is the activity status obtained for a person during a reference period of seven days preceding the date of the survey. According to this, a person is considered a worker if he /she has performed any economic activity for at least one hour on any day of the reference week, and is obtained on the basis of daily activities performed on each day of the reference period.

CDS of a person is determined on the basis of his/her activity status on each day of the reference week using a priority-cum major time criterion (day to day labour time disposition). Broadly, a person is considered working (employed) for the full day if he/she worked for four hours or more during the day and half day if he/she pursues at least one hour in a day.

India's labour market is characterized by a low female participation rate, visible in its poor labour sex ratio and also low worker-total population ratio.

Most of the workers in India have very low education and skill levels. Less than 30 per cent of the workforce in 2011-12 had educational attainments up to secondary and above (see Appendix Table 3.12). Further, as per the NSSO 68th round survey, as of 2011-12, less than one-tenth of the workers had received vocational training, either formal or informal, with the former comprising only 2 per cent of all workers. Although NSSO surveys grossly underestimate several types of skills of workers acquired informally (by those working in cottage and handicraft household enterprises), there is no doubt that levels of skill are very low in the country.

Less than one-tenth of workers have formal or informal vocational training. Most workers have low levels of education and skills.

Another important feature of the Indian workforce is that agriculture still accounts for about half of the total workforce. As in the most developing countries, the open rate of unemployment is quite low. It is around 2.2 per cent on the basis of the UPSS measure. Even using the most comprehensive measure of unemployment, current daily status (CDS), which takes into account labour force participation on a daily basis, the rate of unemployment goes up to only around 6 per cent (See Box 2.1 for various concepts of employment). On the other hand, the level of poverty as mentioned earlier, is very high. This obviously means that a large proportion of the workers are poor and as such poverty, and not open unemployment, is the main problem. This is typical of a labour-surplus economy where most people are engaged in low-income activities who cannot afford to be 'unemployed'. With about half of the workers being self-employed, they share whatever work is available, leading to widespread underemployment and poverty.

Standard definitions of employment and unemployment are not always sufficient to adequately capture all dimensions of the labour market in India which is dualistic in nature, and

Box 2.2

Some Important Terms

Formal/Organized Sector

It consists of the government/public departments and public/private enterprises plus the private enterprises which employ 10 or more workers.

Unorganized/Informal Sector

Enterprises that employ less than 10 workers and are not government/public and public/private limited are in the unorganized/informal sector. These enterprises can belong to any of the following five categories: (i) proprietary, (ii) partnership, (iii) co-operative societies/trusts/other non-profit organizations, (iv) employer's households (private households employing maid servants, watchmen, cook etc.), and (v) others.

Formal Workers (Formal Employment)

Formal workers consist of those working in the unorganized/informal sector, who are regular workers with social security benefits provided by the employers and the workers in the formal sector with any employment and social security benefits provided by the employers.

Informal Workers (or Informal Employment)

Informal workers consist of those working in the unorganized/informal sector enterprises or households, excluding regular workers with social security benefits provided by the employers and the workers in the formal sector without any employment and social security benefits provided by the employers.

Note: These definitions are largely based on the definitions adopted by the NCEUS. For details, see NCEUS (2006).

Table 2.2

Status of Employment (UPSS), 1983 to 2011-12

Share (%) in Total Employment of :	1983	1993-94	1999-2000	2004-05	2009-10	2011-12
Regular wage employment	13.5	13.2	14.0	14.3	15.6	17.9
Formal	-	-	5.4	5.6	6.4	6.8
Informal	-	-	8.6	8.6	9.2	11.0
Casual wage employment	29.0	32.0	33.2	28.9	33.5	29.9
Self-employment	57.5	54.7	52.8	56.9	51.0	52.2
Casual and self employment	86.5	86.7	86.0	85.8	84.5	82.1
Organized sector	-	-	9.3	11.1	14.0	16.4
Unorganized sector	-	-	90.7	88.9	86.0	83.6

Note: Formal employment includes the regular workers with social security in organized sector.
Source: Computed from unit level data of various NSSO rounds.

has a large traditional or low-income economy coexisting with high level of growth, productivity, surplus and modern economy. The former is called the unorganized sector and the latter the organized/formal sector.[1] The unorganized sector (consisting of private enterprises employing less than 10 workers or own account workers, including both agriculture and non-agriculture) has low productivity and jobs are temporary: irregular or casual. The sector is extremely

1. In official statistics in India 'organized' and 'unorganized' sectors are often used instead of 'formal' and 'informal' sectors. In this report, as in case of the National Commission for Enterprises in the Unorganized Sector (NCEUS), these terms have been interchangeably used (See Box 2.2). The NCEUS report was a pioneering piece of work which brought to the public domain for the first time, the magnitude of vulnerability and deprivation that informal workers are faced with. See NCEUS (2009).

heterogeneous comprising big cultivators, wholesale traders, large shopkeepers and an increasing number of professionals with high earnings on the one hand, and petty producers, small and marginal farmers, and own account workers on the other. Segments within the sector that have strong forward linkages with the organized sector are more dynamic than the rest. The workers in this sector are neither protected by government regulations nor unionized in any way to wield any collective bargaining power. On the other hand, organized sector employment carries the benefits of social security and other non-wage benefits. Jobs are regular and wages and salaries are governed by regulations and protected through collective bargaining. Consequently, wages and other benefits are much higher than in the unorganized sector (See Box 2.2 for definitions of some important terms used frequently in this report).

> The Indian labour market is dualistic, where a large traditional economy coexists with a high level of growth, surplus, productivity, and modern economy.

The broad features of the labour market and employment prevailing in India are provided in Table 2.2. As can be seen from the table, regular wage employment constitutes about 18 per cent of the total employment. There was a somewhat significant rise in the percentage of regular workers after 2004-05 which was stagnant for two decades prior to that. However, over 60 per cent of the regular workers are informal workers with no social security and only around 40 per cent are formal workers. In other words only 6.8 per cent of the total workers have regular formal jobs which can be categorized as good or decent jobs. It is also important to note that since 2004-05, there has been a one percentage point increase in regular formal jobs. A little less than one-third of the total workers are casual workers and this has been more or less stable (ranging between 30 and 33 per cent) during the three decades from 1983 to 2011-12. Over half of the workers were self-employed in 2011-12 and the figure has declined by five percentage points since the middle of 2004-05 (Table 2.2 and Figure 2.1).

Figure 2.1

Percentage Share of Employed by Work Status: 1983 to 2011/12

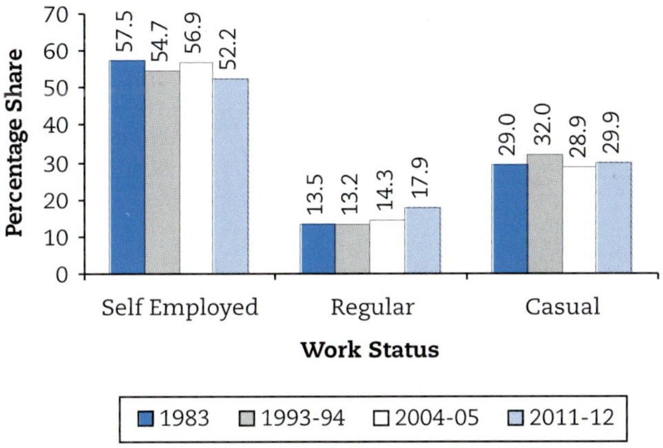

Source: Computed from unit level data of various NSSO rounds.

About one-sixth of the total workers are in the organized sector and the rest (about 84 per cent) are in the unorganized sector. It is also seen that since the early 1990s, there has been slow but steady growth of workers in the organized sector. While there has been some increase in regular formal wage employment, the bulk of the increase in regular wage employment has been in the informal component. This is a fact of considerable significance and is illustrative of the limitations of the employment impact of the Indian growth experience.

The above-mentioned features of the labour market, in which a large majority are casual and irregular workers or petty self-employed producers and own account workers, are hardly in line with an economy which has experienced 6 to 7 per cent growth in per capita income and 8 to 9 per cent growth in GDP. The employment performance *vis-à-vis* growth has obviously not been satisfactory and suggests distorted and exclusionary growth. Thus, the Indian labour market is highly dualistic in nature and this dualism has sharpened over time, more so during the high-growth period. However, as mentioned earlier, since 2004-05, it seems that there has been a small but noticeable change in the trend. The shares of regular employment, regular formal employment and organized sector employment have shown some increase, which is indeed healthy. This significant development needs to be studied carefully to see whether it is indeed an exception.

2.3 Trends and Patterns of Employment Growth

Aggregate employment has grown at an average annual rate of 2 per cent in India during the past four decades since 1972-73, although during the last few years the growth of employment has been substantially reduced. This pattern of employment growth has not been experienced by many countries historically. However, as mentioned in the earlier section, a large part of this growth of employment simply indicates growth in labour force. The growth of organized sector employment and particularly, formal employment has been slow. Of course, the rise in productivity and earnings of workers in the unorganized sector indicate some improvement in the employment conditions of informal workers.

Notwithstanding the quantitative expansion in employment growth, some disconcerting features of employment growth have emerged in recent years:

- Employment growth has decelerated.
- The employment content of growth has shown a decline.
- Sectors with higher employment potential have registered relatively slower growth.
- Agriculture, despite a sharp decline in its importance in gross domestic product, continues to be the largest employer because the non-agricultural sectors have not generated enough employment to effect a shift of workforce.
- Most of the employment growth has been contributed by the unorganized sector, which is characterized by low incomes and poor conditions of work.
- Though employment growth in the organized sector has picked up in recent years, it has largely been led by an increase in employment of casual and contract labour.

There has been a steady growth of workers in the organized sector in the recent decade; while there has been some increase in regular formal wage employment, the bulk of this increase has been in the informal component.

2.3.1 Growth in Employment, GDP and Employment Elasticity

Although long-term employment growth over the period of about four decades, as noted earlier, has been around 2 per cent per annum (which was only a little less than labour force growth), it has seen a declining trend from one decade to another: it was 2.4 per cent during 1972-73/1983, 2.0 per cent in the following ten year period and 1.8 per cent during 1993-94/2004-05 (Table 2.3). There has been a sharp deceleration in employment growth between 2004-05 and 2011-12, as revealed by the latest round of NSSO. This has been largely due to a sharp fall in the workforce participation rate (WFPR) of women, particularly in rural areas as mentioned in Section 2.2.

Table 2.3

Sector-wise Growth of Employment (UPSS) and Employment Elasticity

Sectors	*Employment Growth*				*Employment Elasticity*			
	1972-73/ 83	1983/ 93-94	1993-94/ 2004-05	2004-05/ 2011-12	1972-73/ 83	1983/ 93-94	1993-94/ 2004-05	2004-05/ 2011-12
Primary	1.70	1.35	0.67	–1.98	0.46	0.49	0.26	–0.42
Secondary (including								
Mining & Quarrying)	4.43	2.82	3.97	4.46	0.87	0.53	0.59	0.48
Tertiary	4.21	3.77	3.41	2.09	0.77	0.57	0.43	0.17
Non Agricultural	4.30	3.36	3.64	3.15	0.81	0.55	0.48	0.28
Total	2.44	2.02	1.84	0.45	0.52	0.41	0.29	0.04

Source: Estimates based on various rounds of NSS data on employment and unemployment, adjusted by census population.

The long-term trend of decline in the rate of employment growth is a fact that cannot be ignored. What is particularly intriguing is that this decline has been accompanied by acceleration in the rate of economic growth. Thus, when GDP grew at 4.7 per cent per annum during 1972-73 to 1983, employment growth was 2.4 per cent; GDP growth increased to 5 per cent, but employment growth declined to 2.0 per cent during 1983/1993-94; during 1993-94/2004-05, GDP growth accelerated to 6.3 per cent, but employment growth further declined to 1.8 per cent; and during the period 2004-05/2011-12, when GDP growth was as high as 8.5 per cent, employment grew at an insignificant rate of 0.5 per cent (Appendix Tables 1.2 and 3.6). The declining trend in the employment component of growth is quite clearly seen in terms of the values of employment elasticity (ratio of employment growth to growth in value added) in Table 2.3. It was 0.52 during 1972-73/1983, which declined to 0.41 in the next 10-year period and further to 0.29 during 1993-94/2004-05. During 2004-05/2011-12, it declined to almost zero.

2.3.2 Patterns of Employment Growth at a Disaggregated Level

The employment growth rates have of course varied across sectors and activities. In the secondary sector, (consisting of mining, manufacturing, electricity, water and gas, and construction) growth has been relatively high—in fact the highest among the three sectors, during 1972-73 to 2011-12. It has declined, over this period, with some fluctuations over the shorter periods, but has shown a significant increase during 1994 to 2012. Even during 2004-05 to 2011-12, when overall employment had virtually stagnated, it grew by around 4.5 per cent in the secondary sector. Employment growth in the tertiary or services sector has also been relatively high but has consistently declined over the three periods of 10 years each since 1972-73. The growth of employment in the primary sector, as expected, has been the lowest and has sharply declined between 2004-05 and 2011-12.

Primary Sector

The slow and declining growth of employment in agriculture is a result of the slow and declining rate of GDP growth of this sector and a decline in employment elasticity that turned negative in 2011-12. The negative growth in employment in agriculture also indicates that the sector is not able to absorb the existing workers and they are moving to non-agriculture. In the secondary sector, a high employment growth despite moderate rates of GDP growth has been possible due to relatively high and stable employment elasticity. But in the tertiary sector, a high GDP growth has not been accompanied by high growth in employment and this is reflected in a steep decline in employment elasticity (Table 2.3, Figures 2.2 and 2.3).

Figure 2.2

Sector-wise Employment Growth 1972-73/1983 to 2004-05/2011-12 (UPSS)

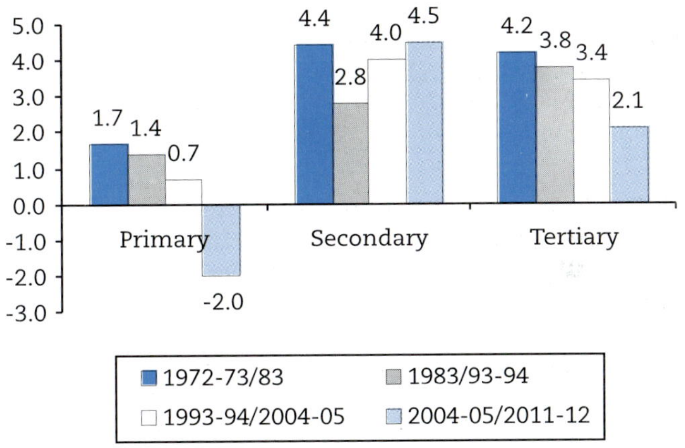

Source: Computed from unit level data of various NSSO rounds.

Figure 2.3

Sector-wise GDP Growth 1972-73/1983 to 2004-05/2011-12 (UPSS)

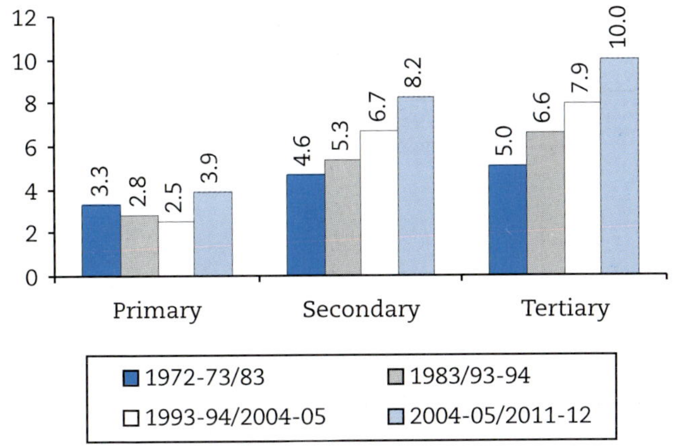

Source: Computed from unit level data of various NSSO rounds.

Secondary Sector

Within the secondary sector, the construction sector experienced a relatively high and increasing rate of employment growth; it was over 7 per cent during 1994-2005, almost similar to its GDP growth. It has recorded almost double digit employment growth between 2004-05 and 2011-12, when the total employment has virtually stagnated (Appendix Table 3.6). Appendix Table 7.1 provides some details about the quantum and quality of employment generated in the construction sector during 2004-05/2009-10 at disaggregated level of 4-digits. Most of the employment generated in construction was of low quality, casual and irregular with low wages.

Employment growth in manufacturing has also been moderately high, and after declining during 1983/1993-94, it registered an increase in the next period, 1994-2005. But it experienced a decline in employment growth during 2004-05/2011-12. The employment elasticity in manufacturing has been relatively high except during 2005-12 (Appendix Tables 3.6 and 3.10a). As can be seen from Appendix Table 7.3, which provides employment growth at 4 digit level, there have been rather significant changes in the pattern of employment in manufacturing industries between 2004-05 and 2009-10 with some industries showing decline and others showing reasonably good growth. The quality of employment as expected, has been better than the construction sector.

Services Sector

In the services sector, trade and transport have shown the best employment performance, with both registering a growth of over 5 per cent during 1994-2005, after having seen a decline in growth rate, sharper in transport than in trade, during 1983-94, over 1973-83. Financial services, however, have recorded the highest increase in employment over the period 1993-94/2004-05. Even during 2004-05/2011-12, this sub-sector of services has registered an employment growth of about 8 per cent, while the trade and transport sub-sectors experienced about 2 per cent growth in employment. Thus it appears that all sub-sectors of the tertiary sector with the possible exception of community, social and personal services have shown reasonably high potential for employment generation (Appendix Table 3.6). The employment growth rates at disaggregated level for selected services are provided in Appendix Table 7.1. The sub sectors at disaggregated level also show the better quality of jobs in trade and transport.

There are a few emerging sectors like 'computer hardware consultancy', 'software publishing', 'data processing' and 'maintenance and repair of office accounting and computing machinery', where although the share of total employment is not very large, their growth rate varies from 17 per cent to 54 per cent annually and the share of regular employment varies from 60 to 95 per cent with relatively high earnings (Appendix Table 7.2). It must, however, be noted that in most sub-sectors of services, while the GDP has seen high and increasing growth, employment growth has been on the decline. Employment elasticity has, therefore, declined sharply during the periods 1972-73/1983 to 2004-05/2011-12 from 0.81 to 0.16 in trade, from 0.91 to 0.13 in transport and from 0.71 to 0.12 in community, social and personal services. In financial services, it has declined from 1.25 to 0.39 during 1972-73/83 to 1983/1993-94 but again increased during 1983/1993-94 to 2004-05/2011-12 from 0.39 to 0.59 (Appendix Tables 3.6 and 3.10a).

Overall Sectoral Pattern

Thus, it may be inferred that the employment content of growth has declined over time; Although it has varied across the sectors, the primary sector, consisting of mainly agriculture, has witnessed least employment growth, which in itself is not worrisome as this sector is home to the bulk of surplus labour. The sub-sectors of the tertiary sector such as financial services which are linked to globalization have witnessed faster growth of employment. However, the manufacturing sector, which has significant multiplier effects with other sectors, has not registered high growth of employment during the recent period due to primarily low growth of output. The quality of employment generated in manufacturing sector, although better than agriculture and construction, was generally not good. Construction has witnessed high growth rate of employment but quality of employment is poor. But for the first time, there is an indication of a structural shift in employment, albeit small, from agriculture to other sectors which is a positive trend.

2.3.3 Gender Differentials in Employment Growth

Female employment, which accounts for around one-third of all employment, grew less than male employment during the past three decades (Table 2.4). During the period 2005-12, the available estimates indicate a steep decline in the growth of employment. But the pattern of employment growth has an important gender dimension; there was an absolute decline in employment for rural females. In this period, for males, in both rural and urban areas, a slowdown in employment growth has occurred; but the sharp absolute decline for rural female warrants further investigation. India has the lowest participation rate for women in the workforce when compared to all its South Asian neighbours except

Table 2.4

Growth of Employment (UPSS)

Years	*Rural*			*Urban*			*Total*		
	Male	*Female*	*Total*	*Male*	*Female*	*Total*	*Male*	*Female*	*Total*
1983-94	1.92	1.39	1.72	3.14	3.38	3.19	2.21	1.64	2.02
1994-2005	1.40	1.54	1.45	3.10	3.30	3.14	1.86	1.81	1.84
1983-2005	1.65	1.47	1.58	3.12	3.34	3.17	2.03	1.73	1.93
2005-2012	1.06	−2.76	−0.22	2.54	1.07	2.23	1.51	−2.04	0.44

Source: Computed from unit level data of various NSSO rounds and various decadal census reports.

Pakistan. A number of experts and commentators have attributed it to the marginalization of women in the labour market because of the absence of suitable jobs for them. Others have termed it as a healthy development indicating rising enrolment of women in schools and colleges as well as withdrawal of a large number of women from work due to rising income (called income effect in economic discourse).

A large percentage of women in India, particularly in rural India, are involved in various part-time economic activities, along with their domestic care duties, which are often not measured by national surveys; this results in under-reporting of economic participation of women.

Certain deficiencies in the way WFPR for women is measured should also be mentioned here. In a poor country like India and more so in rural areas, a very large percentage of women are involved in various part-time economic activities, along with their domestic and care duties, which are very often poorly counted and captured by the national statistical surveys resulting in under-reporting of economic participation of women. This 'invisibility' of women's work has been widely documented and analysed in economic literature. The problem is not unique to India but extends to other poor developing countries. In India, this is a rather significant reason behind the low rates of female LFPR. This is revealed by an extensive survey conducted by the Institute for Human Development (IHD) during 2009-10, with a stratified random sample of 36 villages in Bihar. As against a very low estimate of LFPR of women reported from rural Bihar—around 14 per cent in 2009-10 and 6 per cent in 2011-12 by the NSSO, the IHD survey reports 37 per cent participation of women. Notwithstanding some differences in survey tools and approach, the under-reporting of women's work is strongly evident from the findings of this survey (see Box 2.3).

In fact, the undercounting of women workers may be one of the most important reasons for the recent reported decline in female LFPR. That is not to say that other factors have not played their part. There is significant increase in enrolment of women in educational institutions; at the elementary levels it is now universal and at other levels also it has increased significantly. The female student population increased from 118 million in 2004-05 to 151 million in 2011-12. In case of rural females, the average year of schooling was 2.7 years in 2004-05 which increased to 3.8 years in 2011-12. In case of urban females too, it has increased from 5.9 years to 6.8 years during the same period. That is why the drop in female LFPR during 2005-12 is sharpest in the age group of 15-24 years. The tightening in the labour market among certain groups due to enhanced income and efforts at motivating women to withdraw from the labour force is also considered to be one of the factors behind the decline in female LFPR. In part, the slowdown of female employment during the period 2005-12 may be due to an increase in their enrolment rate as well as withdrawal from distress employment due to improved family earnings during this period.

It is also important to understand the sub-sectors in which female employment has grown or declined; the sub-sectors characterized by odd working hours, challenges of community or cultural barriers are generally not attractive for women workers. In the three important non-farm sectors: (i) manufacturing, (ii) trade, restaurants and hotels, and (iii) transport,

Box 2.3

Women's Work

Women's work remains under-reported, undercounted and undervalued in national statistics. There are serious problems with the estimation of women's participation in the workforce in conventional data sources such as the NSSO. Field studies such as IHD's survey data from 36 villages in Bihar provides some insights which are not captured by secondary data. For instance, the female LFPR is as high as 37 per cent, even using a narrow definition of LFPR (see table below). This is more realistic than the 14 per cent estimated by the 66th Round of Employment–Unemployment Survey of the NSSO for female LFPR in Bihar.

Labour Force Participation of Workers Aged 15-59 (%) in Bihar

	*Narrow Definition**			*Wide Definition***		
	Primary Activity	*Secondary Activity*	*Total*	*Primary Activity*	*Secondary Activity*	*Total*
Men	78	41	81	86	65	94
Women	14	28	37	20	56	64

Notes: * Narrow definition of worker = employer, own account worker/self-employed, regular wage worker/salaried, casual wage worker and attached labour; **Wide definition of worker = the above five categories + unpaid family worker, and beggar

Source: Rodgers, Gerry, Amrita Datta, Janine Rodgers, Sunil K. Mishra and Alakh N. Sharma (2013). *The Challenges of Inclusive Development in Bihar*, New Delhi: Institute for Human Development (IHD).

storage and communication, employment growth of women was much lower than men during the period 1994-2012. In trade, restaurants and hotels, male employment growth (9.9 per cent) was almost double the female growth in employment (5.1 per cent). In manufacturing it was 4.4 per cent for females as compared to 5.7 per cent for males and in transport, storage and communication it was 10.5 per cent for females as compared to 13.1 per cent for males. In the seven years during 2004-05 to 2011-12, there has been an absolute decline of rural female employment in these three sectors (Appendix Table 3.6 and NSSO Surveys, 61st and 68th Rounds). The dynamics behind such changes need to be investigated in depth.

Gender discrimination is evident in the greater proportion of women engaged in low productivity, low-income and insecure jobs in the unorganized sector including in farms.

If we compare the industry-wise share of employment for males and females, in agriculture and related activities (a low productivity sector), the ratio of female workers in the sector to total female workers in the workforce is much higher than that of males. In the year 2011-12, 62.8 per cent of female workers were engaged in agriculture and allied activities as compared to 43.6 per cent of total male workers. The percentage of females employed in agriculture and allied activities to the total female employment in rural areas is as high as the 75 per cent. In all other activities of the non-agriculture sector (a more productive sector), the proportion of female workers is less than that of their male counterparts in the year 2011-12, with an exception of manufacturing where the share was marginally higher for females. It shows that there is higher degree of disguised unemployment among female workers in rural areas, who are mainly employed in agriculture, and they are less likely migrate in search of non-farm employment (Appendix Table 3.7).

With the decline in the share of agriculture in the economy, it is quite obvious that more and more workers would move out of agriculture into non-agriculture work. However, these opportunities are limited and more easily available to males than to females. Consequently, while rural males increasingly move into non-farm work, particularly in trade, hotels and restaurants, construction and transport, storage and communication, women appear to be stuck in agriculture.

Figure 2.4

Percentage Shares of Male and Female Workers by Select Indicators (2011-12)

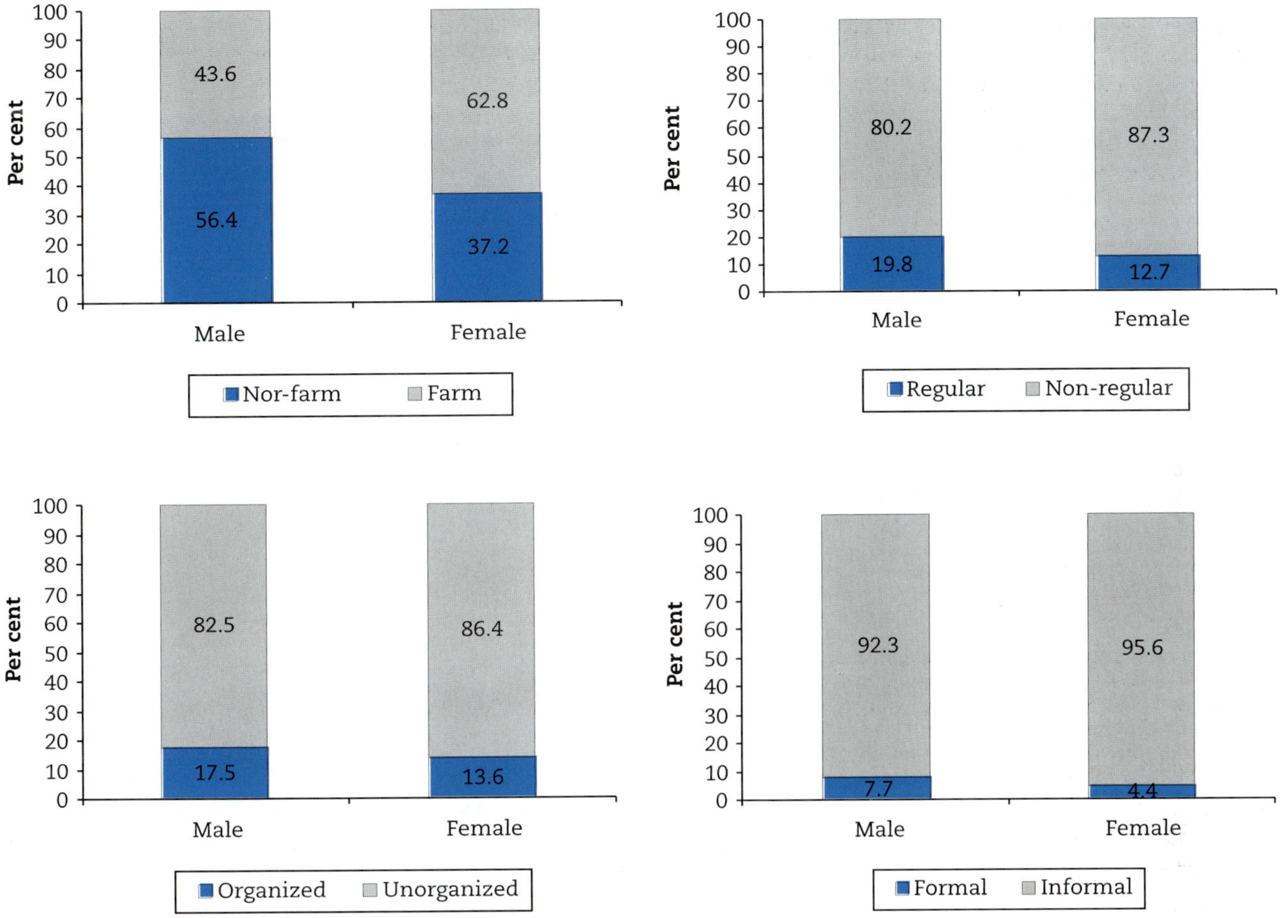

Source: Computed from unit level data of NSSO, 68th Round.

While the rising income of some households may cause some decline in the female LFPR, the other factor due to limited employment opportunities in rural areas cannot be dismissed. The absence of women from the non-agricultural sector for a continuous period makes them invisible in this sector and reduces the job opportunities for those females who need work. The decline in female employment, in the non-agriculture sector in rural areas, for the continued period may also create large gaps between urban and rural incomes. It may also affect the status of women and their role in household decision-making. This means that there is need to identify the ways by which we can create job opportunities for females in the non-farm sectors of the rural areas.

Labour market discrimination on the basis of gender evolves with time, changes in technology and culture change. Jobs in the emerging sectors of information and communication technology, business process outsourcing, media, entertainment and hospitality are influenced by gender roles and divides. Certain jobs known to be women-oriented or almost exclusively being carried out by women such as nursing, primary school teaching and so on are increasingly witnessing more and more employment of men.

Gender discrimination is conspicuous in the quality of employment accessed by woman. Out of the total female workforce, greater proportions are engaged in low productivity, low income, and insecure jobs on farms in the unorganized and informal sectors, as compared to the similar statistics for men (see Figure 2.4). Although in many spheres, gender

Table 2.5a

Percentage Distribution (Row-wise) of Total Workers (in millions) by Unorganized/Organized Sectors and Formal/Informal Workers: 1999-2000, 2004-05 and 2011-12

Year	Unorganized Sector	Organized Sector	Total
Informal Workers			
1999-2000	95.7	4.3	100.0 (367.5)
2004-05	93.9	6.1	100.0 (427.3)
2011-12	89.4	10.6	100.0 (436.4)
*Formal Workers***			
1999-2000	22.2*	77.8	100.0 (29.3)
2004-05	6.7	93.3	100.0 (30.1)
2011-12	5.2	94.8	100.0 (35.6)
Total Workers			
1999-2000	90.2	9.8	100.0 (396.9)
2004-05	88.2	11.8	100.0 (457.4)
2011-12	83.0	17.0	100.0 (472.0)

Note: Figures in parentheses are of workers in millions.

* *Lesser number of enterprise codes in 1999-2000* did not allow to disaggregate to get proper share of formal workers in informal sector and therefore it is overestimated.

** Formal workers include the regular workers with social security in organized sector as well as unorganized sector.

Source: Computed from unit level data of various NSSO rounds.

Table 2.5b

Percentage Distribution (Column-wise) of Total Workers (in million) by Unorganized/Organized Sectors and Formal/Informal Workers: 1999-2000, 2004-05 and 2011-12

Year	Unorganized Sector	Organized Sector	Total
Informal Workers			
1999-2000	98.1	41.1	92.6
2004-05	99.5	48.0	93.4
2011-12	99.5	57.8	92.4
*Formal Workers***			
1999-2000	1.8*	58.8	7.4
2004-05	0.5	52.0	6.6
2011-12	0.5	42.2	7.5
Total Workers			
1999-2000	100.0 (358.0)	100.0 (38.9)	100.0 (396.9)
2004-05	100.0 (403.4)	100.0 (54.0)	100.0 (457.4)
2011-12	100.0 (391.8)	100.0 (80.2)	100.0 (472.0)

Note: Same as Table 2.5a.

Source: Computed from unit level data of various NSSO rounds.

Figure 2.5a

Percentage Workers in the Organized Sector

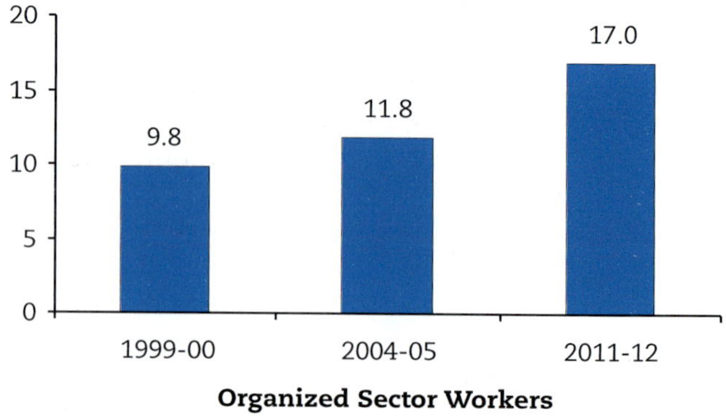

Source: Computed from unit level data of various NSSO rounds.

Figure 2.5b

Percentage Workers in Formal Employment across both Organized and Unorganized Sectors

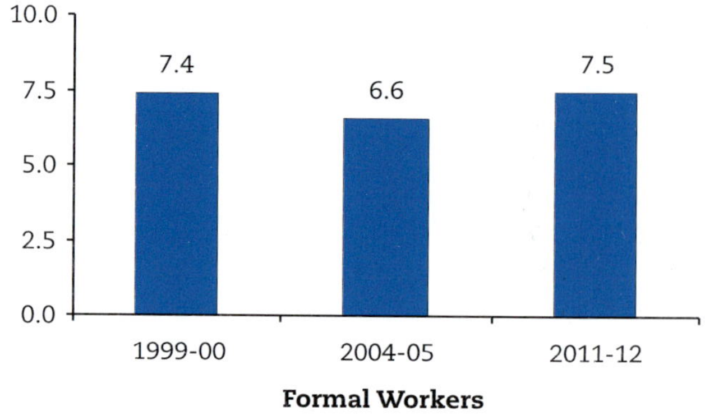

Source: Computed from unit level data of various NSSO rounds.

Figure 2.6

Percentage of Informal Workers in Formal Sector: 1999-2000 to 2011-12

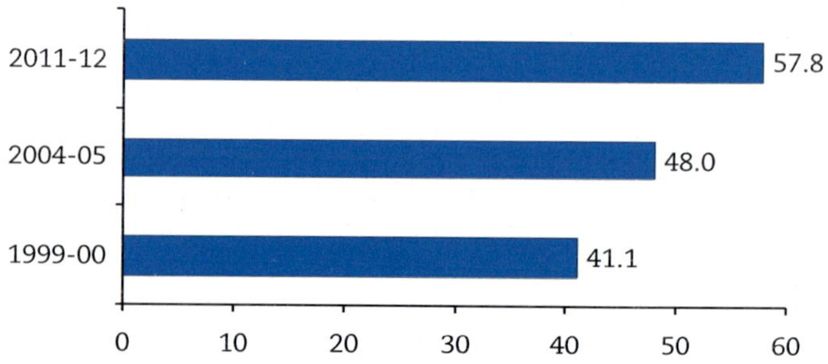

Source: Computed from unit level data of various NSSO rounds.

discrimination is declining, it is obvious that India still has a long way to go in terms of ensuring gender equality in work opportunities.

It is a matter of concern that the employment structure of women is comparatively rigid and not adequately responsive enough to socio-cultural change. With rising educational enrolments, the coming years will witness a surge in the number of educated women; a significant percentage of then would be graduates. The LFPR of women who are at least graduates is 33.3 per cent as opposed to the average of 22 per cent for all women. Hence, these graduate women will enter the workforce in large numbers in the foreseeable future without adequate opportunities of employment on the offer for them which are gainful, equal and conducive (Datta and Sharma, 2013).

2.3.4 *Organized Versus Unorganized Sector/ Formal versus Informal Employment*

Agricultural employment by its very nature is largely informal. It had been a widely held belief that as an economy matures, structural shift of workers from the primary to the secondary and tertiary sectors would improve conditions of work as it would lead to formalization of employer–employee contracts. This belief has been challenged in recent years when informal employment in the secondary and tertiary sectors is seen to have grown at the expense of formal labour. Most of the sectors within the services sector—financial services, real estate business, education, health—have witnessed greater employment of informal workers. Contract labour has been increasing steadily in factories.

Trends in 'Informalization'

As per the NSSO surveys, the organized sector accounted for only about 10 per cent of total employment in 1999-2000 and 12 per cent in 2004-05. The proportion is found to have further increased to 17 per cent in 2011-12 (Figure 2.5a). However, all those employed in the organized sector are not formal workers; only 7.5 per cent of the total workers are formally employed and enjoy regular jobs with social security benefits (Figure 2.5b).The organized sector which comprises about 80 million workers, has 58 per cent (i.e., 46 million) workers in the 'informal worker' category, with neither secure tenure of employment nor any protection against the contingent risks during or after employment. In fact, the proportion of informal workers has been rising over time from 41 per cent of organized sector employment in 1999-2000 to 48 per cent in 2004-05 and further to 58 per cent in 2011-12 (Tables 2.5a, 2.5b and Figure 2.6). Thus, of all the workers in the organized and unorganized sectors together, 92.5 per cent were in 'informal employment'. Only 7.5 per cent had secure job tenures and social security against contingent risks of work and life. Their proportion declined slightly during 1999-2000/2004-05 but rose to 7.5 per cent in 2011-12 (Figure 2.5b).

Most of the sectors within the services sector like financial services, real estate business, education, health, have witnessed greater employment of informal workers. Contract labour has been increasing steadily in factories.

The employment data on the organized sector is also provided by the Director General of Employment and Training (DGE&T).[2] DGE&T collects the data from secondary and tertiary units in the private sector employing 10 or more persons and all public sector units. Although it has limited coverage and there are some inacuracies in figures, due to non-response of some units but it is interesting for the employment trends.

According to the DGE&T, organized sector employment peaked at 28.3 million in 1997 before showing a continuous decline till 2005. It rose again after 2005 to reach 29.0 million in the year 2011. It should be noted that the decline has been mainly in public sector employment which has continued to decline except during 2009 and 2010. So far as the private sector is concerned, it showed a small decline during 2001-04, but increased to an all time high at 11.5 million in 2011. Decline in public sector employment is visible across manufacturing, construction, transport as well as community, social and personal services. Mining is the only sector where some increase has taken place in public sector employment in recent years (Appendix Table 5.1). The

2. According to the DGE&T, the unorganized sector includes the operating units whose activities are not regulated under any statutory act or legal provision and/or which do not maintain regular accounts and the rest are treated as oganized. The two estimates of oganized sector as discussed from NSSO and DGE&T may differ marginally.

Figure 2.7

Trends in Employment in Organized Sector in India, 1981-2011 (in '000)

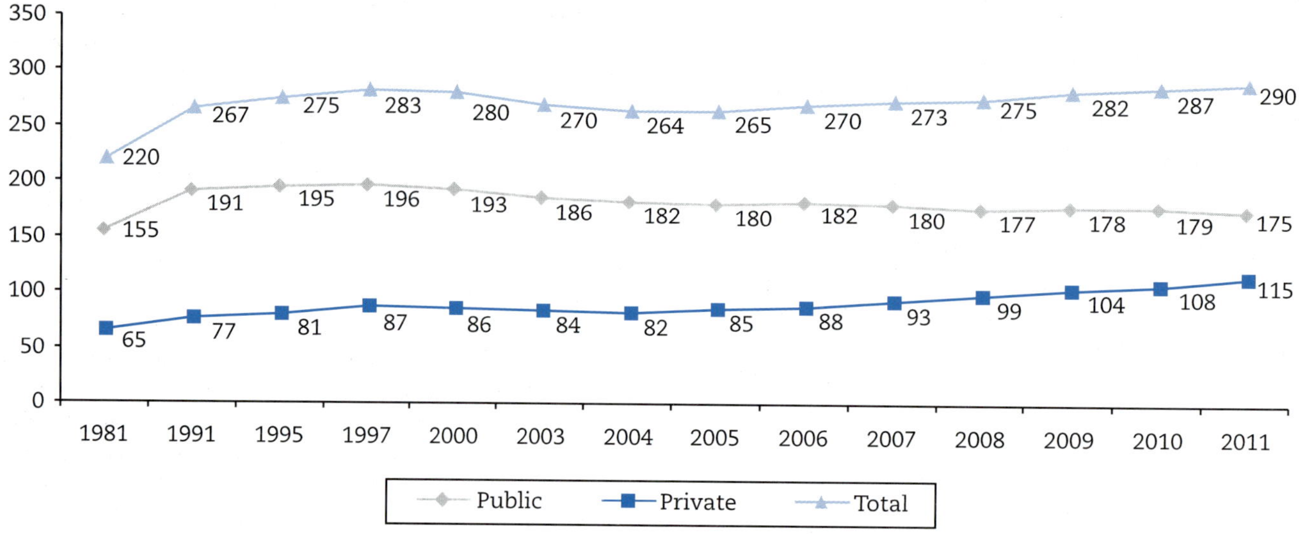

Source: Economic Surveys, Government of India, Various Years.

trend in organized sector employment, both public and private, since the introduction of economic reforms can be more clearly seen in Figure 2.7.

> In the organized manufacturing sector, the growth of contract workers has been much higher than the increase in regular workers in recent years.

The decline in public sector employment has come in the wake of economic liberalization policies which led to downsizing of government agencies, reduction in overstaffing of public enterprises and withdrawal of the government from commercial activities. Employment in all segments of the private sector except manufacturing has continuously risen since 1991, and even in manufacturing the trend appears to have reversed, with an increase since 2004, which can also be seen from the data of *Annual Survey of Industry* (ASI). During 2001-2004, employment in manufacturing declined before a reversal during 2005 and 2009, when there was significant growth in employment in both public and private sectors (Appendix Table 5.1 and NSSO Survey, 66th Round). However, this employment growth is mostly because of the employment of contract workers at the expense of regular workers. The analysis of data from the ASI shows that in the organized manufacturing sector during 2000s, while regular workers increased by little more than 2 per cent per annum the growth of contract workers has been around 10 per cent per annum. This has resulted in a significant increase in the share of contract workers from around 13 per cent in 1990-91, to around 20 per cent in 1990-2000 to as high as 34 per cent in the year 2010-11. This trend of increasing contractualization in the organized manufacturing sector has been evident from the early 1990s when the process of economic reforms had started but has accelerated during the 2000s, as is evident from Figure 2.8.

Figure 2.8

Percentage of Contract Workers in Organized Manufacturing Industries: 1990-91/2010-11

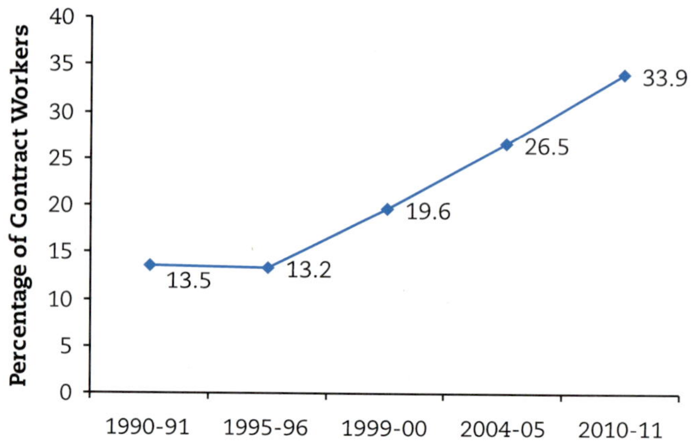

Source: Annual Survey of Industries (various years), Ministry of Statistics and Programme Implementation, Government of India.

Conditions of Work in the Informal Sector

Rising trends of informalization and flexbilization have serious implications for quality and conditions of work. Annual Survey of Industries (ASI) provides information on manufacturing, processing and repairing units registered under sections 2 m(i) and 2 m (ii) of Indian Factories Act of 1948 on annual basis with certain time lag. The Factories Act (1948) lays down norms to ensure decent work conditions, minimum earnings and security of work. However, several research studies have shown the lack of seriousness in their implementation. The NCEUS report (2007) and surveys undertaken by the Labour Bureau of the Government of India provide a detailed account of the defiance of law. In industries such as chemicals, leather tanning, fire works, brick kilns, workers are exposed to life-threatening chemical fumes due to lack of proper ventilation in hot and humid conditions. Lack of proper lighting in weaving workshops, manufacture of leather products, embroidery, etc., leads not only to injuries, but also income penalties in case of poor quality of work. Norms of physical conditions of work are also flouted. Informal workers are rarely provided with basic amenities such as drinking water, first-aid, rest rooms, canteens, etc. The law entitles all workers, regular and contractual, to these facilities. Industries such as mining and construction, which employ informal labour in clusters located far away from their residences, provide housing and sanitation facilities which offer immense scope for improvement. Industries which pose severe occupational hazards, such as mining and quarrying, printing presses, ship breaking, etc., also employs a large share of informal workers. In these industries, loss of lives, amputations, adverse health outcomes are commonplace due to lack of adequate precautions and safety measures. Informal workers in such industries are vulnerable as compensation for injuries and illnesses contracted in the course of work (say due to inhalation of toxic fumes or particles) are minimal or non-existent.

> The lack of housing and sanitation, deplorable working conditions in informal enterprises and within the premises of home-based workers, the plight of the petty self-employed working in streets and pavements and the insecurities of work, add to the vulnerability of the working poor in India.

There is pervasive job insecurity even among workers—as of 2011-12 around two-third of these workers are also contractual. The rising proportion of informal/contract workers even in the government and public sector enterprises amply reflects the high levels of uncertainty of livelihoods, both in terms of income and social security. Even in the case of regular workers, the incidence of social security has fallen over time. In 2009-10, less than 50 per cent of regular workers were insured (NSSO Survey, 66th Round).

Since a large proportion of informal labour is remunerated on a piece-rate basis, workers usually prolong their work hours in order to earn higher incomes. A stipulated work week for all adult workers should not exceed 48 hours in a week and 10.5 hours in a day. In reality, work days of domestic workers, security guards, coolies, rag pickers, fisherfolk, several other categories of both self-employed and wage workers and more recently, employees in Business Process Outsourcing (BPO) sector often stretch to over 12 hours. Informal workers have no paid benefits such as casual leave, sick leave and maternity leave. Wages are earned on a daily, no-work-no-pay basis. In an economy where a large pool of unskilled labour is available, there will be no labour shortage as long as higher skills are not required. The number of workers employed each day can be increased or decreased easily based on the needs of that day and the employer is not bound to guarantee work or pay to any worker.

The effectiveness of trade unions has reduced over time with lower collective coverage and union density. The number of inspections, prosecutions and convictions for violation of labour laws has been abysmal, posing little threat to rampant violations.

2.3.5 *Employment Share by Sector*

The majority of Indian workers are engaged in agriculture and allied activities (primary sector). With economic development, agriculture is expected to decline in importance in terms of its share in employment and output. The proportion of agriculture in total employment has declined over the years: from 74 per cent in 1972-73 to 56 per cent in 2004-05. It has declined further to 49 per cent in 2011-12. But the decline in the employment share of agriculture has been much slower than its share in GDP from agriculture. Thus, while share of agriculture in GDP declined from 41 per cent in 1972-73 to 14 per cent in 2011-12 (Table 2.6), that in employment declined from 74 per cent to only 49 per cent during this period. Decline in GDP share has been faster during 1993-94 to 2011-12, from 28 to 14 per cent; while the rate of decline in employment share during this period has been relatively slow, from 64 per cent to 49 per cent.

The decline in the employment share of agriculture has been mostly compensated by an increase in the share of the tertiary sector in the pre-reform period (before 1991); but ever since the economic reforms, the secondary sector has been the main gainer of the shift in employment. Yet, the increase in its employment share has not been commensurate with the increase in its share of GDP during 1993-94 to 2011-12. The share of secondary sector in employment has increased at a relatively faster rate while its share in GDP has remained constant at about one-fourth of the total. Within the secondary sector, construction has sharply increased its share in employment. Manufacturing increased its share, both in employment and GDP, but rather slowly. In the tertiary sector, trade experienced a fast increase in its share in employment, and a significant increase in its share in GDP in the post-reform period. Financial services registered a faster increase both in its employment and GDP share, though its share in employment is small (2.6 per cent)—about one-seventh of its share in GDP (18.1 per cent). Community, social and personal services which used to be the largest activity in the tertiary sector, both in terms of employment and GDP, in the pre-reform period, saw a marginal decline in their share both in employment and GDP (Appendix Tables 1.1 and 3.5).

The asymmetry in the rate of change in employment and GDP shares of different sectors and divisions has serious implications for earnings across sectors. In 1972-73, when agriculture employed about three-fourth of the workers and produced a little over two-fifth of GDP, the output per worker in agriculture was already significantly lower than in non-agricultural activities; the ratio being 1:3.6. In 2011-12, the differential has considerably increased, the ratio going up to about 1:6. Consequently, there has been a large decline in the relative earnings of those engaged in agriculture. That is partly because agricultural growth has been consistently slower than that in the non-agricultural sectors; but, mainly, because a shift of workers from agricultural to non-agricultural activities, as expected in the process of economic development, has not taken place at the desired level. Agriculture has grown at an average rate of 2.8 per cent per annum as against a 6.8 per cent growth in the non-agricultural sector during the period under consideration. It is not generally realistic to expect a much higher growth rate in agriculture. But even if it grows at a rate of about 4 per cent per annum, as was envisaged in the Eleventh Plan, it cannot employ many more persons productively. The output per worker in agriculture is so low that even at a higher growth rate it would need to reduce its workforce significantly in order to provide a reasonable level of income to those engaged in it. It is precisely for this reason that the Planning Commission projected no increase in the number of workers in agriculture during the Eleventh Plan (2007-12) and a decline of 4 million during the Twelfth Plan period (2012-2017). (Planning Commission, 2012, Vol. I, pp.76-77).

In most of the backward and poor states, there is a large concentration of the workforce in agriculture. In some of the eastern states (such as West Bengal and Bihar) due to high density of population in rural areas, more than 90 per cent of the farmers are small and marginal, and are barely able to make both ends

Table 2.6

Percentage Shares of Employment (UPSS) and GDP in India

Sectors	*Sectoral Share in Employment*					*Sectoral Share in GDP*				
	1972-73	*1983*	*1993-94*	*2004-05*	*2011-12*	*1972-73*	*1983*	*1993-94*	*2004-05*	*2011-12*
Primary	73.92	68.6	63.98	56.3	48.90	41.1	35.5	28.4	19.0	14.1
Secondary (including Mining and Quarrying)	11.3	13.8	14.96	18.78	24.37	24.4	25.8	26.8	27.9	27.5
Tertiary	14.78	17.6	21.07	24.92	26.73	34.5	38.7	44.8	53.0	58.4
Non-agricultural	26.08	31.4	36.02	43.7	51.10	58.9	64.5	71.6	81.0	85.9
Total	100.0	100.0	100.0	100.0	100.0	100.0	100.0	100.0	100.0	100.0

Source: Estimates based on various rounds of NSS data on employment and unemployment.

Figure 2.9

Sector-wise Output Per Worker (in ₹ thousands at 2004-05 Prices): 1993-94/2011-12

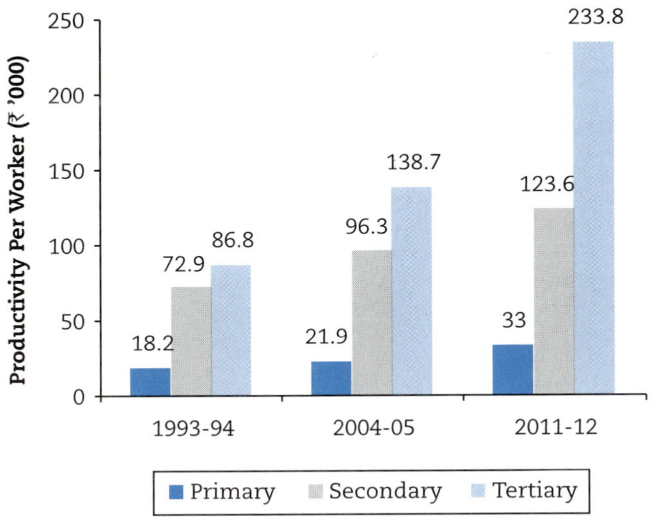

Source: Computed from unit level data of various NSSO rounds and various issues of the National Accounts Statistics.

Figure 2.10

Industry-wise Output Per Worker (in ₹ thousands at 2004-05 prices): 2011-12

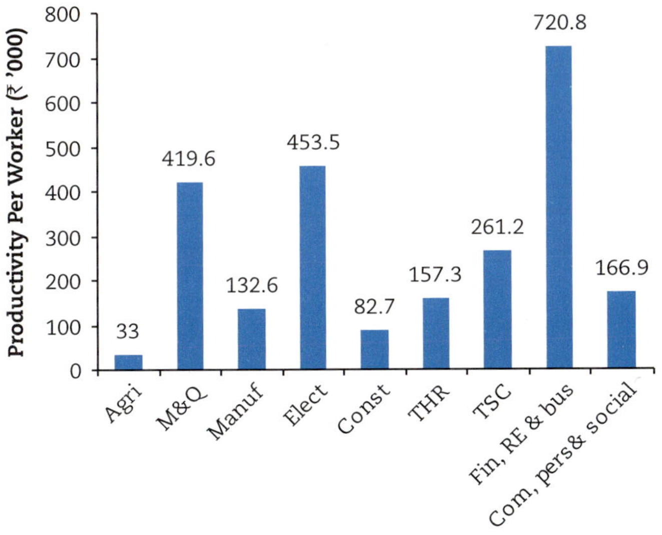

Source: Computed from unit level data of various NSSO rounds and various issues of the National Accounts Statistics.

meet through agricultural activities. Thus, the shifting of the workforce from agriculture to non-agriculture, more so in backward states, is urgently needed. Along with this, agriculture and allied activities have to grow at a faster rate than in the past. This requires measures to improve agricultural productivity, especially among small and marginal farmers.

If we compare the output per worker per annum (at 2004-05 prices) between the secondary and tertiary sectors, there was only a difference of about 20 per cent in the year 1993-94 (i.e., secondary: ₹ 72,900 and tertiary: ₹ 86,800); but after liberalization it increased to 100 per cent in the year 2001-12 (Figure 2.9). Within the secondary sector, from employment point of view, there are two major industries at one digit level *viz.*, manufacturing and construction. The output per worker in manufacturing has increased by more than 130 per cent during 1993-94 to 2011-12, but in construction it remained almost same during this period (Appendix Table 3.10b). As a whole, the growth in the output per worker in the tertiary sector was higher than in the secondary sector. Within the tertiary sector, the increase in the output per worker during 1993-94 to 2011-12 was highest in case of transport, storage & communication (210 per cent) followed by trade, hotels & restaurants (120 per cent) and financing, real estate & business services (25 per cent) (Appendix Table 3.10b and Figure 2.10).

In keeping with the above facts, new jobs that are required to be created have to come from the non-agricultural sectors. In a 20 to 25 years perspective, the employment structure must be envisioned as consisting of about 20-25 per cent in agriculture and 75-80 per cent in non-agricultural activities as against 50 per cent in agriculture and 50 per cent in non-agriculture in 2011-12. It would imply that all new employment opportunities will be located in non- agricultural activities in the coming years.

The pattern of growth led by the services sector in India seems to be distorted and contrary to the historical experiences of the developed countries where the shift of employment had taken place from agriculture to first industry and then to services. The late industrializing countries of south-east and east Asia, including China, have similar experiences.

As can be seen from India's employment share of manufacturing, it is much lower than that of China and other Asian countries. It is widely believed that the neglect of the manufacturing sector has been one of the most important causes of the slow growth of employment in the country; as the manufacturing sector has direct and indirect linkage with other sectors of the economy, leading to larger creation of employment.

Serious doubts have been expressed over pursuing such a growth path, in a labour-surplus country like India, where industrialization has been retarded. The services-led growth has resulted in high wage and non-wage earnings, providing enormous benefits to the middle class. In fact, the rapid growth of services over a long period of time seems to be unsustainable now. The difficulties in the balance of payments, high level of current accounts deficit, the growing anomaly between domestic absorption and domestic production, and slowdown in growth are the results of this pattern of distorted pattern growth (Ghose, 2013).

2.3.6 The Working Poor

The analysis in the preceding sections shows that in India, the problem of those underemployed and working but poor—'the working poor'—is more acute than open unemployment, although the latter dimension is becoming increasingly more important because of the youth bulge (visible in Section 2.6). 'The working poor' exist in massive numbers in India as is evident from the high incidence of poverty on the basis of even the modest 'official' poverty line. One-fourth of all workers were poor in 2011-12, with the percentage being as high as 36 per cent among casual workers. If the poverty line is enhanced to US$ 2 (PPP), around 58 per cent of all workers will slip below it. No less than 75 per cent casual and 60 per cent own account self-employed workers would also be categorized as poor (Table 2.7a). By the current poverty line, the number of working poor is around 118 million (2011-12). Of the 118 million poor, 59.5 million are self-employed and 51 million casual workers (Table 2.7b). On the basis of US$ 2 (PPP), the number of poor would be around 276 million. Indeed, this is a huge number which shows the qualitative dimensions of the employment challenge in India.

In India, the problem of those underemployed and working but poor, "known as—working poor"—is more acute than open unemployment.

In fact, the statistics do not adequately capture the vulnerability of the 'working poor' in the country. The lack of housing and sanitation, deplorable conditions of work in the informal enterprises and within the premises of home-based workers, the plight of the petty self-employed working in streets and on pavements and insecurity of work and life are plainly visible. Unfortunately, the national statistical system has not been able to document and capture these critical dimensions of vulnerability of the working poor in India.

Table 2.7a

Percentage of Poor Workers by Employment Status: 2011-12

Status	*Tendulkar Poverty Line*			*US$ 2 (PPP)*		
	Rural	*Urban*	*Total*	*Rural*	*Urban*	*Total*
Own Account Workers (including UFW)	26.5	17.5	24.6	67.2	34.4	60.4
Employer	6.3	1.6	4.4	30.3	4.4	19.6
Regular Employed	13.2	7.1	9.3	43.6	17.8	27.0
Casual Worker	36.4	33.7	36.0	78.6	57.6	75.9
All	28.6	15.0	25.0	68.8	30.0	58.5

Note: UFW: Unpaid Family Worker.

Source: Computed from unit level data of NSSO, 68th Round.

Table 2.7b

Number of Poor as per Current Poverty Line by Employment Category: 2011-12

Employment Categories	*No. of Poor ('000)*
Self-employed workers	59,500
Regular workers	7,800
Casual workers	51,000
All employed	118,300

Source: Computed from unit level data of NSSO, 68th Round.

2.4 Migration of Workers

Mobility in the labour market may be across sectors, occupations, work statuses, and location. Geographical migration is the most important and possibly most complex form of worker mobility, which takes many forms and has an equally diverse set of causes behind each. Distress migration by the rural poor, due to the lack of local livelihood opportunities, is most common. The Census and the NSS mainly identify permanent or semi-permanent migration but fail to capture seasonal migration, the magnitude of which is both large and growing (Srivastava and Sasikumar, 2005; Srivastava, 2011[3]).

3. Parts of this section and most estimates on migration from secondary data sources have been drawn from Srivastava (2011).

Box 2.4

The Migration Story from Bihar

Conventional data sources such as the Census and NSSO are unable to capture the dynamics of migration in their entirety. Owing to their conceptual framework, survey design and empirical shortcomings, they have a bias towards long-term and permanent migration, and tend to miss out on a significant proportion of short-term and circular migration. Micro-level studies are a very useful source of in-depth information related to migration, its characteristics and pattern. Recent longitudinal survey data of the IHD's Bihar Research Programme shows that more than one-fourth of all workers constituted out-migrants in 2010 in the state. It also reveals that there has been a substantial increase in the incidence of migration from rural areas over the last three decades (Figure 2.11).

While the better-off sections of the population too migrate, the disadvantaged and marginalized sections appear to be resorting more to migration. As such, in order to understand the nuances of migration both from the motivations perspective as well as from the outcomes or benefits viewpoint, it requires more in-depth survey-based enquiry.

Figure 2.11

Percentage of Migrant Workers to Total Workers, 1981-2010

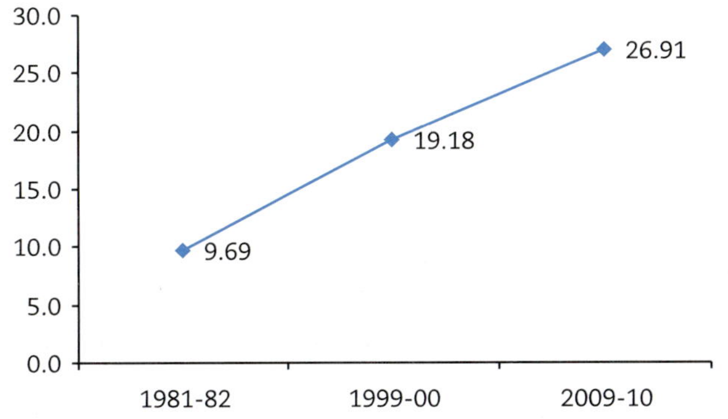

Source: Gerry Rodgers, Amrita Datta, Janine Rodgers, Sunil K. Mishra and Alakh N. Sharma (2013). *The Challenges of Inclusive Development in Bihar.* New Delhi: Institute for Human Development (IHD).

Most of the circular or internal migration remains outside the coverage domain of the limited secondary data definitions. Only primary surveys tend to reveal the high incidence of migration that is seasonal, intermittent, circular or temporary.

> The economic and non-economic costs of moving to cities are prohibitively high, as are barriers to formal employment markets and productive self-employment, for migrants to urban areas.

About 314 million persons or 32 per cent of the Indian population could be described as 'ever migrant' in 2001 using the change in Usual Place of Residence (UPR) definition (Registrar General and Census Commissioner, Population Census, 2001). The National Sample Survey estimates that in 2007-08, 326 million people or 28.6 per cent of people were 'ever' migrants by the UPR definition. However, the bulk of the migrants in India are women who migrate out of their villages due to marriages.

> A majority of migrants to urban areas are the poor and vulnerable employed in the informal economy. Women migrants are often absorbed as domestic workers.

The Census and the NSS show that migration (including rural-urban migration) for economic reasons has gone up. The 2007-08 NSS survey collected information on characteristics of both in-migrants and out-migrants, which clearly establishes that migration rates are positively associated with educational attainment, social group status and per capita consumption. Those who migrate for employment have a high propensity to migrate to urban areas. While female out-migrants usually migrate shorter distances; 45.8 per cent of male migrants from rural households and 33.3 per cent from urban households were found to be inter-state migrants. Notably, 78.3 per cent males (32.6 million) and 2.4 per cent (1.7 million) females migrated for economic reasons. The percentage of interstate out-migrants, among all out-migrants, was very high in the poorer states such as Bihar (61.8 per cent), Jharkhand (54.8 per cent), Uttarakhand (45.5 per cent), Uttar Pradesh (35.1 per cent) and Odisha (35.5 per cent) (Srivastava, 2011).

A decline in short duration migration rates was also noticed. Furthermore, the presence of poorer migrants in cities seems to be shrinking which suggests that the cities are becoming more unfavourable to poor rural migrants (Kundu, 2009). Rural migrants are finding it increasingly difficult to move permanently to urban areas along with their families. The economic and non-economic costs of moving to cities are prohibitively high as are the barriers to formal employment markets and avenues of self-employment. But the result is not less migration but more circulatory and seasonal migration to cater to the accumulation needs of high urban growth. In other words, the changing pattern of urban migration co-exists with a large, and possibly growing, mass of informal migrant workers. The trend and pattern of seasonal migration represents the most vulnerable segment of migrant workers.

The socio-economic profile of the short duration seasonal out-migrants is very different from the other migrants. These migrants are much more likely to be from socially deprived and poorer groups, have low levels of education, and are more likely to be engaged in casual work. More than two-thirds of short duration out-migrants moved to urban areas. About 45 per cent of these migrants went to other states (8.6 per cent to rural areas and 36.5 per cent to urban areas of the destination states). But inter-state migration was more among males (47.9 per cent) compared to females (27.5 per cent). The highest percentage of migrants was in the construction industry (36.2 per cent), followed by agriculture-related sectors (20.4 per cent) and then manufacturing (15.9 per cent) (Srivastava, 2011).

There is no hard secondary data to establish any increase in seasonal and circulatory migration. However, a number of detailed empirical studies show both a high incidence of such migration as well as its growth. A longitudinal survey in 36 villages in Bihar conducted by IHD shows a significant increase in migration between 1981-82 and 2009-10 (see Box 2.4). In the out-migration endemic rural areas of central and tribal Andhra Pradesh, Bihar (particularly north Bihar), or eastern Uttar Pradesh, the incidence of families with at least one out-migrant, ranges from 30 per cent to 70 per cent. An industry or sector-wise picture also reveals a very high incidence of seasonal and circulatory migration in many industries and sectors. Seasonal migratory labour is concentrated in agriculture, construction, brick kilns, textiles, mines and quarries, sericulture, head loaders and *coolies*, rice mills and other agro-processing, salt plants, rickshaws and other types of land transportation, leather manufacture, diamond cutting and polishing and other unorganized industries which have a seasonal nature. Circulatory labour is also concentrated in many other industries including textiles (power looms and garments), manufacturing, domestic and other support services, land transport, head loaders and others. Rough estimates by Srivastava (2011) show that there could be about 80 million migrant labourers concentrated largely in the non-agricultural sector. These numbers are still smaller than the recent estimates of labour migration in China; but nonetheless, they contribute a very large proportion of the waged and self-employed workers in the non-agricultural informal economy (Srivastava, 2011: 423).

Irrespective of urban or rural areas, men migrate into non-agricultural work. The majority of urban migrants are poor and vulnerable workers employed in informal economy. The unbalanced pattern of regional growth has largely led to such a phenomenon. Urban women migrants are generally absorbed in the services sector, often as domestic help. The basic human rights of such workers are often violated and a coherent policy which could support migrant workers needs to be formulated and implemented (Srivastava, 2011).

A large survey of around 8000 households conducted by IHD in 2012 for the Government of Delhi shows that while the rate of migration has declined in the metropolis, the shift has taken place to peripheral and other areas of the National Capital Region (NCR). Big cities like Delhi are becoming more exclusive and more skilled and educated workers are migrating to Delhi at the expense of the poor and less educated workers (DHDR 2013, Chapter 2). This is happening because of higher cost of living, more so housing, as well as policy measures which discourage and obstruct the migration of poor to these cities. On the other hand, the prosperous and growing cities are absorbing more better off migrants with higher educational levels. It was observed during the survey that proportion of migrants in search of employment and better employment opportunities have shown a declining trend in Delhi during the decade from 2002 to 2012 and those who are migrating for the purpose of education and training have shown an increasing trend. The survey found that poor migrants are migrating more to peripheral areas of Delhi (Ibid). Obviously the bigger cities are becoming inhospitable for the poor migrants.

As these patterns in urbanization and migration endure in the coming decades, the challenge of planning for urban growth and employment creation will only become more acute.

2.5 The Employment Perspectives

India's employment challenge is enormous in quantitative terms and multidimensional in qualitative terms. Quantitatively, it goes beyond the growing labour force and the number of unemployed to encompass a large number of workers who are severely under-employed and live below the poverty line. Qualitatively, a majority of the Indian workers are low skilled and unable to find decent work that ensures regularity and stability of employment, humane and safe working conditions and social security protection against the risks of work and life. Some of these aspects are explored further in other chapters of this report.

2.5.1 Quantitative Projections

The Twelfth Five Year Plan (2012-2017) has projected employment opportunities and given two estimates. The first estimate is based on the assumption that the economy and its sectors continue to grow at the Eleventh Plan rates and projects the employment (15 and above age group) on a pure demand side basis. As per this estimate, total employment at the end of the Twelfth Plan period would be 508.9 million. It would generate additional employment of about 41 million during the five year period. This would lead to a reduction in the unemployment rate, and when adjusted for LFPR, the employment in agriculture is expected to decline. The farm sector share in employment is expected to drop to 47.3 per cent in 2016-17 from 49 per cent in 2011 and the shift from the farm to non-farm sector would be small, if the skill up-gradation and expansion of employment opportunities in manufacturing and services does not take place (Govt. of India, Twelfth Five Year Plan, Vol. 3).

The second method is based on the assumption that the manufacturing sector becomes an engine of growth, by growing at the targeted two percentage points above the overall growth rate (11 per cent); and the agriculture sector grows at 4 per cent. As per this estimate, projected employment in 2016-17 would be 502.4 million, generating additional employment of 34 million. In fact during the five-year period, as per this estimate, about 50 million additional employment opportunities would be generated in the non-farm sector and there would be a reduction of 16 million jobs in the farm sector (Govt. of India, Twelfth Five Year Plan, Vol. 3).

Historically, efforts at projecting employment have not been very successful because the projections were purely based on the past and projected GDP growth and employment elasticities for different sectors. These were no more than educated guesses and were conceptually flawed. The employment elasticity observed, is in fact the result of both supply and demand factors, a mix of positive employment creation in growing sectors and the absorption of excess labour supply in others. It is therefore unlikely to be stable in a changing labour market, and is not a good basis for forecasting. Even in theory it depends on relative factor prices, which are not taken into account. The 'backlog of unemployment' is in reality not a meaningful target for employment policy, because, as we have seen above, it is to a large extent a structural feature of the labour market, determined by job search, on the one hand, and social exclusion, on the other, rather than a temporary surplus that can be absorbed if new jobs are created. The Twelfth Five Year Plan has also projected employment on the basis of past and projected GDP growth and employment elasticities for different sectors. But, in addition, it has emphasized on shifting the farm sector employment to non-farm sector through skill development and by assuming the manufacturing sector as engine of growth. A more qualitative assessment of the future is likely to be more helpful.

2.5.2 Long Term Perspectives

In the long run, if India's high growth path is sustained the employment pattern will eventually move towards larger shares of the organized sector, non-agricultural activities and wage/salaried jobs; but it will take time. In 2011-12, agriculture employed about 49 per cent of workers but accounted for only 14 per cent of GDP; so the output per worker in agriculture is only one-sixth of that in non-agricultural activities. Differentials in productivity and the quality of work are likewise large between organized and unorganized enterprises, more so in urban areas. This asymmetry is a source of both macro-economic imbalance and income inequality, and points to the need for rapid growth of modern employment. Although private organized sector employment is now growing, but it is doing so from a low base, and so even higher rate of employment growth translates only into a rather small absolute number of additional jobs, compared to the size of the labour market. Moreover, the decline in public employment shows no signs of abating.

Rapid growth of the manufacturing industry and modern services is needed to bring about a quicker shift of the workforce from agriculture to non-agriculture, reduce the disparity between the two and lead to an improvement in the quality of employment. But it is clearly not sufficient. There is no plausible rate of growth of employment in the private organized sector which would make this the main driver of employment growth in the Indian economy in the coming decades. So it is important to identify the patterns of growth of organized sector or of specific sectors on industries that have stronger links with the unorganized sector, and whose growth is more likely to have a positive impact on the growth of unorganized sector, so that the labour productivity and earnings in the sector becomes high. In fact, such a trend has been witnessed in India recently between 2004-05 and 2009-10, when growth of productivity and wages in the unorganized sector was higher than those in the organized sector. This has very important implications for the transfer of labour from the unorganized sector to the organized sector and consequent gradual transformation of the labour market (Ghose, 2012).

It is important that the organized sector, particularly organized manufacturing, grows. Among other reasons, improvements in productivity, wages and the quality of work in the organized sector may indirectly filter through to the economy as a whole through its linkage with the unorganized sector. But unorganized employment is continuing to grow, and will continue to be the main source of employment for many years. Moreover, even in the organized sector, informal employment at least till recently has been increasing. It follows that the route towards a formal high productivity economy does not lie merely in organized sector growth. It is necessary to enhance the productivity of unorganized sector enterprises and ensure that the employment created in these enterprises meets minimum quality standards. In other words, a strategy for the formalization of informal work is needed. In reality, for the vast majority of Indian workers, the main issue is not so much more work as better paid work. If the recent growth in labour productivity and wages in the unorganized sector is accelerated in future, it will make a significant dent on poverty and will also facilitate and accelerate the transfer of labour from subsistence agriculture sector to a more productive modern sector.

As mentioned earlier, it is essential to rely on manufacturing-led growth for facilitating this process. This has been the path of growth in East and South-east Asia coupled with effective policy of human resource development and India has to learn a lot from the experiences of these countries. In fact, China has also adopted this path and consequently wages and labour productivity in China are almost two and half times to three times the Indian levels and the country is now widely believed to have passed the Lewis-turning point, thereby increasing the pressure of rising wages (Fang, 2008).

2.6 Unemployment and the Challenge of the Youth Bulge

The measurement and interpretation of unemployment is complex. In the absence of unemployment insurance, most workers face great pressure to find work and this is often reflected in low productivity self-employment. As such the open unemployment rate is not a good indicator of job short-falls. Some workers are able to invest time in search for decent jobs, for instance, if other family members are working. At the same time, there are severely deprived groups that face particular forms of discrimination or exclusion from the labour market; there are occupations subject to seasonal fluctuations; casual workers may find work one day but not the next; and so on. One has, therefore, to make use of more than one tool or approach to measure the different facets of worklessness exhibited by an economy such as India, where open unemployment coexists with under-employment and disguised unemployment.

As mentioned earlier in this chapter, the NSSO has been adopting four approaches to capture these different aspects of employment and unemployment situation in India (see Box 2.1). Estimates of unemployment derived from the UPS criterion represent chronic unemployment. The UPSS criterion takes note of the subsidiary gainful status of those classified as 'not working' under the UPS criterion and thus represents the core of open unemployment. The CWS criterion leads to the estimation of open unemployment in the reference week. The CDS measures employment or unemployment in terms of person days and represents the extent of under-utilization of labour force in terms of person days. In other words, the CDS estimate is the most inclusive measure of unemployment and visible underemployment, but it does not represent the actual number of persons unemployed in a particular year. The disconnect between work and income or the phenomenon of the working poor is another aspect of the employment/unemployment scene. The working poor may no doubt be 'employed', as per any of the three criteria referred to above, but could be earning incomes at or below subsistence level as discussed in Section 2.3.

Table 2.8 shows these different measures of unemployment over a long period. The CDS shows the highest rate, fluctuating between 6 and 8 per cent (5.60 per cent in 2011-12 and 8.34 per cent in 2004-05), and UPSS the lowest, fluctuating between 1.6 and 2.6 per cent. None of these rates show any clear long term trend. The years with overall lowest rates were recorded in the years 1993-94 and the latest round survey in the years
2011-12. But the changes are quite small. A more realistic picture of unemployment could be made by looking at the unemployment rates across gender, location education and age groups which has been discussed in the following sub-sections.

Table 2.8

Unemployment Rates

Year	UPS	UPSS	CWS	CDS
1972-73	3.80	1.61	4.32	8.35
1983	2.77	1.90	4.51	8.28
1993-94	2.56	1.90	3.63	6.03
2004-2005	3.18	2.33	4.53	8.34
2011-12	2.70	2.20	3.70	5.60

Source: Various NSSO Rounds.

2.6.1 *Rural-Urban and Gender Differentials in Unemployment Rates*

The unemployment rates by any criterion are higher in urban than in rural areas, both for males and females, except the CDS rate for males which is slightly higher in rural areas (Table 2.9 and Figure 2.12). As most of the wage employment in rural areas is casual and seasonal, higher CDS rate is not surprising. This clearly indicates labour under-utilization because there is wider access to low income self-employment in rural than in urban areas. Urban unemployment rates for the other measures are quite substantial, it shows that longer term open unemployment is a real concern in urban areas.

Table 2.9 also shows that unemployment rates for women are higher than those for men, irrespective of the concept used and the location, with the longer term rates of females varying between 5 and 7 per cent, and the daily rate being 8 per cent in urban areas. Gender differences are much sharper in the urban areas. We should also note that female LFPRs, as measured by the NSSO surveys, are very low in urban areas, fluctuating between 16 and 18 per cent by UPSS since 1983, which suggests that there may also be a substantial discouraged worker effect and considerable disguised unemployment of women (Appendix Table 2.1).

Table 2.9

Unemployment Rates across Sex and Location, 2011-12

Criterion	Rural			Urban			All		
	Male	Female	Person	Male	Female	Person	Male	Female	Person
UPS	2.1	2.9	2.3	3.2	6.6	3.8	2.4	3.7	2.7
UPSS	1.7	1.7	1.7	3.0	5.2	3.4	2.1	2.4	2.2
CWS	3.3	3.5	3.4	3.8	6.7	4.4	3.5	4.2	3.7
CDS	5.5	6.2	5.7	4.9	8.0	5.5	5.3	6.6	5.6

Source: Computed from unit level data of NSSO, 68th Round.

Figure 2.12

Unemployment Rates (CDS) across Sex and Location, 2011-12

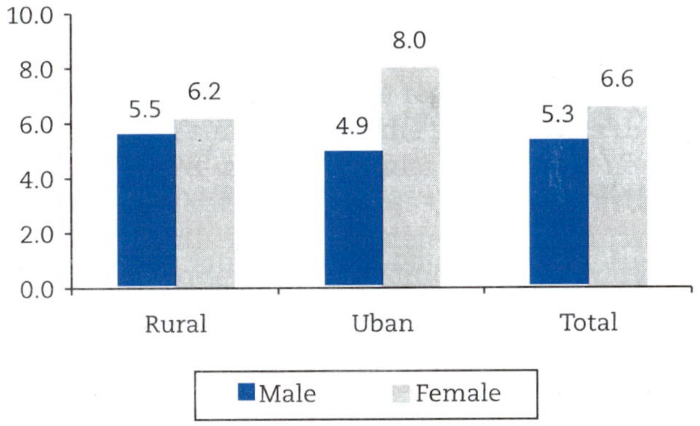

Source: Computed from unit level data of NSSO, 68th Round.

As discussed earlier women's work remains under-reported, undercounted and undervalued in national statistics. An IHD study of 36 villages in Bihar shows that female LFPR is as high as 37 per cent as compared to only 14 per cent by NSSO for the state in the year 2009-10 (see Box 2.3).

2.6.2 *Education and Unemployment*

A precondition to turn the 'demographic bulge' into the 'demographic dividend' is education and skill formation. Educational and skill levels of Indian workers are abysmally low (Table 2.10). Thirty one per cent of workers are illiterate. Only 29 per cent have had secondary or higher level of education.

Among women workers, only 16 per cent have this level of education while 51 per cent are illiterate. In case of vocational training only 11.6 per cent of persons in the age group 15-59 were either receiving or had received some vocational training (formal or informal) in 2011-12; and about 3 per cent were receiving or had received such training in formal vocational institutions. The position of women with regard to vocational training was worse: only 7.4 per cent have had or were undergoing any training, only 2.3 per cent have had or were receiving formal training (NSSO, 68th Round).

There is now a steady reduction in illiteracy rates among the employed as better educated young people join the labour force. But projections made by the NCEUS (2009) suggest that even by 2017, 28 per cent of India's labour force will still remain illiterate. And altogether, over half of the labour force will still have no more than primary schooling.

Table 2.10

Percentage Distribution of Workers (UPSS) by Level of Education, 2011-12

Educational Categories	*Male*	*Female*	*Total*
Not Literate	23.5	51.3	31.2
Below Primary	10.8	9.4	10.4
Primary & Middle	32.4	23.0	29.7
Secondary & Higher Secondary	21.7	9.8	18.4
Diploma/Certificate	1.6	0.8	1.4
Graduate and above	10.0	5.7	8.8
Total	100.0	100.0	100.0

Note: Age 5 and above years.

Source: Computed from unit level data of NSSO, 68th Round.

Secondly, imparting education is not enough, there must also be jobs for the educated. At present, the unemployment rate as per UPS increases consistently with increasing levels of education for both males and females in rural as well as urban areas. It is true that generally the more educated are able to remain unemployed until a suitable offer comes along. Some part of the higher unemployment rate for the more educated reflects this greater waiting period. At the same time, it is undeniably true that males as well as females, more so the latter, with higher secondary and above education, have very high unemployment rates in both urban and rural areas (Table 2.11 and Figure 2.13).

Unemployment rates among those with a diploma or a certificate are also very high. This shows that even the persons with certificates or diploma from technical institutions are also not getting employable training.

If we look at the share of unemployed by level of education, about 30 per cent of the total unemployed in the year 2011-12 were at least graduates or more qualified (Table 2.11). Out of these 30 per cent, 22 per cent were graduates and 8 per cent were post graduates. The share of unemployed at-least-graduate females was higher (36 per cent) as compared to males (28 per cent). If we compare by location the share was much higher for urban areas (43 per cent) as compared to rural areas (22 per cent). Another important point is that this share has been increasing; it was 21 per cent in 2004-05 as compared to 30 per cent in 2011-12.

The distribution of enrolment of higher education (diploma and degree holders) by field of study for the year 2011-12 shows that more than 60 per cent of the students were in general education (Arts, Science and Commerce). Out of 60 per cent who were in general education, 30 per cent were in Arts and the remaining 30 per cent were in other fields. This means that only 40 per cent were in professional fields namely engineering, medical, agriculture etc. (Govt. of India, Twelfth Five Year Plan). Thus, the supply of general graduates, which was much more than the technical and professional graduates and diploma holders, should be reduced.

2.6.3 *Unskilled Labour Force and High Rates of Youth Unemployment: A Constraint on the 'Demographic Dividend'*

The demographic dividend is considered as a rise in the rate of economic growth due to rising share of working population. But in the transition period it is second stage. In the first stage due to suitable policies, fertility falls significantly and youth dependency rate decreases (IIPA, 2011).

In the demographic dividend model, it is the dependency ratio (that is, dependent population relative to the working-age population) rather than the absolute increase (or decrease) in the size of the working-age population that is economically most relevant for the supply side. If the dependency ratio declines, i.e. if the working-age population as a share of the total population increases, per-capita growth is likely to accelerate. In the same way, a rising dependency ratio is likely to be a 'drag' on growth.

India witnessed a growth in the share of working age populatin from 59 per cent in 2001 to 63 per cent

Table 2.11

Unemployment Rate by Education (UPS), 2011-12

Education Level	*Rural*			*Urban*			*Total*		
	Male	*Female*	*Total*	*Male*	*Female*	*Total*	*Male*	*Female*	*Total*
Not Literate	0.6	0.7	0.6	0.9	1.0	0.9	0.6	0.8	0.7
Below Primary	1.0	1.4	1.1	2.9	2.1	2.8	1.4	1.6	1.4
Primary	1.6	1.1	1.5	1.9	1.9	1.9	1.7	1.2	1.6
Middle	2.2	4.2	2.5	2.3	4.7	2.6	2.2	4.4	2.5
Secondary	2.6	8.8	3.5	2.3	8.3	2.9	2.5	8.7	3.3
Higher Secondary	4.3	14.2	5.5	4.9	10.7	5.7	4.5	12.7	5.6
Diploma/Certificate	10.0	25.9	12.6	6.1	11.2	7.0	8.0	18.3	9.7
Graduate	8.0	23.7	10.2	5.8	14.8	7.4	6.6	17.5	8.4
PG and above	10.0	23.2	12.6	4.5	12.4	6.5	6.1	14.9	8.2
Total	2.1	2.9	2.3	3.2	6.6	3.8	2.4	3.7	2.7

Note: Age 5 and above years.

Source: Computed from unit level data of NSSO, 68th Round.

Figure 2.13

UPS Unemployment Rate by Education, 2011-12

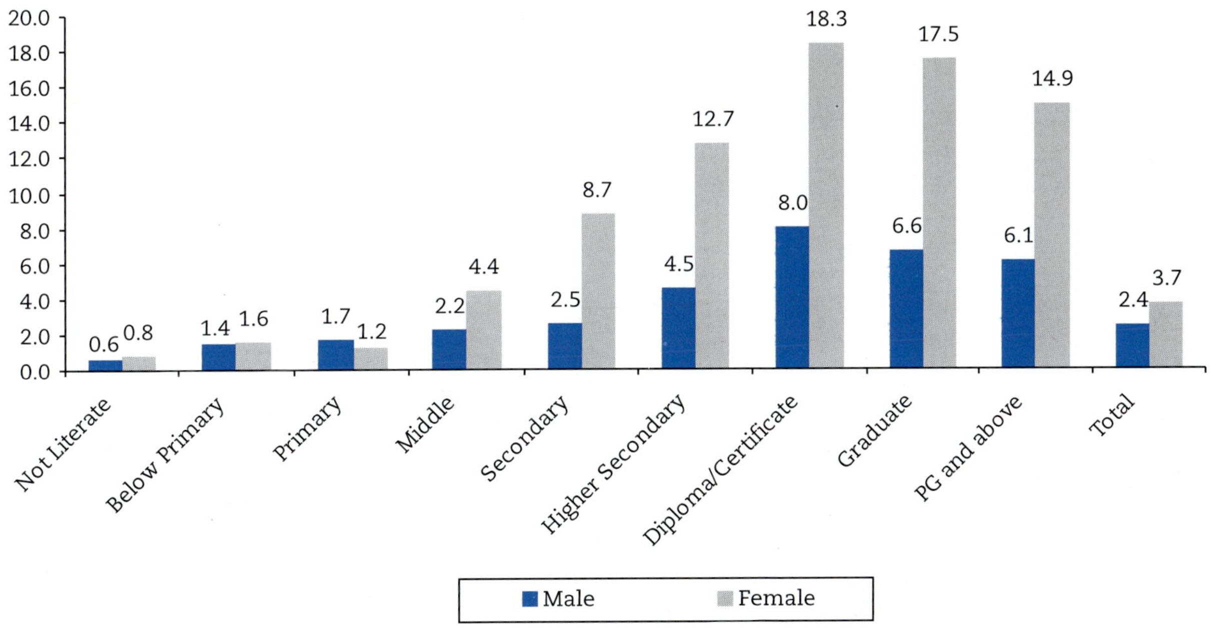

Source: Computed from unit level data of NSSO, 68th Round.

in 2011. It is now widely believed that the stage has now come for the country to reap the demographic dividend which may last for nearly three more decades. Already some states of India—Tamil Nadu, Gujarat and Karnataka—have experienced this between 1961 and 2001 when the incomes sharply rose and working age population increased (Aiyer and Mody, 2011).

The distribution of the Indian population by age group and gender is shown for the years 2011 and 2026 in Figures 2.14 and 2.15 respectively. These figures also reveal that young population of the year

Figure 2.14

Age Pyramid of India's Population in 2011 (in '000)

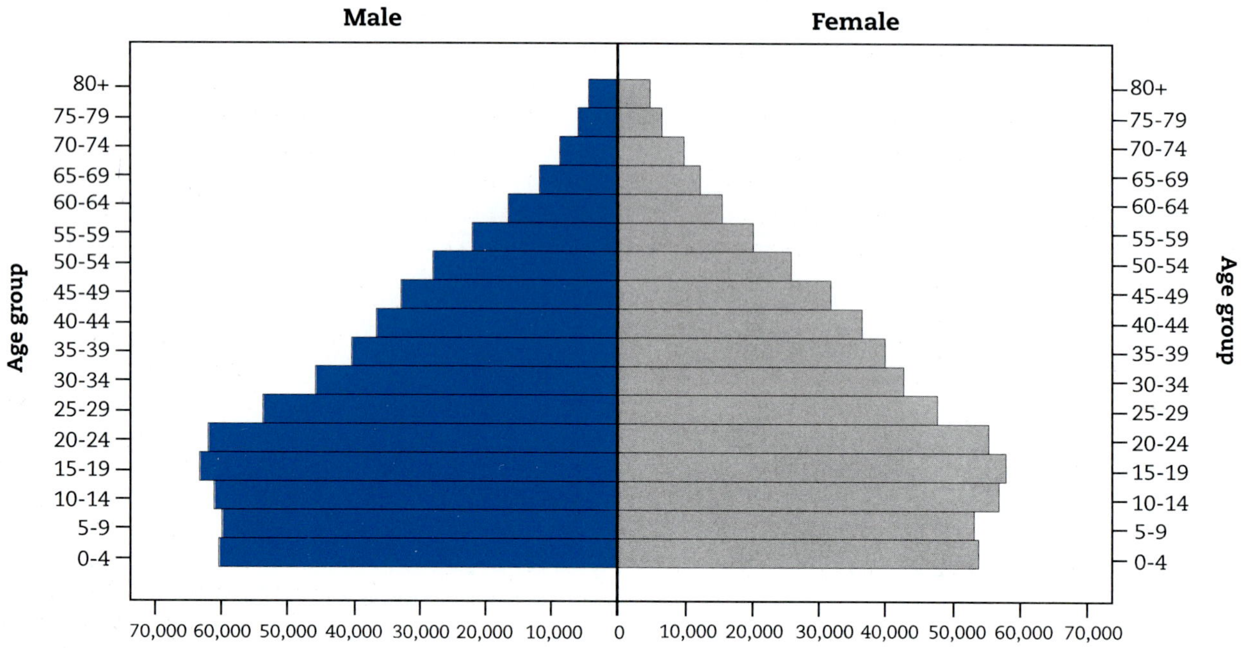

Note: The figures are projected.[4]

Source: RG&CCI, *State-wise Population Projection 2001-2026*, New Delhi, 2006.

Figure 2.15

Projected Age Pyramid of India's Population in 2026 (in '000)

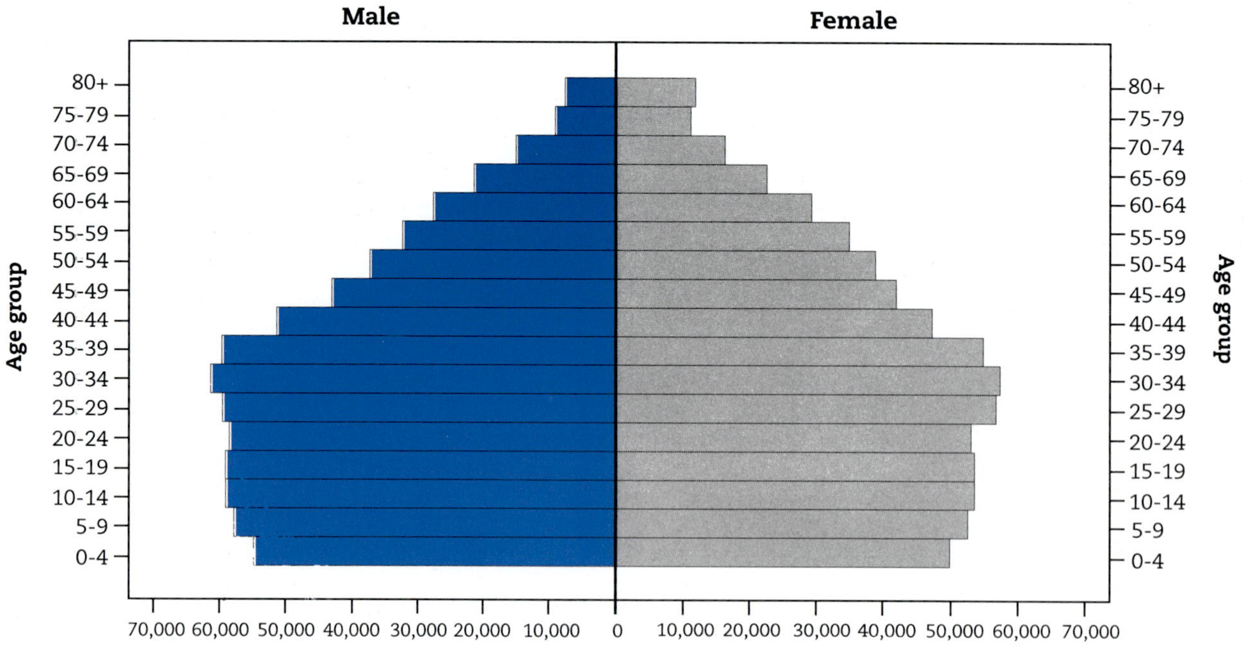

Source: RG&CCI, *State-wise Population Projection 2001-2026*, New Delhi, 2006.

4. The projections based on 2011 census results will be giving different results, although the broad trends may be similar.

2011 will transform to the working age population in the year 2026. It can be seen that broad bottom gradually shifts upward and the middle ranges start bulging. If population growth rate does not drastically fall as a result of sudden drop in birth rate, we can stretch the population dividend a little longer. India will have a rising number of persons in the labour force, despite the fact that more young people are opting to prolong their years of education and the number of senior citizens is rising. If properly harnessed, the demographic potential can result in a change in savings and investment behaviour, improving financial market growth prospects and finally economic growth prospects.

> A pre-condition to turn the 'demographic bulge' into the 'demographic dividend' is education and skill formation.

The young population would be an asset only if it is educated, skilled and finds productive employment. Providing skills to this large and growing young population from an exceedingly small base would be a big challenge for India. The skill strategy for the country has to be planned accordingly. An important aspect of reaping the demographic dividend is that it would increase the female labour force participation; hence properly educating and training women labour force should form an important strategy.

Structural shifts in the economy in terms of an increase in the contribution of secondary and tertiary sectors to GDP can have implications for the skill development strategy. This would also increase the demand for decent employment opportunities. It depends on the generation of adequate decent employment opportunities in the secondary and tertiary sectors and upgradation of skills of the existing as well as new entrants to the workforce.

Table 2.12

Unemployment Rates (CDS) across Broad Age Groups

Age Group	1993-94	2004-05	2009-10	2011-12
15-24	11.2	14.8	14.3	13.3
25-34	6.6	8.5	6.3	5.9
35+	3.3	5.3	4.2	3.1
Total	6.0	8.3	6.6	5.6

Source: Various NSS Rounds on Employment and Unemployment.

Unfortunately, the record of the Indian economy has not been very encouraging in case of the youths who are new entrants to the workforce. The unemployment rate has been very high among the young in the labour force. Using the CDS measure, for instance, unemployment is highest for the 15-24 age cohort, 11 per cent in 1993-94, about 15 per cent in 2004-05 and more than 13 per cent in 2011-12 (Table 2.12). This age group accounted for 16.7 per cent of the UPSS workforce in 2011-12. Thus, the new entrants in the labour market are seen to be much more prone to unemployment and account for quite a significant proportion of the total magnitude of the unemployed problem. Even at the present overall lower level of education, the young female educated unemployment is alarmingly high. The future years will witness a sharp rise in the number of job seekers by both males and females for which both the educational system and labour markets have to be prepared. The youth bulge is both an opportunity as well as a big challenge. If the country does not get fully prepared to leverage the opportunity, it will prove to be a disaster, leading to huge social unrest and instability.

2.7 Summing Up: Key Features of the Employment Situation

The labour markets have witnessed significant churning in the three decades since the initiation of the process of liberalization and globalization of the Indian economy. Sometimes there have been contradictory trends and patterns as well. The main findings emerging from the above discussions may be summarized as below:

- Although the employment share of agriculture has been declining, while that of the secondary sector (including mining and quarrying) and the tertiary sector has been increasing, the pace of change has been slow compared to changes in the output share, leading to huge asymmetry.

- In the secondary sector, employment growth has been relatively high during 1972-73 to 2011-12. It has shown a significant increase during 1993-94 to 2011-12. Employment growth in the tertiary sector has also been relatively high, but has consistently declined over the three periods of 10 years each since 1972-73.

- The manufacturing sector which has significant linkage effects with other sectors has not registered high growth of employment primarily due to low growth of output and other institutional bottlenecks.

- The share of regular work in total employment has increased only marginally despite the apparent transformation of the economy. The share of casual work has not fallen and that of self-employment has declined slightly.

- An important trend has been a decline in the female LFPR during 2005-12, largely in rural areas. While enrolment in educational institutions and rising income of the households may account to some extent for this trend, the lack of appropriate employment opportunities for women could also be behind such a decline. Further, the share of females in more productive and secure jobs is much lower than their male counterparts, indicating the gender discrimination in the labour market

- The unorganized sector is dominant, accounting for about 83 per cent of all workers. Informal workers constitute about 92 per cent of the total workforce. There has been rapid increase in the percentage of contract workers, particularly in the organized manufacturing sector. There has been a small increase in the growth of organized sector and formal employment since 2005, a trend which needs to be analysed in depth.

- While public organized employment has been declining for some time, organized private employment has been on the rise since 2004.

- There is considerable segmentation and dualism in the Indian labour market in terms of various categories—sectors (organized *versus* unorganized/formal *versus* informal), occupations, locations (rural vs urban and migration status), gender, castes, tribes, etc. Contrary to expectations, the labour market dualism has not narrowed. While there is evidence that mobility of labour has increased; the dualism is so strong, that even now each segment is largely dominated by its own characteristics and interaction across segments is limited.

- The population structure in India will display a 'youth bulge' in the form of a rapid expansion in the number of younger workers at least for two more decades. By 2030, India will have the largest workforce in the world, providing the country with the opportunity for reaping the demographic dividend. However, this also entails that the country will face the gigantic task of meeting their aspirations in terms of providing education and jobs in the labour market. Unless they are better educated and trained and provided suitable jobs, this bulge, instead of becoming a dividend, may prove to be a 'disaster' leading to huge social unrest

- As the pace of urbanization and migration is likely to accelerate in future, there will be a massive challenge of planning the urban growth and urban labour market policies for the vast number of new entrants in the labour force.

- Unacceptable poor working conditions and lack of occupational safety are widespread and the basic rights of a majority of the workers are often violated.

- The challenge of employment in India is not so much the problem of unemployment, as a vast majority of workers who are employed, but that of poverty due to underemployment and low productivity of work.

- Due to the youth bulge, the problem of open unemployment is likely to be much more acute in future with immense implications for education and skill requirements.

- The lack of social protection among informal workers exposes them to high levels of uncertainty of livelihoods.

The challenge of employment in India is simply huge, both in terms of quantity and quality, which is likely to exacerbate in the coming decades due to the youth bulge. An employment strategy in the medium to longer term, should be envisaged wherein the organized sector, particularly the manufacturing sector, grows much more rapidly than in the past and leads to a process of economy-wide productivity growth, along with employment expansion and rising wages. Even in the organized sector, informal employment should not grow. Regulatory interventions in informal enterprises should ensure that a minimum quality of employment is maintained and the basic rights of workers are not violated. The recent growth in the productivity and wages of workers in the unorganized sector is an important and welcome development. Although small, it has important implications for employment and development policies of the country. The need is to sustain and accelerate this process so that India is able to reach the Lewisian turning point in the next five to ten years. Better health and education facilities and minimum social security for all workers should be an integral part of this strategy.

3

Access to and Exclusion from Employment: Social and Regional Dimensions

3.1 Introduction

As discussed in the preceding chapter, aggregate employment in a labour-surplus economy like India is not a good measure of access to employment. A majority of jobs in India are low-paying opportunities in the informal sector, which often are also insecure, intermittent, and precarious. Quality employment has an influence on productivity and wages and can be instrumental in improving livelihoods. The high economic growth in India so far has resulted in widening disparities in wages and incomes between skilled and unskilled workers, capital and labour, and workers in the informal sector and the formal, and these will be discussed in greater detail in the next chapter (Chapter 4). In this chapter, the focus is mainly on the issue of access to employment, particularly quality employment, with respect to social and regional dimensions.[1]

Inequality in income and wealth has been on the rise within socio-religious groups as has the trend of exclusion of disadvantaged regions from the gains of high economic growth of the last several years. Policy concern in this context is well reflected in the very sub-title of the approach paper to the Eleventh Five Year Plan—*The Challenge of Inclusive Growth*. The recent move to expand the reservation policy to private sector jobs and reservation of seats in educational institutions for disadvantaged groups also originates from the same concern regarding unequal access to assets, skill building, education, and employment opportunities.

> A majority of the jobs in India are low-paying opportunities in the informal sector, which are insecure, intermittent and sometimes hazardous.

As such, Planning in India has had a particular focus on the need to provide support to historically disadvantaged groups such as the Scheduled Tribes (STs), Scheduled Castes (SCs), the Other Backward Classes (OBCs), and also other marginalized and vulnerable groups suffering from handicaps which includes persons with disabilities, senior citizens, street children, beggars and so on. Over the years, several steps have been taken to bridge the gap between these marginalized groups and the rest of the population. But disparities still persist and further efforts are needed so that the deprived groups share the fruits of economic development as well. This calls for inclusive growth which provides equal opportunities for all to participate in the growth process combined with schemes that would either deliver benefits directly or, more importantly, empower these groups to access opportunities offered by the development process, in general.

Economic exclusion of the disadvantaged groups is driven primarily by three important factors: i) skewed distribution of assets (land and capital), ii) unequal access to education and skill endowment, and iii) discrimination in the labour market. These factors, taken together, result in unequal access to 'good' and 'quality jobs' in the labour market perpetuating a vicious circle of deprivation. Where affirmative policies exist in providing access to quality jobs, the 'creamy layer' within the groups often appropriates the benefits of such measures.[2] These factors are further exacerbated by or even owed to the fact that these groups are often geographically concentrated in underdeveloped regions (rural, inaccessible, and 'backward districts').

Keeping in mind the issues discussed above, this chapter focuses on the social and regional dimensions of access to employment opportunities in India.

3.2 Historical and Geographical Profile of Socio-religious Groups in India

The STs and SCs have special status under the Indian Constitution. People belonging to SC communities are, by and large, spread all over the country, with about 80 per cent of them living in the rural areas. Around half of the SC population is concentrated in the five states of Uttar Pradesh, West Bengal, Tamil Nadu, Andhra Pradesh and Bihar. Unlike the SCs who are dispersed throughout the country, STs have traditionally been concentrated in about 15 per cent of the country's geographical area, comprising mainly of forests, hills and other inaccessible pockets, which makes it difficult to deliver essential services to them. The geographical segregation has also made it more challenging for the STs to benefit from the accelerated growth process than other deprived

1. The analyses in this chapter, to a large extent, are updation and extension of the arguments made in Sharma (2002).

2. In this chapter, affirmative action policies are understood to go beyond the idea of formal reservation. It includes policies that give access to jobs, education and other drivers of empowerment.

Table 3.1

Religious Composition of Social Groups, 2011-12

Social Groups	*Religion*					
	Hindus	*Muslims*	*Christians*	*Sikhs*	*Others*	*Total*
Scheduled Tribes	86.6	1.8	8.7	0.0	2.8	100.0
Scheduled Castes	93.9	0.2	0.2	3.0	2.6	100.0
Other Backward Classes	81.9	16.0	1.4	0.6	0.1	100.0
Others	70.7	23.3	2.3	2.9	0.9	100.0

Source: Computed from unit level data of NSSO, 68th Round.

communities. Recognizing the fact that SCs and STs have historically suffered grave social and economic deprivation, the Constitution provides special provisions for the advancement of their interests.

OBCs comprise the castes and communities common to the lists included in the Mandal Commission Report and those of individual state governments. The Constitution does not make any specific provisions for OBCs, but Article 15 of the Constitution empowers the states to make special provisions for the advancement of any socially and educationally backward group of citizens. Article 16(4) also empowers the State to make provisions for reservations in appointments in favour of any backward class of citizens, which, in the opinion of the State is not adequately represented in the services under the State. The Directive Principles of State Policy of the Constitution (Article 46) also state that: 'The State shall promote with special care the educational and economic interests of the weaker sections of the people'.

The Indian Constitution is also committed to the ideas of equality and protection and assurance of rights of minorities, which cover six religious communities, namely, Muslims, Christians, Sikhs, Buddhists, Jains and Zoroastrians (Parsis). These communities accounted for 18.4 per cent of the population and the remaining 81.6 per cent were Hindus in 2011-12 (National Sample Survey Organization, NSSO 68th Round). The largest proportion among the minorities comprised Muslims (13.8 per cent), followed by Christians (2.1 per cent), Sikhs (1.7 per cent), Buddhists (0.6 per cent), Jains (0.3 per cent) and Zoroastrians (0.01 per cent). Depending on their distribution across states and Union Territories, these communities do actually enjoy 'majority' status in some states, for example Muslims in Lakshadweep (98.8 per cent), and Jammu and Kashmir (61.5 per cent); Christians in Nagaland (96.3 per cent), Mizoram (90.2 per cent) and Meghalaya (84.3 per cent); and Sikhs in Punjab (56.3 per cent). Among these, the Muslims, the largest minority in the country, are seriously lagging behind on all human development indices, as has been extensively documented by the Sachchar Committee.

There is also significant religious diversity within social groups (Table 3.1). Contrary to popular belief, there exist SCs, STs and OBCs, among non-Hindu groups as well, albeit in varying proportions. Most notable are the relatively significant proportion of non-Hindu 'Others', as well as Muslim OBCs (16.0 per cent) and Christian STs (8.7 per cent). This suggests a case for exploring within-group variability in access to employment, especially among certain religious minorities.

Figure 3.1

Percentage Distribution of Population and Workers by Socio-religious Group, 2011-12

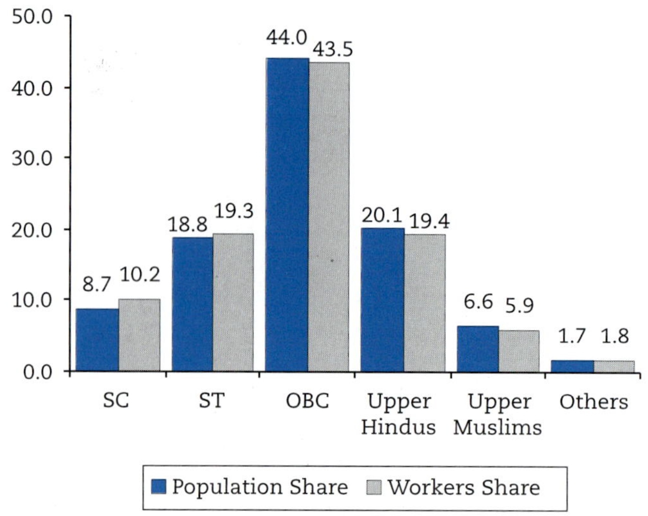

Source: Computed from unit level data of NSSO, 68th Round.

Official documents as well as researchers usually classify the population into four categories, namely STs, SCs, OBCs and Others, for identifying and formulating schemes for the disadvantaged groups. Given that these groups cut across religious persuasions, a factor that may obfuscate the extent of disadvantages in employment faced by certain religious groups represented in the 'Others', a more detailed classification has been used in this chapter. The new classification disaggregates the 'Others' (which includes upper sections from all religious sections) into Upper Hindus, Upper Muslims and Others, which along with SCs, STs and OBCs forms the basis of our analyses into the social dimensions of access to employment. As per this classification, the relative share of the different groups in the population in the year 2011-12 is presented in Figure 3.1. It shows that in India, OBCs are the largest socio-religious group followed by the Upper Hindus.

3.3 Poverty by Socio-religious Groups and Regions

Despite the various measures taken by the government, there is widespread disparity within different socio-religious communities, giving credence to the view that each community is largely a differentiated category with multiple identities and different socio-political and economic aspirations (Govt. of India, Planning Commission, 2012). Therefore, patterns of poverty experienced by socio-religious group and by urban-rural locations are important in the study of social and economic exclusion in India.

> Socio-religious groups that have been identified to be disadvantaged in the past continue to suffer from gross inequalities even today.

Table 3.2 shows a high proportion of poor among the STs, SCs, OBCs and Upper Muslims. This suggests that the socio-religious groups that have been identified to be disadvantaged in the past continue to suffer from gross inequalities even today. It is also important to note the locational dimension of marginalization in India, evident in the higher proportion of poor being located in rural areas as compared to urban areas.

It is also clear from the table that although poverty has been on a decline from 2005 to 2012, the pattern has varied across social groups and locations. It is interesting to note that the decline in poverty for SCs, STs, OBCs and Upper Muslims, particularly in rural areas, has generally exceeded the national average between 2005 and 2012. This reduction in

> There is a lacational dimension to marginalization in India, evident from the higher proportion of poor located in rural and backward regions.

Table 3.2

Poverty by Socio-religious Groups: 2005-2012

Socio-religious Groups	*Population (%), 2012*	*Poverty (%)*		*Change (Percentage Points)*
		2005	2012	
		Total		
Scheduled Tribes	8.7	59.6	40.6	19.0
Scheduled Castes	18.8	50.1	29.9	20.2
Other Backward Classes	44.0	38.9	21.9	17.0
Upper Hindus	20.1	17.0	9.1	7.9
Upper Muslims	6.6	41.7	23.1	18.6
Others	1.7	4.0	1.8	2.2
Total	100.0	37.8	21.9	15.9
		Rural		
Schedule Tribes	11.1	61.9	42.7	19.2
Schedule Castes	20.8	52.7	32.3	20.4
Other Backward Classes	45.0	41.0	24.0	17.0
Upper Hindus	16.0	21.6	12.3	9.3
Upper Muslims	5.7	42.9	25.6	17.3
Others	1.4	4.2	1.7	2.5
Total	100.0	41.8	25.7	16.1
		Urban		
Schedule Tribes	3.5	35	23.3	11.7
Schedule Castes	14.6	40.0	21.6	18.4
Other Backward Classes	41.6	31.4	16.2	15.2
Upper Hindus	29.8	9.9	4.8	5.1
Upper Muslims	8.0	39.3	18.7	20.6
Others	2.5	3.5	2.0	1.5
Total	100.0	25.7	13.7	12.0

Source: Computed from unit level data of NSSO, 55th and 68th Round.

Table 3.3

Distribution of Workers (UPSS) by Social Groups and Industry, 2011-12

Industry	*Scheduled Tribes*	*Scheduled Castes*	*OBCs*	*Upper Hindus*	*Upper Muslims*	*Others*	*Total*
Agriculture, etc	70.4	49.0	50.6	39.7	32.0	41.3	48.9
Mining & Quarrying	0.6	0.8	0.5	0.5	0.2	0.4	0.5
Manufacturing	5.2	10.9	13.3	14.3	24.5	9.5	12.8
Electricity, Gas & Water supply	0.3	0.5	0.3	0.6	0.6	1.1	0.4
Construction	12.0	17.3	9.8	5.1	11.3	6.9	10.6
Trade, Hotel & Restaurants	4.0	7.3	11.9	16.6	17.0	16.8	11.5
Transport, Storage & Communication	2.0	4.6	4.4	4.6	6.8	4.9	4.4
Finance, Business, Real Estate, etc	0.4	1.6	2.2	5.7	1.6	6.3	2.6
Public Admn, Health, Education, etc	5.2	8.1	7.0	12.9	6.0	13.0	8.2
Total	100.0	100.0	100.0	100.0	100.0	100.0	100.0

Note: UPSS: Usual Principal and Subsidiary Status.

Source: Computed from unit level data of NSSO, 68th Round.

poverty may be attributed to two main reasons: high economic growth over the last decade that created new jobs for the rural poor and government public schemes which targeted vulnerable sections of the society (Panagariya and More, 2013). However, there still remains a disproportionate representation of the poor amongst the disadvantaged socio-religious groups when compared to the all-India level and to the 'Upper Hindus' and 'Others'. In fact, 'Others' (comprising mostly minorities like Christians, Sikhs, Jains and Parsis) are best placed in the country in terms of incidence of poverty. Furthermore, the rural dimension to poverty in India is obvious from the higher percentages of rural poor across all social groups, except 'Others' in 2012.

It is widely accepted that creating 'quality employment' opportunities lies at the core of poverty alleviation. For the poor, labour is often the only asset they can use to improve their well-being. Hence, the creation of productive employment opportunities is essential for achieving poverty reduction and sustainable economic and social development.[3] It is crucial to provide decent jobs that secure both income and empowerment for the poor, who, as seen in Table 3.2, largely comprise of the socially excluded groups. The following sections look at the different types of industries and work that workers from different social groups are employed in so as to identify issues related to access to employment, particularly productive employment.

3.4 Access to Employment by Socio-religious Group

In India, in spite of increasing urbanization and mobility of people, there exists considerable dualism in the labour markets and there are sharp differences in the quality of employment. The best 'quality employment' includes employment in the public sector (government, semi-government and similar organizations) and organized private sector (including private corporate sector and other large private enterprises).[4] In fact, these 'quality jobs' are most sought after. However, as we have seen in the preceding chapter, a large percentage of jobs, even in the organized sector, are contractual and temporary in nature without social security. Although these jobs are, in comparison, much better than the casual and a large majority of the self-employment options. While central and various state governments have reserved a maximum of 50 per cent of jobs in the public sector for SCs, STs and OBCs, there is a strong demand for extending the reservation to the corporate sector

3. *http://undesadspd.org/Poverty/PovertyandEmployment.aspx*

4. Corporate sector includes public and private limited companies. Co-operative societies which have a share of about 2 to 3 per cent in total employment are not included because of two reasons: i) The co-operative societies' data relating to employment, which is available from NSSO, includes Trusts and NGOs; ii) some of the larger societies like Mother Diary in Delhi are in the public sector.

also.[5] In this context, it will be insightful to see the access for 'quality jobs' by various socio-religious groups and differentials in 'quality jobs' across the regions.

3.4.1 Share of Employment in Low Paid Activities by Socio-religious Groups

The share of workers in low paid agriculture and related activities during the period 2004-05 to 2011-12 has decreased as a result of an overall change in employment in this sector (see Chapter 2). However, out of the six groups—STs, SCs, OBCs, Upper Hindus, Upper Muslims and 'Others'—the proportion of STs, SCs, and OBCs workers in the low-paid 'agriculture and related activities' and 'construction' is much higher in comparison to the other three groups in the year 2011-12 (Table 3.3). The share of Upper Hindus and 'Others' is lower in agricultural activities and much higher in sectors such as finance, business and real estate, public administration, health, education etc. In comparison, Upper Muslims have a high share in 'agriculture', 'manufacturing' and in 'trade, hotel and restaurants', the latter largely because of their greater presence in urban areas compared to other communities (Table 3.3). This shows that the socially excluded groups are mainly occupied in sectors that are less productive, with poorer income streams.

> The proportion of STs, SCs and OBCs among workers in the low paid 'agriculture and related activities' and 'construction' sectors is much higher in comparison to other groups.

3.4.2 Employment Shares by Socio-religious Groups

'Upper Hindus' and 'Others' have a higher proportion of workers in regular employment (as regular workers) in comparison to their share in workforce. In case of Upper Hindus, share of regular employment is 31.7 per cent and their share in workforce is only 19.4 per cent, whereas in case of 'Others' share of regular workers in 2.8 per cent and their share in workforce is only 1.8. In contrast to this STs (5.0 per cent) and SCs (16.5 per cent) have much lower share of regular workers in comparison to their share in the workforce viz. 10.2 per cent and 19.3 per cent respectively (Table 3.4).

Table 3.4

Percentage Distribution of Workers (UPSS) by Social Group and Work Status, 2011-12

Socio-religious Group	*Share of Workforce (2011-12)*	*SE*	*RW*	*CL*
Scheduled Tribes	10.2	10.4	5.0	12.8
Scheduled Castes	19.3	13.6	16.5	30.4
OBCs	43.5	46.1	38.5	42.0
Upper Hindus	19.4	21.4	31.7	8.6
Upper Muslims	5.9	6.5	5.5	5.1
Others	1.8	2.1	2.8	0.7
Total	100.0	100.0	100.0	100.0

Note: UPSS: Usual Principal and Subsidiary Status; SE: Self-employed; RW: Regular worker; CL: Casual labour.

Source: Computed from unit level data of NSSO, 68th Round.

3.4.3 Share of Regular Workers in the Organized Sector by Socio-religious Group

Table 3.4 shows that the STs, SCs and OBCs have a large proportion of their workforce in the lowest paid type of casual employment that are concentrated largely in agriculture and construction. It is important to further disaggregate the socio-religious background of the workers employed as regular workers.

> The proportion of STs and SCs employed in the public sector is higher than their proportion in the private sector, indicating the efficacy of the reservation policy.

Comparing the share of regular workers in the organized sector (public and private combined), by social groups and their share of population, it is seen that in the case of STs, SCs, OBCs and Upper Muslims, share of regular workers is much lower than their share in the workforce. On the other hand, in case of Upper Hindus and Others, the share of regular workers is much higher than their workforce share. The percentage shares of STs, SCs, and Upper Muslims in regular workers are only 5.2, 15.2, and 4.0, respectively, whereas their percentage shares in the workforce are 10.2, 19.3 and 5.9, respectively (Table 3.5). For OBCs, the comparable figure is 35.8 per cent

5. Some states such as Tamil Nadu have a higher level of reservation (as high as 69 per cent).

regular workers in the organized sector which is closer to their workforce share (43.5 per cent).

Table 3.5

Percentage Distribution of Regular Workers (UPSS) in Organized Sector by Social Group and Enterprise Type, 2011-12

Socio-religious Groups	*Public Sector*	*Private Sector*	*Total*	*Share of Workforce (2011-12)*
Scheduled Tribes	8.3	2.7	5.2	10.2
Scheduled Castes	17.9	12.9	15.2	19.3
OBCs	33.4	37.8	35.8	43.5
Upper Hindus	34.4	38.7	36.7	19.4
Upper Muslims	3.5	4.4	4.0	5.9
Others	2.4	3.5	3.0	1.8
Total	100.0	100.0	100.0	100.0

Note: UPSS: Usual Principal and Subsidiary Status.
Source: Computed from unit level data of NSSO, 68th Round.

In the public sector, the percentage of STs and SCs employed is higher than their proportion in the private sector, which could be indicative of the effectiveness of the reservation policy. Whilst the figures for public/private sector employment for OBCs do not follow the same trend, a relatively high proportion of OBCs are employed as regular workers indicating their relatively better economic position, more so for some of the dominant castes among them, alongwith the benefits from reservation accruing to them as a group. However, it is more worthwhile to look at the distribution of regular formal workers by social group as all regular workers, taken together, are not always representative of those employed in good jobs. In some cases, it can be argued that the regular informal workers are only marginally better off than casual labourers.

Table 3.6

Percentage Share of Regular Formal Workers by Socio-religious Group, 1999-2000 to 2011-2012

Socio-religious Group	1999-2000		2011-12		*Share of Workforce, (2011-12)*
	Public	*Private*	*Public*	*Private*	
Scheduled Tribes	7.2	3.3	8.1	2.2	10.2
Scheduled Castes	16.1	10.1	16.3	10.2	19.3
OBCs	24.1	27.6	32.6	36.1	43.5
Upper Hindus	44.9	50.0	37.2	45.0	19.4
Upper Muslims	4.3	3.9	3.2	2.4	5.9
Others	3.4	5.1	2.5	4.0	1.8
Total	100.0	100.0	100.0	100.0	100.0

Source: Computed from unit level data of NSSO, 55th and 68th Round.

3.4.4 Share in Regular Formal Workers by Socio-religious Groups

Although the largest proportion of regular formal jobs (which are considered the 'best quality' jobs) both in the public and the private sector, are largely appropriated by the Upper Hindus, the situation has been improving over the years (Table 3.6). Most striking is the increase in OBCs share in regular formal work in the public sector, which can largely be attributed to the affirmative policy in their favour since early 1990s, as also to the higher economic status that some groups within the OBCs enjoy. Furthermore, there has been an increase in the proportion of OBCs engaged in the private sector with an accompanying decline in the share of Upper Hindus. It is possible that the reservations that OBCs enjoy in educational institutions are opening up better job opportunities for them in the private sector as well. There has also been small increase in the proportion of STs in formal regular jobs comparing 1999-2000 to 2011-12 in the public sector, but there has been a decline in their share in the private sector. The most striking is the decrease in the shares of both Upper Hindus and 'Others' (comprising Christians, Jains, Sikhs and Parsis) in both public and private sector formal jobs between 1999-2000 and 2011-12 as well as the decline in the share of Upper Muslims in both public and private sector formal jobs during this period.

Reservation of OBCs in educational institutions is possibly resulting in better job opportunities for them in the private sector as well.

Thus, while it is clear that ST and SC workers are the worst placed and 'Upper Hindus' and 'Others' best placed (although their relative access to good jobs is on the decline), on the whole, it seems that the affirmative policy has helped the OBCs in accessing public sector formal jobs, although their participation in proportion to their total workforce is still low.

Table 3.7

Percentage of Population in Various Social Groups by Consumption Expenditure Class, 2011-12

	Scheduled Tribes	*Scheduled Castes*	*OBCs*	*Upper Hindus*	*Upper Muslims*	*Others*	*Total*
Poorest	39.6 (17.2)	26.4 (24.9)	19.9 (43.9)	8.0 (8.0)	17.6 (5.8)	2.7 (0.2)	- (100)
Poor	23.9 (10.4)	23.9 (22.5)	21.0 (46.2)	12.9 (13.0)	23.1 (7.6)	3.6 (0.3)	- (100)
Medium	17.1 (7.4)	21.3 (20.0)	21.2 (46.8)	17.1 (17.2)	24.0 (7.9)	7.3 (0.6)	- (100)
Rich	12.3 (5.4)	17.8 (16.8)	20.6 (45.3)	24.1 (24.2)	19.5 (6.4)	22.6 (1.9)	- (100)
Richest	7.1 (3.1)	10.7 (10.1)	17.3 (38.1)	37.9 (38.1)	15.8 (5.2)	63.9 (5.5)	- (100)
Total	100 (8.7)	100 (44.0)	100 (44.0)	100 (20.1)	100 (6.6)	100 (1.7)	- (100)

Note: Figure within brackets are row-wise percentage.

Source: Computed from unit level data of NSSO, 68th Round.

3.5 Access to Employment within Socio-religious Group

Several experts have questioned the efficacy of the reservation policy for the socially excluded groups, especially in light of the argument that the elites or the 'creamy layer' within these groups have cornered the benefits of the same. However, proponents of the affirmative action policy have taken a strong position against doing away with reservation, given the socio-economic exploitation of these groups by virtue of their historical position in the caste hierarchy, and the continued deep-rooted prejudices faced by them. This controversy has taken centre stage in view of the judgment of the Supreme Court to exclude the 'creamy layers' from among the beneficiaries of reservation. Although due to data limitations, it is not possible to directly comment on the issue of 'creamy layer', it will be seen in the later sections that disproportionate access to educational endowment by richer classes within the social groups is indeed indicative of appropriation of reservation benefits by a select few.

3.5.1 Population Share of Each Socio-religious Group in Different Consumer Expenditure Classes (Quintiles)[6]

In the context of looking at within group differences, it is interesting to see the distribution of various social groups vis-à-vis the expenditure classes (Table 3.7). A majority of the STs (63.5 per cent) and SCs (50.3 per cent) belong to the poorest and the poor categories while 62 per cent of Upper Hindus and 86.5 per cent of the 'Others' are either rich or richest. In case of OBCs and to some extent Upper Muslims, there is very low variation in the population distribution across different classes. It is pertinent to note here that in India 38.1 per cent of the richest and 45.3 per cent of the rich are OBCs.[7]

3.5.2 Share of Poorest and Richest in Organized Sector (Public and Private) Jobs within Socio-religious Group

Figures 3.2 and 3.3 present the shares of workers belonging to various social groups in the highest consumption expenditure class (CEC) (richest) and the lowest CEC (poorest) with respect to access to public and private (organized) sector jobs. The results are quite revealing. The richest in all class groups also have a larger share of organized sector jobs. But differences in the shares of poorest and richest are much higher for OBCs, Upper Hindus, Upper Muslims and Others. In case of OBCs, share of poorest quintiles in public (organized) and private sectors are only 7.4 per cent and 7.3 per cent, respectively, whereas share of richest are 42 per cent and 43 per cent respectively. A similar pattern of a linear increase in share in organized jobs with class can be seen for Upper

6. The population is divided into five equal proportions on the basis of their monthly per capita household expenditure.

7. Are the 'rich' rich because they have better jobs, or do they get better jobs because they are rich? Since it is difficult to determine the causality, we cannot directly make inferences about the creamy layer and, to that extent, the analysis suffers from limitations.

Figure 3.2

Percentage Share of Workers by Class in the Poorest and Richest Expenditure Categories in Organized Public Sector Employment: 2011-12

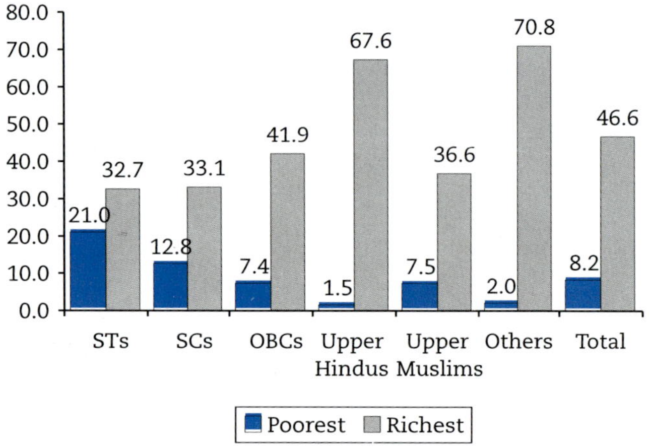

Figure 3.3

Percentage Share of Workers by Class in the Poorest and Richest Expenditure Category in Organized Private Sector Employment: 2011-12

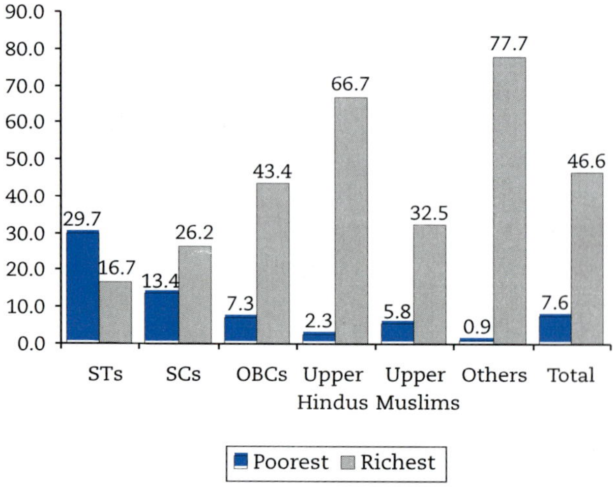

Hindus, Upper Muslims and Others. But in case of STs and SCs, the situation is different. For the STs, 21 per cent jobs in the public sector and 30 per cent jobs in the private sector are in the poorest class group. In the case of the SCs, the comparable figures for the poorest classes are 12.8 per cent (public) and 13.4 per cent (private). This suggests that the STs and SCs, although employed in the organized sector, probably have access to the low paying jobs (viz. sweepers, peons, etc.) which require low level of skills within that sector. Secondly, the share of STs and SCs in the poorest class is very high, viz. 40 per cent and 27 per cent, respectively. It could also be that these workers belong to poor class households and have benefited from the reservation policy. This also shows that the persons in the higher income group of SCs and STs are not getting the regular jobs because of their low level of skills or discrimination.

Table 3.8

Distribution of Self-employed Individuals in Non-agriculture Employment (UPSS) by Social Groups and CEC, 2011-12

	Poorest	*Poor*	*Medium*	*Rich*	*Richest*	*Total (Row %)*
Scheduled Tribes	29.8 (9.3)	18.1 (4.2)	18.6 (3.6)	18.2 (2.9)	15.1 (2.0)	100.0
Scheduled Castes	19.9 (23.6)	22.5 (20.1)	22.2 (16.4)	21.8 (13.2)	13.7 (7.0)	100.0
OBCs	12.9 (47.2)	17.1 (47.1)	21.5 (49.0)	24.8 (46.6)	23.6 (37.5)	100.0
Upper Hindus	4.2 (8.4)	9.3 (14.0)	14.4 (17.9)	24.9 (25.4)	47.1 (40.6)	100.0
Upper Muslims	12.7 (1[illegible])	21.6 (14.3)	22.8 (12.5)	22.7 (10.2)	20.3 (7.7)	100.0
Others	1.8 (0.3)	2.1 (0.3)	6.2 (0.6)	19.7 (1.7)	70.2 (5.1)	100.0
Total (Col%)	12.2 (100.0)	16.2 (100.0)	19.6 (100.0)	23.8 (100.0)	28.2 (100.0)	100.0

Note: Figures within bracket are in percentages.

Source: Computed from unit level data of NSSO, 68th Round.

Table 3.9

Percentage of Graduates and above across Social Group and CEC, 2011-12

	Poorest	*Poor*	*Medium*	*Rich*	*Richest*	*Total (Row %)*
Scheduled Tribes	6.7 (12.3)	8.3 (7.0)	11.0 (4.9)	23.4 (4.2)	50.6 (2.0)	100.0
Scheduled Castes	5,8 (19.9)	7.8 (16.7)	13.8 (15.7)	23.5 (13.4)	49.1 (7.0)	100.0
OBCs	3.7 (50.0)	5.8 (47.1)	10.5 (46.4)	22.2 (42.1)	57.9 (37.5)	100.0
Upper Hindus	0.9 (14.1)	3.6 (23.7)	6.8 (26.3)	16.3 (33.0)	72.4 (40.6)	100.0
Upper Muslims	1.6 (3.6)	4.5 (26.3)	12.4 (5.7)	20.9 (5.0)	60.7 (7.7)	100.0
Others	0.2 (0.2)	0.9 (5.7)	2.5 (1.0)	9.8 (2.3)	86.6 (5.1)	100.0
Total (Col %)	2.4 (100.0)	4.7 (1.0)	8.8 (100.0)	19.0 (100.0)	65.1 (100.0)	100.0

Note: Figures within brackets are column percentages.

Source: Computed from unit level data of NSSO, 68th Round.

The high proportion of poor STs and SCs amongst those employed in the organized sector suggests that they have access to low paying jobs within the sector.

3.5.3 Distribution of Self-employed (Non-agriculture Sector) Workers of Different Socio-religious Groups by Consumption Expenditure Class

Self-employment represents the highest proportion of employment compared to regular or casual status (Table 3.4). It is a highly heterogeneous category with poor artisans and others with meagre capital, on the one extreme, and high-earning business persons, on the other. Table 3.8 gives an idea of the well-being of the various social groups, where the distribution of self-employed (non-agricultural work) is presented by social group and expenditure group (quintiles). The table shows that a large proportion of the self-employed among SCs, STs, OBCs and Upper Muslims belong to the poor class suggesting that these groups are the disadvantaged within this employment category because of skewed distribution of assets (land and capital). This reiterates the disparities that exist within social groups, that is a challenge to any blanket positive discrimination policy based only caste classification.

Disparities that exist within social groups pose, a challenge to any blanket affirmative action policy based only on caste classification.

3.5.4 Share of Graduates and Above among Different Socio-Religious Groups and Classes

It is well recognized that education is the principal means of accessing quality jobs, either public or private. Table 3.9 looks at the distribution of graduates (and above) across various CECs across social groups. Unsurprisingly, the proportion of graduates in richer households is much higher than the proportion of graduates in poorer households and this is the case across all social groups. Moreover, Upper Hindus (88.7 per cent) and 'Others' (96.4 per cent) have the highest percentage of graduates in the combined rich and richest CECs. In contrast only, 15 per cent ST graduates, 13.6 per cent SC graduates

Reservation of seats for SCs, STs and OBCs in educational institutions allow greater access to education without translating into high paying jobs.

Table 3.10a

Poverty by Households Occupation and Socio-religious Group, Rural, 2011-12; Poverty Reduction (Change in Percentage Point) in 2012 over 2005

Occupation		*SEAG*	*SENAG*	*RE*	*CLAG*	*CLNAG*	*OTH#*	*TOT HH*
Share population		35.6	15.4	9.2	22.4	14.3	3.1	100.0
STs	Poor (%)	40.1	28.9	19.1	55.3	51.7	22.2	42.7
	Change	15.8	20.3		20.1	15.7	7.4	19.2
SCs	Poor (%)	30.9	24.5	10.6	40.8	34.1	17.2	32.3
	Change	12.3	23.3		24.1	16.5	8.1	20.4
OBCs	Poor (%)	21.8	21.8	9.9	33.8	31.7	13.2	24.0
	Change	13.4	16.1		26.7	10.5	12.1	16.9
Upper Hindu	Poor (%)	11.4	10.0	6.0	24.4	19.8	6.2	12.3
	Change	8.5	6.9		21.3	6.3	3.6	9.3
Upper Muslim	Poor (%)	26.8	18.2	13.8	38.5	26.9	16.7	25.6
	Change	8.0	23.0		22.9	23.5	10.1	17.3
Others	Poor (%)	1.8	1.6	0	7.8	2.1	0	1.7
	Change	-0.2	-0.4		15.6	5.9	2.0	2.5
Total	Poor (%)	23.9	18.7	10.2	41.1	34.7	13.1	27.1
	Change	9.2	17.2		23.0	13.5	5.2	15.3

Note: SEAG—self employed in agriculture; SENAG—self employed in non-agriculture; RE—regular employed; CLAG—casual labour in agriculture; CLNAG—casual labour in non agriculture, OTH#—Others and TOT HH—Total Households.

Source: Computed from unit level data of NSSO, 55th and 68th Round.

Table 3.10b

Poverty by Occupation and Socio-religious Groups, Urban, 2011-12; Poverty Reduction (Change in Percentage Point) in 2012 over 2005

Occupation		*Self-employment*	*Regular Employment*	*Casual Labour*	*Others*	*Total*
Share population (2011-12)		38.5	43.4	11.4	6.6	100.0
STs	Poor (%)	24.8	8.7	54.2	11.9	23.3
	Change	18.9	5.3	17.3	3.5	11.7
SCs	Poor (%)	23.5	12	36.5	18.4	21.6
	Change	23.4	10.9	28.7	7.8	18.4
OBCs	Poor (%)	18.6	7.6	29.8	10.4	16.2
	Change	16.9	9.8	25.6	12.9	15.2
Upper Hindu	Poor (%)	6.1	2.6	18.7	3.9	4.8
	Change	5.0	3.9	18.8	4.2	5.0
Upper Muslim	Poor (%)	20.3	10.4	36.8	11.1	18.7
	Change	15.7	24.9	31.2	15.9	20.6
Others	Poor (%)	2.4	0.9	9.4	1.2	2.0
	Change	0.5	1.9	15.4	1.6	1.5
Total	Poor (%)	12.5	5.9	34.6	7.8	11.9
	Change	10.6	7.9	26.0	5.7	10.7

Source: Computed from unit level data of NSSO, 55th and 68th Rounds.

and 9.5 per cent OBCs graduates are in the poor and poorest CECs (these figures are less than 5 per cent for Upper Hindus and Others). Clearly, though the reservation of seats for these groups in educational institutions is perhaps allowing greater access to education, this is not necessarily translating into higher incomes in all cases. At the same time, there does exist a class bias within these disadvantaged groups, wherein 74-80 per cent (ST/SC/OBC) graduates belong to the richer classes. This suggests that the 'creamy layer' indeed gets better access to education even in disadvantaged social groups, although there are some differences between groups. Educational endowment opens up better opportunities in the labour market, where access to public sector jobs too is facilitated by the reservation policy. This linkage between income and access to education warrants revisiting the reservation policy for disadvantaged groups, especially in the context of the 'creamy layer' argument. This raises some questions regarding affirmative action policies that do not take into account the within-group differences. In the case of India, the relevant question is whether positive discrimination for the more deprived sub-groups within the reserved groups is called for, particularly among the OBCs, wherein a few economically and politically dominant OBCs have appropriated most of the benefits of the reservation policy. There is an additional concern as to whether certain groups of Muslims, who are currently classified as Upper Muslims, should be designated as OBC keeping in mind the large disparity within that group (Sharma, 2002).

> A few economically and politically dominant sections amongst the disadvantaged groups have appropriated most of the benefits of the reservation policy.

Thus, it seems that segmentation in the labour market is not only between socio-religious groups but also with regard to income and wealth within each group which is further reflected in the possession of educational endowment. Segmentation on an economic basis is much greater among the Upper Hindus and 'Others' than among the STs, SCs and OBCs. Among Muslims there is high inequality in terms of income and access to education, but the disparity is less than that among the Upper Hindus and the of category 'Others'.

3.6 Regional Exclusion

The previous sections of this chapter discussed the disadvantages faced by some of the socio-religious groups in India and the under representation of these groups in high paying and 'good' occupations. This is particularly challenging given that gainful employment can be instrumental in elevating the status of the disadvantaged. Another depiction of the link between the quality of employment exclusion can be seen from the distribution of poverty amongst those employed in different occupations and resident in urban/rural areas. This captures both the socio-religious and regional dimensions of deprivation in India.

Tables 3.10a and 3.10b present poverty estimates based on household type or occupation in rural and urban areas.[8] If we compare the rural and urban areas, the households below poverty are much higher in rural areas (27.1 per cent) as compared to urban areas (11.9 per cent). However the reduction in poverty during the period 2005 to 2012 was more in rural areas (15.3 per cent point) as compared to urban areas (1.7 per cent point). Furthermore, analysis of poverty and occupation type establishes that casual labourer households in both agricultural and non-agricultural sectors have the highest poverty ratio in the rural areas. Amongst casual labourers households, the STs and SCs have the highest poverty rates. So not only are these groups over represented in low paid jobs and low growth industries, they are the most deprived of the workers engaged in these occupations and for that matter in all occupations. This strongly suggests an element of discrimination in the labour market against these groups. Furthermore, this pattern with respect to casual labour households in rural India is replicated in the poverty rates in urban areas. On the other hand, regular employed households which has a lower proportion of poor, also has a smaller proportion of poor OBCs households. This may be indicative of OBCs benefiting from some of the policies, especially with respect to reservations in jobs.

8. The NSSO identifies household type or occupation based on the main source of income for the household during the 365 days preceding the survey. For this purpose, only the household's income (net income and not gross income) from economic activities is considered. Surveys identify different categories of occupations for rural and urban areas. In rural areas, these categories are: non-agricultural self-employed, agricultural self-employed, agricultural labour, other labour and a catch-all category called other rural. In 2011-12, wage or salaried workers that were earlier part of the other category have been separately identified. In urban areas, the categories include self-employed, wage or salaried, casual and a catch-all category called 'other urban'.

The stark decline in poverty is also observed across household occupational categories with the highest decline amongst casual workers in agriculture and lowest in other categories including regular workers in rural areas. In the urban areas, there is a 26 percentage point reduction in poverty among casual workers as compared to 11 percentage point for all households.

3.7 Regional Dimensions of Unemployment

Regional exclusion can play out at various levels. Just as urban–rural geographical locations can have implications for the level of exclusion experienced, so can the region or state location. Quality of employment available in a state has a direct bearing on the access to employment for social groups.

3.7.1 Employment Growth and Incidence of Unemployment

Aggregate national estimates and trends in employment conceal large regional variations. States differ widely in employment structure and growth, and in the incidence of unemployment. Andhra Pradesh, Haryana, Himachal Pradesh, Madhya Pradesh, Karnataka, Orissa, Tamil Nadu and West Bengal (besides Delhi), recorded high employment growth during 1983-94, each showing a growth rate of over 2.5 per cent comparable to the national average of 2.08 per cent per annum. During the period 1994-2005 there was a deceleration in the rate of growth: the national average declined to 1.84 per cent and most states in this group also experienced a similar deceleration. On the other hand, several states with low rates of employment growth during 1983-94 had higher growth in the subsequent decade. During 2005-12, further deceleration in the growth rate of employment was observed. A few states (Jammu & Kashmir, Chhattisgarh, West Bengal and Himachal Pradesh) only achieved close to 1.0 per cent growth in employment. Assam, Haryana, Karnataka, and Uttarakhand depicted absolute decline in the number of persons employed during this period (Appendix Table 3.13).

Unemployment rates also vary widely among states (Appendix Table 4.3). It is the highest (by the UPSS criterion) in Kerala at 7 per cent, followed by Assam (5 per cent). It is relatively high at 3 to 5 per cent in Bihar, Jammu & Kashmir, and West Bengal and low (less than 2 per cent) in Gujarat, Madhya Pradesh, Rajasthan and Maharashtra. It is difficult to explain these unemployment differences in terms of some common variables like per capita income or GDP growth or structure of growth. Furthermore, the pattern of the current daily status (CDS) unemployment measure also differs from UPSS. Keeping this in mind, the following section looks at access to employment and quality of employment across states and regions (a cluster of states, assumed to have similar characteristics). It also analysis relative employment situation in the states, based on a number of dimensions, which allows comparison between the states.

3.7.2 Employment Situation Index of States

While different variables can be used to measure employment quality, this section uses a composite index—the Employment Situation Index (ESI)—for the different states in India. The purpose of constructing this index is to get a single aggregate ranking, synthesizing the information of some important attributes of employment quality relevant in a country like India at the state level.

The various state level indicators that are used for the construction of the ESI are:[9]

- Percentage employed in regular formal work,
- Work participation rate,
- Percentage employed as casual labour,
- Percentage of self-employed workers below the poverty line,
- Average wage of casual labourers,
- Unemployment rate of secondary educated and above, and
- Percentage of unionized informal workers.

The state wise distribution of different indicators used in the construction of the index is presented in Tables 3.11 and 3.12. The data was used to construct separate index for males and females.

The methodology used is an average ranking method. Under this method, the different states are given a rank on the basis of each of the indicators mentioned above. In 21 major states, rank of '1' implies that the state has the best performance on that indicator and a rank of '21' means that the state is the worst in the group. An appropriate direction

9. A correlation matrix was generated to establish the efficacy of combining these indicators in the index.

Table 3.11

Employment Situation Indicators by State, 2004-05

	CL			WPR (UPS)			UR (UPS), Secondary+			UIW			FR			WPD (₹)			SEP		
Major States	M	F	P	M	F	P	M	F	P	M	F	P	M	F	P	M	F	P	M	F	P
Andhra Pradesh	36.4	46.2	40.2	82.5	52.0	67.0	7.1	10.9	7.8	8.6	4.2	7.6	6.0	2.8	4.7	92	55	76	25.9	31.6	28.1
Assam	19.0	33.4	21.2	82.5	16.7	51.4	13.0	30.0	15.3	6.0	4.0	5.7	6.5	5.0	6.3	111	95	107	32.3	16.9	30.6
Bihar	33.5	46.6	35.4	83.3	13.9	49.1	6.0	10.2	6.1	2.9	8.9	3.4	2.1	0.8	1.9	83	72	79	41.7	41.4	41.6
Chhattisgarh	37.5	45.8	40.8	82.7	56.4	69.7	6.0	11.2	6.5	3.3	1.6	3.0	5.8	1.4	4.1	69	53	62	43.5	49.3	45.8
Delhi	4.2	5.9	4.4	72.7	10.6	45.0	5.7	9.3	6.1	1.8	0.4	1.6	19.9	38.3	21.8	151	95	143	14.5	20.1	14.8
Gujarat	30.3	41.3	33.3	84.8	34.7	60.5	3.2	7.0	3.7	2.0	1.2	1.8	9.7	2.9	7.8	97	76	90	24.3	31.1	26.3
Haryana	18.1	12.2	17.2	75.9	15.5	47.4	6.6	18.1	7.9	4.7	5.8	4.8	10.9	6.4	10.2	136	104	128	17.5	24.6	18.9
Himachal Pradesh	22.6	3.1	14.5	76.2	52.0	63.9	7.8	19.6	11.6	3.7	8.6	4.4	13.6	4.8	9.9	151	111	146	21.3	27.3	24.5
Jammu & Kashmir	13.3	7.9	12.8	75.5	9.4	44.3	6.8	26.2	9.0	3.7	7.1	4.0	12.2	11.3	12.1	178	100	172	16.6	14.5	16.3
Jharkhand	26.2	23.9	25.5	81.6	33.2	57.9	6.5	4.8	6.3	1.9	2.6	2.0	6.4	1.8	5.1	93	72	88	41.1	43.6	41.8
Karnataka	36.7	47.3	40.4	83.7	45.9	64.9	4.0	15.2	6.1	3.2	6.7	3.9	7.8	4.1	6.5	97	56	81	30.2	34.9	31.8
Kerala	41.6	31.2	38.9	71.5	22.2	45.2	13.2	54.0	29.6	22.6	15.8	20.8	7.2	13.4	8.8	238	120	213	15.0	16.9	15.4
Madhya Pradesh	28.2	36.0	30.6	84.2	41.4	63.7	3.5	5.8	3.7	5.1	2.1	4.4	5.6	1.6	4.4	76	56	69	38.2	49.0	41.5
Maharashtra	27.7	42.6	32.9	78.1	44.0	61.5	5.3	6.4	5.5	2.7	2.4	2.6	11.6	4.6	9.1	95	53	77	34.3	39.5	36.1
Odisha	34.3	42.9	36.5	82.1	28.3	54.8	12.6	49.6	18.8	6.6	7.8	6.8	5.6	3.0	4.9	76	53	69	56.8	74.3	61.2
Punjab	25.3	18.5	24.7	79.8	8.1	44.9	5.8	36.0	10.8	3.0	2.0	2.8	8.7	21.1	9.8	136	97	132	12.1	13.4	12.2
Rajasthan	19.4	10.5	16.7	80.8	35.7	58.4	4.3	11.6	4.9	2.9	2.2	2.8	5.8	2.0	4.7	113	92	107	30.2	33.4	31.3
Tamil Nadu	35.0	40.1	36.9	81.3	47.6	64.1	5.4	15.1	7.7	8.0	3.3	6.8	10.0	4.8	8.1	128	65	104	22.4	28.9	25.1
Uttar Pradesh	19.0	18.0	18.9	81.1	18.3	50.3	2.9	9.6	3.3	1.2	3.2	1.4	4.3	1.9	3.8	97	72	92	38.9	51.7	41.4
Uttarakhand	15.3	7.3	12.6	75.4	39.0	57.0	5.6	11.5	6.7	6.1	5.9	6.0	10.9	3.5	8.3	121	99	118	30.1	32.1	30.9
West Bengal	33.6	32.3	33.4	80.4	14.3	48.3	8.4	34.9	11.6	8.3	4.5	7.8	7.1	5.7	6.9	92	70	88	29.9	40.4	31.3

Notes: CL: Casual labour; WPR: Work participation rate; UR: Unemployment rate; UIW: Unionized informal worker; FR: Formal regular; WPD: Wage per day; SEP: Self-employed poor.

Source: Computed from unit level data of NSSO, 61st Round.

Table 3.12

Employment Performance Indicators by State, 2011-12

Major States	*CL*			*WPR (UPS)*			*UR (UPS), Secondary+*			*UIW*			*FR*			*WPD (₹)*			*SEP*		
	M	F	P	M	F	P	M	F	P	M	F	P	M	F	P	M	F	P	M	F	P
Andhra Pradesh	31.8	45.1	36.6	78.1	42.5	59.9	6.0	11.3	6.9	8.7	6.4	8.2	8.3	2.7	6.3	168	111	143	11.2	14.5	12.5
Assam	17.6	23.2	18.3	78.4	11.2	45.8	10.8	29.9	12.9	7.9	6.8	7.8	6.2	7.9	6.4	145	106	139	28.5	17.8	27.6
Bihar	41.2	55.2	41.9	74.2	4.8	41.4	4.1	29.8	5.2	4.2	16.5	4.9	2.2	6.0	2.4	132	95	129	33.8	50.1	34.3
Chhattisgarh	34.8	42.5	37.6	79.3	47.4	63.5	6.0	8.7	6.5	8.8	11.0	9.4	4.0	1.6	3.1	96	83	91	36.0	43.1	38.5
Delhi	3.5	0.8	3.1	73.0	13.7	45.5	4.0	5.8	4.3	1.7	0.0	1.4	24.6	39.4	26.6	265	93	253	9.6	11.9	9.8
Gujarat	21.5	34.7	24.2	82.3	23.5	54.5	1.4	0.7	1.3	2.8	8.9	3.7	7.8	5.2	7.3	123	104	117	22.5	35.8	25.2
Haryana	21.1	22.7	21.2	72.3	9.3	42.6	4.2	11.0	4.8	4.1	3.4	4.0	12.2	18.3	12.8	204	159	199	7.1	2.7	6.8
Himachal Pradesh	21.9	5.1	14.4	74.2	55.2	64.3	3.0	5.5	3.9	5.0	9.3	5.8	13.7	3.7	9.2	173	122	164	12.0	14.8	13.6
Jammu & Kashmir	26.0	15.9	25.2	71.6	7.0	40.6	6.4	31.4	9.7	5.3	3.8	5.1	13.6	20.9	14.2	211	207	210	15.2	7.0	14.7
Jharkhand	29.4	21.7	28.4	79.3	12.6	46.3	4.3	34.6	7.1	5.0	3.3	4.8	6.7	5.0	6.5	141	82	136	36.8	42.7	37.7
Karnataka	27.1	36.6	29.7	79.2	30.9	55.3	3.1	6.3	3.7	5.1	2.9	4.6	11.7	9.8	11.2	170	99	148	22.3	20.5	21.8
Kerala	42.3	34.2	40.3	71.9	20.7	44.3	7.1	32.7	15.8	20.7	10.7	18.0	7.1	13.4	8.7	350	168	310	9.2	9.0	9.2
Madhya Pradesh	29.2	35.7	30.6	79.8	24.1	53.1	2.4	6.8	2.8	2.6	2.5	2.6	6.3	3.1	5.6	113	100	110	31.5	37.6	32.8
Maharashtra	22.6	37.2	26.6	75.7	30.5	53.7	2.0	5.9	2.7	4.1	3.1	3.9	12.6	7.0	11.1	142	95	123	20.6	24.3	21.5
Odisha	28.6	34.2	29.7	82.0	18.7	50.1	7.4	20.9	8.6	4.0	2.0	3.6	5.6	4.4	5.3	127	92	120	29.5	44.6	32.3
Punjab	24.2	12.2	23.1	76.5	8.6	43.9	4.1	9.5	4.7	4.4	2.5	4.1	8.2	16.9	9.0	203	153	198	6.7	15.0	7.2
Rajasthan	25.5	17.8	23.4	74.3	28.8	51.8	3.7	10.6	4.4	4.3	4.2	4.3	5.7	2.7	4.8	167	118	156	16.4	20.4	17.7
Tamil Nadu	39.3	43.3	40.5	77.7	32.6	54.7	4.4	10.8	5.7	7.2	1.9	5.8	11.1	8.5	10.3	204	106	168	10.3	12.8	11.1
Uttar Pradesh	28.3	17.9	26.9	77.1	12.9	45.3	5.3	10.1	5.6	2.0	5.0	2.2	4.1	2.6	3.9	137	97	132	31.4	36.5	32.2
Uttarakhand	18.3	3.2	14.3	68.9	23.9	45.8	5.7	27.3	10.0	3.0	5.1	3.2	12.0	5.1	10.2	177	128	171	15.3	19.0	16.6
West Bengal	40.3	31.2	38.9	78.6	14.7	47.1	7.1	20.6	8.9	8.4	4.0	7.7	6.7	7.6	6.8	128	107	125	15.1	22.0	16.1

Notes: CL: Casual labour; WPR: Work participation rate; UR: Unemployment rate; UIW: Unionized informal worker; FR: Formal regular; WPD: Wage per day; SEP: Self-employed poor.

Source: Computed from unit level data of NSSO, 68st Round.

Table 3.13

Employment Situation Index (ESI) for Major States, 2004-05 and 2011-12

	Overall		*Male*		*Female*	
	2011-12	2004-05	2011-12	2004-05	2011-12	2004-05
North						
Haryana	3	5	4	4	3	5
Punjab	5	8	3	7	7	9
Himachal Pradesh	1	1	1	8	1	1
Delhi	2	2	2	2	5	6
Rajasthan	11	9	14	11	9	10
Jammu &Kashmir	9	4	9	1	4	3
Central						
Madhya Pradesh	18	15	17	12	18	18
Uttar Pradesh	19	17	20	16	17	16
Uttarakhand	12	3	12	4	6	4
Chhattisgarh	17	20	18	20	16	20
North-East						
Assam	14	11	13	10	13	7
East						
Bihar	21	19	21	19	19	19
Odisha	20	21	19	21	20	21
West Bengal	15	16	15	16	14	17
Jharkhand	16	18	16	18	20	11
West						
Gujarat	12	9	9	6	8	12
Maharashtra	7	12	7	14	15	14
South						
Andhra Pradesh	7	13	8	15	11	12
Karnataka	4	14	5	9	10	15
Kerala	10	7	11	13	2	2
Tamil Nadu	6	6	6	3	12	7

Notes: Although Himachal Pradesh is ranked '8' in terms of male employment in 2004-05, the overall rank is '1' because the state has been able to perform remarkably well with respect to female employment relative to the other states lifting its overall rank. Also, Maharashtra and Andhra Pradesh are both ranked '7' and Gujarat and Uttarakhand are both ranked '12' in 2011-12. This is because of their identical ranking score aggregate.

Table 3.14

Regional Distribution of Regular Jobs by Social Group, 2011-12, UPSS

Sector		*Scheduled Tribes*	*Scheduled Castes*	*OBCs*	*Upper Hindus*	*Upper Muslims*	*Others*	*Total*
Public	North	17.0	18.2	10.2	22.5	29.7	40.9	17.2
	Central	24.9	19.1	16.7	19.1	14.2	14.0	18.6
	North-East	18.6	2.6	2.7	3.3	12.3	1.4	4.8
	East	11.7	18.6	11.7	22.4	21.4	1.4	16.1
	West	12.9	13.7	13.0	17.7	13.3	9.3	14.4
	South	12.8	27.8	45.3	14.3	8.6	31.6	28.3
	Others	2.2	0.1	0.3	0.6	0.4	1.4	0.6
	Total	100.0	100.0	100.0	100.0	100.0	100.0	100.0
Private organized	North	13.5	18.2	8.1	18.7	11.7	24.2	14.0
	Central	18.5	18.3	13.8	12.0	8.9	5.0	13.7
	North-East	4.8	0.7	1.0	1.2	3.9	1.1	1.3
	East	18.6	17.5	7.4	13.7	37.0	3.2	13.2
	West	32.4	16.2	19.8	37.9	23.8	27.0	25.8
	South	10.7	29.1	49.8	16.1	14.5	39.1	31.7
	Others	1.4	0.0	0.1	0.3	0.1	0.4	0.2
	Total	100.0	100.0	100.0	100.0	100.0	100.0	100.0

Source: Computed from unit level data of NSSO, 68th Round.

Table 3.15

Distribution of Formal Regular Jobs by Social Group and by Region, 2011-12, UPSS

	Scheduled Tribes	*Scheduled Castes*	*OBCs*	*Upper Hindus*	*Upper Muslims*	*Others*	*Total*
North	2.8	20.0	16.3	48.6	4.7	7.7	100.0
Central	4.8	14.0	29.8	45.8	3.9	1.7	100.0
North-East	28.9	9.1	19.7	27.8	13.9	0.5	100.0
East	5.8	15.9	18.8	54.1	4.9	0.5	100.0
West	4.6	17.0	26.0	44.8	3.8	3.7	100.0
South	2.1	14.6	48.5	28.3	2.7	3.7	100.0
Others	34.7	3.4	12.6	37.0	2.7	9.6	100.0
Total	4.8	15.9	29.7	41.9	4.2	3.5	100.0

Source: Computed from unit level data of NSSO, 68th Round.

Figure 3.4

Region-wise Population Share and Shares of Public and Private Sector (Organized Sector) Jobs in 2011-12

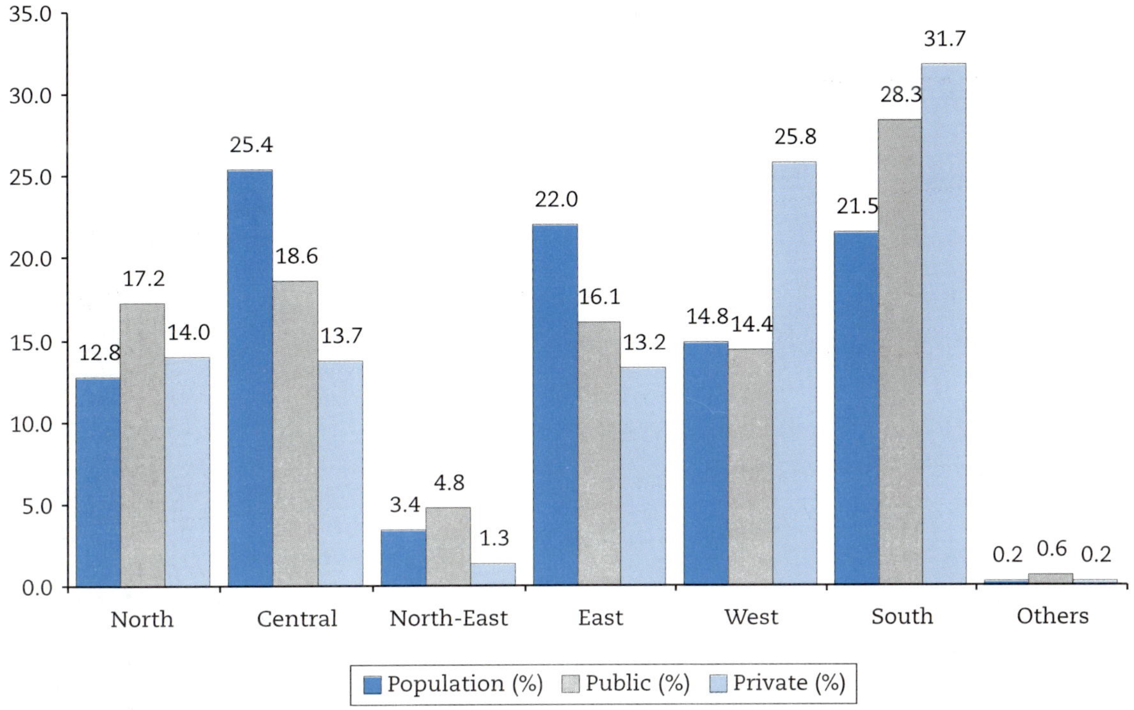

Source: Data computed from unit level data of NSSO, 68th Round.

of ranking is used depending on the indicator under consideration. For example, while a rank of '1' is given to a state with the highest percentage of 'formal regular workers', a state which has the highest percentage of 'casual workers' is ranked '21'. A total score is calculated for each of the states, based on a summation of rankings on the different dimensions, and an average score is calculated. The states are then ranked on the basis of their final scores, with the lowest score denoting the state with the best employment situation.[10]

Inevitably, the overall economic situation in a state affects the employment quality that it is able offer, and has a bearing on the inequality in access to employment for different social groups. Table 3.13 shows how the states rank on the index, over the two time periods, 2004-05 and 2011-12, for which the ESI is calculated. This ranking of states shows that in 2011-12, Himachal Pradesh was best amongst the major states in terms of employment outlook. Bihar, on the other hand, was the worst. The employment scenario has also changed in the states over the years. While Karnataka and Maharashtra have shown substantial improvement in their relative ranking, Kerala, Gujarat, Uttarakhand and Uttar Pradesh have shown a decline *vis-à-vis* the other major states.

> The overall employment condition in states affects the employment quality that it is able to offer; it also has a bearing on the inequality with regard to in access to employment for various social groups.

It must be kept in mind that poorly ranked states such as Bihar, UP, Chhattisgarh and Odisha have large proportions of population that comprise socially excluded groups, which are concentrated in the backward districts within these states. For these groups, access to employment and the quality of employment continue to pose challenges. Therefore, affirmative action policies facilitating access to employment must have embedded in them, policies that recognize and eradicate regional disparities.

10. The formula used for the calculation of the ESI is $\frac{1}{n} \times [\sum_i^n RI_i]$, where RI_i is rank by indicator i, i=1...7

> Affirmative action policies, facilitating access to employment, must have embedded in them policies that recognize and correct for regional disparities.

Comparing the relative ranking for men and women, it can be seen that Jammu & Kashmir, Kerala, and Rajasthan offer a better economic environment for women as compared to men. On the other in Jharkhand, Karnataka, Maharashtra, Punjab and Uttarakhand, women are clearly at a disadvantage compared to men.

Several factors would be responsible for the differing performance of the states and between males and females. They range from levels of economic development to labour market policies as well as structural and social factors in case of gender differences. There is clearly a need for investigating such factors in depth.

3.7.3 Access to Regular Jobs by Region and Socio-religious Group

This section looks at region, defined here as a geographical cluster of states, to establish broad patterns of regional and social exclusion.[11]

Broadly, the states comprising the eastern and central regions have the worst ranking as the ESI. The inequalities in access to employment for social group also vary widely across regional clusters. Tables 3.14 and 3.15 show that the central and eastern regions of India which have the highest incidence of poverty, account for only 35 per cent and 27 per cent of the public and private organized sector jobs respectively, while accounting for about 47 per cent of the country's population. On the other hand, southern, western, and northern regions together, with 49 per cent of the country's population, account for 64 per cent of public sector and 72 per cent of the organized private sector jobs.

Further, inequality is also reflected in the access to jobs by different groups in different regions (Table 3.14 and 3.15). Among the STs, those belonging to the central and north-eastern region (population share of 18.6 and 4.8 per cent respectively), have a significant presence in public sector jobs (24.9 per cent and 18.6 per cent). In case of private sector organized jobs, the STs are best off in the western region (32.4 per cent compared to 25.8 per cent population share). The SCs in South and Central regions have disproportionate access to both public and private jobs. SCs in the Eastern region have disproportionate access to public sector jobs (18.6 per cent compared to population share of 16.1 per cent) and for private sector jobs, SCs in North, Central and Eastern regions have greater access (18.2 per cent, 18.3 per cent and 17.5 per cent respectively) compared to their population share (14.0 per cent, 13.7 per cent and 13.2 per cent respectively). The regional disparity is more obvious in case of the OBCs, where those belonging to central and eastern India with a population share of around 47 per cent, account for just 28 per cent of the public sector jobs and 21 per cent of the private organized sector jobs. The OBCs belonging to southern and western regions with a population share of 42 per cent, account for around 58 per cent of the public sector jobs and 70 per cent of the total private organized sector jobs. Share of public sector jobs among Upper Hindus and Upper Muslims (who constitute only 17 per cent and 9 per cent respectively of the total population) is 23 per cent and 30 per cent in north region. Similarly share of private organized sector jobs captured by Upper Hindus and Upper Muslims in the western region is 38 per cent and 24 per cent, respectively, compared to their population shares of 23 per cent and 15 per cent respectively in that region (Tables 3.14 and 3.15).

Table 3.15 shows that in all regions of India, barring the south, the highest proportion of formal regular jobs is appropriated by the Upper Hindus. In the southern region; the OBCs have a higher share of these most coveted jobs. In the North-east, a high proportion of ST workers are employed as formal regular workers. The distribution of formal regular workers by region confirms some of the patterns observed above with respect to the distribution of organized sector jobs.

The employment patterns examined here are clearly corroborated by the variations in the levels of economic and human development in different regions of the country. The question is whether, over

11. The country is divided into six regions: North (Haryana, Punjab, Himachal Pradesh, Chandigarh, Delhi, Rajasthan and Jammu & Kashmir), Central (Madhya Pradesh, Uttar Pradesh, Uttarakhand, Chhattisgarh), North-East (Assam, Meghalaya, Manipur, Mizoram, Nagaland, Tripura), East (Bihar, Orissa, West Bengal, Jharkhand), West (Gujarat, Maharashtra, Goa, Daman and Diu), South (Andhra Pradesh, Karnataka, Kerala, Puducherry, Tamil Nadu, Andaman and Nicobar) and Others, for the analysis here. The percentage share of population among these regions as per the NSSO survey 2011-12 was 12.4 per cent, 25.4 per cent, 3.4 per cent, 22.0 per cent, 14.8 per cent, 21.5 per cent and 0.2 per cent, respectively.

the years, some groups among the OBCs (which were earlier lagging behind the development ladder) have climbed up to appropriate disproportionate share of the benefits from affirmative policy. Or whether because of competitive politics a few prosperous groups have been added to the list of OBCs enabling them to grab the benefits of reservation which should have gone to the more deserving groups. What can be seen is that in regions (south and central), which have the highest OBC population share who are politically very mobilized also have OBCs well represented in quality jobs. This is also true of SCs in these regions.

The inequalities and disparities that exist in access to employment across regions and for social groups remains a huge challenge.

3.8 Conclusions

- There are significant differences in the access to quality employment across different social groups and regions. While economic growth in India has resulted in an increase in the quantity of employment, the access to quality jobs is still very low and needs to be addressed in the employment policy. Policy particularly needs to take into account both social and regional dimensions to access to employment.

- The poverty rate amongst the disadvantaged socio-religious groups when compared to the all-India level is disproportionately high. Furthermore, the rural dimension to poverty in India is obvious from the higher percentages of poor in rural India across all social groups (except for Upper Muslims).

- The disadvantaged social groups are mostly concentrated in low productivity sectors and in low-paying jobs.

- The percentage of STs and SCs employed in the public sector is higher than their proportion in the private sector. The reverse is true for OBCs. Affirmative action policy has helped these disadvantaged groups in accessing jobs in the public sector, although their participation in proportion to their total workforce is still very low.

- There is a marked within-group difference in terms of occupational attainments, with the Upper Hindus and 'Others' being the foremost beneficiaries of employment growth. Also evident is that the 'Others' comprising of Jains, Parsis, Sikhs and Christians have disproportionate share of good jobs and educational endowment, more than that of the Upper Hindus.

- Affirmative action policies have played a role; but some states and regions, and certain social groups, are better off than the others. The OBCs of South India, in part due to the political clout they wield in the region, are doing better than their counterparts in other regions.

- The overlap between poverty and poor quality of employment is strongly evident; a large proportion of the poor belonging to the disadvantaged groups and resident in rural areas, are also employed in 'bad' jobs.

- In both urban and rural areas, there has been a sharp decline in poverty, even among casual labourers in the period between 2005 and 2012.

- Given the limited access of the socially excluded groups to regular formal jobs and jobs in the organized sector, there is a need to upgrade job quality in the informal sector. High rate of expansion of productive and remunerative employment is pertinent to secure better livelihoods, especially in the case of socially excluded groups.

- There has been a decline in poverty across all socio-religious groups, with the largest decline observed amongst the SCs, STs, OBCs and Upper Muslims.

- Questions regarding the scope of reservation policy in India that were relevant ten years back are relevant even today (Sharma, 2002). The main concern is that any affirmative action policy in India should take into account the various dimensions of exclusion that have emerged in this chapter—social and regional. There is also a need to examine whether only the sub-groups within the reserved groups, the poorest amongst the high caste groups, and certain sections of minorities, need to be included within the gamut of affirmative action policies.

4

Wages, Earnings and Inequality

4.1 Introduction

Rising inequality in income and earnings in India in the post-liberalization period since the early 1990s has been an area of major policy concern. Since official statistics on income are not available, scholars have analysed inequality based on consumption data compiled from various quinquennial rounds of the National Sample Survey Organization (NSSO). Consumption data has consistently shown rising inequality over time, both in rural and urban areas, but more so in the latter (Dev and Ravi, 2007; Himanshu, 2007; Sarkar and Mehta, 2010; Vakulabharanam, 2010). The Gini Coefficient for rural areas declined from 0.319 in 1983 to 0.298 in 1993-94, but increased sharply to 0.320 in 2004-05 but again declined marginally to 0.309 in 2009-10. In urban areas, the corresponding estimates increased from 0.367 to 0.357 and 0.389 to 0.406 and for all areas 0.337 to 0.347 and 0.376 to 0.394 in these four years (Mazumdar, Sarkar and Mehta, 2013). However, it is widely recognized that consumption expenditure is a poor proxy of income and as such the analysis based on this has led to gross underestimation of overall income inequality.

A study based on individual income tax returns, examining the evolution of top incomes and wages from 1922 to 2000 shows that the share of top 0.01 per cent, 0.1 per cent and 1 per cent of the population in the total income shrank substantially from the 1950s to the early mid-1980s, but then rose again, so that these shares in 2000 were only slightly below what they were in the 1920s and 1930s. The top 1 per cent had a share of around 13 per cent of income in the early 1920s, which then rose to a peak of nearly 18 per cent during the late 1930s before returning to around 13 per cent during the late 1950s. Subsequently, it came down to around 4.5 per cent in the early 1980s, and then steadily increased to 9 per cent by 1999-2000. It seems that the very rich people were able to corner most of the income gains from the liberalization process in the 1990s (Banerjee and Pikeety, 2005).

This trend seems set to accelerate in the future. A study on wealth inequality in terms of assets or net worth showed that in 2002, the bottom 10 per cent of the population possessed a mere 0.4 per cent of the total wealth; further, the bottom 50 per cent captured less than 10 per cent of total wealth (Jayadev, *et al.*, 2007).

While an important aspect of income inequality in India is wage inequality, there are certain data limitations. Wage workers constitute only about half of the workforce while the rest are self-employed for whom data on earnings is unavailable. Further, wage data provided by various NSSO quinquennial rounds suffers from inadequate coverage and problems of incorrect reporting particularly among the higher end of workforce. Despite these shortcomings the data from NSSO and *Annual Survey of Industry* (ASI) do provide insights into wage and labour market inequality in India, although this also is somewhat underestimation.

The second section of this chapter analyses the trends in wages and inequality among various groups of wage earners. The third section extends the analysis by locations, occupations, gender etc. Based on ASI data, the fourth section analyses the trends in wage, non-wage and profits in organized industry. The fifth section provides an analysis of workers who receive minimum wages and thus the implementation of the Minimum Wages Act. Finally, the discussions in the chapter have been summarized along with some perspectives for policy.

The Indian labour market is highly segmented by location, sector, and size of enterprise on the demand side, and skill level, social group, and gender on the supply side. As a result, the structure of wages and earnings of workers varies widely. The most pervasive characteristic of the wage situation in India is the low level of earnings among a large majority of workers. Over one-fourth of the working population earns less than the modestly defined official poverty line.

> There is a wide gap in wages between workers as over one-fourth of the working population earns less than a modestly defined official poverty line.

The self-employed are extremely heterogeneous in terms of both the nature of occupation as well as earning levels with no systematic data available on them. But one broad caveat is that most of those who work in agriculture and the informal sector have relatively low levels of income. In 2006-07, while the overall GDP per worker (including both wage-earners and the self-employed) was estimated to be ₹ 9000 per month, the average monthly income of a cultivator (own account farmer) worked out at ₹ 2000 (Planning Commission, 2008c, Vol. III). The

Table 4.1

Trends in Urban–Rural/Regular-Casual Daily Wages, 1983 to 2011–12

Type of Worker	*Wages per Day in ₹*				*Compounded Annual Growth Rate (CAGR) (in %)*		
	1983	1993-94	2004-05	2011-12	1983 to 1993-94	1993-94 to 2011-12	1983 to 2011-12
Regular							
Rural	127	183	251	298	3.5	2.8	3.0
Urban	202	266	348	445	2.7	2.9	2.8
Total	169	232	307	392	3.0	3.0	3.0
Casual							
Rural	53	69	92	138	2.5	3.9	3.4
Urban	84	102	126	173	1.8	3.0	2.6
Total	58	75	99	143	2.5	3.7	3.2

Note: Wages are at 2011-12 prices and pertain to workers in the 15–59 years age group.

Source: Computed from unit level data of various NSS rounds.

average monthly income of a self-employed person in unorganized manufacturing, estimated on the basis of the NSS Survey in 2005-06, worked out to be ₹ 2698 (₹ 1601 in rural areas) and that of a worker in unorganized services to be ₹ 2014 (₹ 1175 in rural areas). Since then these differences have certainly not narrowed down; rather they are likely to have increased.

The average earnings of regular wage/salary workers (for whom data is available on a more systematic basis from NSSO surveys and other sources) were ₹ 298 per day in rural and ₹ 445 per day in urban areas in 2011-12 (Table 4.1). The differences are much larger in the unorganized sector as casual workers do not get work on all the days. Within the organized sector, the average salary in the public sector is more than twice than that in the private sector. Variations across regions and states are also very wide. For example, wages of casual labour in rural Chhattisgarh were less than one-third (30 per cent) of the corresponding wages in Kerala in 2011-12. At all India level, it can be observed that a female worker on an average received only two-third of wages of a male worker (Appendix Table 6.2b).

4.2 Wage Patterns

4.2.1 Overall Wage Levels and Trends

In 2011-12, regular workers received an average daily wage of ₹ 392, which was about three times that of the casual workers at ₹ 143 (Table 4.1). Wage levels of casual and regular workers hide the true earning differential between the two categories because regular workers get paid for all days in a week whether they work or are on leave. Further, availability of work is assured on all working days of the week. But casual workers are paid only for the days that they actually work. Apart from the daily wage rate, the earnings of the casual workers get directly affected by the number of days of work and availability of work on a given day.

Differences between urban and rural wages vary with the nature of employment. The urban–rural differential among regular workers is higher at 49 per cent compared to 23 per cent among casual workers. The segmentation between regular and casual is much sharper than that between urban and rural workers.

The urban–rural differential among regular workers is higher at 49 per cent compared to 23 per cent among casual workers.

As Table 4.1 shows, there has been a substantial increase in real wages from 1983 to 2011-12. During the period as a whole, real wages/salary of regular workers and casual workers displayed compounded annual growth rate (CAGR) of 3.0 per cent and 3.2 per cent, respectively. All categories, rural, urban, regular and casual, benefited from this rise, though not to the same extent. Casual workers did marginally better

Figure 4.1

Trend in Urban-Rural/Regular-Casual Wages, 1983 to 2011-12

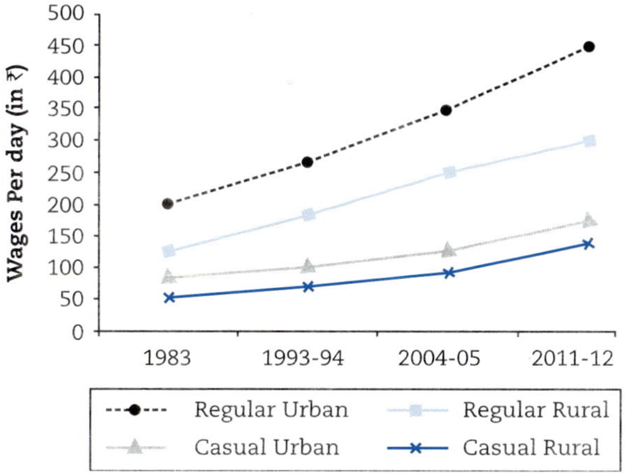

Source: Computed from unit level data of various NSS rounds.

Figure 4.2

Urban–Rural Wage Ratios for Regular and Casual Workers, 1983 to 2011-12

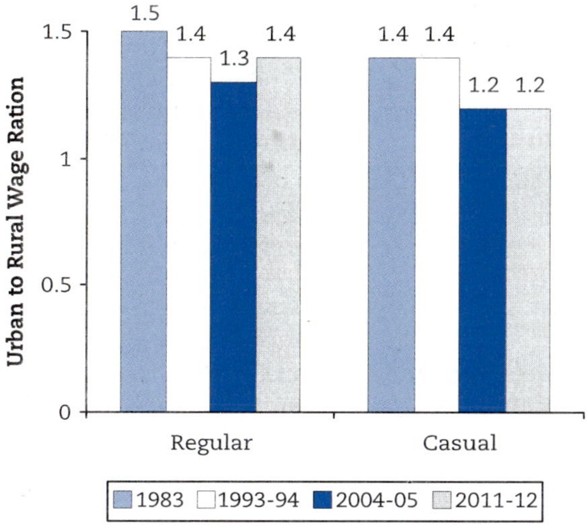

Source: Computed from unit level data of various NSS rounds.

than regular workers and rural areas did better than the urban areas with casual workers in the urban areas as an exception in recent years. Figures 4.1 to 4.3 show that the wage differential between rural and urban areas has been declining over time whereas the differential between regular and casual workers has been rising within both urban and rural areas. However, in 2011-12, the urban–rural wage differential increased for regular workers (Figure 4.2) and it declined between regular and casual workers in rural areas (Figure 4.3).

Figure 4.3

Regular–Casual Wage Ratios for Rural and Urban Workers, 1983 to 2011-12

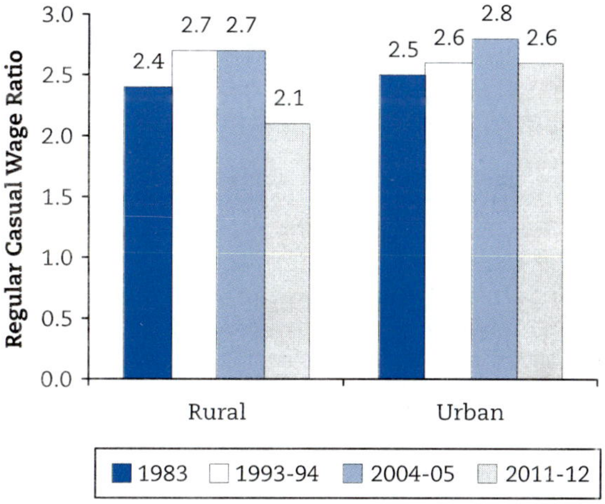

Source: Computed from unit level data of various NSS rounds.

4.2.2 Wages by Sector

Rural Areas

In rural India, the agricultural wage rate is considered to be one of the most robust indicators of economic well-being, not only of agricultural labourers, but also of the rural population as a whole. The overall trend in agricultural wages has been similar to that of rural wages, in which there was a substantial rise over the period 1983 to 2011-12 as a whole (Table 4.2). Casual agricultural workers, however, saw a higher growth in their wages than regular workers (Table 4.2). One plausible explanation is that regular workers who are largely attached to labour find that the advantage of their relative wage differential is eroded by the market-determined wage rate of casual workers (who are also free to pursue non-agricultural occupations).

During the post-liberalization period, rural non-agricultural wages have shown a higher growth rate than that during pre-liberalization for only casual workers (Table 4.2). The rural non-agricultural wage rate has historically been higher than the agricultural wage rate. There has, however, been a decline in the relative difference between the two over the time period between 1983 and 2011-12. But even in 2011-12, the wage of non-agricultural workers was more than twice the agricultural wage for regular workers and around 1.3 times in the case of casual workers.

Table 4.2

Trends in Rural Agricultural and Non-agricultural Daily Wages of Regular and Casual Workers, 1983 to 2011-12

Sector	Wages per Day in ₹				CAGR (%)		
	1983	1993-94	2004-05	2011-12	1983 to 1993-94	1993-94 to 2011-12	1983 to 2011-12
Regular							
Agricultural	65	84	126	149	2.5	3.2	3.0
Non-agricultural	155	200	265	304	2.5	2.3	2.4
Casual							
Agricultural	48	65	81	123	2.8	3.6	3.3
Non-agricultural	74	94	123	162	2.2	3.1	2.8

Note: Wages are at 2011-12 prices and pertain to workers in the 15–59 years age group.
Source: Computed from unit level data of various NSS rounds.

Table 4.3

Trends in Urban Daily Wages by Sector, 1983 to 2011-12

Sector	Wage per Day (in ₹)				CAGR (%)		
	1983	1993-94	2004-05	2011-12	1983 to 1993-94	1993-94 to 2011-12	1983 to 2011-12
Regular							
Primary	193	276	480	721	3.5	5.5	4.7
Secondary	197	242	283	359	2.0	2.2	2.1
Tertiary	207	276	373	476	2.8	3.1	3.0
Ratios							
Tertiary/Primary	1.1	1.0	0.8	0.7	0.8	0.6	0.6
Tertiary/Secondary	1.1	1.1	1.3	1.3	1.4	1.4	1.4
Casual							
Primary	69	79	90	141	1.3	3.3	2.6
Secondary	90	114	138	183	2.3	2.7	2.5
Tertiary	83	100	121	169	1.8	3.0	2.5
Ratios							
Tertiary/Primary	1.2	1.3	1.4	1.2	1.4	0.9	1.0
Tertiary/Secondary	0.9	0.9	0.9	0.9	0.8	1.1	1.0

Note: Wages are at 2011-12 prices and pertain to workers in the 15-59 years age group.
Source: Computed from unit level data of various NSS rounds.

During the post-liberalization period, rural non-agricultural wages for casual workers have shown a higher growth rate than that during the pre-liberalization period.

Urban Areas

In urban areas, the wage gap between the two main sectors—secondary and tertiary—is much smaller (Table 4.3). The size of the primary sector, included in the table for completeness, is small in urban areas.

Casual wages are relatively higher in the secondary sector, while regular wages are relatively higher in the tertiary sector. The gap between regular and casual wages is much higher in the tertiary sector (regular wages were on an average 2.8 times the casual wages in tertiary sector in 2011-12) compared to the secondary sector (regular wages were on an average 1.9 times the casual wages in the secondary sector in 2011-12). This reflects a particularly strong dualism in the tertiary sector (Mazumdar and Sarkar, 2007). Tertiary employment includes both better paid public sector jobs as well as a variety of low income services. Even in the lowest public sector grade (P1), annual earnings (at ₹ 1.14 lakh) were found to be higher than the average annual wage of regular workers in the tertiary sector as a whole (at ₹ 1.03 lakh) in 2007-08 (NSSO, 64th Round). The top government grade of officers was eight times the sector average in the same year. As noted earlier, growth in wages has been slower in urban than in rural areas (more so for casual than regular workers as can be seen in Table 4.1). Some interesting features of sector wise wage differentials in terms of levels and trends may be summed up as follows:

- Wages for regular workers have been rising faster in the tertiary sector than in the secondary sector, while the reverse is true for wages for casual workers, which are rising faster in the secondary sector than the tertiary sector.
- In the tertiary sector, dualism is not only strong, but it is also increasing.
- Compared to the secondary sector, the tertiary sector pays 32 per cent more to its regular workers on an average, but close to 8 per cent less to its casual workers.

Growth in wages has been slower in urban than in rural areas (more so for casual than regular workers.

4.2.3 Regional Wage Differentials

There are wide variations in casual as well as regular wages across states. Table 4.4 shows that in 2011-12, the variations were much wider (coefficient of variation or CV=31.6) in the case of rural casual wages due to the predominance of informal sector, and it was comparatively less (CV=21.8) in the case of urban regular wages, which is due to a relatively higher share of organized economic activities. Madhya Pradesh (₹ 107 per day) and Chhattisgarh (₹ 87 per day) reported the lowest levels of rural casual wages while Kerala (₹ 309 per day) stood out as the best paying state. Wages of regular workers show much smaller variations across states. In rural areas, daily regular wages varied between the highs of ₹ 483 in Jharkhand and ₹ 450 in Uttarakhand and the lows of ₹ 209 in Karnataka and ₹ 239 in Chhattisgarh. In urban areas, the variations are still smaller, the lowest being ₹ 322 in Gujarat and the highest ₹ 754 in Haryana.

What does the above pattern of wage differentials tell us? It appears that the labour market is most integrated across the states in the case of regular jobs in the urban market (CV=21.8%) and least integrated for casual workers in rural areas (CV=31.6%). Labour markets for regular workers in rural areas and for casual workers in urban areas also seem reasonably integrated.

This pattern of wage differentials across states can be explained in terms of two factors—the role of institutional factors in the determination of wages and inter-regional mobility of labour. Wages for urban regular workers are to a considerable extent institutionally fixed and regulated and those institutions are similar, if not the same, across the states. Therefore, wages of regular workers do not show very high variations across the states. Casual wages, on the other hand, are determined primarily by the local labour market conditions, which vary widely among regions. Also there is greater mobility among workers across urban than rural areas, and therefore, urban wages vary less widely than rural wages across the states. Labour mobility per se may also be an important sector in levelling wage differentials.

Do the states perform similarly with respect to wages for casual and regular workers in rural and urban areas? For example, it has been argued that the poorer states pay lower and developed states higher wages (Bhalla, 2004; Deaton & Dréze, 2002; Sen, 1998). Is that so for all types of workers and locations?

It appears that the labour market is most integrated across the states in the case of regular jobs in the urban market and least integrated for casual workers in the rural market.

Table 4.4

Average Regular and Casual Daily Wages in Rural and Urban Areas in Different States, 2011-12

State	Regular				Casual			
	Rural	Rank	Urban	Rank	Rural	Rank	Urban	Rank
Andhra Pradesh	246	16	395	16	138	10	178	6
Assam	303	10	607	2	138	11	154	13
Bihar	413	4	415	14	128	14	159	11
Chhattisgarh	239	19	337	19	87	20	112	20
Gujarat	254	15	322	20	113	18	148	15
Haryana	396	6	754	1	198	4	203	4
Himachal Pradesh	398	5	398	15	163	6	168	10
Jammu & Kashmir	433	3	510	4	211	2	210	2
Jharkhand	483	1	553	3	133	12	154	14
Karnataka	209	20	490	5	143	9	174	8
Kerala	318	8	458	8	309	1	315	1
Madhya Pradesh	244	17	434	10	107	19	130	19
Maharashtra	357	7	482	6	118	17	155	12
Orissa	241	18	431	11	119	16	131	18
Punjab	285	11	360	18	199	3	192	5
Rajasthan	304	9	415	13	153	8	174	7
Tamil Nadu	267	13	378	17	156	7	210	3
Uttar Pradesh	279	12	481	7	131	13	144	16
Uttarakhand	450	2	446	9	171	5	171	9
West Bengal	260	14	428	12	124	15	133	17
CV	27.3		21.8		31.6		25.7	
India	298		445		138		173	

Notes: 1. Wages are in ₹.

Source: Computed from unit level data of NSSO, 68th Round.

In fact, contrary to common perception, better developed states do not in general pay higher wages and vice versa. Gujarat, Maharashtra, Tamil Nadu and Punjab do not feature among the four highest wage states (out of 20) in any of the four categories, namely rural casual (RC), urban casual (UC), rural regular (RR) and urban regular (UR). Nor do states necessarily figure as consistently high or low wage paying in all labour market categories. The ranking of a state varies widely with respect to the wages paid to regular and casual workers in rural and urban areas. Kerala, no doubt, pays the top wages for casual workers both in rural and urban areas, but its rank is as low as 8 in wages for regular workers in both rural and urban areas respectively. Jharkhand is among the lowest quarter of states in respect of casual wages but close to the first quarter in regular wages. Contrarily, Punjab is among first quarter of casual wage but falls in third and fourth quarter of regular wages for rural and urban areas. Haryana and Jammu & Kashmir feature consistently among the relatively higher wage paying states in all categories while, West Bengal, Orissa, Chhattisgarh, Gujarat and Madhya Pradesh are in the lowest quartile in all categories. It should also be noted that a large part of the differences in the wages of regular workers, more so in rural areas, across states, is also due to the presence of several public and private sector industries and other enterprises (e.g., Jharkhand).

Table 4.5

Spearman Rank Correlation (N=20) across States in 2011-12

		RR	UR	RC	UC
RR	Correlation coefficient	1.000	.401	.505(*)	.394
	Sig. (2-tailed)	.	.080	.023	.085
	N	20	20	20	20
UR	Correlation coefficient	.401	1.000	.254	.131
	Sig. (2-tailed)	.080	.	.279	.581
	N	20	20	20	20
RC	Correlation coefficient	.505(*)	.254	1.000	.887(**)
	Sig. (2-tailed)	.023	.279	.	.000
	N	20	20	20	20
UC	Correlation coefficient	.394	.131	.887(**)	1.000
	Sig. (2-tailed)	.085	.581	.000	.
	N	20	20	20	20

Note: * Correlation is significant at the 0.05 level (2-tailed).
** Correlation is significant at the 0.01 level (2-tailed).
RR = Rural Regular, RC = Rural Casual, UR = Urban Regular, UC = Urban Casual.

Source: Computed from unit level data of NSSO, 68th Round.

Coefficients of rank correlation between different states suggest that states which pay higher wages to casual workers in rural areas also pay higher wages to casual workers in urban areas. The same is true of rural regular and rural casual wages and to a small extent of regular wages in rural and urban areas (Table 4.5).

Institutional factors and inter-regional mobility of labour are the principal factors determining wage differentials.

These features again go to suggest that labour markets are segmented by category of workers much more than by region. Also, it appears that the role of institutional factors is being reinforced here: wages in a particular segment in a state are high if it is mostly institutionally covered. As such in Kerala, regular fixation and monitoring of minimum wages keep the wages of casual workers high, while most regular jobs, outside the government, are in small and unorganized establishments. Chhattisgarh is in the top quarter in respect of regular wages, because most of its regular employment is in the government or organized manufacturing, while it ranks very low in wages for casual workers, as there is very little union or government intervention in the casual labour market. Maharashtra and Karnataka's relatively high ranking in urban wages and low ranking in rural wages could also be explained in similar terms.

States which pay higher wages to casual workers in rural areas also pay higher wages to casual workers in urban areas.

It may also be noted in general that less developed and poor states show very high rural-urban differentials in both the casual and regular wage segments. For example, the rural casual wage is less than one-fourth of the urban regular wage in Bihar and Jharkhand. Maharashtra also shows a similar ratio despite being a relatively developed state; it has always reported some of the lowest rural wages in the country. In most of the less developed states the ratios are broadly similar (as also in Gujarat, though it is not a backward state). In contrast, most of the developed states show a lower disparity between casual and regular wages and also between rural and urban areas. The least disparity in this regard is found in Kerala, where the rural and urban casual wages are almost equal and rural casual wages are approximately two-thirds of the urban regular wages.

4.3 Other Aspects of Wage Inequality

We have already noted earlier that there have been some increases in wage differentials over the last two decades between regular and casual workers as well as across sectors. These appear to be part of the wider trend of increasing inequality in India today. This section extends the analysis to look at the overall pattern of wage inequality, and other key wage differentials between groups of workers.

The accelerated growth in inequality from 1993 till 2004-05 can largely be traced to a growing gap between the best paid workers and the rest.

4.3.1 The Overall Pattern of Inequality

All measures of aggregate wage inequality showed a rise since 1983, with a sharper increase in inequality in the first decade of the post-liberalization period. But in 2011-12 it showed mild decline. This can be seen, for example, in the Gini coefficient (Table 4.6). More disaggregated measures show that the accelerated growth in inequality from 1993 till 2004-05 can largely be traced to a growing gap between the best paid workers and the rest. This can be seen clearly by comparing the three Generalized Entropy measures, GE(0), GE(1) and GE(2). GE(0), which gives greater weight to inequality at the bottom of the income distribution, rises steadily between 1983 and 2004 and declines thereafter. GE(2), on the other hand, gives greater weight to inequality at the top of the distribution; it rises much more sharply after 1993 till 2004-05 and also declines at a faster rate in 2011-12. This suggests that in the general stretching of the income distribution, the gap between a high income elite and the rest is playing the pivotal role in the movement of aggregate wage inequality. An important reason behind overall decline in the wage earning inequality in recent years can be due to the fact that between 2004-05 and 2011-12 for the first time since the introduction of liberalization measures there was rather substantial absorption of labour in the formal segment of labour market as was seen in the previous chapter.

The gap between a high income elite and the rest is playing the pivotal role in the movement of aggregate wage inequality.

Table 4.6

Trends in Earning Inequality of Wage Workers

Period	*Gini*	*GE(0)*	*GE(1)*	*GE(2)*
1983	0.483	0.420	0.395	0.503
1993-94	0.506	0.477	0.458	0.687
2004-05	0.542	0.534	0.570	1.305
2011-12	0.510	0.452	0.508	0.923

Note: GE classes of measurements are Generalized Entropy measures. GE(0) gives more weight to the lower level of wages, GE(1) gives equal weight and GE(2) gives more weight to the higher levels of wages.

Source: Computed from unit level data of various NSS rounds.

Table 4.7

Measures of Inequality (Gini Coefficient) in the Earnings of Regular and Casual Workers, 1983 to 2011-12

	1983	1993-94	2004-05	2011-12
Regular				
Rural	0.451	0.409	0.485	0.482
Urban	0.374	0.384	0.477	0.499
Total	0.419	0.400	0.484	0.501
Casual				
Rural	0.318	0.276	0.274	0.298
Urban	0.353	0.308	0.298	0.305
Total	0.329	0.288	0.282	0.303

Source: Computed from unit level data of various NSS rounds.

It is noted that there are large wage differences between regular and casual workers; within these groups also there is considerable inequality. Table 4.7 shows the Gini coefficients for each group separately. Wage inequality among regular workers is consistently higher than for casual workers. This is probably because regular wage workers have much greater variation in skills and qualifications, whereas a large proportion of casual workers consist of unskilled daily labourers. It is interesting to note that wage inequality has increased among regular wage workers, especially in the first decade of the post-liberalization period; but among casual wage workers it has declined continuously from 1983 to 2004-05. It did however, rise high enough in 2011-12 to erase the gains made in the first decade of post-reform period. This is consistent with the changes in the overall trend in inequality discussed above, since highly skilled workers whose wages have increased much faster than the others, are included in the regular workers category. The sharp increase in the skill premium for wages comes out more clearly in the analysis of education–wage linkages.

Skill variations between regular and casual workers also contribute to the wage inequality between these groups of workers.

4.3.2 Wages by Educational Level

An important aspect of rising wage inequality has been the sharp rise of wages of skilled workers relative to the unskilled (Mazumdar and Sarkar, 2008). This might be due to skill-biased technological change or the dismantling of a structure of trade protection that formerly favoured relatively unskilled, labour-intensive sectors.

In the absence of any direct measure of skills, the usual approach is to use the educational level as an indicator of skills. In this case, the expectation is that wages will progressively rise with increasing levels of education (Abraham, 2007). This may be more so in the case of regular workers, as education levels play a much smaller role in determining the wages of casual workers. As the data in Table 4.8 shows, wages indeed do rise with each educational level, but the rise is steeper after the middle level of education, and tertiary education brings a particularly large increase over secondary education. Wage differentials across educational categories for regular workers have been fairly stable. It is only for graduates and above that the differentials with other levels of education have widened during the first decade of post-liberalization period but in the most recent year of 2011-12, this differential has shown some decline.

Table 4.8

Wage Differentials between the Educated Regular Workers and the Non-literate by Level of Education

Level of Schooling	*1983*	*1993-94*	*2004-05*	*2011-12*
Not literate	1.0	1.0	1.0	1.0
Up to primary	1.4	1.3	1.3	1.1
Up to middle	1.5	1.4	1.3	1.3
Up to secondary and higher secondary	2.3	2.1	2.3	2.1
Tertiary	3.7	3.6	4.6	4.1

Source: Computed from unit level data of various NSS rounds.

Table 4.9

Wage Differential within the Educational Groups of Regular Wage Workers

Schooling	*Percentile Level*	*Wage Rate*				*Wage Ratio of 50th and 75th to 25th percentile*			
		1983	1993-94	2004-05	2011-12	1983	1993-94	2004-05	2011-12
Not literate	25th	39.3	50.9	55.9	90.2	1	1	1	1
	50th	85.4	113.2	126.1	135.3	2.2	2.2	2.2	1.5
	75th	106.4	146.8	147.8	210.2	2.7	2.9	2.6	2.3
Up to primary	25th	56.3	72.5	75.9	105.1	1	1	1	1
	50th	119.0	146.1	159.0	150.2	2.1	2	2.1	1.4
	75th	157.6	203.4	190.2	224.8	2.8	2.8	2.5	2.1
Up to middle	25th	67.1	79.0	87.8	112.5	1	1	1	1
	50th	129.5	153.6	168.5	168.5	1.9	1.9	1.9	1.5
	75th	165.4	209.2	195.9	259.7	2.5	2.6	2.2	2.3
Up to secondary & higher secondary	25th	118.0	121.0	114.2	157.3	1	1	1	1
	50th	195.9	233.2	286.1	250.2	1.7	1.9	2.5	1.6
	75th	236.6	314.9	399.0	491.6	2	2.6	3.5	3.1
Tertiary	25th	197.0	248.5	253.6	281.0	1	1	1	1
	50th	316.3	401.7	574.3	561.7	1.6	1.6	2.3	2.0
	75th	380.7	508.5	760.7	912.9	1.9	2	3	3.3
Total	25th	67.5	97.0	101.4	140.3	1	1	1	1
	50th	167.8	230.9	307.5	229.5	2.5	2.4	3	1.6
	75th	211.5	314.9	420.0	525.5	3.1	3.3	4.1	3.7

Source: Computed from unit level data of various NSS rounds.

Figure 4.4

Female–Male Wage Ratios across Categories

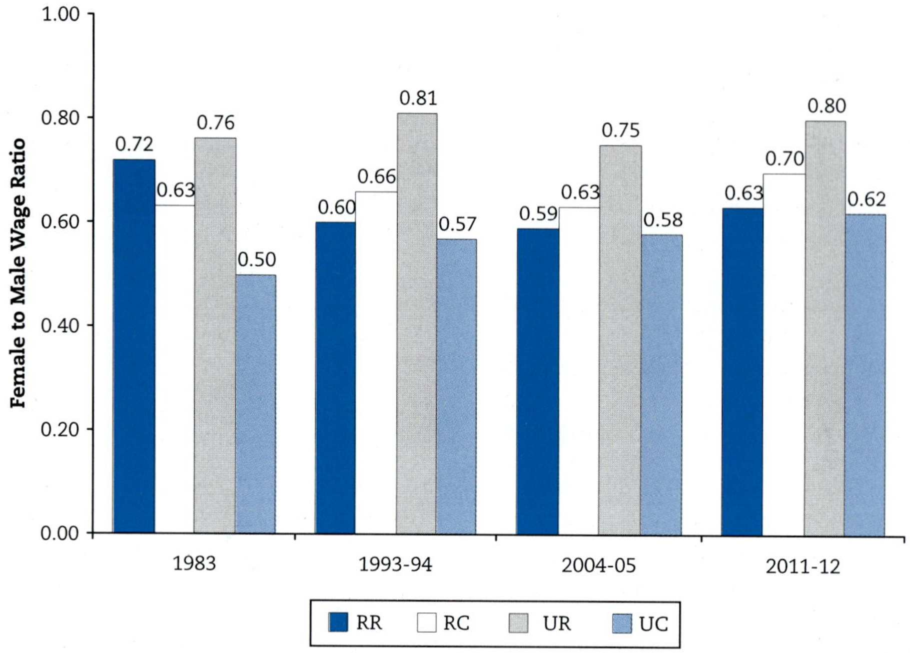

Source: Computed from unit level data of various NSS rounds.

The increase in wage inequality appears to reflect both increased differentials between educational categories, and increased inequality within them, but this is confined to higher educational levels.

What has happened to wage inequality among workers within the same educational category? Inequality within educational categories (Table 4.9) showed remarkable stability in the pre-reform period (1983 to 1993-94). In the first decade of the post-reform period, for those who had attained secondary schooling and above, the ratio between wages at the 50th percentile and 25th percentile and between the 75th percentile and 25th percentile showed a perceptible increase. The biggest rise occurred for graduates and above. However, this pattern was not observed for lower educational levels. However, in the most recent period of 2011-12, only the ratio of wage between the 75th percentile and 25th percentile showed some increase for graduates and above. For all other ratios one can discern a clear decline. It is premature to conclude on the basis of only recent year data that it is a reversal of trend observed in the first decade of post-reform period. Looking at it in totality, the increase in wage inequality appears to reflect both increased differentials between educational categories, and increased inequality within them, but this is confined to higher educational levels.

4.3.3 Gender Differentials in Wages

As is well known, the wages of female workers are lower than those of men across most employment categories and locations. The range of difference can be seen in Table 4.10, which gives wages of regular and casual male and female workers in rural and urban areas, as recorded in the various rounds of NSS quinquennial surveys (1983 to 2011-12).

Table 4.10

Average Daily Wages of Male and Females, 1983 to 2011-12

(Wages in ₹)

	1983		1993-94		2004-05		2011-12	
	Male	Female	Male	Female	Male	Female	Male	Female
RR	17.6	12.8	58.5	34.9	144.9	85.3	320.2	202.8
RC	7.8	4.9	23.2	15.3	55.1	34.9	150.4	104.6
UR	25.7	19.5	78.1	63.3	203.3	153.2	462.8	368.8
UC	11.1	5.6	32.4	18.5	75.1	43.9	185.0	114.9

Note: RR = Rural Regular, RC = Rural Casual, UR = Urban Regular, UC = Urban Casual

Source: Computed from unit level data of various NSS rounds.

The wages of women workers are at least 20 per cent, and at the maximum 50 per cent less than male wages across different categories, locations and years. Male–female differentials in regular wages in rural areas have widened: average female wage was 72 per cent of average male wage in this category in 1983; it fell to 59 per cent in 2004-05 and increased marginally to 63 per cent in 2011-12 (Figure 4.4).

Across all other categories, rural casual, urban regular and urban casual, the gap between male and female wages has narrowed in 1983–2011 to a greater or smaller degree with the maximum improvement visible in urban regular employment wherein the female wage was 80 per cent of the male wage in 2011-12. An improvement of 12 percentage points was seen in the case of urban casual workers as well though the category exhibits the widest differential at 62 per cent.

Average wage rates and differences therein may not, of course, indicate differentials within similar jobs, occupations and activities, but do reflect, to a larger or smaller extent, differences in structure of employment: women may be found in low wage jobs more often than men. It must, however, be pointed out that significant differences in wages are found within the same type of economic activity as well. For example, in casual employment in urban areas, women in services related to community and social work received wages which were only half of that of men, while in economic services it was 63 per cent (Table 4.11). Women's wages come closest to that of men in regular urban manufacturing and services (economic) to the tune of 75 per cent and 79 per cent respectively. Extreme outcomes thus tend to be located in the services (social, community & personal). Urban manufacturing appeared to be maintaining greater gender equity in wages across both regular (75 per cent) and casual workers (60 per cent) as compared to other sectors.

Does education reduce the gender gap in wages? It appears that it does in regular employment but not in casual employment. In fact in the latter, it seems to widen the wage gap between men and women. According to the data from NSSO, 2011-12, the wage disparity between men and women declined with increasing level of education in both rural and urban areas in regular work except for graduate & higher education level in urban areas (Figure 4.5).

A woman worker, with no education, received only 53 per cent of a man's wage in a regular job in rural areas, but with a graduate degree she received 70 per cent of the wage as her male counterpart. In urban areas, the gap was lower: a non-literate woman received 62 per cent of male wages, on an average, while secondary level education enabled her to reach 86 per cent of male wages (though with a graduation degree this fell to 76 per cent). In general, education acted as a leveller between men and women as far as regular jobs were concerned.

Table 4.11

Urban Wage Rates in Select Sectors, 2009-10

Sector	*Wage Rates (₹)*		
	Male	*Female*	*F/M Ratio*
	Regular Workers		
Agriculture	312.6	91.9	0.29
Manufacturing (agro based) (15-22)	237.1	129.3	0.55
Manufacturing (others) (23-37)	344.7	260.2	0.75
Services (economic) (65-74)	533.6	423.1	0.79
Services (community, social, personal) (75-93)	506.9	335.0	0.66
	Casual Workers		
Agriculture	112.0	73.8	0.66
Manufacturing (agro based) (15-22)	117.1	67.7	0.58
Manufacturing (others) (23-37)	130.5	78.3	0.60
Services (economic) (65-74)	141.3	89.7	0.63
Services (community, social, personal) (75-93)	125.3	63.8	0.51

Source: Computed from unit level data of NSSO, 66th Round.

Figure 4.5

Female–Male Wage Ratios by Educational Level of Regular Workers, 2011-12

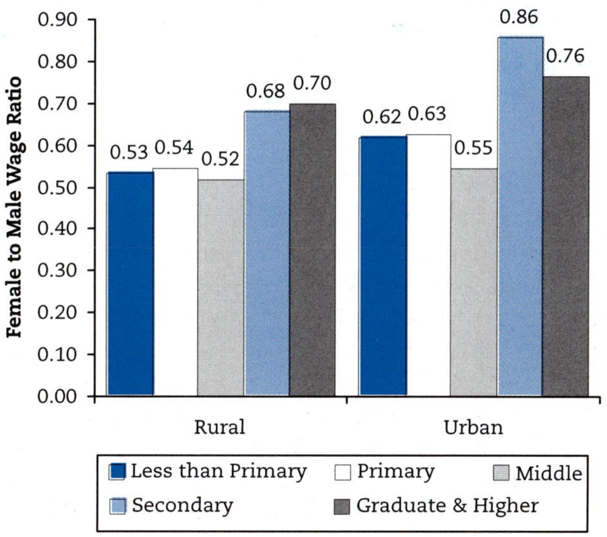

Source: Computed from unit level data of NSSO, 68th Round.

In the casual labour market, however, education seems to put women at a relative disadvantage (Figure 4.6).

Across both rural and urban geographies, women with primary education are seen to be worse off than the non-literate women in terms of female–male wage differentials. It must also be noted that, in general, education has brought little improvement in wages in casual employment for male as well as female workers.

Table 4.12

Wage by Educational Level of Regular Workers, 2011-12

Education	Rural		Urban	
	Male	Female	Male	Female
Non-Educated	178	95	208	129
Primary	189	102	222	139
Middle	217	112	252	138
Secondary*	338	229	383	328
Graduate and higher	550	378	792	607
Total	320	203	463	369

Note: *also included higher secondary

Source: Computed from unit level data of NSSO, 68th Round.

Figure 4.6

Female–Male Wage Ratios by Educational Level of Casual Workers, 2011-12

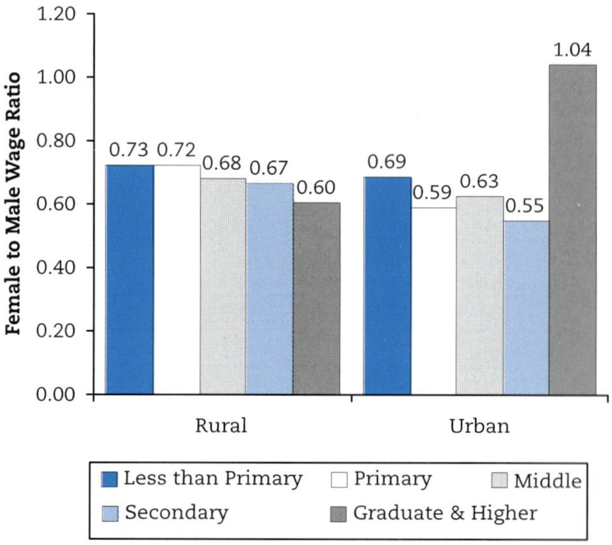

Source: Computed from unit level data of 68th NSS round.

Figure 4.7

Trend in Non-worker–Worker Wage Ratio in Modern Industry, 1981-82 to 2009-10

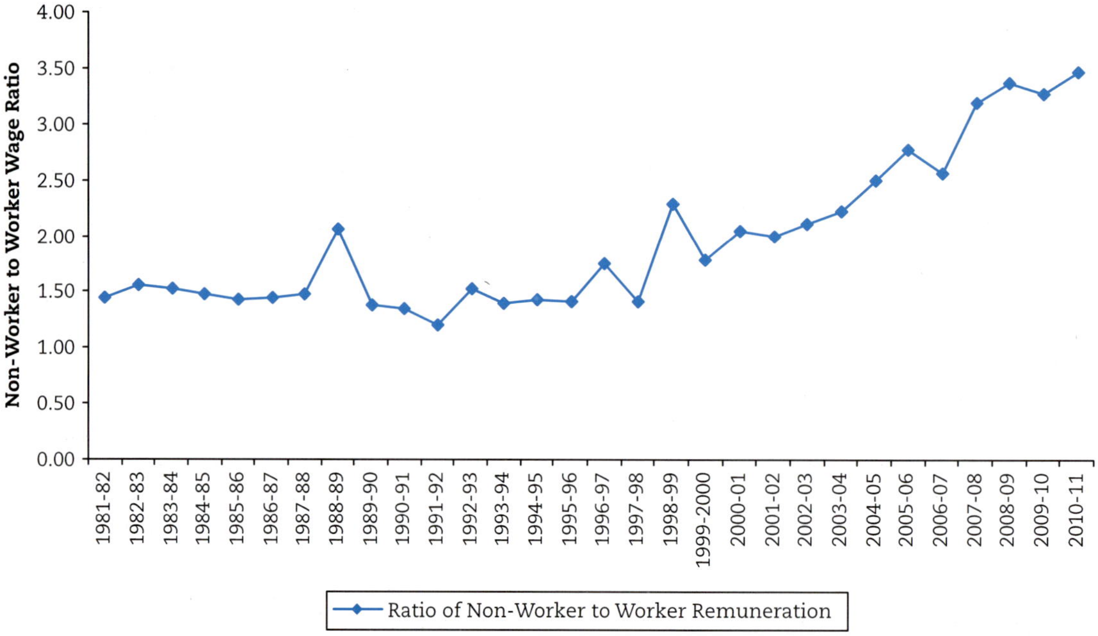

Source: *Annual Survey of Industry* and Central Statistical Organization.

Education has brought little improvement in wages in casual employment, for male as well as female workers.

In the case of regular employment, however, education led to a significant increase in wages of both men and women. In fact, the wages of female workers rose faster with education than those of male workers, in regular jobs. It, therefore, appears that regular employment is a necessary condition for education to benefit workers in general, and to reduce the gender wage gap in particular.

Wages of female workers rose faster with education than those of male workers, in regular jobs.

4.3.4 Wages by Occupation in the Organized Industry Sector

As was shown earlier, wage differentials between regular and casual workers have been growing till 2004-05. There is, of course, some regular work in the unorganized sector and a lot of casual work in the organized sector, but it seems likely that the wage differential between organized and unorganized sectors has also been growing. Recent pay awards in the public sector are likely to have reinforced this trend. Increasing wage differentials by education for regular workers suggest that there is also greater differentiation within the organized sector.

There is some additional evidence to support the latter assertion. ASI data may be used to compare the average compensation of workers with that of non-worker employees (clerical, supervisory and managerial staff).[1] The ratio between mean wages in these two categories gives some insight into the widening wage differentials. From Figure 4.7 it may be observed that till the first half of the decade of the 1990s, the wage differential remained more or less stable at around 1.5. However, from 1996 onwards, the ratio rose steadily, reaching 3.46 by 2010-11. By 2010-11, the average wage of a non-worker employee in modern industry was 3.5 times the average compensation of the worker.

It is likely that inter-sectoral differentials also contribute to growing inequality. There is, for instance, evidence that some export-oriented sectors pay higher wages than domestically-oriented sectors. In the IT sector, for instance, wages are considerably higher as compared to other industries in the country. Graduates employed in IT earn much more than graduates in other sectors (Sarkar and Mehta, 2010). However, it is not obvious that the same is true of casual workers. Another source of wage inequality is enterprise size. As shown by the data from ASI (2005-06), average wages in the largest firms are more than three times than that in firms with less than 50 workers in the factory sector (Mazumdar and Sarkar, 2013). These are issues which merit further investigation in future research.

4.4 Wages, Non-wage Incomes, and Profits

One important issue in analysing wage levels and trends is the distribution between wage and non-wage income. In 2011-12, GDP per worker (wage workers and self-employed) was estimated to be ₹ 175,539 per annum, while the average income of wage and salary earners worked out to ₹ 81,819 per annum. While these figures are not strictly comparable, they give a first indication of the scale of the non-wage share in value added. Over the years (1983-2011) this gap has been increasing sharply, with real wages/salaries rising at a rate of about 3.1 per cent per year, and value added per worker increasing at a rate of about 4.8 per cent per year.[2]

In India, where a large proportion of work consists of self-employment, the calculation of wage and profit shares is rather problematic, because dividing self-employed income into a return to capital and a return to labour is difficult even in principle. However, the division between wage and profit shares is rather more meaningful in organized industry, where self-employment is much less important, and the ASI data for the manufacturing sector permits us to track the changes over an extended period of time.[3]

1. ASI estimates are for the factory sector (organized sector), which is defined as enterprises with 10 or more than 10 workers with electricity and 20 or more than 20 workers without electricity.

2. The values in this paragraph are estimated from various issues of National Accounts Statistics (NAS) and unit level data of NSS employment schedules for 38th and 68th rounds.

3. ASI estimates are for the factory sector (organized sector), which is defined as enterprises with 10 or more than 10 workers with electricity and 20 or more than 20 workers with or without electricity. Although this does not cover the service sector, it might be expected that modern services such as banking, insurance, IT services and the like would show a pattern similar in nature to that for modern industry, since both capital and labour can, in principle, move between them.

Figure 4.8

Wage and Profit Shares in Organized Industry, 1981-82 to 2009-10

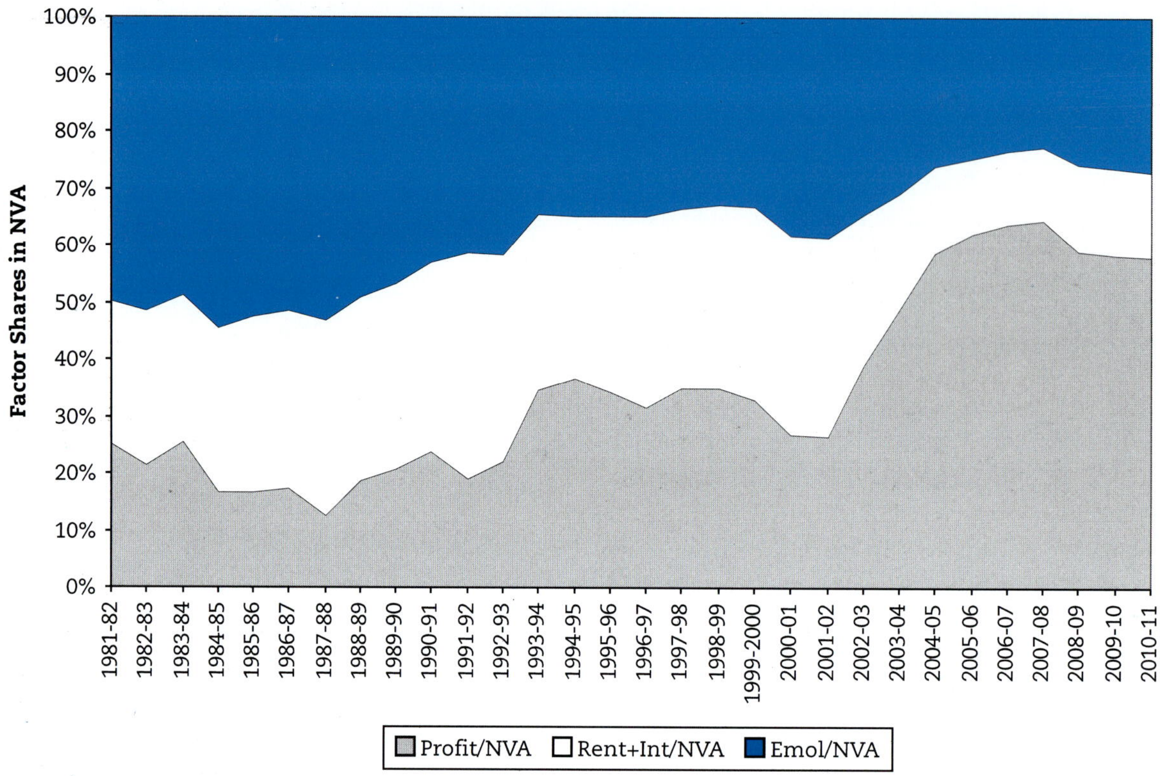

Source: *Annual Survey of Industry*, various years.

Figure 4.9a

Profits, Fixed Capital and Emoluments per Employee

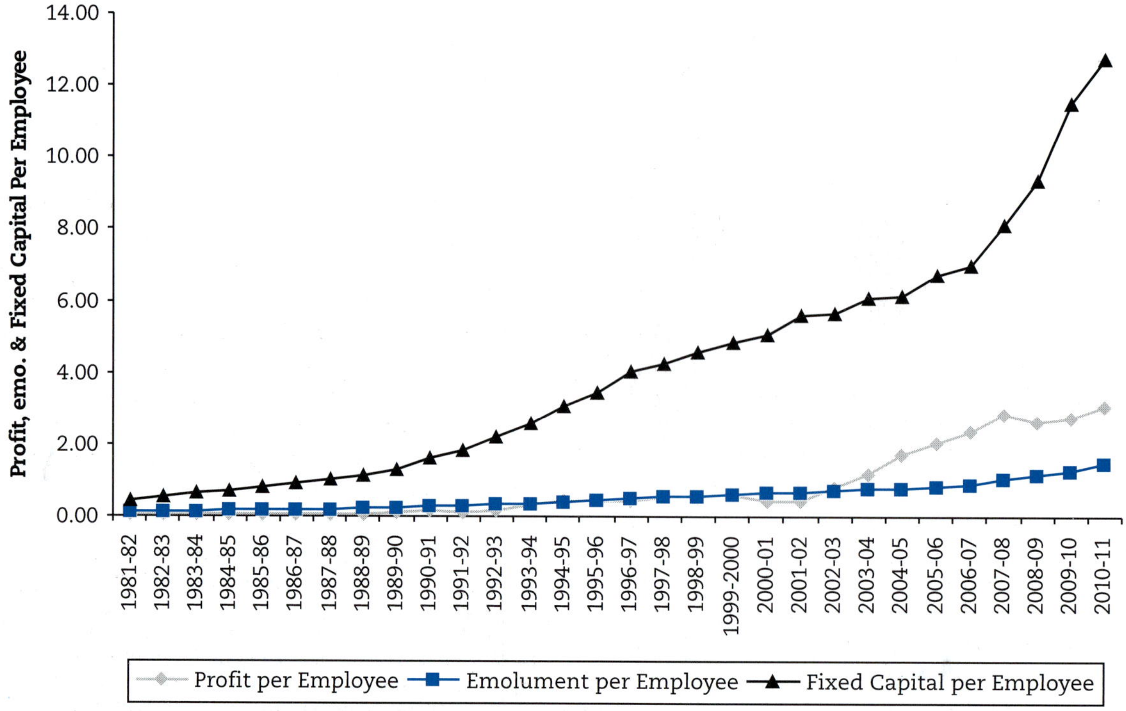

Source: *Annual Survey of Industry*, various years.

Figure 4.9b

Percentage of Total Labour Cost in Production

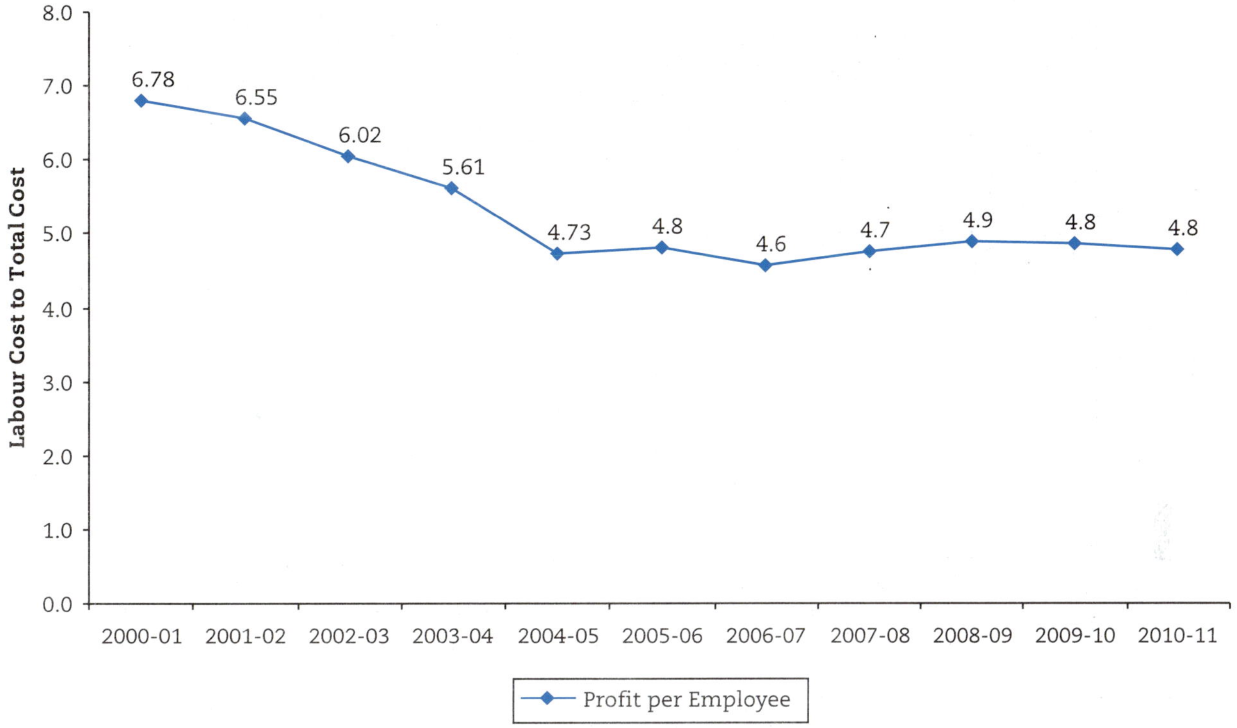

Source: Annual Survey of Industry, various years.

Figure 4.8 shows profit, wage and rent/interest shares in net value added in industry since the early 1980s. The pattern is striking. The profit share, which remained around 0.2 during the 1980s, rose to a new plateau of around 0.3 in the 1990s after the economic liberalization. Then, after dipping at the turn of the century it shot up after 2002-03, to reach 0.58 in 2010-11.

The share of wages in the total value added has been declining consistently, interrupted only by a short reversal in 1999-2002. From around 0.45 in the 1980s it has now fallen to around 0.25 in 2010-11. The share of rent and interest, after rising in the pre-reform period and witnessing a period of relative stability has also declined sharply after the turn of the century. The shift from wages to profits, and, to a lesser degree, from rent and interest to profits, is large, and is obviously closely connected with the acceleration of growth in the last few years, though direction of cause to consequence is not clear. In any case, it amounts to a substantial shift in income towards capital, thus contributing to the overall increase in income inequality.

The share of wages in total value added has been declining consistently, interrupted only by a short reversal in 1999-2002.

Another way of looking at the same data is by converting into per employee terms. This is done in Figure 4.9a, which shows profits and wages per employed worker. This data is in current prices, so the increase in the wage bill per employee reflects both an increase in real wages and an increase in prices. We cannot interpret the change over time without deflating for price changes, but we may reasonably compare profits per employee and the wage bill per employee at different points in time.[4]

The pattern is broadly consistent with that found for wage and profit shares. In the 1980s, wages per

4. The price index would not necessarily be the same for profits and wages, but the two can reasonably be compared in current prices as a first approximation.

Figure 4.10a

Percentage of Casual Rural Farm Workers (15-59 years) Not Getting Minimum Wages in Major States, 2009-10

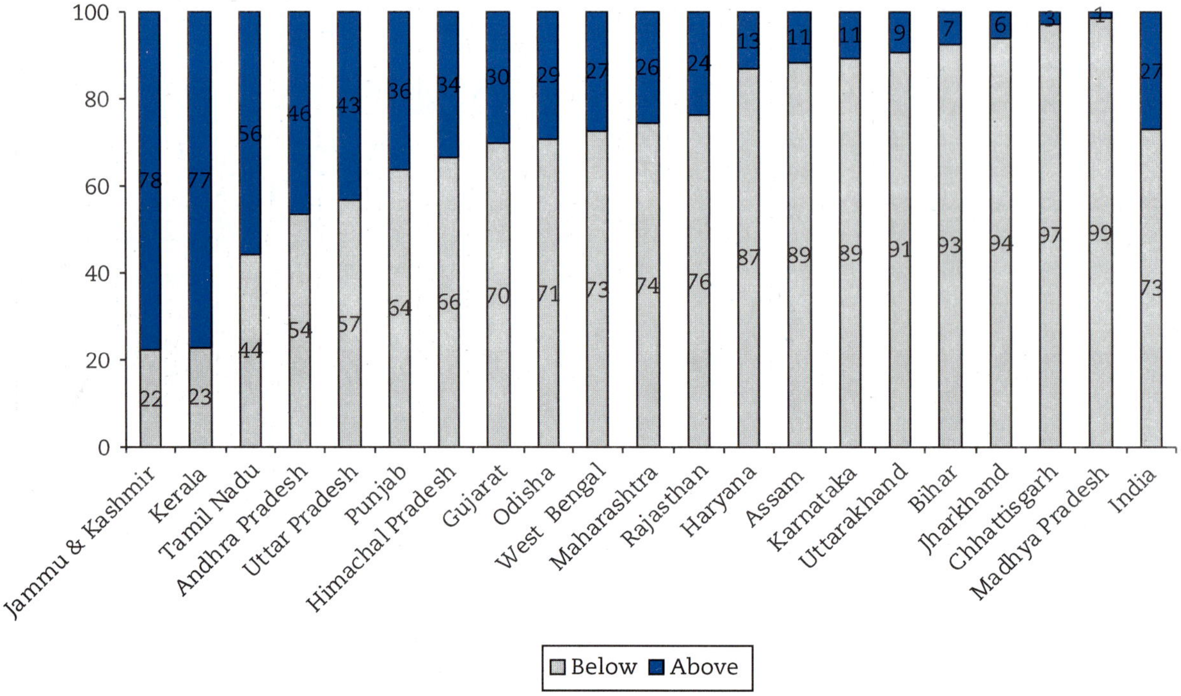

Source: Computed from unit level data of NSSO, 66th Round.

employee were two to three times higher than profits per employee. After the first round of liberalization in the early 1990s the gap narrowed, with profits per employee rising to almost the same level as wages. And in the first decade of the twenty-first century, profits per employee jumped much more sharply than wages, to reach little over two times wages by 2010-11.

There are many possible reasons for the increase in the profit share. One obvious possibility is an increase in the capital intensity of production. Figure 4.9a also shows the change in fixed capital per employee, as estimated in the ASI survey. It can be seen that there is some increase in capital intensity, in the sense that fixed capital per employee rises faster than the wage bill per employee, but the relative increase is modest, and certainly not enough to explain the substantial increase in the profit share.[5]

A distinct shift in labour practices has been observed in the last couple of decades where businesses are showing greater proclivity to hiring workers under casual or other flexible contracts which are comparatively cheap at the expense of regular formal workers. This has enabled the employers to reduce the labour cost in production as shown in Figure 4.9b for the last decade.

In the last couple of decades, businesses have been showing greater proclivity to hiring workers under casual or other flexible contracts which are comparatively cheap at the expense of regular formal workers.

4.5 The Implementation of the Minimum Wages Act 1948

Government intervention in wage determination takes various forms. While the fixing of public sector wages is an important activity that impacts the organized sector directly, the intervention which has the most pervasive economy-wide implication

5. However, it should be borne in mind that capital stock estimates are unreliable.

Figure 4.10b

Percentage of Casual Rural Non-farm Workers (15-59 years) Not Getting Minimum Wages in Major States, 2009-10

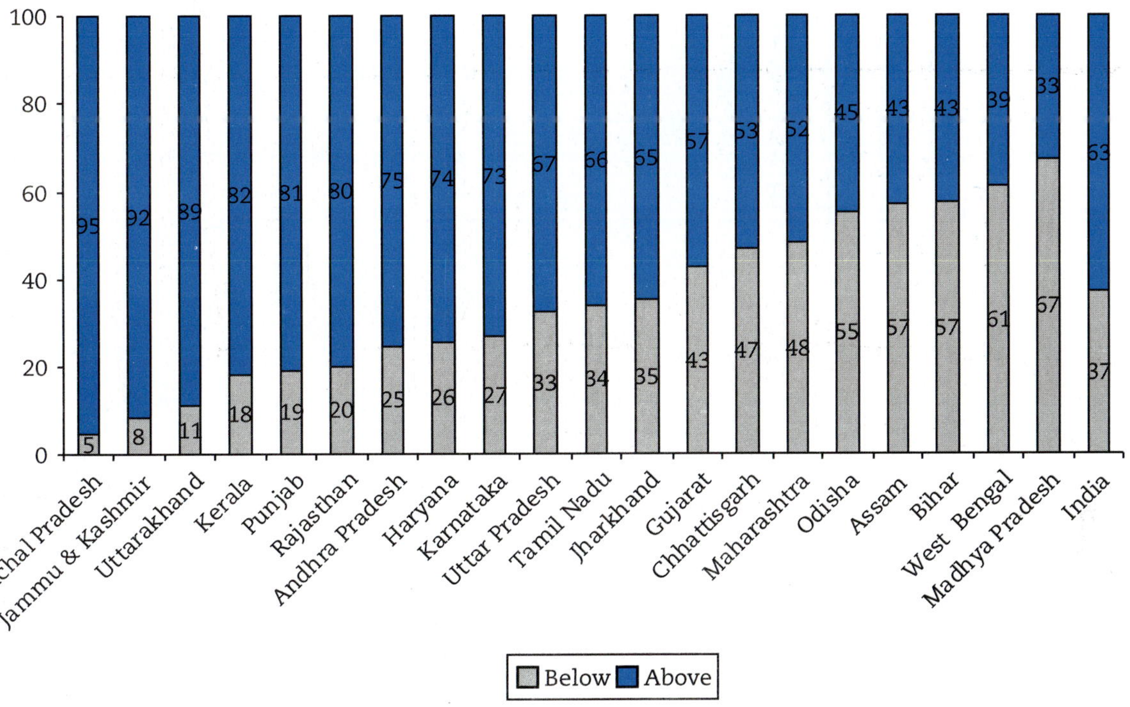

Source: Computed from unit level data of NSSO, 66th Round.

related to the norm for minimum wages. Both central and state governments fix minimum wages for their respective jurisdictions under the Minimum Wages Act, 1948, to be implemented by all employers in both the organized and unorganized sectors. Minimum wages are announced periodically for a variety of occupations.[6]

> The Minimum Wages Act, 1948, has not been properly implemented as casual workers continue to receive wages lower than the prescribed minimum wages.

The basic idea behind the enforcement of minimum wages was to prevent the exploitation of labour by payment of unduly low wages. However, apart from the fact that doubts have been raised about the efficacy of minimum wages (set at almost subsistence level) as a means to provide a minimum standard of living, a number of studies show that the Act has not been implemented properly and casual workers have continued to receive wages lower than the minimum prescribed (Ghanekar, 1997; Anant, 2004).

Figure 4.10a presents the proportion of farm casual labour in rural areas receiving wages below the minimum applicable in different states in 2009-10. For India 73 per cent of casual farm labourers received less than the minimum wages. Even in the agriculturally developed states of Haryana and Punjab approximately 87 and 64 per cent of workers, respectively, did not get minimum wages. In most of the states in southern India, the proportion of casual labourers getting less than the minimum wage was lower than in other parts of the country. In the less developed states of Bihar, Chhattisgarh, Jharkhand and Madhya Pradesh more than nine-tenths of farm casual labourers did not receive the minimum farm wages declared by the respective state governments.

6. Nearly 1,200 scheduled occupations are covered under the Minimum Wages Act. Of these, 1,140 come within the jurisdiction of the different state governments. See *http://labour.nic.in/wagecell*, accessed in April, 2012.

Figure 4.11

Percentage of Casual Urban Non-farm Workers (15-59 years) not Getting Minimum Wages in Major States, 2009-10

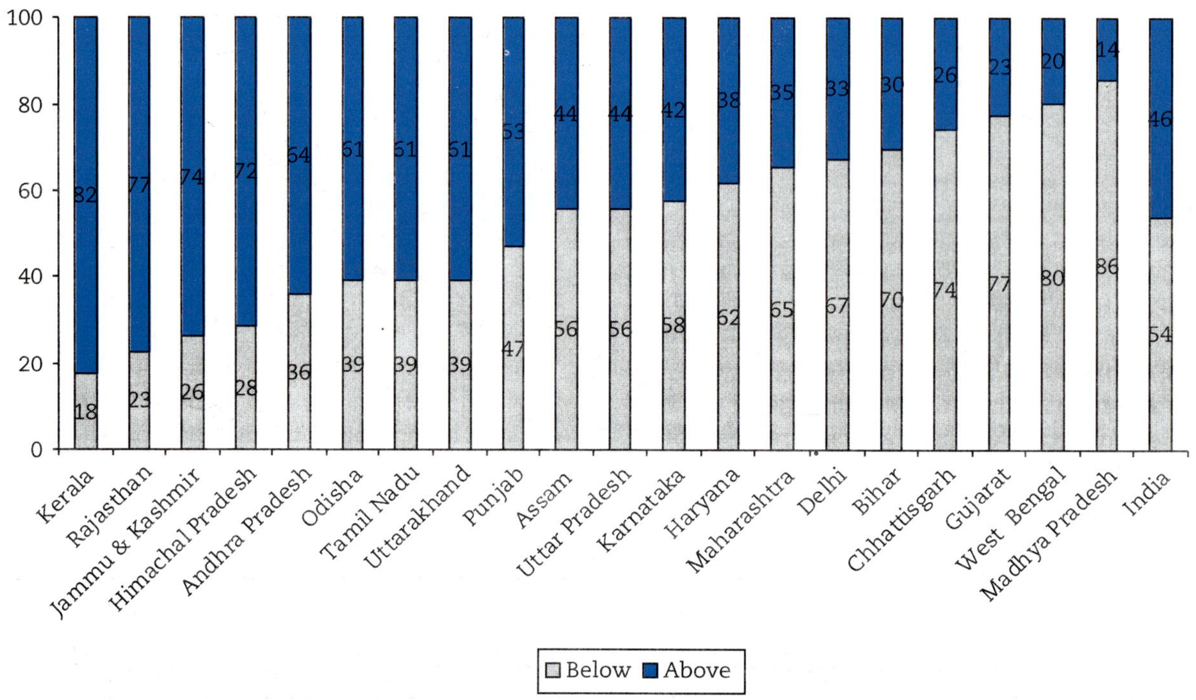

Source: Computed from unit level data of NSSO, 66th Round.

The implementation of declared minimum wages, on the whole, is far better in the case of rural non-farm casual labourers (Figure 4.10b). At the all-India level, 37 per cent of workers of this category were paid wages below the declared minimum. One possible reason for better performance in the non-farm sector in comparison to the farm sector seems to be the implementation of the Mahatma Gandhi National Rural Employment Guarantee Act 2005 (MGNREGA). Hill states like Himachal Pradesh, Jammu & Kashmir and Uttarakhand are the best payers of minimum wages in this category. In contrast, in the eastern states of Assam, Bihar and West Bengal and also in Madhya Pradesh, more than half of non-farm rural casual labourers do not get minimum wages. One possible reason could be that Eastern states have not done well in implementing MGNREGA schemes.

> The worst performing states are Madhya Pradesh, West Bengal and Gujarat where more than three-fourths of urban casual workers do not get minimum wages.

In urban areas, the implementation of minimum wages is better than in the farm sector but worse than in the rural non-farm sector (Figure 4.11). At the all-India level, more than half of casual labourers do not get minimum wages. Worst performing states are Madhya Pradesh, West Bengal and Gujarat where more than three-fourth of urban casual workers do not get minimum wages. It is surprising that this should be the case for Gujarat which is one of the most industrialized and developed states of India.

As a whole, non-compliance is much higher in the rural farm segment compared to the non-farm segment. In agriculture, actual wages are often lower than the minimum wages on a daily basis but the hours of work may not be longer than stipulated. On the other hand, in urban areas and in many rural non-agricultural enterprises, employers may appear to pay the prescribed minimum wages, but most of the workers work for much

Figure 4.12

Index of Average Annual Wage/Salary of Rural Casual Labour, Regular Workers and Central Government Public Sector Employees, 1983-2011-12

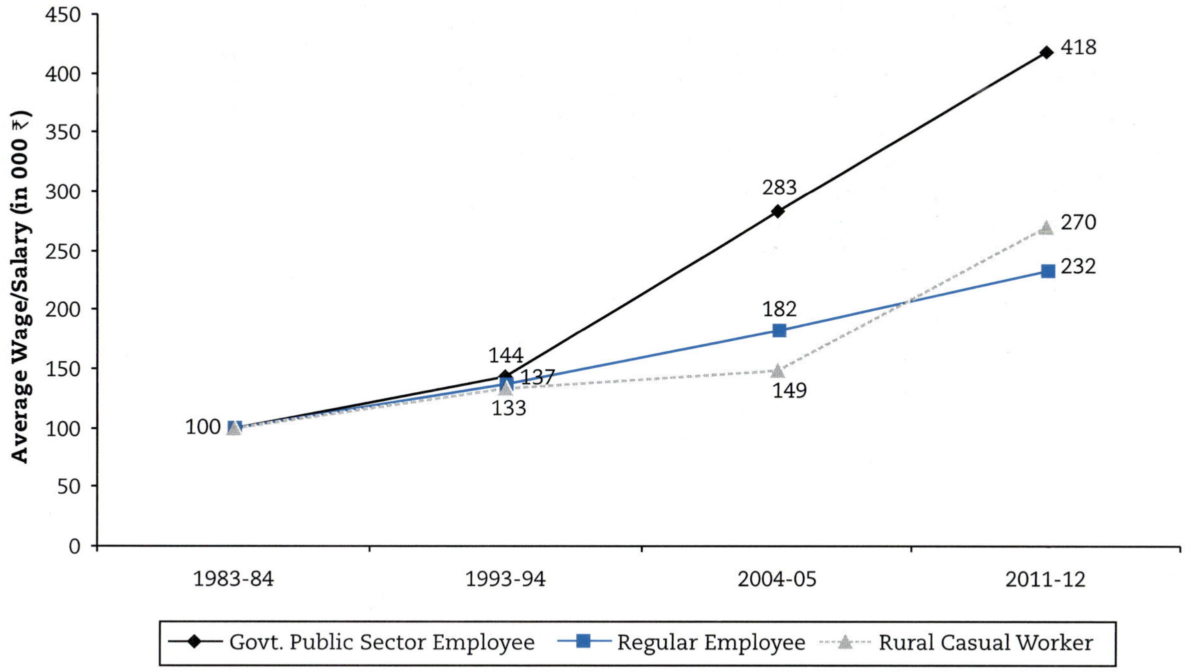

Source: Computed from unit level data of various rounds of NSSO.

longer hours than stipulated in the Act (Saget, 2006). Besides the lack of countervailing power, the reasons for non-compliance with the norms may include poor inspection of the enterprises, complexities of the minimum wage regulations, multiplicity of the rates, and inadequate efforts by the governments to communicate the existence of rules and rates in this regard. However, despite the various problems with the implementation of the Minimum Wages Act, the role of the Act in propping up actual wages is widely acknowledged (Parthasarthy, 1998; Saget, 2006).

4.6 In Conclusion

Available evidence on wage trends by different categories of workers, sectors and regions, as analysed in this chapter, clearly brings out the following points:

- There has been a significant increase in real wages, 3.2 per cent per year on an average, during the period of over two and half decades, 1983-2010.
- Wage disparities have generally increased, particularly in the first decade of post-liberalization (1994-2005) period. The most striking is the disparity between the regular–casual and organized–unorganized sectors,: where the average daily earnings of a casual worker in 2011-12 were estimated at ₹ 138 in rural and ₹ 173 in urban areas, and that of a regular worker was ₹ 298 in rural and ₹ 445 in urban areas. The average earnings of an employee of a central public sector enterprise was estimated at ₹ 2005 per day.
- Further, wage disparity has, in fact, worsened during the three decades 1983 to 2011-12, more so during the two decades of the post-liberalization period. As can be seen from the index of average annual salary/wage of government public sector employees, regular workers and rural casual workers in Figure 4.12, during the period 1983-84 to 2011-12 in the first ten years although the wages of government public sector employees

increased at higher rate in comparison to regular and casual workers but there was not much variation. In the next two decades of the post-liberalization period, the inequality became very high whereas the salary of central government public sector employees increased more than four times (4.2), the wages of rural casual workers increased only by 2.7 times and those of regular workers by 2.3 times. Thus, over the years the gap in the wage salary of government employees and other regular and rural casual workers has been further widened, although the gap between the latter two has declined by small extent.

- The disparity between income from wages and salaries and income from other sources has increased sharply, particularly in the period when the economy has grown relatively fast.

Trends in wages and wage differentials provide strong evidence that income inequality has been rising in the Indian economy as a whole, especially in the first decade of the post-liberalization period. Tentative estimates based on the consumption expenditure data from various rounds of NSSO also show that income inequality measured in terms of Gini index and Generalized Entropy measures shows a sharp increase, especially during the post-liberalizaion period. Moreover, inequality of consumption expenditure is much less than inequality of income because those in higher income groups consume only a small part of their income; while those in the low income groups may, in fact, be consuming more than they earn.

The disparity between income from wages and salaries and income from other sources has increased sharply, particularly in the period when the economy has grown relatively fast.

Overall income inequality is, to a large extent, a function of the distribution of assets, particularly productive assets in the economy, which is highly uneven. There is acute dearth of credible comparable data on assets for India. The disparities in wage and salary incomes as analysed in the preceding sections are also extremely large: for example, in 2011-12, a rural casual worker earned hardly 7 per cent of the salary of a central public sector employee. Although the wages and earnings in general have shown increase over the last three decades or so, the increase is much less in case of the poorest group—say, rural casual labourers—as compared to the better off groups, say, central government public sector employees. If comparison is made between the lowest earning group and the richest group of class one government officers as well as the managerial staff of private sector enterprises (including both salaries as well as perks), the inequality will be extremely high. The averages hide the extreme disparities in wages and salaries between different categories of workers and privileged section of the society. A large part of the income and earnings at the higher end is not properly accounted for by the statistical system. Failure to generate more regular and formal sector employment, which is forcing more and more workers to find work in the unorganized sector and in casual and contract jobs, along with inability to ensure the payment of even very frugally determined minimum wages in the majority of cases, has contributed to a sharp rise in wage and salary inequality. The rise in the categories of flexible workers (contract, etc.) has been rapid since the initiation of liberalization and globalization. It has been an important instrument of the employers to reduce labour cost. Inequality in many other countries, including China, has also risen considerably with the process of globalization. But it should be noted that in China and many other countries, the minimum level of earning is much higher than India (China on an average has about two and half times higher earnings of manual labour than in India). The extreme inequality in a country like India where a significant proportion of workers is afflicted with widespread poverty and

The rise in the categories of flexible workers has been rapid since the initiation of liberalization and globalization.

deprivation is simply unacceptable and detrimental to achieving the goal of inclusive economy and society.

Rising labour unrest and other aspects of inequality are not only matters of concern because of considerations of equity and social harmony but also for the very sustainability of the growth path itself.

5

Labour Institutions and Industrial and Employment Relations

5.1 Introduction

Labour laws in India have a long history dating back to the colonial period, but a comprehensive legislative framework for regulating and strengthening industrial relations was developed only during the decades immediately following political Independence. Labour laws, building on the regulations and codes from the colonial period, sought to regulate various aspects of industrial relations such as industrial disputes, terms and conditions of employment, minimum wages, conditions of work and social security. The main objective of these laws was to ensure that labour was not employed in sub-human conditions nor subjected to unfair practices with respect to payment of wages, dismissals and retrenchments. The laws defined both substantive and procedural aspects of industrial relations, which in the Western democratic countries were determined by collective bargaining.

In the early decades after Independence, the labour policy of the government was mainly inspired by the provisions on social policy in the Constitution of India, especially its Preamble and the Directive Principles of State Policy which mandated the Indian state to steer society towards a more egalitarian socio-economic system. State intervention through labour laws was justified by three main reasons—power imbalances between labour and capital, the need for ensuring social justice, and to promote conducive industrial relations to ensure uninterrupted industrial production. It was a period of state-led industrialization with the state constitutionally mandated to act as a 'model employer'. State intervention in the Industrial Relations System (IRS) was thus a part of the larger strategy to promote faster economic growth.

However, as the labour laws and institutions evolved in response to the demands of organized labour, they tended to develop in a piecemeal and inconsistent way. For instance, while labour laws were developed focusing mainly on the organized sector, few laws—like the Minimum Wages Act, 1948—were enacted either to deal directly with unorganized workers or contained provisions that could be indirectly applied to unorganized sector workers. Labour laws were further characterized by several deficiencies such as being too numerous, having a complex legal structure, different definitions of the same terms in different laws, and so on. However, the major defect of the legal system remained in the fact that there were too many labour laws concerning too few workers in the organized sector, and too few labour laws relating to too many workers in the unorganized or informal sector. Trade unions, dominated by political parties operating mainly in the urban formal sector, largely ignored informal-sector workers and their concerns.

As a result, organized sector workers enjoyed better terms and conditions of work and employment and social security while millions of workers in the informal sector remained unprotected. Labour laws and trade union power were seen to cause wage inflation and poor employment generation, on the one hand, while creating huge disparities between formal and informal sector workers, on the other. The initiation of reforms relating to the product market led to demands for labour market reforms. Labour laws and labour institutions such as trade unions were considered incompatible with the market-led economic regime. Labour reforms were considered to complement product-market reforms and also to reap the positive benefits of the latter. There was a widespread view that the existing framework of regulation and industrial relations undermined the capacity of industry to address the challenges of the competitive environment of a globalized economy. Critics argued that the institutional framework of the labour market, which was designed in the planning period, was ill-suited to the competitive and globalized economic environment and needed re-defining in a manner that would ensure and enhance competitiveness of firms and attract investment.

The huge and the growing informal sector further fuelled the skewed nature of labour institutions such as trade unions and collective bargaining and labour laws. Thus there were powerful demands to re-orient not only the labour laws but other complementary regulatory institutions and the public policy focus to address the concerns arising out of a dualistic labour market, as well. These issues will be examined in this chapter. The chapter will briefly present the legal framework before examining labour relations, labour institutions, industrial conflict, and the machinery for social dialogue.

State intervention through labour laws have been justified by three main reasons—power imbalances between labour and capital, the need for ensuring social justice, and to promote conducive industrial relations to ensure uninterrupted industrial production.

5.2 Legal Framework and Labour Administration

Since matters relating to labour are part of the 'Concurrent List' under the Constitution of India, both the central and state governments are empowered to legislate. There are over reportedly 50 central labour laws and over 150 state labour laws that seek to regulate various aspects of the labour market and employment relations such as working conditions, wages, industrial relations, social security and labour welfare. These labour laws may be classified into four groups: (i) laws relating to conditions of work; (ii) laws on wages and remuneration; (iii) laws on social security; and, (iv) laws on industrial relations and employment security. The main lows are given in Table 5.1. The scope of each of these labour laws is limited by specific provisions regarding their applicability. The thresholds are defined by criteria which include types of employment, size of enterprise and so on. In this sense, the organized and unorganized sector divide is created by the legislative structure itself, though some labour laws apply also to the unorganized sector.

As can be observed in Table 5.1, even if we only consider 'hired workers', with the exception of minimum wages, the coverage is very low. The laws regulating conditions of work apply to less than 9 per cent of the wage workers. Among the social security laws, the Employees Provident Fund Act covers the largest number of workers, but that amounts to only 8 per cent. The two pieces of legislation concerned with industrial relations and employment security, viz. the Industrial Disputes Act and the Industrial Employment (Standing Orders) Act, apply only to 12 per cent and 6 per cent of the workers, respectively. Only the laws related to wages have somewhat larger coverage. Although the coverage of the various labour laws shown in Table 5.1 pertain to the year 1999-2000, there has been hardly much improvement in the coverage over time.

While most labour laws apply only to the organized sector, a few, enacted at both the central and state level, also apply to specific groups within the unorganized sector. The most important of these is the Minimum Wages Act, providing the widest eligibility coverage.

While most labour laws apply only to the organized sector, a few, enacted at both the Central and state level, also apply to specific groups within the unorganized sector. The most important of these is the Minimum Wages Act, providing the widest eligibility coverage among all the laws identified in Table 5.1. Some notable State laws covering unorganized workers include the Kerala Agricultural Workers' Act, 1974; Kerala Headload Workers Act, 1978; and Maharashtra Mathadi, Hamal and Other

Table 5.1

Coverage of Major Labour Laws (% of Workers)

Law	*Workers Eligible as per Law*		*Workers Actually Covered*		
	Total Workers	*Hired Workers*	*Eligible*	*Total Workers*	*Hired Workers*
Factories Act	3.0	6.6	73.5	2.2	4.9
Shops and Commercial Establishment Act	3.9	8.5	44.7	1.7	3.8
Minimum Wages Act	38.1	83.3	9.3	3.6	7.8
Payment of Wages Act	10.5	22.9	50.0	5.1	8.2
Payment of Bonus Act	5.2	11.4	60.0	2.5	5.1
Worker's Compensation Act	3.3	7.2	20.3	0.7	1.5
Employees State Insurance Act	2.2	4.5	87.5	1.9	4.2
Employees' Provident Fund Act	3.7	8.1	100.0	6.6	14.5
Industrial Disputes Act	5.5	12.1	47.6	2.6	5.7
Industrial Employment (Standing Orders) Act	2.7	5.9	49.2	5.1	8.2

Source: Adopted from NCEUS (2009), Table 7.1.1; Papola and Pais (2007); and Papola, *et al.* (2008).

Table 5.2

Structure of Unions in India

Nature of Trade Union Organization (TUO)	*Comments*	*Level*
Central TUOs	Mostly political, affiliated to central political parties	National
Regional TUOs	Political or non-political affiliated to regional political parties	Regional
Industry/sector organizations/federations	Mostly in public sector like banks, insurance, railways, aviation, electricity, affiliated to political parties, or independent, e.g., All India Stock Exchange Employees Federation).	National/regional
Caste-, ethnic-, or gender-based organizations	Organizations by Scheduled Castes and Tribes (SC, ST) tribals, and women employees	Enterprise/regional/industry
Craft organizations	Railways, textiles, coal, aviation	Industry/national/regional
White-collar organizations	Clerical/managerial/professional	Enterprise/sectoral/national
Enterprise unions	Mostly non-affiliated	Enterprise
Enterprise unions' firm-level federations	Non-affiliated	National
Unity organizations	Political or non-political	National/regional/enterprise
Informal sector organizations	Trade unions (political/non-political), NGOs	National/regional/industry

Manual Workers (Regulation of Employment and Welfare) Act, 1969. Several states, especially Kerala and Tamil Nadu, have provided for a number of statutory Welfare Funds and Boards for various segments of unorganized sector workers. At the national level the Unorganized Workers Social Security Act, 2008, is an important milestone which is discussed in the next chapter.

The institutional framework of the industrial relations system and some aspects of the labour market are defined by four main labour laws: the Trade Unions Act, 1926; the Industrial Employment (Standing Orders) Act, 1946; the Industrial Disputes Act, 1947 (the ID Act); the Contract Labour (Regulation and abolition) Act, 1970 (the Contract Labour Act). The labour laws fix the administrative responsibility by defining the 'appropriate government' in the introductory part of the laws. In the federal set up of India, labour administration functions at two levels, Central and state: the Ministry of Labour and Employment discharges the functions of labour administration at the Central level and the State Labour Departments at the state level.

5.3 Workers' Organizations in India

There developed a mutually beneficial relationship between trade unions and the political parties involved in the freedom movement during the colonial rule, which trait continued even after Independence. This political origin is one of the factors which led to the trade-union movement being dominated by 'political unionism', where each union or union's leadership owed allegiance to a political formation. Political unionism is not just restricted to the national level but has percolated to the sectoral and regional levels as well. Regional political parties like the Dravida Munnetra Kazhagam (DMK) and All India Dravida Munnetra Kazhagam (AIADMK) (in Tamil Nadu), Shiv Sena (in Maharashtra) and several others have also formed their own labour wings. These factors, among others, have resulted in fragmentation or 'involution' (Rudolph and Rudolph, 1987) of the union movement which considerably weakened it. The weaknesses and the inadequacies of political unionism have facilitated the rise of 'enterprise unions' (Bhattacherjee, 1987; Ramaswamy 1988). This reflected the preference of the workers to have organizations independent of the political parties which contributed to the growth of a number of decentralized and non-political unions. There are other forms of unionism, namely craft unionism, industry or sector unionism, regional unionism and so on (see Table 5.2). The overall result is a highly fragmented and diverse pattern of organization of workers.

5.3.1 *Trends in Trade Union Organization*

One of the main problems in analysing trends in union growth is lack of reliable data.[1] The information provided by the Labour Bureau, based on returns from registered trade unions, suffers from serious limitations. Since trade union registration is voluntary, not all unions register, not all registered unions submit annual returns (in contravention of the legal requirement to do so), and even if they do, not all of them submit on time and accurately (Das, 2008; Shyam Sundar, 1999). The 'response rate', i.e., the proportion of the number of trade unions submitting complete and timely annual returns in relation to the number of [estimated] registered trade unions, has always been low and in recent times it has worsened considerably—during 1991-2008, 11.32 per cent of the estimated registered trade unions submitted annual returns (see Table 8.2 in Appendix) on which the trade union membership and other related data are based. In view of these, the Labour Bureau itself cautions the users in its annual review of trade union data published in its website that 'The data ... are not strictly comparable with those of the earlier years' (*Trade Unions in India, 2008*, Labour Bureau, Government of India). The presumable exercise of repeating earlier year's data at least for the number of registered trade unions (in 2008 only 13 states and union territories submitted returns and registered trade union data reported only for them. Of these 6 are big and significant states)—affects the annual growth rates, and hence should be interpreted with caution. The available data, however, help in discerning certain trends.

See Table 8.1 in Appendix for time-series data on trade unions

Although the slow-down in the rate at which legal unions have been formed began in the post-Bombay textile strike period, as Table 5.3 shows it worsened during between 1992 to 2008, in the post-reform period. The average annual rate of growth of registered trade unions picked up in the 2000s in general; it could be statistical as the year-on-year growth rates during 2005-07 were higher, at 5 per cent, 12 per cent and 8 per cent, respectively and due to the practice of repeating the data of earlier years, which could lead to over-reporting. Further the trends in the 'actual' numbers would depend on the consistency of the reporting states and their unionization. To be sure, the annual average growth rate of around 3 per cent of registered trade unions in the post-reform period, notwithstanding the frailty of the data, is not unimpressive. Nevertheless, a few regional studies and the struggles on trade union formation and registration even in large industries, would tend to support the 'slow-down hypothesis' typical of the globalization discourse.

Table 5.3

Average Annual Growth Rates of Registered Trade Unions, 1980-2008

Period	%
1980-84	5.30
1986-90	2.93
1991-95	1.97
1996-99	2.88
2000-2004	3.04
2005-2008	3.71
1992-2008	2.85

Note: Growth rates calculated from the data in *Indian Labour Year Book and Indian Labour Statistics, Labour Bureau*, Shimla (various issues); for 2008 see 'Trade Unions 2008', *http://labourbureau.nic.in*, accessed on 1 April 2013.

During the post-reform period, new union formation showed a decline in some major industrialized states such as, Maharashtra, West Bengal, Uttar Pradesh (*Uttar Pradesh Statistical Diary*, various years) and Andhra Pradesh (Reddy, 2008; Shyam Sundar, 2008b; Banerjee, 2008). The recent major struggles such as those at Hyundai Motors, Foxconn, Madras Rubber Factory (MRF) in Tamil Nadu, Honda Motor Cycles and Scooters, Rico, Sunbeam and Maruti Suzuki Motors in Haryana centred on union formation issue. The employers' resistance to trade union formation and their preference for the nature of unions and trade unions' allegation of delays in union registration provoked many a conflict, sometimes bloody (conflicts in Hyundai Motorcycles and Scooters of India, Pricol, Rico, Maruti Suzuki, etc.).

1. According to the Trade Union Act any seven workers, or even employers, can form a union and register the same. The registered unions are required by law to submit annual returns to the Registrar of Trade Unions giving the details of membership, income and expenditure and other aspects as provided in the rules framed by the state governments. The State and Central Labour Departments compile the returns received from their respective spheres and send the information to the Labour Bureau, which in turn, consolidates the data and publishes the statistics in its annual publications.

> Several labour market factors such as decline in employment in the organized sector, decline of union conducive industries and growth of non-unionizable sectors, political factors such as withdrawal of state support to unions, and managerial strategies of retrenchments, parallel production, etc., can be used to explain the decline in unionism in the organized sector.

Statistics regarding the number of registered unions does not tell us much on the bargaining power of workers, which is reflected by the proportion of workers unionized, popularly known as union density or degree of unionization. There are several statistical issues with regard to the choice of statistics for both the numerator and the denominator in calculating union density statistics (see Shyam Sundar, 2008b). The volatility of year-on-year growth of trade union members of the trade unions submitting returns (Labour Bureau statistics on trade unions) in Figure 5.1 should discourage the users from making any categorical statements with regard to the union density figure. However, several use this conventional source of information on union density. The alternative database is the National Sample Survey Organization's (NSSO's) labour-force survey. The NSSO collects information on the union status of respondents (workers) in its labour-force

Figure 5.1

Annual Fluctuations in the Trade Union Membership and the Number of Trade Unions Submitting Returns, 1992 to 2008

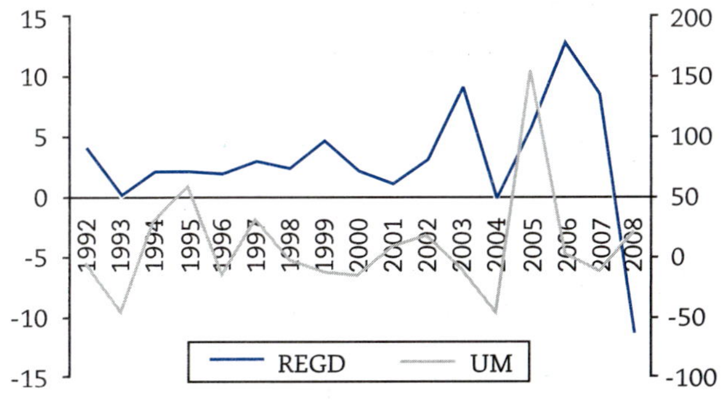

Note: See the text for the explanation with regard to the 'response rate' which primarily explains the wide fluctuations in the union membership data.

Source: Statistics, Labour Bureau, Shimla (various issues); for 2008 see 'Trade Unions 2008', *http://labourbureau.nic.in*, accessed on 1 April 2013.

surveys which can give us some idea about union membership. The NSSO asks each respondent whether she/he is a member of a union or not. Based on this data we define union density (also known as degree of unionization) as the proportion of the estimated workers in each sector as reporting being a member of a trade union.

See Table 8.1 in Appendix for time-series data on trade unions.

As per the Labour Bureau statistics on trade unions, we find that the union density for the aggregate work-force is very low at 2 per cent. It works out at 5 per cent for the non-agricultural workforce. However, it is somewhat higher—in the range of 20 to 30 per cent—for those in organized sector employment, based on statistics collected by the Employment Market Information of Directorate General of Training and Employment (DGE&T) (ILO, 1997: 238; Visser 2003: 385; see also Table 8.1 in Appendix). Union density, measured as the proportion of union members to the total number of organized sector workers, has been fluctuating almost in a cyclical fashion (see data in Table 8.1 in Appendix) primarily owing to fluctuations in the proportion of unions submitting regular returns. As we see from Figure 5.2, the NSSO data (which covers both the organized and the unorganized sectors) also show a decline (though marginal at the aggregate level and a somewhat steep fall in some sectors, such as in public utilities) at the disaggregate level in union density from between 2004-05 and 2009-10. Also, micro-level data on certain sectors like textiles and knitwear do suggest a decline in the union following in the post-reform period (Gurumurthy, 2006; Vijayabaskar, 2006).

Union density is higher in public utilities like electricity, gas and water supply, public administration, transport, storage and communication and mining and quarrying. Union density is significant in the financial sector as well. Trade unionism in the government sector has been historically higher in India such as banking, and insurance sectors, as well as in the electricity and mining industries. The union density is moderate in manufacturing, trade and hotels and low in construction and agriculture.

Several labour market factors [such as a decline in employment in the organized sector, increasing employment of flexible categories of workers (like contract and casual workers), increase in employment in non-unionizable sectors (like information technology), and decline of union-

Figure 5.2

Union Density (%) by Sectors, 2004-05 and 2009-10

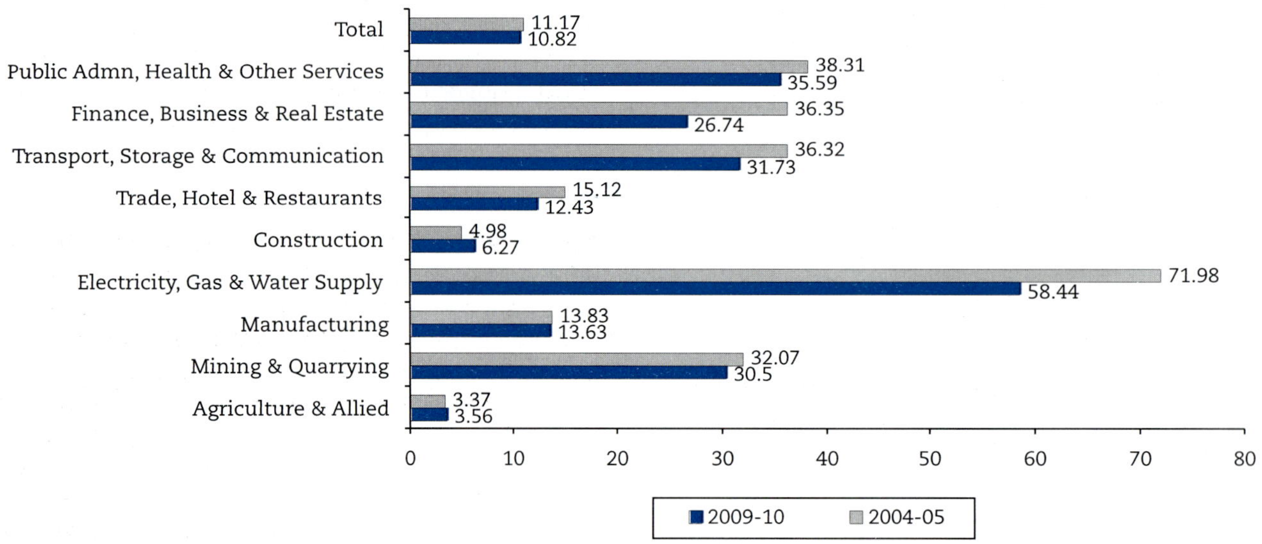

Source: Unit-level data for NSSO Rounds 2004-05 and 2009-10.

conducive industries (like textiles)], political factors (such as withdrawal of state support to unions) and managerial strategies (such as retrenchments, closures, prolonged lockouts, union avoidance, reduction in bargainable categories of workers, partial production, relocation, parallel production and so on especially in large firms and organizational factors like 'saturation' of unionization in organized sector) could explain the decline in unionism in the organized sector in India (see Das, 2008: 978; Nagaraj, 2004; Shrouti and Nandkumar, 1995; Ramaswamy, 2006; Shyam Sundar, 2008a).

5.3.2 *Workers' Organizations in the Informal Economy*

In a country where informal workers constitute over 90 per cent of the workforce, the importance of organizing them for a fair representation of their demands could hardly be exaggerated. But at the same time, organizing the informal workers poses formidable challenges. The diversity of activities, the smallness of units of work, often the lack of any identifiable employer, the dominance of self-employment or home-based work, the casual nature of work, widespread illiteracy among workers, lack of legal entitlements or agency to work with, all come in the way. However, with stagnation or even decline in the organized sector work-force and with much of the increase in employment growth being informal in nature (see NCEUS, 2009), there has been growing concern and intensification of interest in organizing informal workers. Besides the conventional union model, new forms of organizations like union-cum-cooperative institutions such as the long-established and well-known Self Employed Women's Association (SEWA) and Kagaz Kach Patra Kashtakari Panchayat (KKPKP) (union of rag-pickers and waste collectors) in Pune, new informal sector union networks like the National Alliance of Street Vendors in India (NASVI), workers' cooperatives, self-help groups (such as Building and Woodworkers International, Delhi) and so on, have emerged in organizing particular groups of unorganized workers (Bhowmik, 2008; Ahn, 2007).[2]

Organizing the informal workers poses formidable challenges. The diversity of activities, the smallness of the units of work, often the lack of any identifiable employer, the dominance of self-employment or home-based work, the casual nature of work, widespread illiteracy among workers, lack of legal entitlements or agency to work with, all come in the way.

2. Also see, *http://swachcoop.com/about-swachpune.html*, accessed 10 January 2013.

5.3.2.1 Mainstream Trade Unions and Unorganized Workers

The mainstream trade unions have, of late, taken increasing interest in organizing informal workers and addressing their concerns (Datt, 2008; John, 2007; Shyam Sundar, 2009). The verified membership of the Central Trade Union Organizations (CTUOs) increased from 12.27 million in 1989 to 24.88 million in 2002. This was mainly because of the increase in the membership of unorganized sector workers who constituted 39.4 per cent of the total membership of CTUOs (Datt, 2008; John, 2007). The increase in the membership of agricultural and rural workers itself accounted for nearly 30.7 per cent of the total verified membership (Datt, 2008: Table 3).

Mainstream trade unions have adopted five different strategies to organize and address the concerns of unorganized workers: (i) they have organized particular occupational groups among informal economy workers such as *hamals*, hawkers, maid-servants, bullock-cart drivers, and so on at various places under their banner (see Ahn, 2007, for a number of instances); (ii) they have taken up issues and demands of the informal economy workers in their mass campaigns through rallies, strikes, petitions, etc.; (iii) they have been principally demanding some form of regularization of employment of informal workers such as contract and casual workers; (iv) responding to the criticism that the regular workers disregard the interests of contract and casual labourers, they have encouraged regular workers to lend solidarity to the struggles of these workers;[3] and (v) they have attempted to build an all-encompassing organization to wage combined struggles on the policy front. The National Platform for Mass Organizations (NPMO) was formed in the 1990s and comprises organizations of workers in both organized and unorganized sectors.

In spite of the growing involvement of mainstream trade unions in the organization of informal workers, there are certain inherent limitations. For instance, trade unions formed on and sustained by an 'adversarial' orientation are not well-adapted to a situation where there is no clearly-defined employer and there is lack of a common work-site and existence of elements of self-employment. Therefore, specific strategies to organize the unorganized workers have been designed by combining a variety of pragmatic forms and ideas, for instance to represent the interests of self-employed informal workers (Ela Bhatt of SEWA, quoted in Ramaswamy, 2000). The informal economy is a vast area and it is not possible to describe here all the organizing efforts. However, some important initiatives that serve as examples are highlighted below.

5.3.2.2 Self Employed Women's Association

SEWA grew out of the women's wing of the Textile Labour Association (TLA), an Ahmedabad-based workers' organization inspired by Mahatma Gandhi. It faced obstacles in getting itself registered as a trade union since its members were self-employed, and so were not in a conventional employment relationship. Eventually, it won the battle and got registered as a trade union in 1972. But even after more than three decades of significant work, it did not gain legitimacy from the conventional trade unions. It had to seek judicial intervention to be counted as a CTUO in the 2004 membership verification exercise, as the mainstream CTUOs protested against such a move. Again, its move to seek affiliation to International Confederation of Free Trade Unions (ICFTU, now International Trade Unions Congress or ITUC) was contested by some of the ICFTU-affiliate CTUOs in India. Eventually, SEWA has been counted as a CTUO and affiliated to the ICFTU (Ramaswamy, 2000; Venkata Ratnam, 2000). SEWA is also affiliated to organizations like the International Union Federation (IFU), International Textile Garment and Leather Workers' Federation (ITGLWF), and International Federation of Chemical, Energy, Mine and General Workers' Union (IFCEMGWU). It played an important role in securing the ILO Convention on home-based workers (Convention No. 177).

By 2009, SEWA had acquired a membership of 1.25 million, mostly in Gujarat (0.63 m million) and Madhya Pradesh (0.05 million), but it has extended to several other states including Bihar, Delhi, West Bengal, Rajasthan, Uttar Pradesh, Kerala and Uttarakhand.[4] Besides organizing and assisting self-employed women in their economic activities as well as provisioning of social protection, SEWA has also extended its activities to home-based workers engaged in incense stick making, cotton pod shelling and embroidery. But SEWA has also realized some of its objectives through the formation of cooperatives to buy raw materials and market their goods collectively. Skill training, marketing assessment,

3. For example, in some of the meetings/conferences of the employees of Central Public Sector Undertakings held in 2008, a large number of contract workers and their union leaders participated, and the conferences had resolved that the permanent workers would fight for the cause of the contract workers also in addition to their own.

4. *http://www.sewa.org*

health and social security are other complementary services that SEWA has helped to provide.

5.3.2.3 National Alliance of Street Vendors of India (NASVI)

Street vendors constitute an important component of the informal economy. In 2005 they were estimated to account for around 2.5 per cent of the urban population (Bhowmik, 2005: 2262). Their number is estimated to be around 250,000 in Mumbai, 200,000 in Delhi, 150,000 in Kolkata and 100,000 in Ahmedabad. Not only are they found to work under difficult conditions, their earnings are low and a part is appropriated by the municipal authorities and police. The National Alliance of Street Vendors of India (NASVI), initiated in September 1998, started as a networking organization mainly to bring together street-vendor organizations so as to collectively struggle for policy initiatives to support the livelihood of around 10 million vendors operating in different locations in the country. But as it grew in size and activities, in 2003 it was registered as an independent organization under the Societies Registration Act, 1860. Its membership is open to trade unions, non-union forms of organizations (like cooperatives, community-based organizations), non-governmental organizations (NGOs), individual professionals like lawyers, teachers, doctors, etc., who have been associated with the cause of street vendors. It has 373 organizations representing nearly 0.3 million street vendors as dues paying members from 20 states of India (Bhowmik, 2005). Its activities include highlighting the role and magnitude of street vendors, advocacy through organizing interfaces with policy-makers and public officials, creating awareness programmes by petitions, memoranda, conducting *dharnas* and demonstrations, providing support to street-vendor organizations in their programmes and actions, organizing educational programmes to highlight the problems of street vendors, maintaining communication via newsletters, documentation centres and so on. In fact, the efforts of NASVI have led to drawing up the National Policy on Street Vendors.[5] A National Policy on Urban Street Vendors was adopted in 2009 and is in different stages of implementation in different urban areas of the country.

5.3.2.4 National Centre for Labour (NCL)

This is an apex organization of several organizations engaged with the unorganized sector workers. The main objective of the organization is to highlight the problems and issues relevant to vast sections of the unorganized sector workers. Its organizational structure conceives of committees for sectors such as agriculture, fishery, construction, domestic servants, migrant workers, and contract workers. It has played an important role along with others in mobilizing workers for the enactment of the Building and Other Construction Workers Act in 1996, in framing the rules for the welfare boards both at the central and state levels (e.g., Karnataka), in lobbying for the need-based minimum wage especially for unorganized sector workers, in conducting struggles for protection of rights of forest and fish workers and in the development of social security legislation for the unorganized sector workers.

The organizational forms of informal workers are as diverse as the situation of their work. The strategies of organizing them range from pragmatic unity to that of class, and activities/occupation based mobilization. The issues and concerns of their struggle are different from those concerning their counterparts in the organized sector. Their issues in essence, concern 'livelihood'. The principal demand of many of these organizations has been 'identity' and 'dignity'. Some of their priorities are the right to place of work, end of harassment, ensuring minimum wages and social security to informal workers. Though many of these organizations shun political affiliation, their strategies often depend on mass mobilization. Their presence is being felt and voices heard, though gradually, as can be seen from some of the legislative measures relating to construction workers, welfare boards and social security.

5.3.3 *Challenge of Unionizing Workers in the Emerging Sectors*

The 'new sectors' like information technology (IT) and IT-enabled services (ITES), hospitality, new retail establishments like shopping malls, and units in the special economic zones (SEZs) present formidable organizational challenges to the trade unions. Though the government's stated policy is that all labour laws will be applicable in SEZs, the SEZs have proved to be 'impenetrable' for unions for several reasons.

> Unionization in case of 'new sectors' such as information technology, hospitality, new retail establishments etc. has been a formidable organizational challenge. Though all labour laws are to be applicable to SEZs, the SEZs have proved to be impenetrable for unions.

5. *www.http://nasvinet.org*

Physical factors like tight gate security, less scope for socialization of workers (as workers are transported by company buses in and out under security), the absence of 'home contact' strategy as workers are dispersed unlike in the past, affect the logistics of organizing by trade unions. Institutional factors, like relaxations offered in the applicability of labour laws affect the institutional conditions that enable unionization. For example, most of the state governments have declared the establishments in the SEZ, and IT and ITES sectors as 'public utilities' under the Industrial Disputes Act, 1947 which render strikes (and lockouts) well-nigh impossible. Further, some state governments have provided employers in the SEZ sectors the much demanded labour flexibility by relaxing the provisions in the labour laws such as permitting free employment of contract labour, and relaxing labour inspections (Shyam Sundar, 2009; 2010a). Women workers are predominant in the SEZs and unionization of women workers poses additional problems. Owing to these reasons, trade unions have not been able to organize the workers in the SEZs and as a result the labour rights in the SEZs remain a matter of concern (see Gopalakrishnan, 2008).

5.4 Industrial Conflict in India

5.4.1 Legal Framework Relating to Industrial Disputes

The Industrial Disputes (ID) Act, 1947, provides the basic legal framework for settling industrial disputes. The important objectives of the Act are to reduce the incidence of industrial disputes, ensure that disputes do not result in work stoppages and settle them expeditiously if they do. The Act does not apply to persons employed in a managerial or administrative capacity. The processes provided under the ID Act for the settlement of disputes are: (i) conciliation, (ii) investigation, (iii) collective bargaining, (iv) voluntary arbitration, and (v) compulsory adjudication. The formal conciliation machinery according to the ID Act can intervene in not only actual but also apprehended industrial disputes. If the conciliation succeeds, it results in a settlement under Section 12(3) of the ID Act. Otherwise, the conciliation officer submits a 'failure report' to the government. Apart from disputes in public utilities which the government is duty-bound to refer for adjudication, it enjoys wide and sweeping discretionary powers to refer, or refuse to refer disputes in others. It is compulsory in two senses: (i) the parties in dispute have no option but to accept the intervention; (ii) the award of the adjudicatory body is binding. The conciliated settlements are placed on a higher footing than the bargained settlements, in that the latter is binding only on the parties to the agreement, while the former have much wider applicability (not only to parties to agreement but also to heirs and successors of the employer and employees employed presently and in future). Voluntary arbitration was added to the provisions under the ID Act in 1956. It received a much-needed boost as various judicial pronouncements strengthened the role, place, scope of voluntary arbitration.

5.4.2 Work Stoppages

Though there is no change in the basic legal framework of settlement of industrial disputes, globalization has brought about a climate of constraint on the ability of the workers to pursue demands that would precipitate work stoppages. The current phase of globalization has brought in its wake intense competition among countries for attracting investments. The terms set by capital are such as to make governments compromise on labour regulation. It weakens the organizational base of workers, restricts the economic options available to bargainers in an environment of greater competition, and reduces the government's ability to sanction workers' demands as in the past. 'Footloose' corporations use the 'threat of exit and relocation' not only against workers but also against governments. The threat to exit not only affects labour's ability to negotiate but is also used to challenge the presence of unions in the formal sector and its organizing drives in unorganized segments (Brofenbrenner, 2000; Epstein, 2000). The spatial organization of production across national frontiers means that the firm facing or foreseeing of labour problems at one site can transfer the orders to another place free of labour problems. The flexibility and cost-cutting strategies of employers intensify the sense of insecurity of employment and render unions more likely to agree to concession-bargaining, that is, to accepting less favourable terms and conditions of employment.

Though there is no change in the basic legal framework of settlement of industrial disputes, globalization has brought about a climate of constraint on the ability of the workers to pursue demands that would precipitate work stoppages.

The term 'work stoppages' includes both strikes and lockouts. The statistics on work stoppages in India relate to those stoppages in which at least 10 workers are involved directly and/or indirectly and exclude political and sympathetic strikes. The information on work stoppages is provided voluntarily by the employers to central and state government agencies dealing with labour matters, which in turn, are compiled by Labour Bureau and published in the *Indian Labour Year Book*. There are three basic measures of work stoppages, *viz.*, the number of work stoppages, the number of workers involved in these work stoppages and the number of work days lost.

Table 5.4

Indicators of Work Stoppages in India, 1992-2011

Period	WS/N	WI/N	WDL/N	WI/WS	WDL/WI	WDL/WS
1992-94	5.28	37.40	888.36	708.57	23.75	16828.57
1995-97	4.23	34.77	639.65	822.81	18.40	15138.75
1998-2000	3.32	47.70	921.33	1437.54	19.32	27768.14
2001-03	2.20	43.70	983.08	1985.13	22.50	44658.53
2004-06	1.71	85.06	924.41	4986.19	10.87	54186.17
2007-09*	1.40	42.06*	701.46	-	-	54843.3
2010-11	1.33	31.34	641.73	2346.75	20.48	48031.51

Notes: * - excluding 2009 for workers involved statistics

WS/N – Number of work stoppages per one lakh employees in the organized sector

WI/N – Number of workers involved in work stoppages per one thousand employees

WDL/N – Number of workdays lost in work stoppages per one thousand employees

WI/WS – Workers involved per work stoppage (Average Size)

WDL/WI – Workdays lost per worker involved (Average Duration)

WDL/WS – Workdays lost per work stoppage (Average Volume Lost)

Source: *Indian Labour Year Book* and *Indian Labour Statistics*, Labour Bureau, Shimla (various issues); for 2008 see Trade Unions, 2008, *http://labourbureau.nic.in*, accessed on 1 April 2013.

We observe from Table 5.4 that the frequency of work stoppages as given by the number of work stoppages (per lakh employees) declined steeply, though not at a faster rate in the last sub-periods as compared to that in the earlier ones. Though the workers involved in work stoppages fluctuated, a rising trend in the mobilization of workers in work stoppages can be discerned. The trends in the average size of the work stoppages (WI/WS) lend strong support to the 'mobilization thesis' though in the last sub-period (for 2010-11) there is a reduction in the average size of the work stoppages. The workdays lost per work stoppage during the 2000s were higher than those in the 1990s. The inflation in the work stoppages is particularly significant in the context of the press reports and research strongly indicating under-reporting of data on the work stoppages (see Shyam Sundar, 2012b). These and the stories of industrial unrest that consistently hogged the headlines and discussions in the media show that the latter years of the post-reform period has witnessed significant industrial disquiet contrary to the expectations. Indeed the work stoppage record for the post-reform period, i.e., the 1990s and the 2000s are no better in terms of some measures of the work stoppage than that to the earlier decades.

> The spatial organization of production across national frontiers means that the firm facing or foreseeing of labour problems at one site can transfer the orders to another place free of labour problems.

Regional statistics for proneness to work stoppage, given in Appendix Table 8.4, show that West Bengal, Andhra Pradesh, Kerala, Tamil Nadu, Rajasthan and Haryana are highly prone to experience industrial conflicts. It is interesting to note the huge gap in proneness-to-work-stoppage figures between the first ranked state West Bengal and the second ranked state Andhra Pradesh in 1997-99, or Kerala in 2005-07. It is interesting to see from Figure 5.3 that in most states that are highly work-stoppage prone, the share of the total workdays lost due to strikes is less which means lockouts dominate the workdays lost.

Figure 5.3

% Share of Work Days Lost due to Strikes in Total Work Days Lost in Selected States, 1992 to 2009

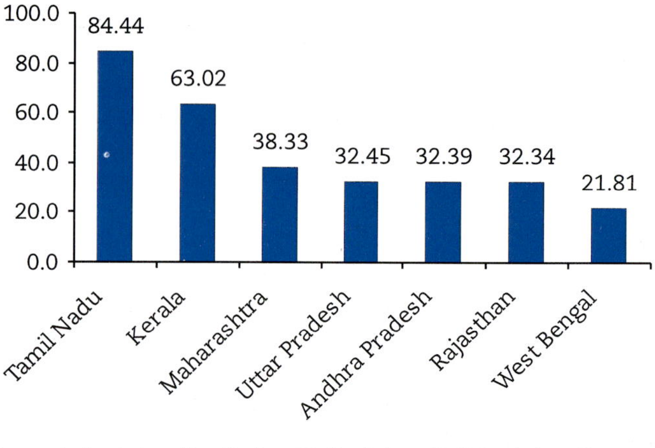

Source: *Indian Labour Year Book and Indian Labour Statistics*, Labour Bureau, Shimla (various issues); for 2008 see Trade Unions, 2008, *http://labourbureau.nic.in*, accessed on 1 April 2013.

It is well known that historically lockouts dominate industrial relations in West Bengal (see Datt 2003; Ramaswamy 2000; Shyam Sundar 2004a), and in the post-reform period lockout incidence has been higher in states like Andhra Pradesh, Rajasthan, Uttar Pradesh and Maharasthra as well.

The width of industrial conflict is evidenced by the fact that strikes and struggles were conducted by workers from public and private sectors, from domestic and multinational companies, from the unorganized sector including the domestic servants, from home-based workers, and workers of all types, regular, casual, contract workers. In fact, in some instances, organized sector employees have forged alliances with agricultural workers and self-employed from the unorganized sector and even students through the National Platform of Mass Organizations (NPMO). The struggle agenda embraced not only industrial issues but also economic, social and other issues.

5.4.2.1 Industrial Unrest

Given the poor validity and reliability of data on work stoppages and indeed the non-availability of detailed statistics post-2008 and the interesting developments and happenings in the industrial relations system prompt us to dwell briefly on the major qualitative features of work stoppages and protests. The strikes and agitations in the 2000s have been marked by violence and unrest. The rise in the share of non-regular workers and the growth of the unorganized sector, arguably due to the globalization drive, has affected the character of industrial conflicts. These are no longer conventional shop-floor disputes to be constitutionally settled, i.e., by resort to set procedures of resolution of conflicts and disputes. As a result, strikes, the conventional expression of protest and conflict, may not occur as often as in the past. But the diminution in strikes does not mean industrial peace. It takes place in various forms including strikes, and thus a climate of 'unrest' prevails. Unrest is more fundamental and widespread and involves even the unorganized sections of workers and can manifest in a wide range of actions such as strikes, sabotage, violence, agitations and other individual forms. It is more comprehensive and encompassing than the conventional forms of industrial conflict.

All-India strikes, workers' conventions, *morchas*, fasting (*satyagraha*), courting arrest (jail *bharao*), road blocking (*rasto roko*), marked protests by workers not only in the organized but also the unorganized sector. In all, 13 all-India strikes/stoppages of work have taken place (on 29 November 1991, 16 June 1992, 9 November 1993, 26 September 1994, 11 December 1998, 12 May 2000, 16 April 2002, 24 February 2004, 26 September 2005, 14 December 2006, 20 August 2008, 7 September 2010, and 28 February 2012), and the recent 2 strikes involved the Congress Party-associated INTUC and the Bharatiya Janata Party (BJP) party-associated BMS. These strikes and protests involved a range of issues including economic policy issues, outcomes such as inflation, foreign direct investment (FDI), etc., labour-policy issues like proposed amendments to provide labour flexibility in terms of hire and fire, disinvestment, minimum wages, etc., and issues concerning unorganized sector workers such as social security law and funds, abolition of the contract labour system, and so on. The strikes and protests in recent years have been prominent for their coverage and width, involving as they did, all types of firms and workers. The struggles by the unorganized sector workers, such as fishermen, waste pickers, domestic workers, *beedi* and *agarbhatti* (incense stick) rollers and so on speak of the spread of protests. It is important to note that much of the unorganized sector workers' protests and strikes target the state owing to the absence of employment relationships and stress the need for state intervention to provide work opportunities and social securities to these workers.

The State seeks to ensure industrial peace and does not hesitate to use the police to curb labour unrest (e.g., the industrial conflict that occurred in 2005 in Honda Motorcycle and Scooters India Ltd. in Gurgaon). As noted above, union recognition and registration issues have provoked many a strike especially in the multinational corporations (MNCs) and in the auto (Honda Motor Cycles, Rico, Sunbeam, Bosch, Toyota Motors, Hyundai Motors, Maruti Suzuki and so on) and food industries (Coca Cola, Nestle, Hindustan Lever tea company and so on). The union organizational issues covered both the regular and the contract workers (e.g., Reliance Energy Limited, Toyota Motors, Holcim Cements, etc.) (see Shyam Sundar, 2010b; 2011b; 2012b).

Much of the unorganized sector workers' protests and strikes target the state owing to the absence of employment relationships and stress the need for state intervention to provide employment opportunities and social securities to these workers.

A disturbing feature of the industrial relations has been the violence by not only the workers but also the employers/contractors and the state agencies. The police has in the recent past often intervened in the industrial conflicts, and clashes between the police and the protestors have become more prominent, e.g., Honda Motorcycles and Scooters India (HMSI) conflict and in Regency Ceramics conflict. Trade unions and commentators have often alleged, and not without substance, on how the use of security guards, bouncers and other musclemen by the employers and contractors to discipline workers degenerated into violent deeds, e.g., Conflicts in Rico, Sunbeam, Maruti Suzuki, Viva Garments and so on (see Shyam Sundar, 2012b). Workers allegedly acting as irate mobs have attacked managerial personnel and the latter have often succumbed to the injuries, e.g., Pricol, Graziano, Regency Ceramics, Maruti Suzuki and so on (Also see Box 5.1). The industrial discontent has been manifested in extreme forms such as attempts to commit suicides and suicides committed by industrial workers as a desperate measure (see Shyam Sundar, 2010b; 2012b). These conflicts clearly reflect the inadequacies and the failures of the institutional framework to govern the labour market and industrial relations system and clearly call for labour reforms. But the labour reform agenda is debatable (see later).

5.4.2.2 Lockouts and Strikes

Employer militancy, as evidenced in terms of lockouts, have been a prominent phenomenon in the Indian IRS (Datt, 2003; Ramaswamy, 2000; Shyam Sundar, 2004a) and it would be interesting to study its incidence in the post-reform period.

Table 5.5

Percentage Share of Lockouts in Totals of Work Stoppages, 1992-2009

Period	*Count*	*WI*	*WDL*
1992-95	35.52	32.01	62.72
1996-99	38.58	30.40	60.41
2000-2004	48.12	24.41	73.57
2005-2009	46.74	6.15	58.82

Source: *Indian Labour Year Book* and *Indian Labour Statistics*, Labour Bureau, Shimla (various issues); for 2008 see Trade Unions, 2008, *http://labourbureau.nic.in*, accessed on 1 April 2013.

The share of lockouts in the total number of work stoppages increased significantly and reached its peak share in the first half of the 2000s. However, the share of workers affected by lockouts declined consistently during the post-reform period and reached its trough level of 6.15 per cent in the second half of the 2000s (Table 5.5). While the share of lockouts in the total workdays lost fluctuated, it reached its peak of about 74 per cent during 2000-04.

Box 5.1

Some Important Instances of Violent Industrial Conflicts

In September 2012 workers of Everest Company in Nashik belonging to CITU, frustrated over the non-resolution of wage demands for over 10 months, attacked management representatives just outside the labour office and one of them stabbed three officers; the non-resolution of wage demands perhaps was related to the facts that the firm was not doing well and the frustration arising out of the realization that the workers in some firms like Volkswagen, Mercedes, General Motors, Thermax, etc. in the neighbouring region, Pune, had been paid an impressive wage hike of around INR 10,000.

On 21 July 2012, workers at the Syndicate Vyper Systems at Mhape in Navi Mumbai (Maharashtra) ransacked the factory, burnt vehicles and attacked the police over an industrial dispute on wage revision, contract labour system and so on. More than 800 contract workers in Regency Ceramics in Pondicherry staged daily protests during January 2012, seeking wage-revision and regularization of services of senior contract workers. According to the workers, wage revision had been pending for over 10 years. S. Murali Mohan, who led their protest, died in the hospital allegedly owing to injuries due to police beating in the protest action towards the end of January. Angered by this news and police action, the irate workers, allegedly encouraged by anti-social elements, damaged the plant and machinery and attacked the President (Operations), K.C. Chandrasekhar, who also succumbed to fatal head injuries. These incidents followed the similar violence-led death of Roy George, the Vice-President–HR of Pricol Ltd. in Coimbatore in Tamil Nadu in 2008.

A wage revision dispute began in Rico Auto Industries at Manesar in October 2010, but deteriorated into labour unrest with alleged clashes between management/contractor-hired goons and workers. This was followed by police firing in which a worker died and several were injured. The workers demanded a compensation of ₹ 5 million and an inquiry into the incident. This was, in turn, followed by the spontaneous occurrence of a day-long general strike involving 0.1 million workers in the region.

Figure 5.4

Percentage Shares of Strikes (STR) and Lockouts (LOC) in Total Work Days Lost, 1960s to 2000s

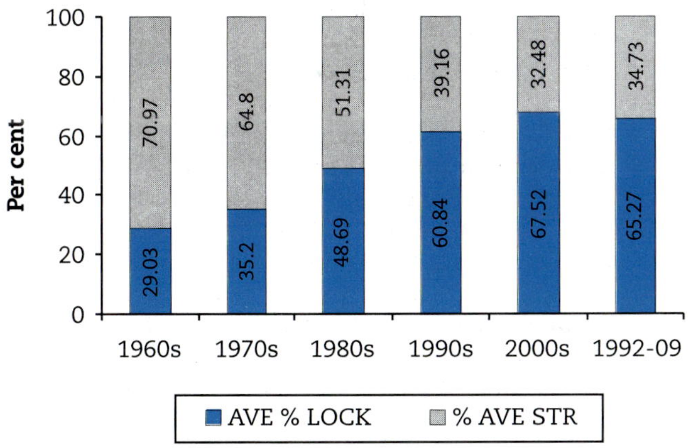

Source: *Indian Labour Year Book* and *Indian Labour Statistics*, Labour Bureau, Shimla (various issues); for 2008 see Trade Unions, 2008, *http://labourbureau.nic.in*, accessed on 1 April 2013.

In general, it can be said that employer-militancy as measured by lockout incidence rose during the post-reform period as evidenced by its rising and/or high shares in total work stoppages and total workdays lost. We do not have adequate statistics on other measures like closures, retrenchment of workers, lay-off of workers, dismissals, defaults in wages, and so on, to be able to draw a complete picture of employer-militancy. However, when seen in a long-term perspective, the share of lockouts in total workdays lost began to rise well before the reform period 1991 onwards (see Figure 5.4); however, the shares of lockouts during the post-reform period reached their peak levels in the 2000s and were generally higher than before.

5.5 Social Dialogue: Tripartism and Collective Bargaining

5.5.1 Tripartism in India

There are two forms of tripartite bodies in India: non-statutory and statutory. Statutory bodies are a product of legislation and they perform the functions that are stipulated by the law. Some notable statutory tripartite bodies are the Contract Labour Advisory Board under the Contract Act, the Minimum Wage Advisory Board under the Minimum Wages Act (central laws), Mathadi Boards under the Maharashtra Mathadi, Hamal and Other Manual Workers (Regulation of Employment and Welfare) Act (a state law) and welfare boards created at the state level to provide social security to the unorganized sector workers. The main non-statutory tripartite bodies at the national level are Indian Labour Conference (ILC) and its complementary body the Standing Labour Committee (SLC) at the central level. Apart from these, other important non-statutory tripartite bodies are the industrial tripartite committees, the State Labour Advisory Boards, the Wage Boards and so on. Some of them, like the Wage Boards, were very active in the initial years, though presently Wage Boards are constituted only for the working journalists.

In the initial years, tripartite bodies such as the ILC and SLC played an important role in law-making, institution-building, evolving consensus and reducing conflict, development of substantive and procedural rules of industrial relations, reviewing and revising laws and institutions (Mathur and Sheth, 1969; NCL, 1969). Over the years, the utility of these institutions has suffered from a decline in the government's initiative, institutional weaknesses and so on. From the early 1970s till the beginnings of the 1990s, these forums were largely non-active bodies for temporary revivals. However, the economic reform process necessitated consultations with social actors and the tripartite forums were revived. The Government constituted a Special Tripartite Committee in 1991 following structural adjustment reforms. A major policy outcome of the consultations in these forums was the creation of the short-lived National Renewal Fund (NRF). In recent years, social partners, especially the trade unions, have been critical of the functioning of these forums and the attitude of the government towards them. The tripartite social dialogue process in India suffers due to three important reasons: (i) The non-inclusion of non-CTUOs and the important organizations working in the unorganized sector. For instance, SEWA was granted CTUO status after a bitter legal and organizational battle by it (see Shyam Sundar, 2009) and this affects the legitimacy and the effectiveness of workers' representation and the social dialogue process itself; (ii) The social actors bring adversarial and ideologically loaded motives to the consultation table, which affects the potential for evolving consensus; (iii) the government has often shown a rather casual attitude towards tripartite forums—non-participation of senior members of the government, delay in calling the meetings, lack of adequate preparation of the items in agenda and the ineffective proceedings, are indicative of an attitude of neglect (see Shyam Sundar, 2011b).

5.5.2 Bipartite Institutions: Consultation and Participation

There are three forms of bipartite institutions prevalent in India, two of which are government-created, non-statutory and statutory bipartite bodies, the third being joint consultation schemes. Non-statutory bodies include bipartite committees for specific industries like jute, engineering, plantations, textiles etc.; the National Apex Body and the Joint Consultative Board of Industry and Labour. Apart from these non-statutory bodies, the labour laws have created bipartite bodies like the Works Committee under the Industrial Disputes Act. The main purpose of these bodies has been to ensure cooperation between workers and employers and establish guidelines and rules for the employment relationship. Further, the government has at various times initiated schemes for joint consultation and workers' participation in management like Joint Management Councils (JMCs) in 1958, Employee Directors in Nationalized Banks in 1970, and shop floor and plant level councils in 1975. In 1975, the Constitution of India was amended to insert Article 43A in the Directive Principles to enable the State to 'take steps by suitable legislation or in any other way to secure the participation of workers in the management of undertakings, establishments, or other organizations engaged in any industry' (Venkata Ratnam, 2006: 536). But the statutory scheme of works committee and various schemes of workers' participation could not achieve the desired results, primarily because of institutional weaknesses such as multiplicity of unions, inter-union rivalry, lackadaisical attitude of the employers and so on (Sharma, 1987). Not satisfied with the progress made in institutionalizing workers' participation in management, the central government introduced a Bill in 1990 in the Rajya Sabha, which sought to provide statutory support to schemes of workers' participation. However, with the winds of reforms blowing all over, the Bill is yet to see fruition (Venkata Ratnam, 2006).

Collective bargaining, which was considered to be the most appropriate and effective method of resolving industrial disputes and ensuring industrial peace in the early years after Independence, is widely preached but very little practised in India. The central industrial relations legislation, the ID Act, which purported to build a system based on collective bargaining, has largely been responsible for reducing it to insignificance due to the elaborate system of state intervention preferred in it. Over the years, the unions and employers, for reasons of their own, have found that the provisions in ID Act suit their convenience, permitting them to refer matters to the government, rather than attempting to take them to the negotiating table. Governments, for their own reasons of power or expediency, have not been averse to intervention, thus discouraging bipartite negotiations and collective bargaining.

The coverage of collective bargaining in any case has been very low in India. It is confined to the organized sector, accounting for only a small percentage (about 8 per cent) of total employment in the country. If we deduct the employment in those sections of the organized sector without bargaining rights or where collective bargaining is rendered redundant by administrative guidelines, then the coverage of collective bargaining is hardly 3 to 4 per cent of the workforce in the country (see ILO, 1997). Yet, it must be noted that there are industries, regions and sectors where the institution is well established, albeit under strain presently. Also worth noting are some developments in the practice of collective bargaining that have taken place in recent years following economic liberalization.

Collective bargaining, which was considered to be the most appropriate and effective method of resolving industrial disputes and ensuring industrial peace in the early years after Independence, is widely preached but very little practised in India. It is confined to the organized sector, accounting for only about 8 per cent of total employment in the country.

There have been decentralizing tendencies in collective bargaining in both public and private sectors (Bhattacherjee, 1999; Kulkarni, 2002; Shyam Sundar, 2010a; 2010b; 2010c). In the public sector, the government has consistently refused to provide budgetary support to the public sector enterprises and asked them to link wage increases to productivity increases in their establishments rather than passing them on in the form of higher prices. For example, the guidelines of the Central Public Sector Enterprises (CPSEs) for the seventh round of wage negotiations, for agreements to be made effective from 1 January 2007, clearly stipulate that no budgetary support would be available for the wage increase and that the resources should be internally generated from increased productivity and profitability. The wage revision should not result in an increase in unit labour costs which means that productivity must increase in the same degree as wages (*Arbiter*, November 2006: 5). Further, the government has rejected the unions' demand for parity of wages

Box 5.2

New Developments in Collective Bargaining with Respect to Contract and Casual Workers in India

The tremendous rise in the numbers of the contract workers—the share of contract workers in the total number of workers in the organized factory sector increased from 13.24 per cent in 1993-94 to about 32 per cent in 2008-09—coupled with the simultaneous fall in the numbers of the permanent workers in the organized sector, and the judicial setbacks suffered by the contract and the casual workers (see below), prompted both trade unions and the workers to resort to the organizational and negotiation route to improve conditions of work of contract and casual workers. The role of global union federations in offering organizational and negotiational support in these efforts is also significant. The trade unions have been able to use this strategy to achieve impressive outcomes with regard to employment security and terms and conditions of employment. The trade unions could (i) secure regularization of services of contract workers as a first best option, and failing which, to ensure continuity of services in the case of contract workers even if the contractors change (e.g., regularization of services of contract and casual workers in Neyveli Lignite Corporation, Tamil Nadu Electricity Board in Tamil Nadu, Glaxo Smithkline (Horlicks) in Nabha in Punjab, Century Rayon in Mumbai; continuity of employment of contract workers in Rashtriya Chemical Factory in Mumbai, Sandvik Company in Pune, Nokia India in Tamil Nadu); and (ii) ensure assured days of work for casual workers in seasonal industries (e.g., Coca Cola Company in Karnataka). Trade unions used the negotiation route to secure impressive terms and conditions of employment and regular tenure-oriented collective agreements similar to the ones reached for permanent workers—a wage structure, variety of allowances, safety equipments, leave and holidays, social security, and bonus as per the Payment of Bonus Act, 1965 and so on (see Shyam Sundar 2011b, and 2012a for details and patterns of wage negotiations).

between the various public sector enterprises. Recently, the National Bankers' Association insisted on holding negotiations with trade unions on wage revision at the individual bank level and not at the industry level as in the past. However, the trade unions in the banking sector have rejected this.

The dominant level of bargaining in many private sector industries is the enterprise-level. In the past, collective bargaining used to take place at the industry (and often industry-cum-region) level as in the case of cotton textiles and plantations. Industry-wide employers' associations, for example cotton textile industry associations like Southern India Mill Owners' Association (SIMA), also exist in some regions.[6] However, the increasingly competitive environment, where individual units have to compete with each other, seems to have played a role in inciting the mills to take independent decisions on economic and workload matters. As a result there unit-wise rather than industry-wide agreements have emerged through decentralized collective bargaining.

A similar shift towards local settlements has occurred in the plantations industry. Product-market factors such as intensification of competition, rise in the raw material and energy prices, cheaper imports (owing to removal of quantitative restrictions), and product differentiation compulsions prompted the firms in textile and plantation industries to break away from the industry-level bargaining depending on the configuration of technological and managerial efficiencies. Competitive pressures prompted the firms to rein in costs, especially labour costs as costs in other areas such as raw materials and energy could not be controlled. In the case of plantation industry in Tamil Nadu, the differences among the trade unions operating in the plantation industry in different regions have led them to negotiate terms and conditions at the district level (see Shyam Sundar, 2010c; Venkata Ratnam, 2003). In the textile industry in Mumbai, the dilution of collective bargaining manifested in informal ways of determining work-load and pay issues, even at the departmental levels (see Kulkarni, 2002).

The dominant managerial objectives in collective bargaining in recent years have reduced labour costs, increased production or productivity, flexibility in work organization, increase in work time, stability in labour conditions, reduction in staff strength via Voluntary Retirement Scheme (VRS), stress on quality, etc. (Krishna Murthy, 2006; Ramaswamy, 2000; Venkata Ratnam, 2003). Trade unions have cooperated, especially in crisis situations caused by external factors. A content analysis of over 200 collective agreements reached during 1991-2001

6. SIMA, which had most of the large and medium sized textile mills and some small mills as its members, facilitated the conduct of industry-wide collective bargaining over the substantive issues, wages and bonus and basic guidelines regarding the workload and technological arrangements Shyam Sundar, 2010c).

(Venkata Ratnam, 2003) shows several instances where trade unions have agreed to wage and allowance cuts, to managerial freedom in work organization, modernization and computerization of work, positioning and transfer of workers, reduction in workforce or substitution of workers with machines.

Productivity concerns now dominate the collective agreements. Trade unions have realized the need for raising productivity in contrast to their earlier opposition to it. They have agreed to the measures and work reorganization leading to increased productivity subject to some conditions such as consultative processes, mechanisms to share productivity gains, etc.

Productivity concerns dominate the collective agreements. Trade unions have realized the need for raising productivity in contrast to their blind and obstinate opposition to productivity raising measures in the past. The trade unions have agreed to the measures and work reorganization leading to increased productivity subject to some conditions such as existence of consultative processes, mutually agreeable productivity measuring and determining agencies, mechanisms to share the productivity gains and so on. The deals are arrived not without ruptures and employment flexibilities. However, the compulsions of intense competition have promoted pragmatism on the part of the trade unions (see Krishna Murthy, 2008; Samant, 2010; Shyam Sundar, 2012c). The same pragmatism has characterized both the employers and the trade unions in dealing with issues concerning the employment security issues of flexi-category workers, which are discussed below.

Along with these trends, there have been attempts in several cases by the temporary and contract workers to bargain for employment security, better wages and other facilities (see Box 5.2).

5.6 Labour Regulation and Labour Reforms

As mentioned at the beginning of this chapter, there exist a large number of laws regulating employment of labour in India. Employers have often complained of the difficulties in complying with them and the costs (both direct and transactions costs) that they involve. As such, there has been a persistent demand for labour law reforms by the employers as well as from sections within the government.

The pitch of this demand has risen since the initiation of economic liberalization, as it is argued that the rigidity imposed by various provisions of law makes it particularly difficult for the enterprises to operate in an internationally competitive environment. As a consequence, growth of output and investment is adversely affected, which in turn, has adverse impacts on the expansion of employment, particularly regular and formal employment.

5.6.1 Labour Law Reform Demands in India

Among the main focuses of the debate on labour law reform is that (i) there are too many laws; often several dealing with the same aspect of employment; (ii) there is a confusing variety of definitions given to the same term such as 'worker', 'wages', 'industry' etc.; (iii) there is a need to codify laws into one or few aspects (condition of work, social security, industrial relations and wages), and streamline concepts and definitions; and (iv) there is a need for simplifying procedures and minimizing harassment and corruption involved in frequent inspection visits by multiple officials under different acts.

There is objection by some sections of the industry to the Minimum Wages Act and a demand that wages be determined by the free play of market forces. Changes in certain provisions in the Factories Act, which are too specific and detailed and also in some cases, antiquated, are also demanded (Debroy, 2005; Papola and Pais, 2007).

Among the main focuses of the debate on labour law reform is that there are too many laws and they lack systematic codification, concepts and definitions require streamlining, procedures need simplification, and issues of harassment and corruption need to be addressed.

However, the issues that have received most attention and generated the most heat concern some provisions of the ID Act and the Contract Labour Act (see Sharma, 2006 for a comprehensive discussion of the labour reform issues in India). In the former, the contentious provisions include the rules for change of conditions of work (9-A Chapter II-A, from 1957) and for lay-off and retrenchment of workers and closure of establishments (Chapter V-A and V-B), in particular the provision under V-B stipulating prior permission of the government to lay-off and retrench works or to close the unit in the case of enterprises employing 100 or more workers. These provisions, it is argued, render the requirement-based adjustment of the workforce difficult, increase labour costs for enterprises and, as a consequence constrain expansion of output, employment and investment (see Sharma, 2006).

The Contract Labour Act provides for prohibition of employment of contract labour in process operations or other work which forms the 'core' activity of industry and is of perennial nature or is done ordinarily by regular workers or where it is sufficient to employ a considerable number of full-time workers. Employers argue that different numbers of workers are needed at different times due to the fluctuating demand for their products, particularly in the contemporary trend towards increased participation in global production networks and supply-on-order mode of operations (see Papola, 2012, for the difficulties in exercising the prohibitory clause in the Act)

These demands for changes in the ID Act and the Contract Labour Act are naturally resisted by the trade unions (see Shyam Sundar, 2012a). They suspect that such changes will give complete freedom to employers to hire and fire at will and make workers highly vulnerable, and will lead to the complete erosion of the limited rights to job security and employment stability, those workers in India have earned through long struggles. They, in fact, demand extension of the scope of application of various laws to hitherto uncovered workers and their more effective implementation.

5.6.2 *Evidence on Labour Flexibility and Regulation*

Demands for changes in provisions of these laws are based primarily on the argument that they render workforce adjustment inflexible. As a result, enterprises have to carry the load of more labour than required, which increases cost and reduces competitiveness. Employers, therefore, are reluctant to hire more labour and entrepreneurs are shy to invest. Growth of industry and employment thus suffers. Is there really such a lack of flexibility that has led to an adverse effect of output and employment?

There have been a number of studies trying to examine the impact of labour regulation on the growth of investment and employment. The studies on labour regulation present a complex set of exercises. One set of studies comprises econometric exercises which have used secondary quantitative data relating to the organized manufacturing sector and proxy variables on labour regulation and generally shown the detrimental effects of restrictive labour regulation in India on employment, output and their implications for poverty reduction (e.g., Ahsan and Pages, 2009; Besley and Burgess, 2004; Dougherty, 2008; Fallon and Lucas, 1993; Goldar and Aggarwal, 2012; Bhattacharya, 2009, for references of various studies). While the earlier studies in this genre principally focussed on the specific restrictive provisions of the ID Act (say Chapter V-B), the latter studies have sought to widen the measurement of labour regulation. Secondly, the labour flexibility measurement exercises by global financial organizations such as the World Bank provide both a database and policy prescriptions for labour reforms to countries including India.

> The debate and the evidence on labour law reforms has remained inconclusive, prompting the government to keep an ambivalent attitude towards it.

Based on the response of employers, World Bank has over the years sought to rank the countries on the ease of doing business based on several areas (five, eight or ten depending on the improvements in the methodologies) including credit, taxes, contract enforcement system, employing workers and so on (see Shyam Sundar, 2008b, for more details on this and other such measurement exercises). The category of 'employing workers' seeks to assess the labour flexibility or its absence of each country and rank them. India shows high levels of rigidity mainly in terms of a 'difficulty of firing' index. In terms of flexibility in hiring, India enjoys maximum flexibility and in case of hours of work index it is not worse off than its Asian neighbours and the separation costs in India are second lowest in Asia (see Table 5.6).

Table 5.6

World Bank Labour Flexibility (Rigidity) Scores for Selected Countries in Asia, 2009

Country	*Difficulty of Hiring Index*	*Rigidity of Hours Index*	*Difficulty of Firing Index*	*Employment Index*	*Firing Costs (weeks of salary)*
Cambodia	44	60	30	45	39
China	11	20	50	27	91
India	0	20	70	30	56
Philippines	56	20	30	35	91
Thailand	33	20	0	18	54
Vietnam	11	20	40	20	87
Sri Lanka	0	20	60	27	169
Pakistan	78	20	30	43	90
Bangladesh	44	20	40	35	104

Note: The index is scored from 0 to 100, where lower scores mean flexibility and higher scores mean rigidity (see the source for further details).

Source: World Bank's 'Doing Business' report, 2009. *http://www.doingbusiness.org/reports/global-reports*

Table 5.7

Some Aspects of Termination of Employment in Countries in Asia

Country	*Prior Permission*
Bangladesh	No
China	No
Hong Kong	No
Indonesia	Yes, collective dismissals of more than 10 workers regulated by law
Japan	No
Malaysia	No
Pakistan	Yes, from Labour Court for closure or termination of employment of more than 50 per cent of workers.
Republic of Korea	Collective dismissals and redundancy allowed for 'urgent managerial needs'.
Singapore	No

Source: *http://www.ilo.org/dyn/eplex/termmain.home*, accessed 3 January 2013.

However, the exercise of measuring and ranking labour flexibility was severely criticized by several, including the ILO and trade unions, for not factoring in ILO's core labour standards (universally valued as 'core human rights'), and provoking a race to the bottom in labour standards in terms of dilution of labour rights and standards to achieve relatively better ranking on labour flexibility (see ILO/GB, 2007). The World Bank's 'Doing Business' report for 2011 and 2012 does not rank countries on the 'Employing Workers Indicators' and also does not include these indicators in the aggregate ranking of the countries.[7] Notwithstanding these developments, critics of labour regulation have used these indicators to call labour reforms in India.

The so-called rigidity in firing index is primarily due to the statutory requirement that employers have

7. *http://www.doingbusiness.org/reports/global-reports/~/media/FPDKM/Doing%20Business/Documents/Annual-Reports/English/DB12-Chapters/Employing-Workers.pdf.*

to obtain prior permission from the government. This provision exists only in a few countries in the world (see Table 5.7). In most countries, including China, the employers are required to follow some procedures (like sending a written notice to stakeholders), intimating the government in case of collective dismissals (dismissals involving at least 10 or 20 workers), consulting the social partners and considering their suggestions before effecting retrenchment or closure. In European countries, employers are required to devise social plans of training, relocation and so on.

Thirdly, some studies based on micro-level data have shown the employers have enjoyed flexibilities in employment and wage determination in the organized manufacturing sector despite the restrictive legal regime; for example, firms, especially the larger ones, have been able to increase or decrease employment though not to the extent that the employers desire (see Deshpande, *et al.*, 2004). Some micro-level studies have principally focused on contract labour flexibility and brought out the adverse conditions of employment faced by contract workers and highlighted the inequities between the contract workers and the regular workers in terms of wages (even for those performing same work) and working conditions in the so-called organized manufacturing sector (see Bhandari and Heshmati, 2006; Maiti, 2009; Rajeev, 2006; Shyam Sundar, 2011b). The data on industrial injuries (see Table 8.6 in Appendix)—which suffers from limited scope (as it covers manufacturing, mining and railways) and under-reporting (which could be used as a proxy for working conditions) shows that industrial injuries, even factoring in under-reporting—continue to pose a concern.

Fourthly, macro level studies on labour regulation which primarily deal with enforcement of labour laws and other regulatory variables have found that the labour regulatory regime in India is not as tough as it is portrayed (especially by the colourful even fanciful phrase of 'inspector-Raj'); this is evidenced by the reduction in the enforcement variables such as labour inspections, prosecutions, the low and declining coverage of labour laws, increasing complaints of non-implementation of labour laws and violations and so on (see for e.g., Papola *et al.*, 2008 and the studies mentioned in it; Papola and Pais, 2007; see also Table 8.6 and 8.7 in Appendix).

With regard to data on labour laws enforcement, there is severe under-reporting or non-reporting from the lower to the higher levels of the labour department in a region. The primary reason is the discourses on globalization and labour reforms. While relaxations in and self-certification of implementation of labour laws affect the scope of labour enforcement data, continued state retrenchment has led to a slim and over-burdened labour department. These factors, in turn, have affected collection and compilation of data not only at the regional levels but also at the national level.

Further, there has arisen critical literature on pro-labour flexibility studies which have identified several 'flaws' in these studies and highlighted their inadequacies (see for e.g., Bhattacharya, 2009; Jha and Goldar, 2008). For example, pro-flexibility studies that have relied on measurement exercises are found to suffer from problems arising out of high aggregation and simplification of complex and contradicting components of regulation variables and faulty methodology (Bhattacharya, 2009).

Thus, the debate and the evidence have remained inconclusive and the government has taken an ambivalent attitude towards labour law reforms. While it (a governmental agency) sometimes seems to accept the rigidity view (*Economic Survey*, 2005-06), it also acknowledged that the ID Act has not proved an obstacle in its downsizing, nor has the scope of prohibition under contract labour been wide (*Eleventh Five Year Plan Volume II*). At the same time, it recognizes that the ID Act does create a psychological block against creating new enterprises, and the latter makes it difficult 'to cope with large-size orders from retail market chains' in some product lines (*Eleventh Five Year Plan Volume II*: 150). It is also argued that an important reason behind absence of 'missing middle' firms in Indian manufacturing is the lack of freedom among enterprises to lay-off workers in the case of downsizing of business. Consequently, it has led to rapid growth of contract labour in the country, more so in the manufacturing sector.

5.6.3 *The Judiciary and Industrial Relations System*

There exists a consensus among researchers in jurisprudence and the activists that the judiciary in general took a pro-active stance, and delivered judgements until the mid-1990s that sought to establish and protect the rights of workers—such as the right to strike, employment security and so on (see Dhavan, 2006; Pavani, 1985; Singh, 2008; Sharma, 2004). However, the judiciary seems to be taking stances in the post-globalization period which have taken away the long-fought for labour rights in the areas of the right strike, workmen's compensation, employment security of casual and temporary and contract labourers, and established a new perspective which aid the process of globalization (see Cox, 2008, 2012; Singh, 2008). In the case of U.P. State Brassware Corporation Ltd. *Versus* Udai Narain Pandey, 2005, the Supreme Court while deciding on the issue of awarding back wages to a fixed tenure worker observed that 'The changes brought about by the [subsequent] decisions of this Court probably having regard to the changes in the policy decisions of the government in the wake of prevailing market economy, globalization, privatization and outsourcing is evident.'[8] In the case of casual and temporary workers, the Supreme Court in 2006 in a case (Secretary, State of Karnataka & Ors *Versus* Uma Devi & Ors) has overruled the earlier pro-labour judgements and held that despite the long and continuous years of service (even more than a decade) casual and temporary workers employed without due selection process do not have the right to be regularized, as they have made backdoor entries into jobs and thus deprive other potential aspirants of employment seeking jobs (see Singh, 2008, for a critical analysis of this judgement).

The Supreme Court in Air India Statutory Corporation Vs. United Labour Union in 1997, took a pro-active stance and ruled that in the event of abolition of contract labour, the tripartite relationship becomes bipartite (as the contractor disappears) and the principal employer should absorb the contract workers and regularize their service (called the 'automatic absorption' argument). This provided a tremendous boost to contract workers and litigation and struggles to reap the benefits of this judgement followed.

The Supreme Court, in another case in 2001 (Steel Authority of India Ltd. *Versus* National Union of Waterfront Workers), reversed the Air India judgement (in the case discussed above) by arguing that the Contract Labour Act does not provide for automatic absorption of contract workers upon abolition (see Cox, 2008). This led to a considerable drop in the litigation for permanency of contract workers (Singh, 2008). However, in a 2011 judgment, the Supreme Court observed that 'in order to avoid their [employers'] liability under various labour statutes, employers are very often resorting to subterfuge by trying to show that their employees are, in fact, the employees of a contractor. It is high time that this subterfuge comes to an end'September 4.[9]

The Supreme Court's denial of the right to strike of the public employees in the case involving government employees and the teachers in Tamil Nadu in 2003 (see Shyam Sundar, 2004), and judgements by some High Courts against *bandhs* (though not on general strikes) hurt the collective rights of the workers and their political action. The trade union movement has been demanding for ratification of ILO Conventions 87 and 98 on freedom of association and the right to collective bargaining. It is disturbing to note that India has ratified only half of the eight ILO Core Conventions called 'fundamental human and labour rights', though dialogue is on for ratification in the case of a couple of them.

5.6.4 State and Labour Reforms in India

There have been widespread 'reforms by stealth' at the state level. In the absence of any change in the central laws, different states have amended acts, reframed rules and changed practices in the implementation of laws. To begin with, a number of states have relaxed inspection routines by ordering less frequent inspections or the conduct of inspections only with the permission of the civil authorities. Self-certification in factory and labour inspections has been introduced, in some states like Punjab, Gujarat, and Maharashtra in the case a set of laws, though with little success (see Shyam Sundar, 2010b, for a comprehensive review of aspects relating to labour inspection debate).

In the absence of any change in the central laws, different states have amended acts, reframed rules and changed practices in the implementation of the laws.

Activities like information technology and units in SEZs have been brought under the provision of public utilities and essential services regulations, thus restricting industrial actions by unions and employers. Although the ID Act has not been amended, states have become more liberal in granting permission for retrenchment, lay-off and closures. Recently, the

8. *http://www.indiakanoon.org/doc/1102187/*, accessed 10 September 2010.

9. *The Hindu*, 4 September 2011.

Government of Gujarat exempted units in a SEZ from the purview of Chapter V-B of the ID Act and similar legal measures are being mulled over by others. Contract labour laws and rules have been amended in some states to make it easier to hire labour on contract basis in more and more activities (Bannerjee, 2008; Reddy, 2008; Papola *et al.*, 2008; Shyam Sunder, 2008a; Sharma and Kalpana, 2008). As a result, the proportion of contract labour has significantly increased in the organized sector, in both the public and private sectors but particularly in the latter.

However, it seems that while some particular aspects of labour reforms have been over-emphasized, some important ones have been rather ignored. It should be recognized that the Indian labour market is generally under-regulated, either in terms of applicability and enforcement of laws or coverage by institutions like the trade unions. As already mentioned earlier the trade union density is very low. Most labour laws apply to workers only in the organized sector. Over 90 per cent of workers in the unorganized sector have hardly any benefit of protective legislation. Further, a large number of them working as informal workers in the organized sector are no better off. In a situation like this, one major item on the agenda for labour reforms should have been to reduce dualism between the two segments of workers by proposing a minimum measure of legislative protection for the informal workers. There has been a deadly silence on this issue. The NCEUS (2009) in its reports had proposed an agenda in this respect. But it does not seem to have resulted in an adequate response, even from the trade unions.

In the emergence of a legal and institutional framework that dealt with labour and employment affairs in India, trade unions had a critical role, political parties were interested supporters, and the governments at the centre and in the states saw this as a part of the necessary social compact. All the ingredients of a comprehensive labour relations system evolved. But the functioning process threw up several weaknesses. Even as the legislative measures multiplied, the effectiveness of their implementation declined. The laws are perceived to be too many, protecting the interests of too few and only in the organized sector, leaving a vast majority of the workforce in the unorganized sector with little protection. While lack of effective organization of informal workers has been one of the reasons for weak representation of their cause, multiplicity of unions and often political rivalry eroded the power of trade unions in the organized sector. With the process of globalization and the state increasingly assuming the role of facilitator of an economic climate that is attractive for investment, labour regulation and labour institutions are painted as obstacles rather than part of a fair and just social system. In earlier days, state governments used to project a pro-labour image, but now they are competing among themselves as to which one of them is pro-industry. Yet there are positive signs in the form of new unionism especially for informal workers, and new political compulsions to pay attention to inclusive growth.

With the process of globalization and the state increasingly assuming the role of the facilitator of an investment-friendly economic climate, labour institutions and regulations are painted as obstacles rather than part of a just social system. State governments now compete among themselves as to which one is more pro-industry.

Automobile manufacturing hubs, such as Gurgaon-Manesar, Bhiwani and Pune, have seen considerable increases in employment in large-scale units. Over time they have also become new centres of workers' struggles. These new centres of worker concentration will play a key role in developing a new agenda for trade unions in dealing with the combination of permanent, contract and casual employment.

5.7 Conclusions

There has been a decline in the strength of organized labour in the country in the wake of liberalization and globalization. The rights of the workers in the organized sector have shrunk while the more insecure informal workers have been expanding, although very recently there seems to have been a halt to this process. Employers and the State have both eroded the rights of trade union, both legal and extra-legal. However, there has been no change in the Constitutional directives on State policy, nor substantive changes in the labour laws. As such there is simmering discontent and sporadic violent actions from workers in some of the industrial areas. There is also the development of new centres of workers' struggles in areas where industrial expansion is taking place. As a whole, while there has been growth of wages, labour has lost *vis-à-vis* capital in terms of its strength as well as rights.

In the polarized debate on labour reforms in the country, there is a need to keep a larger perspective of 'inclusive growth', so that the interests of workers as well as investment and growth are promoted. The proper balance between the interests of labour and capital will not only lead to industrial peace and social justice, but will sustain growth.

- The tendency toward legislative proliferation has led to the severe problem of definitional incompatibilities and administrative overlap and inefficiencies. The major fallout of all this has been a considerable delay in the adjudication of industrial disputes, leading to the clogging of the labour adjudication system (Anant, 2009). The two National Commissions of Labour did make suggestions in this direction. There is an urgent need to move in this direction. Sources of conflict in this issue are limited, except changes in the structure and reach of some of the enactments, which can be reconciled.

- Reasonable flexibility of labour may be needed for capital in a competitive world. The question is how to ensure flexibility for market adjustments without compromising the basic interests of labour. It is necessary to ensure equal pay for equal work for all types of workers—regular, casual, contract, and temporary, and enforce strictly the payment of minimum wages and give social security benefits not less than minimum wages, to retrenched and unemployed workers along with labour market flexibility.

- There is a consensus among both stakeholders and scholars that there are too many complicated labour laws in India that apply to too few workers, and that rationalization, simplification and consolidation are urgently required.

- A wage guarantee fund may also be considered to meet the redundancy needs of the workers in the case of retrenchment and closure.

- It is extremely important to provide a minimum level of social security to all workers, which will certainly promote flexibility. This will reduce the sharpness of dualism and segmentation in the labour market (Papola, 2012). Of course, the major role in this has to be played by the government and it is now widely viewed that at the present juncture of development, it is possible for the country to do this. This has been discussed in more detail in the next chapter.

- The debates on the benefits or otherwise of labour standards unfortunately revolves around the cost that an individual employer would incur. From the perspective of an individual employer, the labour market should be so regulated as to keep labour cheap. But from the perspective of the economy or even an industry as a whole, the existence of firms competing on the basis of cheap labour smothers the incentive to innovate. Moreover, the wage may be a cost to an individual enterprise, but is an important source of revenue for industry as a whole because workers are also consumers. Parallel arguments can be made about other labour standards, which reflect society's interest and cannot be reduced to the competitiveness of an individual enterprise.

- The most vexatious problem concerns the duality in the markets. There has been a tendency to look at those who have some form of protection, and those who do not, in isolation; whereas they should be looked at as integral and integrated. If decent work is to be realized for the informal workers, the granted formalization of informal labour market is the only option. One important means by which this can be realized is for unionization to be actively promoted by the state as a part of active labour market policy. Formalization would also be promoted by insisting on equal pay and benefits for equal work for both formal and informal workers. A large number of informal workers will enter the net of formalization if the enterprise size filter used in various labour laws is reduced or eliminated. This will not only promote formalization and inclusion but will also contribute to a more sustainable and inclusive growth path.

- A mechanism is needed to overcome the problems of effective collective bargaining arising from the multiplicity of unions. This can be done by putting in place mechanisms to identify a collective bargaining agent who would be recognized by all the parties concerned.

- Lastly, the working conditions in the workplace are extremely poor in the small enterprises, more so in the informal sector enterprises. Unfortunately this has not attracted much attention from the government, industry or even trade unions. Assuring a minimum level of working conditions for all workers should be given much higher priority in the policy agenda. Apart from a comprehensive legislation on this issue, it is important that it should form the agenda of labour reforms in the country.

In sum, in the midst of the present polarized debate, there is scope for evolving a common agenda by all the stakeholders which can take into account the interests of both labour and capital. This is essential not only for growth and investment but also for social justice and inclusive and sustained growth.

6

Social Security for Workers

6.1 Issues and Concerns

Social protection has emerged as a very important concern in the current policy discourse in India. This is hardly surprising in the context of the development experience of the country wherein rapid economic growth has not created enough 'good' jobs to absorb the unemployed and expanding labour force. Although the open unemployment level is low, which is typical of a labour-surplus developing economy, poverty levels continue to be very high and the proportion of informal workers without social security is high at around 90 per cent. Undoubtedly extreme poverty, according to the official poverty line, has declined, which may imply a somewhat declining need for social assistance, but the number of the extreme poor is unacceptably high. The proportion of informal workers who were poor and vulnerable in 2009-10 was as high as nearly 70 per cent (Kannan, 2012, Table 1).

In the wake of globalization, there are indications that the already large informal workforce has experienced further flexibilization of employment relations, leading to greater mobility and informalization. Subsequently, the risks and uncertainties in livelihoods have increased. The population and number of workers in need of social protection are simply huge. Over half of the workforce in India in 2011-12 was self-employed, about 30 per cent comprised casual workers, and only about one-sixth of the total number of workers were regular workers. The former two categories of workers consist of a higher percentage of the poor and vulnerable, with the casual workers being the poorest. This suggests that a high level of self-employment, particularly among own account workers and other petty workers, and casualization are associated with high levels of vulnerability and flexibilization. Even in the organized sector, which employs a maximum share of regular workers, there has been increasing informalization and contractualization.

In the context of such a high level of vulnerability and widespread insecurities in livelihoods, the concept of social protection should generally embrace both the measures intended to assure a minimum standard of life, and the means needed to respond to contingencies such as illnesses or accidents, and eventualities such as old age and death. Corresponding to these concerns, one can identify two streams of social security, that is, 'Basic Social Security' (BSS), which is concerned with the promotion of livelihoods for the vulnerable population (also called 'promotional measures of social security') and 'Contingent Social Security' (CSS), which is generally concerned with the protection of workers and their families against the contingent risks of work and life (also called 'protective measures of social security'). Both these dimensions need to be addressed in a developing country like India, where a large number of workers and their families fail to achieve a minimum standard of living (Guhan, 1993; Kannan, 2007).

> Two streams of social security are the 'Basic Social Security', concerned with promotion of livelihoods and 'Contingent Social Security', concerned with the protection of workers and their families against various contengencies.

Since Independence, a number of efforts have been made to secure basic needs for the disadvantaged sections of the population, though this has usually not been treated as part of the broader issue of social security. These efforts include development plans, specially focusing on sectors that could generate income for the poor, and a variety of specially targeted programmes, particularly since the 1970s. Thus, the public distribution system (PDS) has for long been in operation with the aim of ensuring food security; the expansion of education and health systems is intended to provide universal access to these services; there are programmes such as the Indira Awas Yojana (IAY) to provide housing for the poor; the country also has a long history of self-employment and public employment programmes, of which the latest and most important, the Mahatma Gandhi National Rural Employment Guarantee Scheme (MGNREGS) aims to ensure a measure of income security for the poor. Among these, the two most notable programmes currently in operation are the PDS and the MGNREGS.

The PDS, an instrument for improving food security at the household level, ensures availability of essential commodities like rice, wheat, edible oils and kerosene at prices below the prevailing market rates to the consumers through a network of half a million outlets (called 'fair price shops' or FPSs). Through targeted PDS (TPDS), the cereals are made available to the poor at subsidized prices. The prices are subsidized further for the poorest of the poor. The PDS is widely regarded to have contributed towards enhancing food security for the poor as well as maintaining the stability of foodgrain prices and income security to the farmers in several regions of the country. However, the system has also been criticized by a number of scholars as well as the media for inefficient functioning and widespread leakages in large parts of the country. Several states have made important reforms in their functioning in recent years, and considerable improvements have also been noticed in this regard. The state of Chhattisgarh, for instance, which was till some time ago notorious for the poor performance of its PDS outlets, is today known for the successful implementation of universal PDS. The central government has envisaged to statutorily guarantee food with fixed entitlements to the poor and a National Food Security Act has also been passed in 2013 towards this end. The Act covers 75 per cent of the rural population and 50 per cent of the urban population. Under the Act, a beneficiary would be entitled to 5 kg of rice, wheat or coarse cereals at ₹ 3, 2 and 1 per kg a month, respectively, and would be identified by the states on the basis of certain parameters prescribed by the Union Government. The current entitlement of ₹ 35 per kg of grain per month for 24 million to the poorest of poor families has also been retained in the Act. It is estimated that the current food subsidy bill of around ₹ 9000 crore would go up to ₹ 1.15 lakh crore, which is not really large in view of the huge population it is expected to serve.

As regards employment and poverty alleviation programmes, both self-employment and wage employment programmes have been implemented since the middle of the 1970s. As far as self-employment programmes are concerned, mostly subsidized credit is provided to the beneficiaries, along with the provision of technical and other support in many cases. The Government has further strengthened the self-employment programme by constituting a National Livelihood Mission (NLM). Over time, these programmes have been expanded and strengthened. As mentioned above, the most important development in recent years has been the implementation of the MGNREGS, which provides at least 100 days of guaranteed wage employment in a year to all the people who report for manual work. These promotional measures, implemented in the form of wage and self-employment programmes, have been discussed in detail in Chapter 7.

Although the promotional measures have been expanded and strengthened over the years, their impacts have been much less than expected, and rather widespread leakages, though varying across the states and various programmes, have been reported. The major factors cited as being responsible for the unsatisfactory performance of these programmes include the existence of weak institutions, lack of participation of the beneficiaries, the allocation of inadequate funds in some schemes, and deficiencies in programme designs. Perhaps the most important factor is the inherent weakness in terms of targeting in these programmes. Except MGNREGS, most of the programmes are targeted at the poor. Given the enormous difficulties in the identification of the poor and the vulnerable in the midst of widespread poverty, several studies have reported huge exclusion and inclusion errors.

The National Social Assistance Programme (NSAP) of the central government has added a new dimension, in that an increasing proportion of the poor now have access to a series of non-contributory welfare benefits such as old age pensions, widows' pensions, disability benefits, and death benefits, which are, in principle, now available to all households below the poverty line. A number of state governments have further expanded this programme either by enhancing the pension by their own contribution or by adding some other benefits.

In this chapter, we will mainly examine the conventional mode of social security for workers (CSS), which is mostly concerned with the protection of workers and their families against contingent work and life-based risks. At the end of the chapter, however, we return to the issue of BSS, which can also be called 'Social Protection Floor' (SPF), and other means of facilitating better conditions of work in India.

The relatively adequate level of social security available to formal workers is in sriking contrast to the almost total lack of social security for informal workers.

In practice, the CSS, in the sense of statutorily provided social security, is largely confined to around 8 per cent of the workforce, identified as formal workers in the organized sector. The relatively adequate level of social security available to formal workers is in striking contrast to the almost total lack of social security for informal workers. Nevertheless, there have been attempts to overcome this lacuna in social security for the vulnerable sections of the workforce through the introduction of policies and programmes at both the central and State levels. In this chapter, we first consider the main instruments employed for providing social security for formal workers; and then discuss some of the schemes that are aimed at extending protection to particular groups of informal workers, or at providing at least some protection for the population as a whole.

6.2 The Evolution of Social Security for Formal Workers

CSS, with statutorily backed protection against the risks of unemployment, ill-health, maternity, accidents, injury and death at work, old age, and so on, was by and large, non-existent even in the factory establishments during the colonial rule, except in the Workmen's Compensation Act, 1923. The early measures that were implemented in this area were based on the workers' own initiatives in the form of mutual benefit societies, along the lines of their European predecessors, which sought to provide some social protection to select groups of workers. For example, the Amalgamated Society of Railway Servants of India and Burma, formed in 1897, started a series of benefit schemes. The Printers' Union in Calcutta (1905) and the Postal Union in Bombay (1907) introduced mutual insurance schemes, night schools, educational stipends, and funeral allowances. The Kamgar Hitawardhak Sabha, which was formed in 1910, undertook such welfare functions as payment in the event of accidents to industrial workers and improvement in their housing conditions. Concerns about social security received some impetus with the establishment of the International Labour Organization (ILO) in 1919. Domestically, the establishment of the All India Trade Union Congress (AITUC) in 1920 led to a further impetus in this regard. The ILO's Convention on Employment Injury in 1921 paved the way for the demand for protection against employment injury, and consequently, the Indian Legislative Assembly passed the Workmen's Compensation Act in 1923, which provided security against the contingency of employment hazards including industrial accidents and occupational diseases. The Bombay Maternity Benefit Act, 1929, was another early development in this sphere. The Royal Commission on Labour (1929) recommended similar legislations for other provinces also. Although their coverage was limited, these early initiatives were significant steps towards granting access to social protection for the poor.

The evolution of social security for formal sector workers in India had various developments on the labour welfare front during and after the Second World War. The publication of the Beveridge Report in Great Britain ushered in a new welfare state approach and the efforts of the ILO added to this momentum. In response to the demands of the organized labour movement, the British Government in India appointed three Committees in 1943: the Professor B.P. Adarkar Commission to draw up a health insurance plan for workers; the D.V. Rege Committee to investigate the risks that bring about insecurity and the implementation of suitable methods for meeting such risks; and the Sir Joseph Bhore Health Survey and Development Committee to plan for medical care and health services. The most important of these in the sphere of social security was the Adarkar Committee, which went beyond its terms of reference of preparing a health insurance scheme covering only illness, and made a strong case for setting up a unified and integrated system of healthcare, maternity and employment injury insurance.

The Adarkar Commission's recommendations formed the basis for the Employees State Insurance Scheme (ESIS) of 1948. This continues to be a major social security pillar for workers in the formal or organized sector even today. The other important statutory social security provisions are based on the Employees Provident Fund and Miscellaneous Provisions Act of 1952, the Maternity Benefit Act of 1961, the Payment of Gratuity Act, 1972, and the Workmen's Compensation Act, 1936. Table 6.1 provides details of the coverage and benefits under these Acts. It may be noted that except for the Workmen's Compensation Act, all other legislations were enacted after Independence. One of the major factors in the evolution of various social security enactments was political independence as also the drafting of a Constitution that strongly emphasized the values of social justice and welfare.

In this context, it is worth noting that the Constitution of India calls upon the State to secure protection to its citizens against contingent risks under the Directive Principles of State Policy. Thus Article 41 states, "The State shall, within the limits of its economic capacity and development, make effective provision for securing right to work, to education and to public assistance, in cases of unemployment, old age, illness and disability and in other case of undeserved want". And Article 42 asks the State to "make provision for securing just and humane conditions of work and maternity relief".

Table 6.1

Social Security for Organized/Formal Sector Workers

Legislation	*Eligibility*	*Nature of Benefit*
Employees' State Insurance Act, 1948.	Factories and establishments employing 10 or more workers. Further eligibility is confined to those drawing a monthly wage of not more than ₹ 10,000 (revised to ₹ 15,000 in 2010).	Sickness, maternity, disability and death due to employment injury. (coverage about 17 million insured persons and 60 million beneficiaries in March 2012).
Employees' Provident Funds and Miscellaneous Provisions Act, 1952*	All establishments employing 20 or more employees and cooperative societies with 50 or more workers without using power.	Withdrawal of fund on retirement and old age monthly pension (Coverage: 6.6 lakh establishments and 82 million members as of March 2012).
The Maternity Benefit Act, 1961	All shops and establishments employing 10 or more workers other than those covered under The ESI Act, 1948.	Maternity cover for those not covered under ESI Act. Twelve weeks leave and medical allowance.
The Payment of Gratuity Act, 1972	All factories and establishments employing 10 or more workers. Only regular employees with a continuous service of 5 years and above are entitled (amended in 2010 to include any employee).	15 days' wages for every year of service subject to a limit at the time of superannuation, retirement, resignation or death. (The limit was enhanced from ₹ 3.5 lakh to ₹ 10 lakh in 2010.)
The Workmen's Compensation Act, 1936. (Also, the Employees Compensation Act as amended in 2010)	All employees under the Mines Act, the Factories Act of 1948, government employees except armed forces (drawing monthly wages up to ₹ 8000)	Compensation for injury caused by accident, arising out of and in the course of employment, resulting in death or in total or partial disablement.

Note: Employees' State Insurance Act (ESIA) does not apply where the Workmen's Compensation Act (WCA) applies.

6.2.1 Employees' State Insurance Corporation (ESIC)

The ESIC, formed through the Employees' State Insurance Act of 1948, aims at providing protection to employees and their dependents against loss of wages due to inability to work during times of sickness, maternity, disability and death on account of employment injury. The members of the Corporation represent employers, employees, central and state governments, the medical profession and the Parliament. The Union Minister for Labour and Employment is the Chairman of the Corporation. The Medical Benefit Council, a statutory body, advises the Corporation on matters connected with the provisioning of medical care to the beneficiaries of the Scheme. The Director General is the Chief Executive of the Corporation and also the ex-officio member of the Corporation and of its Standing Committee. At the state level, regional boards have been constituted while at the grassroots level, local committees have been formed as advisory bodies to ensure the smooth functioning of the scheme.

The ESIC offers social security cover to workers in factories using power and employing 10 or more workers (and 20 or more workers without the use of power). In addition, it covers specified service establishments such as restaurants, shops, cinemas, theatres, newspaper establishments and transport undertakings with 20 or more workers. The employees of the aforesaid categories of factories and establishments, drawing wages of up to ₹ 15,000 per month, are entitled to social security cover under the ESI Act. Two types of benefits are provided. One is medical care for insured workers and their families through its vast network of panel clinics, ESI dispensaries and ESI hospitals. The other is cash benefits provided in the case of illness, maternity, disablement, retirement, and for funeral expenses. As of 31 March 2012, the scheme covered 17.1 million employees and 66.3 million beneficiaries. The number of factories and establishments covered was 0.58 million (MoL&E, 2013: 64).

The ESI Scheme is mainly financed by contributions from the employers and employees. The rates of the employers' and the employees' contributions are 4.75 per cent and 1.75 per cent, respectively, of wages paid/payable in respect of employees in every wage period. The share of expenditure of the state governments on the provision of medical care is 12.5 per cent of the expenditure of medical benefit (within the per capita ceiling of ₹ 1500/- per insured person per annum) (Ibid.: 65). The state governments also offer medical services under this scheme for employees covered under the ESI Act, 1948.

Even though the ESI Scheme is well-formulated, there are many issues in the management of this scheme. A large number of employers avoid coverage under the scheme; many posts of medical staff remain vacant because of the high turnover and lengthy recruitment process. Other problems include rising costs of speciality treatments; the existence of a poor management information system; low utilization of the capacity of the hospitals; dissatisfaction of the workers with the services offered; and lastly, poor access of the people to these services in rural areas. Notwithstanding these limitations, however, there is a widely shared view that the ESI scheme has largely benefited its members and that there is need for a similar scheme for informal workers as well.

6.2.2 Employees Provident Fund Organization

The Employees Provident Fund Organization (EPFO) is a statutory body under the Ministry of Labour, Government of India. The organization, which was set up in 1952, extends social security cover to workers in both the private and public sector. It administers social security schemes framed under the Employees' Provident Fund and Miscellaneous Provisions Act, 1952 (Central Act), and constitutes a major legislation which was enacted to ensure social security for the organized working class. Establishments employing 20 or more persons and cooperative societies employing 50 or more persons are covered under the EPF. Others can voluntarily join and that is why there are more establishments and employees now participating than statutorily provided. The statutory rate of contribution to EPF is 12 per cent of the emoluments (basic wages, dearness allowance, cash value of food concession and retaining allowances, if any). The employers' rate of contribution is 10 per cent in the case of the brick, *beedi*, jute, *gur* and gum factories, and the coir industry other than the spinning sector. A matching contribution has to be collected from among the emoluments of the employees. As on 31 March 2012, 6,64,000 establishments and factories were covered under the Act, with a membership of over 82.6 million under the EPF scheme (MoL&E, 2013).

The Employees' Pension Scheme (1995) constitutes another dimension of social security provided by the EPFO. Members qualify for superannuation pension on attaining the age of 58 years and on having rendered a minimum of ten years of contributory service. Members who serve for less than ten years are eligible to retain their membership till the age of 58 years or to withdraw the benefit, as the case may be. The Employees' Pension Scheme provides the following benefits to the members and their families: monthly member pension, permanent total disablement pension, widow/widower pension, child pension, orphan pension, disabled child/orphan pension, nominee pension, and pension to the dependent father/mother. With regard to entitlement, every employee, other than the apprentices, is entitled to receive gratuity after he or she has rendered continuous service for five years or more. As of 31 March 2012, there were about 27 million member pensioners, about 8,00,000 spouses, over 14,000 parent pensioners, about 5,74,000 children pensioners, about 15,000 orphan pensioners, and close to 8000 nominee pensioners under the scheme (Ibid.: p.67).

6.2.3 Payment of Gratuity Act, 1972

The Act provides for payment of gratuity equivalent to 15 days of wages for every completed year over five years of continuous service, subject to a ceiling on the amount to be paid. Gratuity is payable at the time of termination of service either: (i) on superannuation, or (ii) on retirement or resignation, or (iii) on death or disablement due to accident or disease. The termination of services includes retrenchment. However, the condition of five years of continuous service is not necessary if the services of the employee are terminated due to death or disablement. In the case of death of the employee, the gratuity has to be paid to the nominee, and if no nomination has been made, then the gratuity goes to the heirs. For every completed year of service or part thereof in excess of six months, the employer pays gratuity to an employee at the rate of 15 days' wages based on the rate of wages last drawn. As per Section 4(3) of the Act, the amount of gratuity payable to an employee shall not exceed ₹ 3.5 lakh, which was amended in 2010 and enhanced to ₹ 10 lakh.

> Main problems pertaining to social security schemes, where they exist, have to do with coverage and delivery of benefits.

As can be seen from Table 6.1, all these measures apply to workers in establishments which are part of what is called the organized or formal sector. It can safely be said that the social security provisioning for workers in the formal sector has sound statutory backing and reasonably takes care of a vast range of contingencies. However, the main problem pertaining to some of the schemes has to do with ensuring the intended coverage and delivery of benefits. The legislation has been enacted in the form of Central laws applicable to the whole country with provision for the state level government to decide on extensions. The legislations provide for two different modes of funding. One consists of the ESI and EPF Acts, which are financed through joint contributions of employers and employees, and administered through dedicated enforcement agencies, including the ESIC and the EPFO. The other Acts, especially those relating to compensation, maternity and payment of gratuity, place the liability on employers. Here, there are frequent complaints of delay or denial of benefits due to various reasons such as inadequate coverage, evasion by employers, and the cost and delay involved in legal remedies.

6.3 Social Security for Workers in the Informal Sector

6.3.1 Initiatives by the Central Government

Prior to the Unorganized Workers' Social Security Act, 2008, the contingent social security schemes for informal workers enforced by the central government were very few in number and limited in coverage. Some legislations, such as the Workmen Compensation Act, the Maternity Benefit Act, and the Building and Other Construction Workers Acts, are directly or indirectly applicable to a section of the workers in the unorganized sector as well. However, both the application and implementation of these laws have been mostly limited and ineffective. A number of welfare funds have been established under laws concerning workers in different industries and occupations to provide social security to the selected groups of workers. These funds are financed through a cess on the respective industries, covered under The Mica Mines Labour Welfare Fund Act of 1946; The Limestone and Dolomite Mines Labour Welfare Fund Act of 1972; The Iron Ore, Manganese Ore and Chrome Ore Mines Labour Welfare Fund Act of 1976; The Beedi Workers Welfare Fund Act of 1976; and The Cine Workers Welfare Fund Act of 1981. These Acts stipulate the meeting of the expenditure incurred in connection with welfare measures and facilities in such fields as healthcare, social security, education, housing, recreation and water supply. Some of these funds are hardly in operation (for example, the one for dolomite mine workers) or cover very few workers. The only significant one relates to *beedi* workers. The significant measures undertaken under the Beedi Workers Fund include the rehabilitation of *beedi* workers displaced due to a decline in employment in the industry as a result of implementation of measures for prohibiting the consumption of tobacco, scholarships for education for the children of *beedi* workers, setting up and upgrading of hospitals for them, and provision of subsidized housing for them, among others.

> The coverage of social security schemes for informal workers often excludes women workers working from home; for example women *beedi* workers, as they get classified as 'self-employed' and not 'employees'.

Table 6.2

Financing and Expenditure of Central Government Welfare Funds, 2011-12

(₹ crore)

Fund	*Cess Collection*	*Utilization of Funds*	*Expenditure on*				
			Healthcare	*Housing*	*Education*	*Recreation*	*Total*
Beedi workers	163.14	209.67	70.29	50.22	81.59	0.21	202.30
Limestone and dolomite workers	5.21	11.26	6.09	0.70	1.03	0.65	8.47
Iron ore, manganese ore and chrome ore mines workers	12.03	12.38	6.93	0.22	2.87	0.20	10.23
Mica mines workers	2.00	1.92	0.99	0	0.44	0.08	1.52
Cine workers	1.51	1.44	1.13	0	0.30	0	1.43

Source: MoL&E, 2013: 74.

Details regarding the actual number of workers covered and the benefits received by them on a regular basis under any of the above-mentioned welfare funds created and administered by the central government, are not available. The available data on the magnitude of collection and utilization of funds and expenditure under various heads pertaining to welfare for the year 2011-12, as given in Table 6.2, adequately reflects the extent and pattern of services provided by these funds. As can be seen from the table, the collection and utilization is relatively substantial only in the case of the *Beedi* Workers Welfare Fund and miniscule in the case of the Mica and Cine Workers Fund. In two cases, *viz.*, *Beedi* and Limestone the collections are much lower than utilization during the year. In the case of *beedi* workers, the largest amount is spent on education, followed by health and housing and the Fund can thus be seen as having a lasting impact on the workers' lives.

Since the early 1990s, some initiatives have been taken to introduce additional social security schemes to cater to the needs of the poor, an overwhelmingly large percentage of whom are informal workers. Most of these are contributory schemes of a contingency social insurance type. The Janashree Bima Yojana (life insurance), which was introduced in 2000, targeted the urban and rural poor living below the poverty line (BPL) or on the BPL margin. Under this scheme, half of the annual premium of ₹ 200 is paid by the central government and the remaining half by the individual or the state government. This scheme met with very limited success. Another scheme called the Varishtha Pension Bima (old age pension insurance) was launched in 2003 for the unorganized sector workers aged 55 years and above. It is fully financed through investment by the beneficiary to receive a pension ranging from ₹ 250 to ₹ 2000 per month, depending on the total investment, and is based on a guaranteed 9 per cent return implemented by the Life Insurance Corporation (LIC). This scheme too has achieved only limited coverage. An Unorganized Sector Workers Social Security Scheme was launched in 2004, but it was introduced only on a pilot basis and was restricted to 50 districts. The implementation of this scheme was an attempt to follow the recommendations of the Second National Labour Commission (2002). Although the scheme provided for an old age pension, and medical and personal accident insurance, only 3,500 workers were enrolled under it. Subsequently, the scheme was virtually closed. Another scheme called the Universal Health Insurance was introduced in 2004, and was slated to be jointly implemented by the four public sector general insurance companies. The targeted group comprised BPL individuals and families, and entailed payment of a premium of ₹ 165 for individuals and up to double this amount for families, depending on the household size. The scheme was expected to cover about 10 million households. However, a Parliamentary Committee that assessed the scheme in 2006 reported that it had benefited only 10,000 families against an initial target of 1,00,000.

A couple of occupation-specific schemes were also initiated by the central government. One of these is the scheme for handloom weavers and artisans, providing a thrift fund, insurance for illness, maternity, accident and loss of dwelling, and a pension plan restricted to master craftsmen. Another such scheme was the Krishi Samajik Suraksha Yojana, which was launched in 2001, and was limited to just 50 identified districts, entailing a coverage of one million agricultural workers. The LIC, as the implementing agency, was to provide insurance cover for death and accidents and survival benefits on a periodic basis. While the worker was expected to pay a contribution of ₹ 30 per month, the Government undertook to pay ₹ 60. However, the scheme did not take off and was terminated in 2004.

Another initiative by the central government was the enactment of an umbrella legislation for construction workers in the form of two Acts in 1996, namely, the Building and Other Construction Workers (Regulation of Employment and Conditions of Service) Act; and the Building and Other Construction Workers Welfare Cess Act. These Acts provide for regulating the employment and conditions of service, safety and health and welfare measures for the construction workers. Under these Acts, welfare funds have to be set up at the state level by levying a cess of 1 to 2 per cent on all construction works. The funds are intended to provide financial assistance to the families of workers in the case of accidents, old age pension, housing loans, payment of insurance premiums, children's education, and medical and maternity expenses, among other expenses. Most states have constituted Welfare Boards, and have notified a one per cent cess along with the central government. So far, a total amount of ₹ 8127.3 crore has been collected as cess by the state governments, though a sum of only ₹ 1081.2 crore has been spent, which indicates a rather slow progress in the preparation and implementation of schemes by the state governments.

Finally, it may be noted that the National Social Assistance Programme (NSAP), which is, in principle, aimed at BPL households rather than informal sector workers, in practice, covers a significant fraction of the population concerned. For instance, the most important component of the NSAP, that is, the Indira Gandhi National Old Age Pension Scheme, which was launched in 2007, reported a total of 22.7 million beneficiaries in October 2012 (MoL&E, 2013: 77). Under this scheme, an amount of ₹ 200 is provided as pension to all BPL citizens above the age of 60 years, with the amount being ₹ 500 for persons aged above 80 years. Further, the states have been asked to add to the central government's per capita grant of ₹ 200 per month, and some states have already implemented these instructions.

A new co-contributory pension scheme called 'Swawlamban' was launched by the central government under the New Pension Scheme (NPS) in September 2010 in order to encourage workers from the informal sector to voluntarily save for their retirement. The central government contributes a sum of ₹ 11,000 to each eligible NPS subscriber, who, in turn, contributes a minimum of ₹ 1000 per annum under the scheme. The Government's contribution is available for five years till 2016-17. Till November 2012, an enrolment of 1.13 million was reported to have been done and over 7 million workers from the informal sector are expected to benefit from the scheme by 2016-17 (MoL&E, 2013: 77).

6.3.2 Initiatives by the State Governments

As mentioned earlier, since the issue of labour is included in the Concurrent List of the Indian Constitution, both the central and state governments have the power to legislate on this subject. As has been observed in the case of the central government, most state governments too have made limited efforts to introduce social security schemes for informal sector workers. A few such initiatives undertaken in various states are described below.

> There has been limited effort by both the central and state governments to introduce social security schemes for informal sector workers.

The state of Kerala has been at the forefront with respect to the welfare of the unorganized workers. It has established over two dozen welfare funds covering informal workers such as agricultural labourers, toddy tappers, coir workers, construction workers, and so on. Most of these welfare funds have statutory backing. They may be classified, in terms of their financing, into two groups, depending on whether they do or do not function with the financial support of the state government. Almost all of them entail a contribution, even if a nominal sum, by the workers. The contributions are collected directly from employers wherever they are identifiable, or raised through a cess when the employers are not visible or are transient. In terms of coverage, the core contingencies taken care of are illness, old age and death. However, many of the funds contain 'children's education' as a notable benefit and very often also include support for the 'marriage of daughters'. 'Funeral expense' is yet another item that finds a place in many welfare funds.

Tamil Nadu is the next most progressive state in terms of social security coverage and benefits offered to the informal sector workers. The occupations covered here include construction workers, washermen, hairdressers, tailors, palm tree workers, handicraft workers, footwear and leather workers, tannery workers, handloom workers, taxi and auto rickshaw drivers, and artists. Initially nine occupation-specific welfare funds and boards were created for the above-mentioned groups, which were later consolidated into the Manual Workers Social Security and Welfare Board in 2004. In addition, a separate Welfare Board for Construction Workers was established in 1995.

Apart from Kerala and Tamil Nadu, there are a number of other states wherein specific groups of informal workers have been able to secure a measure of social security for themselves. One notable and relatively successful example is that of the head-load workers engaged in loading and unloading of goods in Maharashtra, for whom the Mathadi Workers' Welfare Board was created under a legislation passed in the state in 1969. The latest available information indicates that there are around 50,000 registered employers with 1,50,000 registered workers under 39 different Mathadi Boards in the state. Apart from regulation of the conditions of work, the Board provides social security cover with respect to health and illness, accidents, injury and death, housing and the education of children. The Mathadi Boards have set up two hospitals and twelve dispensaries. However, this well-tested working organizational model does not seem to have been extended to other segments of informal workers in the state.

Andhra Pradesh enacted the Andhra Pradesh Unorganized Labour Welfare Fund Act in 2002. Around one million workers have reportedly been enrolled under the scheme, with most of them employed in small factories, shops and other similar establishments. Under the scheme, apart from the workers' contributions, the Government also provides some grants. The benefits provided under the Act include medical aid to workers, funeral expenses, and assistance for children's education.

The government in West Bengal enacted its first legislation in 2001 to benefit unorganized workers through a Provident Fund scheme. This scheme provides for the creation of a provident fund for all wage and self-employed workers between the ages of 18 and 55 years, subject to an income ceiling. There is a worker contribution of ₹ 20 per month with a matching amount contributed by the state government. However, not more than 5 per cent of all informal workers in the state had been covered by 2007. West Bengal also enacted a Building and Construction Workers (Regulation of Employment and Conditions of Service) Act in 2004, in line with the corresponding Central Act of 1996. A Board was then set up to implement the Act but its activities are yet to achieve a significant scale.

Gujarat has established two important institutional mechanisms for providing social security and welfare to the unorganized workers. One of them is the Gujarat Rural Workers Welfare Board, which administers four insurance schemes for particular groups of workers, providing some financial compensation in the event of death or disability. The other is the Welfare Scheme for Salt Workers, which provides assistance for establishing healthcare centres and children's crèches at worksites, and offers financial assistance for housing. The state government has recently taken the initiative of establishing *a department for unorganized sector workers* with a view to improving the welfare and social security of these workers. Although it is too early to evaluate the functioning of this new initiative, it should certainly be seen as a desirable step towards ensuring social security for informal workers.

In Madhya Pradesh, one of the notable initiatives towards providing social security to workers was the passage of the Madhya Pradesh Unorganized Sector Welfare Act in 2003. Under this Act, two Welfare Boards have been set up—one each for the rural and urban areas. The social security cover provided under these two boards encompasses old age pension, family and disability assistance, and assistance for housing and education of children.

Most other states do not have any statutorily backed social security provisioning, specially for meeting the contingent social security needs of informal workers. A few of the states, however, have schemes for extending assistance of one kind or another, but they have made only limited progress.

6.3.3 Unorganized Workers Social Security Act 2008

As is evident from the schemes described above, India has had a long tradition of State-sponsored social security initiatives. However, these initiatives have been fragmented, their coverage has been limited in terms of both workers and contingencies, and their delivery has often been ineffective. In this context, the constitution of the National Commission for Enterprises in the Unorganized Sector (NCEUS) in 2005 was an extremely welcome move, as the agenda of the Commission was to examine the problems faced by enterprises and workers in the unorganized sector, as also to provide for the extension of coverage of social security to the unorganized sector workers.

In its first report, entitled, *Social Security for Unorganized Workers* (NCEUS, 2006), the Commission addressed this issue in detail and recommended a universal (that is, one covering all unorganized workers) national minimum social security framework. The NCEUS scheme offered three types of social security cover: (i) health cover to take care of illness of the workers and members of the family and maternity benefit to the spouse or self; (ii) accident or death of the registered workers; and (iii) old age pension for those belonging to poor households and provident funds to those falling outside this segment. The minimum package to be statutorily provided by the central government could be topped up by individual states by adding one or more benefits. Suggestions were also made for setting up a detailed organizational structure and dedicated fund at the national level. The Commission proposed legislation in this regard, which, after prolonged discussion and deliberations, culminated in the enactment of the Unorganized Workers' Social Security Act in 2008.

> Most state governments do not have any statutorily backed social security provision for meeting the needs of the informal workers.

Although the Unorganized Workers Social Security Act (UWSSA), 2008, did not measure up to the expectations of the NCEUS, it does take forward many of its recommendations, thereby marking a departure from the past on the much neglected issue of social protection for the unorganized workers. The main features of the UWSSA 2008 may be summarized as follows:

i. The Act covers a significant section of unorganized workers, including both self-employed and wage workers.

ii. It provides for the formulation of schemes by the central government for different sections of unorganized workers on matters relating to: i) life and disability cover; ii) health and maternity benefits; iii) old age protection, iv) any other benefit as may be determined by the central government.

iii. It provides for the formulation of schemes relating to provident fund, employment injury benefits, housing, educational schemes for children, skill upgradation, funeral assistance, and old age homes by the state governments.

iv. It provides for a National Social Security Board under the chairmanship of the Union Minister for Labour and Employment. The Board, among others, also provides for representatives of unorganized workers and employers of unorganized workers as well as persons belonging to the Scheduled Castes (SCs), Scheduled Tribes (STs), other minorities and women. The Board is empowered to recommend to the central government suitable schemes for different sections of the unorganized workers, monitor implementation of schemes, and advise the central government on matters relating to the administration of the Act. There is also provision for the constitution of similar Boards at the State level.

V. Realizing the critical deficiency in the database relating to unorganized workers and the need for such information for proper monitoring, the Act prescribes record-keeping functions by the District Administration with the help of the District Panchayats in rural areas and urban local bodies in urban areas.

vi. Provision has also been made for the setting up of Workers' Facilitation Centres to disseminate information on social security schemes available to them and to facilitate the registration of workers by the district administration and enrolment of unorganized workers.

vii. The Act, in Schedule I, lists ten social security schemes for unorganized workers and provides for the inclusion of more such schemes from time to time.

The central rules under the Act have since been framed and the Act came into force with effect from 16 May 2009. Under the Act, the National Social Security Board has been constituted and some states have already constituted their respective Social Security Boards.

The ten schemes included in the Schedule I of the Act are the: (i) Indira Gandhi National Old Age Pension Scheme, (ii) National Family Benefit Scheme, (iii) Janani Suraksha Yojana, (iv) Handloom Weavers' Comprehensive Welfare Scheme, (v) Handicraft Artisans' Comprehensive Welfare Scheme, (vi) Pension to Master Craftspersons, (vii) National Scheme for Welfare of Fishermen and Training and Extension, (viii) Janashree Bima Yojana, (ix) Aam Aadmi Bima Yojana (AABY), or Life Insurance Scheme for Common People, and (x) Rashtriya Swasthya Bima Yojana (National Health Insurance Scheme). The first eight of these ten schemes are existing ones while the last two are relatively new schemes that were announced a few months before the Act was passed. It is important to note that except the schemes for handloom weavers, handicraft artisans, fishermen and landless labour households, the eligibility in all the other schemes is based not on the unorganized/informal work status of the person but on whether those concerned belong to BPL households. We shall briefly discuss the RSBY and the other new scheme, *viz.*, the AABY here.

6.3.3.1 Rashtriya Swasthya Bima Yojana

The Rashtriya Swasthya Bima Yojana (RSBY) has been operational since 1 April 2008, and was later made part of the schedule of ten schemes under the UWSSA. Under the scheme, all workers in the unorganized sector belonging to the BPL category and their families are covered for healthcare. The scheme has attractive features such as: (i) no premium to be paid by the beneficiary since that will be provided by the central and state governments in the ratio of 75:25, (ii) coverage of five members in a household, (iii) provision of cashless insurance cover of up to ₹ 30,000 per annum, and (iv) dealing with migration through the smart card system, which would entitle the beneficiary to avail of hospital services in any designated hospital across the country. All pre-existing diseases are covered, with additional coverage of transportation cost of ₹ 100 per visit. Subsequently, the scheme was also extended to cover building and other construction workers, MGNREGA beneficiaries who have worked for 15 days or more, and railway coolies and vendors, *beedi* workers, and domestic workers, apart from the BPL families.

> RSBY, covering poor households and some other vulnerable groups, is an important initiative for extending financial risk protection against high healthcare expenditure. However, its design remains a matter of concern as it excludes a large number of other vulnerable segments and covers only hospitalization benefits. There is a need for upskiling this scheme in terms of both coverage and benefits.

RSBY is an important initiative for extending financial risk protection against high healthcare expenditure, among the poor and vulnerable households. The scale and coverage of the scheme is huge in absolute terms. The scheme offers cashless hospitalization facilities. During its five years of operation, the RSBY has managed to cover more than 34 million families and has emerged as the largest health insurance scheme globally (RSBY Connect Newsletter, April 2013) and has provided financial support to about 5.2 million hospitalized cases across the country since its inception. Recent data suggests that the scheme has been instrumental in reducing financial barriers for access to the required services among the households enrolled under the scheme; hospitalization rates have increased significantly among the beneficiaries, if compared with population groups with similar economic profile (that is, the poorest 40 per cent of the population) during the pre-RSBY period. From the perspective of universal coverage though, the design of the RSBY remains a matter of concern. By restricting its coverage to those in possession of 'BPL cards', and some other select occupational groups like REGS workers, the scheme excludes other vulnerable segments such as those engaged in low-income and informal employment. Recent studies (IHD, 2012) have also found low awareness and enrolment in RSBY among both migrant households or those engaged in informal occupations. While the RSBY support of ₹ 30,000 for a family of five is an important source of financial risk-pooling among the poor, the amount may be inadequate for paying for major illnesses or surgical procedures, and there are risks of 'unnecessary' or rather trivial illness episodes being disproportionately covered, or of dilution of the impacts. There is need for a flexible design, which could possibly accommodate potentially catastrophic cases keeping in view the economic capacity of the insured persons in a scaled-up RSBY. Taking due note of these considerations, the RSBY is experimenting with suitable mechanisms to extend out-patient care coverage in addition to offering the present hospitalization benefits.

6.3.3.2 Aam Aadmi Bima Yojana

The Aam Aadmi Bima Yojana (Insurance Scheme for Common People) was launched in October 2007 and later brought under the schedule of UWSSA. It provides for insurance to the head of the family of rural landless households against natural death as well as accidental death and partial or permanent disability. In addition, it also provides for a scholarship benefit for children of the members of the AABY, to the tune of ₹ 100 per month for two children studying in standards 9th to 12th. The premium of ₹ 200 is shared by a Central Fund created for the purpose and the state governments on equal basis. The benefits under the scheme include a cover of ₹ 30,000 in case of natural death and ₹ 75,000 in case of death due to accident or fatal permanent disability (₹ 37,500 in case of partial disability). More than 17.7 million lives were covered under the AABY as on 31 March 2012.

6.4 The Way Forward: Steps Towards a National Minimum Universal Social Security or Social Protection Floor

It is clear from the above account of the evolution of social security in India that until recently the primary focus of the statutory provisioning of protection and benefits has been on workers in the organized sector. Practically all the conventionally covered contingencies, including illness, maternity, injuries and disabilities due to accidents at work, old age, and death, have been provided for in the case of these workers. There is, however, no provision for unemployment except in a limited way through retrenchment and lay-off compensation in the event of job loss of workers in relatively larger-sized establishments. The adequacy of the benefits could be questioned, in spite of periodic revisions. The implementation of laws and schemes leaves much to be desired in terms of both the effective coverage of all eligible establishments and workers, on the one hand, and the delivery of benefits to the eligible workers, on the other. It must, however, be pointed out that constant efforts are being made to extend coverage and improve the delivery of social security schemes, as for example, in the case of the Employees State Insurance and Provident Fund schemes.

Implementation of laws and schemes leaves much to be desired in terms of both the effective coverage of all eligible establishments/workers and the delivery of benefits to the eligible workers.

The workers in the unorganized sector—wage earners in small establishments and the self-employed in farming and petty trade, processing and services—as well as informal workers in the organized sector have by and large remained outside the purview of the statutorily provided social security benefits against different contingencies of work and life. The main reasons for this relative neglect are stated to be twofold: first, the lack of resources and second, difficulties in implementing schemes for a large mass of dispersed, variegated and diversely employed workers. The former reason has lost most of its validity today with a rapidly growing economy. The experience of implementing many programmes and schemes in the areas of poverty alleviation and social protection among the poor, unorganized and self-employed over the past few years has provided counter-arguments where the second reason is concerned. However, there is clearly urgent need of innovative design and better implementation from which the country cannot escape.

The recent law on social security for unorganized workers, however, discussed above, represents an important step forward as compared with previous policies in this area. However, the main programmes that are presently being implemented under this law suffer from an important restriction, in that the benefits offered under them are confined to BPL households. This leads to serious handicaps due to two reasons. First, the process of identification of BPL households is deeply flawed; and second, large numbers of vulnerable workers and their families in the unorganized sector, who live precariously just above the poverty line, are excluded from the purview of benefits. If this restriction is removed, considerable progress can be made towards providing adequate protection to all informal workers.

It now seems feasible to work towards universal social security coverage, and the incorporation of protection against the basic contingencies of illness, maternity, disability and death at work, and old age to all workers. It thus seems both desirable and practical to implement the following measures:

(i) Extending the non-contributory old age pension schemes at a reasonable level to the old-age population, including the physically disadvantaged and widows;

(ii) Providing access to health services to the poor, either through public provision as recommended by the Planning Commission High Level Committee, or through a social health insurance scheme such as the RSBY, or both; and

(iii) Expanding within a specified period of time the Unorganized Sector Workers Social Security Act, 2008, in order to ensure that it guarantees statutory and universal provision of national minimum social security.

Social security, in the form of an assured social minimum, can promote self-employed workers, lacking individual or household secuirty, to undertake more productive albeit risky investments.

In addition, the role of social security needs to be re-conceptualized. Hitherto, it has been seen as a means of promoting the well-being of workers and their households falling below some not-so-well-defined minimum level, and in various contingencies. India, however, is an economy that is rapidly undergoing change. It is demonstrating shifts, even if at a relatively slow pace, out of agriculture into various forms of non-agricultural work. There are increasing incidences of migration of various types, including circular migration. In addition, land is being taken over for various mineral and industrial projects with the consequent destruction of older livelihoods. In all these situations, universal social security could play a significant role in making the transitions easier and less painful for workers. There is need for more and newer kinds of jobs, though meanwhile social security can facilitate the transitions from old to new jobs and occupations (Nathan, 2012; Kanbur, 2003). Social security, in the form of an assured social minimum, can promote the self-employed workers, lacking individual or household security in undertaking more productive investments, which are also likely to be more risky. The issue of social security, therefore, needs to be re-conceptualized not only as a mechanism of social protection but also as one that promotes and permits various transitions that are underway in the economy. Expenditure on social security could thus be seen as a productive social investment and not merely as transfer payments. Universal social security, in the form of an assured social minimum, could help shake off the inertia and mindset which oppose change as a risky proposition. It could also facilitate greater flexibility in the labour market as has been mentioned in Chapter 5.

One of the key questions in the debates on BSS, as also on the subjects of an assured social minimum, or a SPF, has been: Can India afford to have such an assured minimum? While we will return to this question *per se* later, here it is necessary to turn around this question: Can India afford not to have an assured social minimum? It is important to provide a social minimum to enable workers to not merely navigate through various contingencies, like a fall in the market for the goods or services produced, but also to successfully face the various transitions that the economy is undergoing. With an assured social minimum, such changes in livelihoods and locations can be undertaken with less cost.

> It is desirable to work towards universal social security coverage, and the incorporation of protection against the basic contingencies of illness, maternity, disability and death at work, and old age to all workers.

An issue that has dominated the debates on social security in India in recent years is that of cash transfer versus the types of transfers.[1] It has been argued by several experts that the introduction of cash transfer in the major programmes of the government with respect to social security could lead to huge savings, which can then be used for other programmes, besides ensuring more effective reach in terms of its target audience. While programmes like Bolsa Familia in Brazil and Opportunidades in Mexico have been generally successful, the blind imitation of these programmes could prove to be counter-productive, as each country has its own specific situations and needs. In a country as complex and diverse as India with huge remote and inaccessible areas, there cannot at present be universal sustainability of cash transfer. An obvious limitation in India is its limited banking network. While one needs to constantly move ahead, at the same time, there should not be hesitation in first experimenting with a few specific schemes with regard to their coverage, nature of recipients, delivery costs and others associated benefits and then extending it to other schemes, if they are proven to be effective.

Recent estimates suggest that it is feasible to finance and implement a system of social security so as to provide a SPF in phases. Srivastava (2013) estimates that both central and state government expenditures on major social protection-related sectors were about 5.25 per cent of the GDP in 2010-11, having increased from 4.42 per cent in 1995-96. The additional average financial requirements under different entitlement schemes to bring all up to the level of the SPF, range between 1 and 3.5 per cent of the GDP in 2013-14 to between 2.26 and 4.37 per cent of the GDP in 2021-22, when the various schemes would be fully in place.

If a rough calculation were to be made on the basis of the national poverty benchmark of ₹ 1000 in urban areas and ₹ 816 in rural areas per capita per month for 2011-12 (Planning Commission, 2013), the estimated total annual budget for providing 90 per cent of the rural population and 80 per cent of the urban population would be ₹ 92 lakh crore, which would account for 9.7 per cent of the GDP in 2012-13. It should be noted that the average social protection expenditure of middle income countries is 8.9 per cent of the GDP (ILO, 2011, *World Social Security Report*, Table 8.2, p. 82), while in India, it is less than half of that average. Such a social minimum consumption would replace and consolidate the numerous existing schemes rather than being envisaged as an addition to the latter.

An important question to be considered in this regard is: Are the fiscal resources for the required expenditures available? The answer would be: Surely

1. See Standing (2012) for a review of the issues in India and Hanlon, *et al.* (2010) for an international review of related issues.

not on the basis of the existing tax system. There have been calls (such as by the Kelkar Committee Report, 2012) to widen and deepen the tax base. The tax to GDP ratio in India is not only lower than in countries of comparable GDPs, but it has also declined in recent years (Srivastava, 2013). The resources for providing a Social Protection Floor could be procured provided the tax to GDP ratio is increased to a level similar to that in other countries of a similar per capita GDP. What is needed is the political voice to make universal social security a reality. However, this political voice also needs to be backed by an appropriate design so that social security can achieve both the goals of providing a Social Protection Floor and contributing to the development process, while also achieving other goals such as enabling a shift to higher-value activities in self-employment, easing the pains of changes in the economic structure, increasing gender and social inclusion, and promoting formalization of the economy. Combined with better public provision of educational and medical services, a universal and portable social protection floor could thus function as an important instrument in pushing the economy on to the high road of not only rapid but also more inclusive and sustainable growth.

Combined with better public provision of educational and medical services, a universal and potable social protection floor could thus function as an important instrument in pushing the economy on to the high road of not only rapid but also more inclusive and sustainable

7

Employment Strategies, Policies and Programmes

7.1 Employment in Development Strategy

Employment has been a part of the development agenda in India since the very beginning of development planning after Independence. The approaches and policies adopted for employment generation have, however, varied with changing perceptions and conditions. During the early years of planning, the strategy of industrialization-based growth was expected to generate adequate employment to absorb the moderately growing labour force (Papola, 2008). The Plans laid out directions for overall and sectoral development in a medium-term perspective for promoting faster economic growth with special emphasis on employment-intensive sectors like the small scale industry (Planning Commission, 1956; 1962). Employment generation in the 1950s was thus perceived as part of the processes of faster growth, and these perceptions marked the strategy adopted for employment in the 1960s as well. However, by the mid-1970s, it was clear that the achievements relating to growth and employment had fallen far short of expectations. The overall growth of the economy was much less (3.5 per cent) than expected and even the employment growth was too little to absorb growth in the labour force (2.5 per cent), resulting in the growth of unemployment and persistence of poverty among more than one-half of India's population.

7.1.1 Focus on Employment during the 1980s and 1990s

Recognizing the urgency to address the problem of growing unemployment as well as of persistent poverty, the Fifth Five Year Plan (1974-79) envisaged a re-orientation of the development strategy towards employment-oriented growth. It introduced special anti-poverty and employment generation programmes. However, by the mid-1980s, the unemployment situation worsened further, thereby necessitating the implementation of the Seventh Five Year Plan (1985-90) to place generation of productive employment at the centre of development strategy (Planning Commission, 1985: 23).

The focus on employment continued during the Eighth Plan (1992-1997), which adopted a strategy for achieving a high rate of growth along with an emphasis on employment generation by promoting the growth of employment-intensive sectors. The Ninth Plan (1997-2002) reiterated the employment-oriented strategy by emphasizing that growth could be made more employment-friendly by 'concentrating on sectors, sub-sectors and technologies that are more labour-intensive, in regions characterized by a higher incidence of unemployment and under-employment' (Planning Commission, 1998: 14).

> Employment generation in the 1950s and 1960s was largely perceived as part of the process of faster growth. However, since the mid-1970s, the planning process envisaged a re-orientation of the development strategy towards employment-oriented growth and target employment and poverty alleviation programmes.

The slow growth in employment in the 1990s, despite a relatively high growth in GDP, led to renewed urgency among the planners to focus on employment by the end of the 1990s. The Planning Commission constituted two Committees in quick succession (a Task Force on Employment Opportunities in 1999, and a Special Group on Targeting 10 Million Employment Opportunities Per Year in 2001) to examine the trends and potential for employment generation, and to suggest a strategy for creating employment opportunities in order to attain the goal of employment for all within a specified period of time. Their assessments and recommendations (Planning Commission, 2001; 2002a) were used in the formulation of the Tenth Plan (2002-2007). This Plan also took into account the fact that mere job growth is not sufficient to address the issue of persisting poverty among more than one-fourth of the workers, commonly termed as the 'working poor', which was mainly the outcome of low levels of productivity and poor skill endowments among them. The strategy, therefore, had to be re-designed for approaching the issue of employment generation on two fronts: (i) accelerating the growth of employment in the formal segment, and (ii) improving the quality of jobs (in terms of the productivity, earnings and protection of workers) in the unorganized segment. A number of special programmes pertaining to different sectors were introduced, particularly in the agriculture sector and related activities, small and medium enterprises, the non-farm rural sector and social sectors like education and healthcare, while policy changes for the faster development of sectors of high labour intensity like construction, tourism, information and communication technology and financial services were also envisaged.

The Tenth Plan period (2002-2007) witnessed the creation of about 47 million employment opportunities, which was quite close to the target of 50 million (Planning Commission, 2008: 92). However, in view of the need for long-term employment growth and enhancing the quality of employment, this expansion left much to be desired. During the period 1999-2000 to 2004-05, the number of unemployed increased by about 8 million and the entire growth was limited to the sphere of informal employment (NCEUS, 2009). The Eleventh Plan (2007-2012), therefore, called for more 'inclusive' growth and envisaged employment as a central element of such growth. While the Plan set a target of generating 58 million employment opportunities, the emphasis since then has been on the productivity and income aspects of employment, in order to address the problems of the working poor, and to effect improvements in the employability of the poor through the implementation of a concerted and large-scale programme for training and for upgradation of skills, particularly among the poor (Planning Commission, 2008). The achievement of the Eleventh Plan in the area of employment generation has been less than satisfactory. There has been an addition of only 2.76 million job opportunities during the period 2004-05 to 2009-10. Although for the first time, there has been an absolute decline in the number of unemployed by 1.8 million between 2004-05 and 2009-10, this has been largely associated with the increased enrolment in educational institutions, and is also partly due to a decline in the participation of women in the labour force. The Twelfth Plan (2012-2017) reiterates the centrality of employment creation for achieving faster and more inclusive growth. The Plan has set the target of creation of 33.8 million jobs. It proposes to make the manufacturing sector a growth engine for employment generation (Planning Commission, 2012).

7.2 Macroeconomic Policies and Employment

The integration of the employment objective with the overall growth strategy is, however, a much aspired goal, which is rarely achieved. The employment generation strategy has, therefore, primarily focused on emphasizing the faster growth of sectors with a high employment potential in order to ensure a relatively higher employment content of aggregate growth. Certain provisions of macroeconomic and sectoral policies are also often used to help promote employment. Although the primary objectives of macroeconomic policies are aimed at controlling inflation, sustaining public expenditure, and attaining fiscal balance, but these policies through monetary and fiscal measures can also affect employment. The use of certain fiscal and credit instruments for supporting the sectors and activities with high employment potential have always been an integral part of economic policies. Tax exemptions and concessions to small-scale industries and decentralized sectors like handicrafts and handlooms are among notable examples of such a support. Credit quotas and lower rates of interest for small and rural industries have also been part of the package of assistance in view of their promotion and development of the employment objective as well (Papola, 2008).

The New Economic Policy, with market-led growth, initiated since 1991, had envisaged to generate a substantial employment by restructuring of production in favour of labour-intensive activities. However, evidences indicate that this expectation has not been realized despite relatively high growth.

7.2.1 *Economic Liberalization and Employment*

During the first four decades of planning in India, credit and fiscal policies were often used for promoting employment by targeted and priority sector lending, by tax and other fiscal incentives, to promote labour-intensive and small industries, and to stimulate industrialization and employment growth in the backward regions. Beginning with 1991, there have been fundamental changes in the content of, and approach to economic policy. The New Economic Policy, initiated in 1991, was aimed at achieving stabilization in the short run and structural adjustment in the long run. The stabilization policies were seen on two fronts: the fiscal policy and balance of payments. The structural adjustment policies aimed at bringing about a series of changes in the existing industrial and trade policies that would lead to a shift from public sector-led investment and growth to market-led private domestic and foreign investment, with an emphasis on efficiency and competitiveness as the drivers of growth. It was argued that liberalization of trade, finance and an increased role for market-driven growth would not only generate a higher rate of output growth but would also lead to a restructuring of production in favour of labour-intensive activities and, therefore, also substantially contribute to an increase in employment. Evidence, however, indicates that this expectation has not been realized despite the achievement of relatively high growth.

The New Economic Policy hardly accorded any priority to employment generation. In fact, the change in macroeconomic policies from inward-oriented public sector-led growth to market-driven outward-oriented liberalization since 1991 resulted in a kind of jobless growth in the 1990s. Under the regime of economic reforms, macroeconomic policies have sometimes led to actions that militated against the goal of employment creation as part of the development strategy. The compulsions to reduce public expenditure in order to contain the fiscal deficit resulted in a reduction in budgetary provisions for employment programmes in the 1990s. Similarly, policies aimed at the reduction of subsidization in interest rates and the non-performing assets (NPAs) of banks also had an adverse impact on the availability and cost of credit for employment-intensive sectors like small and rural industries. However, such instances of conflicts between the objective of employment creation and macroeconomic policies have been few and prevailed for shorter periods, and public expenditure and conducive policy initiatives to promote employment have largely been restored (Papola, 2008).

Foreign direct investment (FDI) increased from 0.3 per cent of the GDP in 1991 to over 3 per cent in 2010. Most of it, however, has been concentrated in the sectors pertaining to chemicals, engineering, transport equipment, and fuel, and very little in the labour-intensive sectors like textiles and clothing. Some of the employment-intensive sectors that attracted a significant inflow of foreign investment during the period 1991-2003 are food processing and services. Although estimates of employment generated through foreign investment are not available, yet the sectoral pattern of investment indicates that the magnitude of jobs directly generated by this process may not be very large. It is, however, expected that its secondary (indirect) impact on employment generation would be significant.

The economic reforms process also resulted in a sharp increase in capital intensity in the organized manufacturing sector, particularly since the latter half of the 1990s. This has been noticed in as many as 47 out of the 51 three-digit industry categories. Interestingly, labour intensity declined not only in the case of capital-intensive industrial units but also in labour-intensive units during the post-reform period (Das, *et al.*, 2009). The relative importance of labour-intensive units in output has also declined during the post-reform period. This also implies that there has been a labour-saving bias in the development process and that the benefits of the resulting increase in labour productivity have largely accrued to capital in the form of profits.

The recent global financial crisis and consequent recession in the developed countries have had an adverse impact on employment in the export-oriented labour-intensive industries like diamond polishing, gems and jewellery, textiles and garments, and leather products, among others. With this situation in mind, the government offered some stimulus packages, which included a reduction in interest rates and an interest rate subvention of 2 per cent to employment-intensive export industries, as also a reduction in duties and an increase in subsidies for exports to select industries.

7.2.2 Trade Policy and Employment

With the adoption of the new economic policy and reforms, characterized by deregulation and liberalization of the trade regime, the exports sector has, of late, been seen as an important source of employment. Trade policy has thus become, for the first time, an important instrument not only for achieving faster growth, but also for facilitating job creation on a larger scale. Trade and the inflow of investment are expected to boost employment in a labour-abundant developing country like India in two major ways: by accelerating the growth rate, and by offering a comparative advantage based on exports and investment in labour-intensive industries. Similar policies had earlier governed the inflow of foreign investment as well. These policies protected employment in industries, but at the same time, they also engendered inefficiency in production and restricted the faster growth of sectors with a comparative advantage and potential for larger productive employment generation. These policies have, however, undergone a sea change, particularly since 1991. The new policies in the realm of trade and investment are characterized by a rapid reduction in tariff rates, the removal of quantitative restrictions, and the opening up of most sectors for FDI and the granting of permission for portfolio investments and automatic approval for up to 100 per cent foreign equity in certain areas.

What has been the experience of the trade policy reforms in India, and what are the emerging trends and their implications with respect to employment? There has been a steady rise in the external trade sector of the Indian economy over the past two decades. The share of trade (exports plus imports) in the GDP has increased from around 15 per cent in 1980 to over 42 per cent in 2009-10. Exports as a percentage of the GDP have also grown considerably.

> There has been labour-saving bias in the development process and the benefits of the resulting increase in labour productivity have largely accrued to capital in the form of profits.

Employment growth, as noted earlier, has been slow in the aggregate, averaging to around 2 per cent during the 1980s, and even lower during the 1990s, but employment in the manufacturing sector has grown reasonably fast, averaging to around 2.5 per cent per annum. As regards the manufacturing sector, while there was no significant difference between the employment growth in export-oriented industries and that between import-competing industries during the 1980s, the employment performance of export-oriented industries was significantly better during the 1990s: employment in these industries grew at the rate of 3.36 per cent per annum, as against the corresponding 2.67 per cent in import-competing industries during the period 1990-97 (Goldar, 2002; Ghose, 2003). Low skill-intensive products dominated the sector of manufactured exports: industries which could be characterized as medium-low or low technology ones accounted for 75 per cent of the total manufactured exports during both the decades of the 1990s as well as the 1980s (Ghose, 2003). However, since 2000-01, there has been a perceptible shift in the composition of trade—from labour-intensive light manufacturing, to heavy manufacturers and petroleum products. The share of labour-intensive industries such as textiles, ready-made garments, gems, jewellery, leather and handicrafts declined from nearly from 24 per cent in 2000-01 to 11 per cent by 2009-10 (MoF, 2010). The conventional theoretical expectation that a labour-surplus developing country like India has a comparative advantage and would, therefore, specialize in the exports of low-skill labour-intensive exports does not seem to hold any longer.

In recent years, information technology-based services have been projected as being important among the fast-growing exports, implying the rapid growth of employment in this sector. Services like professional services, and software agencies, among others, have seen a rapid growth, accounting for a major part of the growth of non-factor services in the invisible account in the balance of payments. Software exports alone were growing at the rate of 35.6 per cent per year during the period 2000-01 to 2004-05. However, in the wake of the global economic crisis, this growth of software exports declined to 25 per cent during the year 2008-09 (GoI-MoF, 2009). The exports of commercial services increased more than three-fold over the period 1980-97, in terms of US dollars (World Bank, 2000), and increased at the rate of 11 per cent per annum during the period 2000-06 (GoI-MoF, 2008).

All these facts and figures show that the positive impact of liberalization-induced expansion of trade on employment, in accordance with the pattern of the Heckscher–Ohlin notion of comparative advantage with regard to labour-intensive aspects, should not be taken for granted in India.

> The positive impact of liberalization-induced expansion of trade on employment, in accordance with the comparative advantage of labour-intensive aspects, should not be taken for granted in India.

7.2.2.1 Tariff Policy

An appropriate tariff policy tailored to the specific requirement of manufacturing could promote competitiveness, the incentive for investment, employment generation and an increase in exports. One of the widely shared views is that India suffers from an 'inverted tariff policy', implying that the tariff structure is biased against intermediate and component imports, and favourable to end-products, particularly in certain lines of production like electronic hardware, electrical equipments (FICCI, 2013), which are also labour-intensive. In comparison to India's inverted tariff structure, crucially for electronic products resulting in the import of these labour-intensive products instead of domestic production, China's exports, on the other hand, represent the processing trade, with no tariffs charged on intermediate imports and the consequent promotion of a huge employment potential through the assembling of final products for exports. Bringing about appropriate changes in the present inverted tariff structure could prove to be an important trade-related policy measure for promoting the assembly of electronics and other similar products.

7.3 Sectoral Policies

In order to achieve the objective of employment growth, some sector-specific policies were also introduced for inducing faster growth of relatively more labour-intensive sectors within the overall development strategy. The Task Force on Employment Generation (Planning Commission, 2001) identified four employment-intensive areas—agriculture and allied activities, food processing industries, small-scale industries, and services—which were given strategic impetus during the Tenth Plan. The Eleventh Plan also continued its focus on promoting these employment-intensive sectors with an increased emphasis on improving productivity through technological upgradation, provision of credit, and the development of both infrastructure and skills.

7.3.1 The Industrial Policy

The industrial policy reforms undertaken during the 1990s were based on the premise that the State intervention by way of assigning a primary role to the public sector in promoting industrialization in basic and key industries, and regulation of private domestic and foreign investment in a large number of industries, was the fundamental reason for the general inefficiency, lack of competitiveness and slow growth afflicting the economy. The policy measures included the removal of industrial licensing for investment, opening up of all but a few strategic areas, which were earlier reserved for the public sector, and according more primacy to competition law over the Monopolies and Restrictive Trade Practices (MRTP) Act. Even as regards the policy for reservation for the small-scale sector, a number of items were de-reserved. The influx of FDI was permitted in a large number of industries. Over the years, the scope of automatic approval was enlarged, 100 per cent foreign ownership was allowed in a number of industries, and majority ownership was allowed in all sectors barring banks, insurance, telecommunications and airlines. However, many of these major changes in industrial policy hardly showed any concern on the impact of these measures on employment, leave alone any specific incentives for employment. On the contrary, the zeal to invite private investment often resulted in deliberate laxity in the administration of protective labour regulatory measures. The continuous decline in public sector employment, coupled with only a small level of growth in organized employment in the private sector in the 1990s, which accelerated somewhat during the 2000s, shows that the present industrial policy regime has hardly facilitated employment generation. However, the dismantling of regulation and the State concern for employment is still not complete in the case of micro and small enterprises.

The continuous decline in public sector employment, coupled with only a small level of growth in organized employment in the private sector in the 1990s, which accelerated somewhat during the 2000s, shows that the present industrial policy regime has hardly facilitated employment generation in the country.

7.3.1.1 Relative Factor Prices

Although there have been drastic changes in the economic policy regime since 1991, and a shift from the industrial policy to market incentives as instruments of inducing investment, there are clear indications that the Indian industrial structure is taking a retrograde turn away from the ideal of a comparative advantage driven labour-intensive path to more capital intensity, which is preventing the much needed structural change that can absorb more labour. This is being blamed on the provision of wrong incentives, leading to distorted relative factor prices, thereby making the relative price of capital cheap and that of labour dear. The depreciation allowance in India has been raised to 20 per cent as against the global norm of about 10-12 per cent, thereby providing an incentive to invest in machinery and equipment-intensive production rather than in labour-intensive production. The Draft Paper on Employment Policy recognizes this and points out, "...between 1995-96 and 2003-04, while money wages rose by 35.6 per cent, the index of the cost of capital fell by 17.6 per cent. This is close to a 53 per cent point negative shift in the price of capital relative to labour, pointing to a major bias in prices that favour capital intensity (GoI-MoLE, 2010). In order to promote labour-intensive manufacturing, it is necessary to reduce the relative price of labour by public investment in areas that would increase real wages and would reduce relative labour costs."

In order to promote labour-intensive manufacturing, it is necessary to reduce the relative price of labour by public investment in areas that would increase real wages and would reduce relative labour costs.

7.3.2 Policy for Micro and Small Enterprises (MSEs)

Like in many other developing countries, Micro, Small and Medium Enterprises (MSMEs) constitute an important source of employment and income generation in India. There are nearly 26 million MSMEs in the country, which provide livelihoods to nearly 60 million people and manufacture more than 6000 products. They contribute to 40 per cent of the exports, account for 45 per cent of the gross value added in manufacturing and contribute 8.7 per cent to the GDP during the year 2009-10 (GoI-MoMSME, 2012). MSMEs generate a high employment per unit of investment. They often provide rural people and people living in isolated areas with a sustainable source of employment and also promote eco-friendly growth, especially in difficult terrains and ecologically sensitive areas.

Since the beginning, the government policy has been supportive for developing modern small scale industries (SSIs). It reserved some 800-odd products for exclusive production in SSIs. This invited criticism over the years that these measures have resulted in distortions in the growth of small enterprises and kept them apart from the formal economy. Economic reforms brought about a reversal in some of the preferential treatment being accorded to these industries. There has been a gradual de-reservation for production exclusively by SMEs with regard to 114 items. Presently, 358 items are reserved for exclusive purchase by the central government, and its PSUs from the Micro and Small Enterprises (MSEs). However, the Planning Commission Task Force on Employment Opportunities (2001) also gave important promotion policy-based suggestions to revitalize the sector. These included: (i) extension of promotion policy to services, (ii) upgradation of common infrastructure support including quality control, and (iii) elimination of harassment caused by a large number of inspection machinery, especially at state-level. Several policy initiatives were undertaken to address the pressing problems relating to access to finance, markets and sickness. The Technology Upgradation Fund Scheme (TUFS), introduced during the Tenth Plan, helped in the modernization of Small and Medium Enterprises (SMEs).

The Micro, Small and Medium Enterprises Development (MSMED) Act, 2006, provides for a statutory consultative mechanism at the national level with a balanced representation of all the sections of stakeholders, and with a wide range of advisory functions which include the establishment of specific funds for the promotion, development, and enhancement of the competitiveness of these enterprises; progressive credit policies and practices; preference to products and services of MSEs in the government procurement; and measures for the mitigation of delayed payments.

The Eleventh Plan views the MSE sector as an engine for sustained and inclusive economic growth and employment. It advocates the granting of loans to MSEs up to ₹ 5 lakh without any collateral, launching of an aggressive marketing campaign, and both infrastructure and skill development. The new initiatives for promoting the growth of MSEs include establishing a Technology Mission to promote new and emerging technologies and to upgrade existing technologies, and removing infrastructure bottlenecks in the areas of power supply, transport and roads (Planning Commission, 2008, Vol. 3). The NCEUS (2009) underscores the need to improve the existing low levels of productivity of workers in MSEs through the introduction of pro-active policies like increased investment in fixed capital, programmes of technology improvement, skill formation, and entrepreneurship development (pp.274-75).

Although the recent policy initiatives have helped in the overall growth of MSEs and have brought about changes in the structure of MSEs with an increasing share of services, and improvement in labour productivity (NCEUS, 2009), the availability of credit still remains a major problem for the growth of MSEs. The RBI (2009) reports that though the growth of credit to the SSI sector picked up in recent years, its share in the total credit to industry tended to decline over the years. Further, the share of the MSEs sector in the total priority sector advances declined from 43.7 per cent in 1998 to 18.6 per cent in 2007. The important schemes for the promotion of MSEs include an exemption in central excise duty to make MSE products price-competitive, priority sector lending to facilitate an improved credit flow to MSEs, a technology upgradation facility for all manufacturing MSEs, credit guarantee schemes for banks lending to MSEs, and the Prime Minister's

Rozgar Yojana for employment generation. The incidence of sickness and resultant closure of units is significant in the case of MSEs. This underscores a need to create an enabling environment for the development of MSEs across various regions of the country.

Incentives such as excise exemption sometimes limit the vertical growth of MSEs into medium-scale industries, simply due to the fear of loss of such exemptions. While this issue must be recognized, it is reasonable to allow MSEs to retain the benefits of excise exemption up to the prescribed limits even after they graduate to becoming medium-scale enterprises (Planning Commission, 2008, Vol. 3: 203).

7.4 Targeted Employment Programmes

After three decades of relatively slow growth, the Indian economy has moved to a high growth trajectory for over two decades now. However, the problem of under-employment, low income and poverty persists and open unemployment is on the rise. This puts a question mark on the exclusionary and inequitable nature of growth. In order to minimize deprivation and provide immediate relief to the under-employed and the unemployed, several direct employment generation programmes have been initiated. A large number of such programmes have been in operation in India, some of them on a continuous basis, and others introduced from time to time. These targeted programmes fall into three broad categories: (i) self-employment programmes, (ii) wage employment programmes, and (iii) self-employment and wage employment programmes.

7.4.1 Self-employment Programmes

Self-employment programmes started with the initiation of a loan-cum-subsidy scheme known as the Integrated Rural Development Programme (IRDP) in 1978. Alongside, two sub-programmes, namely the Training of Rural Youth for Self Employment (TRYSEM) and Development of Women and Children in Rural Areas (DWCRA) were also started. These aimed at building the capacity of youth for self-employment and at organizing women into producers' groups, respectively. All rural self-employment programmes were integrated into the Swarnajayanti Gram Swarozgar Yojana (SGSY) in 1999. The SGSY focused on micro-enterprise development by providing assistance for income-generating assets through a mix of bank credit and government subsidy. It laid an emphasis on social mobilization through the formation of self-help groups (SHGs) and their capacity building. It also incorporated various other aspects like the planning of activity clusters, build-up of infrastructure and technology, training and marketing, aspects that were found to have been neglected in IRDP. Further, it laid special emphasis on the weaker sections: 50 per cent of the SHGs have to be exclusively of women and 50 per cent of those assisted should belong to the Scheduled Castes/ Scheduled Tribes (SCs/STs).

During the last eleven years of its operation (1999-2000 to 2009-10), 3.7 million SHGs were formed and nearly 11.4 million *swarozgaris* (self-employed people) were assisted, and about 2.3 million below the poverty line (BPL) households managed to come out of poverty by the end of 2008-09. The total amount of budgetary funds available for the programme during the period 1999-2000 to 2008-09 was ₹ 17,432 crore (including both Central and state funds) (GoI-MoRD, 2009). However, only ₹ 13,230 crore or about 76 per cent of the total allocated funds were utilized. The relatively small number of assisted *swarozgaris* indicates the modest performance of the programme as compared to the huge rural workforce in need of livelihoods outside the agriculture sector. Also, there is high rate of attrition of SHGs—a large number of them fizzle out mid-way after availing of the revolving fund. Further, a significant number seem to wait for long periods before getting an opportunity to avail of the subsidy assistance.

As against a norm of 10 per cent of the total funds of the SGSY that have been allocated for skill training, an important component of the SGSY, the actual expenditure on this activity was very low, at 6 per cent of the total utilized funds during the period 1999-2000 to 2008-09. The poorer states fared worse in this regard. As a result, there has been a high incidence of untrained SHGs (GoI-MoRD, 2009). The utilization of funds for infrastructure development, which is yet another important component of the programme, is rather small. Only 16 per cent of the total funds were utilized for infrastructure development over the ten-year period of the programme. Still worse, the overall utilization rate declined over the years. Almost two-thirds of funds went in the payment of subsidies, thus making the SGSY earn the epithet of being 'subsidy-driven'! The overall credit achievement under the programme was also low, at about 50 per cent of the targets set (Planning Commission, 2008, Vol 3: 93).

An evaluation of the SGSY showed that more than two-thirds of the assisted *swarozgaris* were engaged in the primary sector—with dairy activity alone accounting for 50 per cent of the beneficiaries. The average monthly income per *swarozgari* was also very low, at ₹ 1228, even in the relatively better performing state of Andhra Pradesh (Purushotham, 2008). Notably, the performance of the SGSY was unsatisfactory in the states that had a high incidence of poverty such as Assam, Madhya Pradesh, Uttar Pradesh, Orissa, Jharkhand, Chhattisgarh, West Bengal and Bihar (GoI-MoRD, 2009). The SGSY has, however, been quite successful in the southern region because of effective bank linkages.

The lessons of implementation of self-employment programmes under the SGSY show that for poor households with negligible or low levels of education, meagre assets and dependence on seasonal low wage employment, one of the major hurdles in moving towards self-employment is the lack of not only adequate financial resources but also of skills and capacity, and sustained institutional support.

The lessons of implementation of self-employment programmes under the SGSY show that for poor households with negligible or low levels of education, meagre assets and dependence on seasonal low wage employment, one of the major hurdles in moving towards self-employment is the lack of not only adequate financial resources but also of skills and capacity, and sustained institutional support. In order to move from casual wage labour status to that of running an enterprise under the SGSY, however tiny it may be, a poor household needs considerable investment in capacity building and institutional hand-holding not only for acquiring credit but also for managing production and marketing of the produce. The SGSY has thrown up certain successful models in the form of the Kudumbashree in Kerala, the Indira Kranthi Patham (IKP) in Andhra Pradesh, and the individual household enterprise model of Gujarat (GOI-MoRD, 2009). The common features of the successful enterprises in Kerala and Andhra Pradesh include the investment of a considerable amount of effort in social mobilization, capacity building of both the household as well as the SHG, and strong political and administrative support. A social climate conducive for individual entrepreneurial activity is behind the success story of Gujarat in self-employment. While the Kerala experience could be a model for states with strong *panchayat raj* institutions (PRIs), the IKP model of Andhra Pradesh needs considerable effort in terms of social mobilization, and institutional and individual capacity building.

Learning from the limitations of the SGSY such as vast regional variations in the mobilization of the rural poor, insufficient capacity building of the beneficiaries, inadequate investments for building community institutions, and weak linkages with banks leading to low credit mobilization and low repeat financing, the government restructured the programme as the National Rural Livelihood Mission, now renamed as '*Aajeevika*' (livelihood), which was formally launched on 3 June 2011 (GoI, MoRD, 2012). *Aajeevika* focuses on building strong institutions of the poor into SHGs, their federations and livelihoods collectives at the village, block, district and state levels. It aims at promoting the larger participation of marginalized groups by ensuring that half of the beneficiaries are from SC/ST households, 15 per cent from the minorities, and 3 per cent are persons with disability. Training and skill development have also been accorded renewed priority with a provision of 15 per cent of the total budget for skill training. During the year 2011-12 (up to December 2011), 10.47 lakh *swarozgaris* were assisted, of which a large majority of 69 per cent consisted of women (GoI-MoRD, 2012).

7.4.1.1 Prime Minister's Employment Generation Programme (PMEGP)

The Prime Minister's Rozgar Yojana (PMRY) was launched in October 1993 for providing self-employment opportunities to one million educated unemployed youth in the country. It was designed to provide self-employment to more than a million persons by setting up of 700,000 micro enterprises by the educated unemployed youth. Projects up to ₹ 100,000 were covered under the scheme in the case of individuals. The cost ceiling for assistance would increase up to ₹ 100,000 for each additional member joining as a partner. An entrepreneur was required to contribute 5 per cent of the project cost as margin money in cash. The balance 95 per cent was to be sanctioned as a composite loan by the banks at the interest rates applicable to the priority sector. The Government of India provided a subsidy at the rate of 15 per cent of the project cost subject to a ceiling of ₹ 7,500 per entrepreneur. In the case of there being more than one entrepreneur, the subsidy was to be increased proportionately.

After evaluating the performance of the PMRY, the government launched a credit linked Central scheme, namely the Prime Minister's Employment Generation Programme (PMEGP) on 15 August 2008, by subsuming the two earlier schemes of the Prime Minister's Rozgar Yojana (PMRY) and the Rural Employment Generation Fund (REGF) for generating self-employment opportunities in both rural and urban areas. This scheme, which is being implemented by the Khadi and Village Industries Commission (KVIC), is estimated to have generated 37 lakh additional employment opportunities during the period 2008-09 to 2011-12, with an expected credit flow of ₹ 15,000 crore. The cost limit for setting up an enterprise under the scheme is ₹ 25 lakh for the manufacturing sector, and ₹ 15 lakh for business and service enterprises. Entrepreneurship development is an important aspect of this self-employment scheme. In view of the allocation of skill training of 3 to 10 days under the previous REGP and PMRY schemes, and the limited success of that training, this new scheme has the provision of training for two to three weeks.

There is a big gap in the demand and supply of credit for the scheme, as has been revealed in the Annual Reports of 2009-10 and 2011-12 of the Ministry of Micro, Small and Medium Enterprises. Nearly half of the applications were rejected on various grounds. Among the approved applications, about one-fourth were sanctioned loans by banks and only one-fourth of the sanctioned loans could actually be disbursed during the year 2009-10.

As a whole, the self-employment programmes have had a very limited impact on livelihoods and employment, and the amount of expenditure has been much less as compared to the overall requirements.

As a whole, the self-employment programmes have had a very limited impact on livelihoods and employment, and the amount of expenditure has been much less as compared to the overall requirements of those looking for such support. Further, the amount per beneficiary has also been meagre, except in the case of the newly introduced PMEGP. The incidence of red-tapism by banks as well as the administrative machinery have been the other factors often cited for the poor performance of these programmes. Wherever these bottlenecks have been overcome, the results have been better as in the case of the Kudumbashree programme in Kerala and SHGs in Andhra Pradesh.

7.4.2 Wage Employment Programmes

India has a long history of the implementation of labour-intensive public works for relief during natural calamities like famines. One of the earliest initiatives of wage employment as a guaranteed right was taken by the state of Maharashtra, which launched the Maharashtra Employment Guarantee Scheme (MEGS) in the mid-1970s in response to severe drought conditions. The use of labour-intensive public works as a poverty alleviation employment programme started with the National Rural Employment Programme (NREP) in 1980, which had the dual aims of providing wage income to the rural poor, and the creation of rural infrastructure. The fulfilment of these twin objectives continued in the new incarnation of NREP as the Jawahar Rozgar Yojana (JRY), which was started in 1989-90. The Rural Labour Employment Guarantee Programme (RLEGP), which was implemented along with the NREP, aimed at providing income to the landless households by guaranteeing each of them 100 days of employment per year, while the Employment Assurance Scheme (EAS), which was introduced in 1993, aimed at providing a similar guarantee of employment in the selected backward and poor areas. The Sampoorna Gram Rozgar Yojana (SGRY) integrated all rural wage employment programmes into one scheme in 2001. The SGRY was subsumed in the National Rural Employment Guarantee Scheme (NREGS) in April 2008.

The earlier wage employment programmes had limited success in providing additional employment for the under-employed in rural areas and thereby supplementing the incomes of their households. For example, the JRY and EAS together generated an equivalent of 4.4 million person years of employment during 1998-99, accounting for about 1.5 per cent of the total employment in rural areas. The poor households comprised about 4.5 per cent of the labour force under it, which is a fairly high proportion of employment, considering the fact that on a current daily basis (CDS), the proportion of rural unemployment is 7 per cent (Radhakrishna and Ray, 2006). According to various evaluation studies, the JRY and EAS generated only 11 to 17 days and 30 days, respectively, of employment per participating worker per year. Yet, the experience of the Maharashtra Employment Guarantee Scheme (MEGS), which has been implemented since the mid-1970s, shows that this programme had succeeded in both mitigating hunger and also preventing rural wages from falling to very low levels (Acharya, 1990).

The failure to build rural assets and infrastructure, even after their long tenure and the huge public expenditure incurred on them, has been one of the major criticisms levied against wage employment programmes.

The failure to build rural assets and infrastructure, even after their long tenure and the huge public expenditure incurred on them, has been one of the major criticisms levied against wage employment programmes. Several attempts have been made, primarily in terms of changes in the wage to material ratio and improvement in the planning of works, to ensure that the objective of infrastructure building is better achieved. The introduction of the Jawahar Grameen Rozgar Yojana (JGRY) in 1999, alongside the JRY and EAS, was an exercise meant to separate the two objectives of employment generation and asset building. The prime objective of the JGRY was to focus on the creation of rural infrastructure without any stipulation of the wage to material ratio, while the JRY and EAS continued with their primary objectives of supplementary wage employment to the rural poor with a stipulated 60: 40 wage-material ratio for works to be undertaken under the programme. The JRY, EAS and JGRY were, however, eventually combined into the Sampoorna Grameen Rozgar Yojana (SGRY) in 2001, which aimed to fulfil both the objectives.

7.4.2.1 Mahatma Gandhi National Rural Employment Guarantee (MGNREGA)

There has been a major shift in the provision of rural wage employment as a programme to that of a right through the enactment of the National Rural Employment Guarantee Act, 2005, now called Mahatma Gandhi National Rural Employment Guarantee Act (MGNREGA), 2005, which provides for a legally-backed employment guarantee. The programme was initiated in 200 poorest districts of the country but since April 2008, it has been extended to all the districts. The fact that it provides for a legally backed employment provision, guaranteeing 100 days of wage employment on demand at statutory minimum wages, to people in all the rural areas of the country, makes it qualitatively different from the earlier rural employment programmes for poverty alleviation. The Act further aims at creating durable assets and strengthening of a rural livelihood resource base of the rural poor. The fact that PRIs are envisaged to implement the scheme is seen as a major step towards the empowerment of the panchayats and local communities. Further, the fact that it would mobilize a large mass of the rural population in an organized manner to secure their rights to employment is seen as a great opportunity for the social and economic empowerment of weaker sections like dalits and women.

Since it is an open-ended and demand-driven programme, more resources would be made available if the demand and actual expenditure exceed the budget. The expenditure pattern in terms of labour and material cost is 60: 40 while the upper limit on the material cost is 40 and the labour cost would go up to 100. Moreover, one-third of the total employment generated should be for women.

The total expenditure incurred on the programme was ₹ 37,638 crore during the year 2011-12, which tripled from the corresponding expenditure incurred during the year 2006-07. The overall utilization of budgetary support in terms of the total expenditure on the NREGS was 87 per cent (GoI-MoRD, website). Nearly 70 per cent of the total expenditure is incurred on the payment of wages to workers.

Altogether, about 50 million households were provided employment under MGNREGA during 2011-12 (during 2009-10 and 2010-11, the corresponding figures were 52.6 million and 55 million, respectively). The total number of person-days of employment generated during 2011-12 was 2117 million (it was 2836 and 2572 million person-days during 2009-10 and 2010-11, respectively). The SCs and STs together accounted for 40 per cent of the total employment generated under the programme, which shows that the programme is reaching the needy. Close to half of the total employment generated under the programme was availed of by women workers.

Within a short period of its operation, the MGNREGA has made a substantial impact on rural employment generation.

Within a short period of its operation, the MGNREGA has made a substantial impact on rural employment generation. For instance, during its very first year of operation in 200 districts, it generated more than three times the number of person-days of employment during 2006-07 as compared to earlier schemes like the SGRY and National Food for Work Programme (NREGA Review by Prime Minister on 20 June 2007, Available at: *http://nrega.nic.in*). Various evaluation studies of the NREGS indicate that it has significantly improved the wage income levels of rural households and also reduced the distress migration (IHD, 2006, 2008; Sainath, 2008). A survey showed that most of the people in the rural areas were aware about the provision of 100 days of guaranteed employment under this scheme. However, there was a lack of awareness about the various components of the programme such as minimum wages, worksite facilities, provision of transportation in case the job is not provided within a radius of 5 km of the prospective worker's residence, and provision of unemployment allowance if no job is provided, among others. Payment of minimum wages still remains a matter of concern. In many places, delays in the payment of wages were also observed (Hirway, *et al.*, 2008). There is a huge gap between the demand and supply of employment, as reflected in the average number of person-days of employment. The stipulation of payment of unemployment allowance is still being circumvented in most of the states through an exploitation of the loopholes in the scheme (Khera, 2008).

MGNREGS appears to be reaching a large proportion of the needy and deserving population, and providing them with much-needed employment opportunities for supplementing their household incomes.

In the context of widespread underemployment and a large number of informal workers in rural India, it is encouraging to note that the MGNREGS appears to be reaching a large proportion of the needy and deserving population, and providing them with much-needed employment opportunities for supplementing their household incomes. On the basis of both secondary data as well as field data, it can be concluded that as a programme of self-selection, MGNREGA is reaching a wide category of workers, including landless labourers, small and marginal farmers, and the SC and ST population. These are the groups that are most vulnerable to poverty and deprivation, and their participation in MGNREGS has contributed to an improvement in both their employment as well as living conditions (Sharma, 2013).

Although there are regional variations, overall, there has been a very high demand for work under MGNREGA, with workers often demanding work for more than the 100 days of work per household, as stipulated under the scheme, and the local government machinery appears to be lagging behind in providing work for various reasons, including lack of technical and managerial capability. However, the workers look for regularity and continuity in the work available under the scheme. In states like Andhra Pradesh, wherein both the regularity of work and a long duration of work are ensured by adjusting the MGNREGS work to the agricultural lean season, the performance of the scheme is better than in other states where these provisions are not ensured. This enables the workers to adjust their employment calendar accordingly, in order to garner the maximum advantage from both agricultural work and public works. However, in states like Bihar and Rajasthan, there is still an overlap of MGNREGS works and agricultural season, and the net result is often a shortage of the overall in-site number of work-days, thereby resulting in workers to migrate for work during the lean agricultural season (Sharma, 2012). The lack of capacity of the PRIs, and of the associated personnel, as also the shortage of technical staff have often been found to be the major factors responsible for the poor performance of the MGNREGA in several states, particularly in the north. It has also been pointed out that not much attention has been paid to the creation of assets in the programme, and that the target of meeting the stipulated expenditure has been single-mindedly pursued. Notwithstanding these limitations, it is widely believed that this programme is much more successful than all its predecessors.

The lack of capacity of the PRIs, and of the associated personnel, as also the shortage of technical staff have often been found to be the major factors responsible for the poor performance of the MGNREGA in several states, particularly in the north.

However, there is no gainsaying the fact that MGNREGS has already succeeded in providing very substantial additional wage employment to the poor at a wage that is not lower than the prevailing wage. The result has thus been an impressive growth in wages. Nevertheless, MGNREGS has not had the expected effect of significantly reducing rural poverty because of inflation. If MGNREGS has to succeed in alleviating poverty, stimulating growth and promoting full employment, two things need to happen. In the short run, the government must find a way of using the accumulated stock of foodgrains it holds in order to curb food price inflation. Alongside, the government must also undertake to increase public investment in agriculture to ensure that food production can grow in the longer run to match the growth in demand. Further, MGNRES cannot be implemented for a long time unless it is firmly integrated with the ongoing development programmes. There is thus a need for the introduction of a lot of innovative measures to ensure the effectiveness and suitability of the programme for at least the next one decade.

7.4.3 Self-employment and Wage Employment Programmes

7.4.3.1 Swarna Jayanti Shahari Rozgar Yojana (SJSRY)

The poverty alleviation and employment generation programmes launched by the government have been mainly implemented in rural areas, which is not surprising in view of the latter's large size as well as the higher incidence of poverty there. However, with the growth in urban population, it was realized that urban areas and the poor there also need focused attention. Thus, a new urban poverty alleviation programme, namely, the Swarna Jayanti Shahari Rozgar Yojana (SJSRY) was launched on 1 December 1997 after subsuming the earlier three urban poverty alleviation schemes, namely, the Urban Basic Services for the Poor (UBSP), the Nehru Rozgar Yojana (NRY), and the Prime Minister's Integrated Urban Poverty Eradication Programme (PMIUPEP). The main aim of the programme was to provide gainful employment to the urban unemployed or under-employed by encouraging the setting up of self-employment ventures or the provision of wage employment. The SJSRY is being implemented by state/UT governments and is funded in the ratio of 75: 25 by the Centre and the states, respectively.

The SJSRY consists of two major components, namely, the: (i) Urban Self-employment Programme (USEP), and (ii) Urban Wage Employment Programme (UWEP). Under USEP, the urban poor are given assistance for setting up their enterprises. Special attention is provided to poor women, SCs and STs through the reservation of a certain proportion of assistance for them. Under the programme, up to 30 per cent of the beneficiaries can be women. Training is also imparted to the beneficiaries under the programme for the purpose of improving their vocational skills. Since its inception till 2010-11, the total financial assistance earmarked for USEP was ₹ 4697 crore. The Central funds released for the scheme fluctuated from as low as ₹ 38.31 crore in 2001-02 to ₹ 515 crore in 2009-10. However, there has been a steady increase in the fund allocation for the programme since 2004-05 and the overall fund utilization improved significantly, by rising to more than 72 per cent. In all, 1.13 million persons were offered assistance under this scheme, including 0.44 million women, up to the year 2010-11. Disabled persons constituted about 5.5 per cent of the total beneficiaries (Ministry of Housing and Urban Poverty Alleviation, *Annual Report, 2009-10*). Skill training was also imparted to 1.87 million urban poor during the last 13-year period.

The UWEP provides wage employment to prospective BPL beneficiaries within the jurisdiction of urban local bodies by utilizing their labour for the construction of socially and economically useful public assets. This programme is implemented only in the jurisdiction of urban local bodies having a population of less than 5 lakh, as per the 1991 Census. A total of 76.13 million person-days of employment was generated under this scheme during the period 1997 to 20010-11 (Ministry of Housing and Urban Poverty Alleviation, *Annual Report, 2011-12*).

So far, however, this programme does not seem to be a visible programme for targeting the urban under-employed and unemployed. Apart from institutional and implementation-related bottlenecks, the major reason for this has been its limited coverage. In view of the size of the urban poor population of 6.71 crore, the overall budgetary support for the SJRY could hardly make any significant dent in terms of reduction of poverty and unemployment in urban areas (Rustagi *et al.*, 2009).

An assessment of the overall performance of the direct employment generation programmes indicates that the impact of the UWEP, as a whole, has been modest. In fact, except MGNREGA, all the other programmes have had a rather limited impact, primarily because of the miniscule nature of their interventions, while the universal nature of MGNREGA has naturally scaled up its coverage and impact. The other oft-cited reasons for the limited impact of these direct programmes have been the weak capacity of the implementation machinery, shortcomings in design and lack of coordination among various agencies, leakages leading to corruption, lack of awareness among the beneficiaries, and non-synergy with other development programmes. Nevertheless, the impacts of the programmes vary considerably across regions. Most of these programmes have been generally better implemented in the southern states than in the northern ones.

> In the current phase of development of the country with widespread poverty, there is strong justification to continue the direct employment generation programmes. At the same time, they should be effectively linked with the infrastructural development programmes so that they can contribute to the growth process.

A pertinent question that is often asked pertains to the proper balance between development programmes and direct employment generation programmes in the development process. Ideally, such programmes should be reduced gradually when the poverty level declines and labour markets get tightened due to the growth process and as such, they should not be seen as permanent features. However, in the current phase of development of the country, wherein widespread poverty prevails with the existence of a huge number of working poor, there is sufficient reason to continue these programmes. The larger question concerns finding ways to make them effective by linking them with the infrastructural development programmes so that they can contribute to the growth process. Strict monitoring and evaluation should be an integral component of the implementation plan of these programmes, and they should be restricted and redesigned whenever required.

7.5 Skill Development Policy and Programmes

A poor skill base is often identified as a major constraint in raising the productivity and incomes of a large number of workers in the unorganized sector (NCEUS, 2009). It is also realized that the benefits of higher rate of economic growth in India hardly reach a large majority of the workforce mainly because of their lower educational and skill attainments, which prevent them from gaining access to emerging employment opportunities.

Lack of requisite skills is also seen as an important reason for unemployment among a large number of young persons. Unemployment rates are highest not only among graduates and post-graduates belonging to general streams but also among technical diploma- and certificate-holders. It is not merely the low levels of education but also the type of education that constrains skill formation. There is a growing mismatch between the demand and supply of skills, as is evident from the number of unfilled vacancies alongside the unemployed. Although the extent of such a mismatch is not exactly known, what is convincingly argued is that the present system of education, training and skill development is neither suitably equipped nor very responsive to be able to meet the pattern of demand for various kinds of skills that is arising in the process of globalization-induced faster growth of the economy. The shortage of workers with appropriate skills in high-growth activities is thus constraining their growth (Mathur and Mamgain, 2004; Papola, 2009).

> There is a growing mismatch between the demand and supply of skills, as is evident from the number of unfilled vacancies alongside the unemployed.

Nearly 70 per cent of the Indian population is literate. As has been seen in Chapter 2, less than 30 per cent of the workers are educated (at the secondary level and above), which is much lower than in the other emerging economies. However, this scenario prevails only in respect of attainments in terms of general education. The situation is worse if one looks at the skill profile of the Indian population, particularly the youth. Only about 8 per cent of the population in the age group of 15-59 years have acquired vocational training, either formally or informally. A large part of the skill training is imparted in non-formal forms, mainly comprising hereditary and on-the-job training (Mehrotra *et al.*, 2013). Industry-wise, the highest percentage of the workforce in manufacturing, that is 27 per cent, has skill training, followed by 17.2 per cent in the services sector, and the least at 5.1 per cent, in agriculture (Mehrotra *et al.*, 2013). A generous estimate of all those who received or were receiving formal or informal vocational training in the age group of 15-59 years in 2009-10 was less than 10 per cent of the labour force (Mehrotra *et al.*, 2013).

The education policy, which aims at achieving universal access to elementary education for all children in the age group of 6-14 years under the

Sarva Shiksha Abhiyan (SSA), ensures accessibility of schools in the rural areas of the country. The Gross Enrolment Ratio (GER) has also improved substantially in elementary education from over 82 per cent in 2001-02 to over 100 per cent in 2007-08. The gender gap in enrolment also substantially declined from 17 to 7 per cent during the same period. Although a great deal of progress has been made under the SSA, the quality of education at the primary level still leaves a lot to be desired. These improvements, however, are shadowed by the higher rate of drop-outs at the school level. Around 43 per cent of the students drop out at the elementary level of education, and this pattern has marginally changed since 2001-02 (Planning Commission, 2010, Mid-term Review). Students need more than eight years of education to acquire the skills needed for the services market, and at least secondary education is required for this purpose. The GER in secondary education is a little over 50 per cent, and the Eleventh Plan aimed to raise it to 75 per cent and 100 per cent by the end of the Twelfth Plan (Planning Commission, 2008). The quality of education is a major issue, which was addressed by the Eleventh Plan by increasing the number of teachers, reducing the incidence of absenteeism among teachers, and the provisioning of quality teaching resources. However, there has been less than satisfactory progress in this respect, as highlighted in the *Mid-term Appraisal of the Eleventh Plan* (Planning Commission, 2010). Several recent studies and surveys have also shown the poor quality of education at all levels.

> Although a great deal of progress has been made in terms of enrolment and increase in school infrastructure the quality of education still leaves a lot to be desired.

In the case of higher education, despite the impressive growth in this sphere in the country, the university and college enrolments in the country accounted for only 15 per cent of the eligible population of 18-23 years in 2009-10. This compares unfavourably with the enrolment figure of about 55 per cent in the developed countries and the world average of over 23 per cent for this age group. What is even more worrisome is the marked decrease in the quality of teaching in the institutions of higher learning (Planning Commission, 2008). The achievement of the promise of allocating 6 per cent of the GDP as public spending on education still remains elusive. During the period 2000-01 to 2007-08, the total public expenditure on education (by both the Central and state governments) as a percentage of the GDP ranged between 3.3 and 3.9 per cent (CBGA, 2009).

7.5.1 Vocational Education and Skill Development

The need for developing a skilled labour force has always attracted the attention of policy-makers in India. Almost every Five Year Plan has aimed at strengthening the vocational education system in the country. The vocationalization of education at the higher secondary stage was, in fact, one of the important reforms included in the Sixth Plan. Measures were also initiated to establish the necessary links for combining vocationalization, skill training, in-plant apprenticeship, and placements in gainful employment as the composite parts of an integrated effort to raise the level of utility of the programme, and to ensure its wider acceptance and success. During the Ninth Plan, the scheme of vocationalization of education at the 10+2 stage was introduced to regulate admissions at the college level. The objective was to divert at least 25 per cent of the 10+2 stage students to self-employment or wage employment, while providing them with vocational competence in their respective fields of choice by the year 2000. In spite of the necessity as also the desirability of vocationalization of education, there has been no significant progress in diverting the students from the general stream to the vocational stream of education. The issue of skill development gained renewed importance in the policy discussion when the Planning Commission appointed two Task Forces on Employment Opportunities, and on Skill Development, respectively. While explicitly recognizing the importance of vocational education and training, the proposals in the Eleventh Plan and their continuation in the Twelfth Plan are expected to help in the expansion of the vocational training infrastructure, in the modernization of Industrial Training Institutes (ITIs), and in the addition of relevant skills and the public-private mode for training.

> In spite of the necessity as also the desirability of vocationalization of education, there has been no significant progress in diverting the students from the general stream to the vocational stream of education.

The Ministry of Labour and the Ministry of Human Resource Development are the major agencies that promote skill development in the country, along with various other ministries/departments. Under the Craftsmen Training Scheme of the Ministry of Labour and Employment, there are 2062 ITIs run by the state governments, and nearly 8250 privately-run Industrial Training Centres (ITCs), which impart training in 133 engineering and non-engineering trades, with a seating capacity of 1.12 million students as in April 2012. There has been a sharp increase in the number of these institutes over the years, with the number of ITCs going up to 2,925 since 2007, which accounts for about 57 per cent of the total number of institutions set up during the first 60 years of Independence in India. Further, there has been a vast expansion in the number of trades being taught under the vocational training curriculum from 63 in 2003 to 133 in 2012.

Since the quality of training has been an issue of major concern in the past, systematic efforts are presently underway for improving the quality of education and training imparted by the ITIs. A scheme for upgradation of 500 ITIs into 'Centres of Excellence' was announced in 2006-07. There has been a definite upward shift in the availability of vocational education since the setting up of the Prime Minister's National Skill Development Council.

The Ministry of Human Resource Development (MoHRD) has a network of over 1200 polytechnics, with a capacity of about 3 lakh students, which impart diploma level education in various branches of engineering. The MHRD has also introduced vocational training at the Plus 2 stage of secondary education as an alternative to the pursuit of studies in science, humanities or commerce. There are presently about 10,000 schools offering about 150 educational courses of a duration of two years in the broad areas of agriculture, business and commerce, engineering and technology, healthcare and paramedical services, home sciences and science and technology, to about one million students.

In the services sector, two bodies are concerned with imparting vocational training. The National Council for Hotel Management and Catering Technology (NCHM&CT) regulates the programmes run by the Ministry in the areas of hotel management and catering training. The Construction Industry Development Council, on the other hand, is a larger developmental body, which, *inter alia*, organizes training programmes in various trades connected with construction and even runs diploma courses in civil engineering.

According to an estimate, the total capacity for various training purposes in all the institutions put together is 3.3 million (MoLE, 2008). However, this compares poorly with the total labour force of 431 million and the annual addition of about 9 million. For meeting the growing requirements of skilled persons in the country, the Ministry of Labour and Employment launched a Skill Development Initiative (SDI) in 2007-08 for organizing short-term courses. The scheme has received a good response, as in less than three years, 1,108 modular employable skill course modules have been developed, covering 48 sectors of the economy, with the course duration ranging from 60 hours to 960 hours. Over 4,67,000 youth have hitherto been trained under the SDI. Since the courses are designed while keeping in view the market requirements, they have achieved notable success in terms of the employment prospects of trainees under the SDI—more than half of the trained youth actually got employment after their training (Planning Commission, 2010).

Apart from developing the capacity for vocational education and training in the formal sector, the government policy has also been supportive in terms of promoting informal training programmes. A large number of ministries/departments, commissions, councils and autonomous bodies undertake informal skill development programmes, which are targeted at workers in the informal sector. Prominent among these are community polytechnics and the Jan Shikshan Sansthans under the SDI, being implemented by the Ministry of Labour and Employment, and Entrepreneurship and Skill Development Programmes of the Ministry of Micro, Small and Medium Enterprises, among others. It is, however, argued that these programmes are being implemented by multiple agencies, which lack coordination and cohesion.

In terms of enrolment in vocational education and training courses, India has a net enrolment of only 3.5 million per year as compared to 90 million in China.

There is a huge mismatch between the supply and demand for high-quality skill training. Employers are increasingly expressing concern about the quality of graduates emerging from colleges and polytechnics as a large majority of them lack employable skills. The focus of policy has also been heavily biased in favour of formal sector training. As a result, despite the existence of a large institutional network for vocational education, training and skill development, this has hardly been beneficial for the informal sector (Gasskov, *et al.*, 2003). The Twelfth Five Year Plan recognizes the enormity of the problem when it sums up the situation as one wherein there is low penetration of vocational education and training in India, and the requisite 'skills are yet to become aspirational among youth'. As regards the overall assessment of enrolment in vocational education and training courses, India has a net enrolment of only 3.5 million per year as compared to 90 million in China and 11 million in USA. India thus needs to learn a great deal from these countries, wherein there is much more involvement of the industry and employers in imparting training to the youth than in India.

7.5.2 National Policy on Skill Development

Although the need for diverse skills in a growing economy has been recognized since the early stages of planning, and efforts have been made to provide a network of training institutions, the magnitude of skill deficiency has come to be realized only in the wake of globalization that fostered high rates of growth and along with that, the challenges of imparting the requisite skills to sustain these growth rates. The fact that India was merely skimming the surface as far as skill development was concerned and the realization that something much bigger was required came when the Planning Commission observed that India was doing too little by covering just 100 skills while China had '4000 short duration modular courses which provide skills more closely tailored to employment needs' (Planning Commission, 2008, Vol. i: 87). Skill deficiencies affect the sustainability of high growth in two ways. The lack of a workforce with requisite skills results in low productivity and poor competitiveness that constrain growth. A workforce with poorly endowed skills would be excluded from the high productive sectors and would earn lower incomes, which, in turn, would result in the lack of an adequate aggregate demand to sustain high growth. It is in the wake of this challenge that the future agenda of skill development in India needs to be examined.

While recognizing the huge gap between the requirements and capacity for the development of skills, the Eleventh Plan (2007-2012) proposed the execution of a major programme in a medium-term (5-8 years) perspective in the form of creation of the National Skill Development Mission (NSDM). This programme includes: (i) upgradation of a large number of existing ITIs; and opening of many new ITIs, particularly in the under-served regions and in industrial clusters and Special Economic Zones (SEZs), as also quadrupling of the ITI capacity through the introduction of multiple shifts; (ii) a similar upgradation of the existing polytechnics and setting up of new ones, and doubling of their intake capacity; (iii) expansion of vocational education in 90,000 schools from 2,500 at present, and an increase in their intake capacity from 1.0 to 2.5 million; and (iv) setting up of at least one Rural Development and Self-employment Training Institute (RUDSETIS) in each of the 600 districts. It was proposed to identify 20 high-growth sectors and to initiate sector-specific actions to meet the increasing demand for skilled workers in each of these proposed sectors.

The Prime Minister's National Council on Skill Development has been set up at the top level for providing policy directions and for laying down broad strategies for skill development. The National Skill Development Coordination Board has been set up for coordinating with different government departments in skill development initiatives. It is mandated to oversee the government's skill development policies and bring about an accelerated growth of formal skill acquisition in both the public and private sectors.

The National Skill Development Policy was formulated in 2009 for the promotion of institution-based skill development as well as learning initiatives of sectoral skill development, organized by different ministries, which includes formal and informal apprenticeship training by enterprises, and training for self-employment, among other measures. The National Skill Development Corporation (NSDC) has been put in place to catalyse the private sector efforts in this direction. The NSDC has been bringing together industry, while also training providers and the academic forum. Meanwhile, industry-led Sectoral Skill Councils (SSCs) are being set up for the identified priority sectors and by March 2013, 11 such SSCs had been set up (Planning Commission, 2013).

The Twelfth Five Year Plan proposes the setting up of a National Skill Development Authority to coordinate the skill development activities and to launch the National Skill Development Mission for providing skills to about 80 million during the Plan period and to increase the percentage of the skilled workforce by imparting them formal skill training.

Notwithstanding the above measures, progress in the direction of skill development in the country has been slow. The challenge of education, training and skill, is a huge one, which is likely to aggravate in the wake of the ongoing 'youth bulge'. The country needs to get fully prepared for this.

Progress in the direction of skill development in the country has been slow. The challenge of education, training and skill, is a huge one, which is likely to aggravate in the wake of the ongoing 'youth bulge'.

7.6 Employment and the Policy of Affirmative Action for Disadvantaged Groups

In addition to the overwhelming informal and unskilled nature of the vast majority of the Indian workforce, discrimination and segmentation are the other factors that need special attention in the Indian context. Caste and religion are the two social categories that carry their imprints on the access to jobs differentiated in terms of quality. As was discussed in Chapter 3, of the six widely recognized socio-religious groups, viz. Scheduled Tribes (STs), Scheduled Castes (SCs), Other Backward Castes (OBCs), Upper Caste Hindus, Upper Muslims, and 'Others', the proportion of SCs and STs in the low-paid agricultural and related activities is much higher than that among the other four groups. The number of upper caste Hindus engaged in agricultural activities is far less than that of the OBCs, while their proportion is much higher in the white-collar occupations such as finance, real estate and public administration. Further, a much higher proportion of upper caste Hindus are regular workers, as compared to that of other groups like SCs and STs. The first placed seem to be the category of 'Others', who are much less dependent on agricultural activity and have the largest share in white-collar jobs and business activities. There are huge intra-group disparities as well, especially among the upper caste Hindus, upper strata of Muslims and 'Others', while the bottom segment belonging to these groups also appears to be deprived.

Caste and religion are the two social categories that carry their imprints on the access to jobs differentiated in terms of quality.

Apart from inter-group, there are huge intra-group disparities, especially among upper social groups, indicating the importance of introducing measures for the inclusion of bottom sections within the social groups which are entitled to the benefits of jobs through affirmative action, including addressing the deficits of human endowment of the poor among the higher social groups.

Recognizing the discrimination based on caste and religion in terms of access to employment and education, the Constitution of India provides for affirmative action by way of 'reservation' in public employment and educational institutions for the SCs and STs, which was later extended to 'Other Backward Classes' (OBCs). There is clear evidence that affirmative action in terms of reservation for these communities improves their access to better quality jobs. As was seen in Chapter 3, a higher share of SCs and STs in regular jobs in the public sector than in the private sector shows that the reservation policy has played a positive role in correcting the caste-based discrimination and ensuring a certain level of fairness and justice in the disbursement of jobs. However, it was also mentioned that the richest 20 per cent, regardless of their eligibility for reservations, cornered a very large share of all public sector jobs, which is much more than their population share. In contrast, even with the share of the poorest 20 per cent, with an eligibility for reservation, managed to secure only a very low share of the public sector jobs. This shows that a very large share of public sector jobs in the case of SCs, STs and OBCs were cornered by the elite among them, giving rise to the question of the 'creamy layer' within the social groups, which has been endowed with the benefit of affirmative action on the basis of social justice (Sharma, 2002). This also highlights the importance of introducing measures for the inclusion of poorer groups within the social groups entitled for the benefits of employment through affirmative action. The vulnerability of the poor among the higher social groups shows that some affirmative policies may be required to address the issue of deficits in terms of their human endowment and income as well. These are indeed complex issues that need to be discussed in depth and addressed with a high degree of seriousness.

7.7 National Employment Service (NES)

The NES came into existence in July 1945, soon after the advent of the Second World War, for settling the demobilized defence service personnel, and in the aftermath of the Partition of India, handled work pertaining to persons displaced from Pakistan. Subsequently, in 1948, the scope of the NES was extended to cover employment service to all categories of job-seekers through the Directorate General of Employment and Training (DGE&T). Presently, the NES functions within the conceptual framework of the ILO Convention No. 88 on Organization of Employment Service, with the primary objective of settlement of job-seekers either through regular jobs or through self-employment. The services offered by the NES are free. The network of employment service consists of about 940 Employment Exchanges run by the state governments. The main functions of the NES include the collection, compilation and dissemination of information relating to the various vacancies notified, employment in various industries, types of occupations in existence, the qualifications required for various occupations, and the emerging trends of employment in various industries, among other issues, etc, to facilitate an assessment of the demand and supply of the labour market and to adjust them, as also to create the requisite database for manpower planning and management, career counselling and vocational guidance with a view to effectively guiding the job-seekers. A very ambitious agenda of activities indeed! However, the NES has concentrated excessively on placement activity and over the years, the significance of the NES has been reduced by the emergence of various other factors such as the decline in the scope of the public sector to provide jobs, the setting up of several public sector employment boards, the Supreme Court judgments delinking of the condition that all recruitments in the organized sector should be through registration with the employment exchanges, and the emergence of a large number of private recruitment organizations, have all reduced the significance of the NES. The insignificant status of the NES is also the consequence of its singular concentration on job placements to the utter neglect of its other functions (Chandra, Khanijo and Mamgain, 2006). In the context of the growing informalization of employment and the need for a requisite database, career counselling including guidance regarding appropriate training centres, and the launching of self-employment enterprises, the NES should now be restructured and strengthened to serve as an agency that maintains the requisite database and provides proper guidance for employment in both the informal as well as formal sectors.

In the context of the growing informalization of employment, the National Employment Service should be restructured and strengthened to serve as an agency that maintains the requisite database and provides proper guidance for employment in both informal and formal sectors.

7.8 Concluding Remarks

Employment has been one of the major development objectives of the planning process, but it received special focus in the Five Year Plans only from the Eighth Plan onwards. Since then, a plethora of policies and programmes have been experimented with over the years to create employment opportunities. Yet the challenge of creating productive employment opportunities for a growing labour force and the working poor remains huge. The challenge is likely to exacerbate in view of the 'youth bulge', which India would experience during the next three decades or so. The employment strategy of the country thus needs to be envisaged in the context of the following perspectives:

- Macroeconomic policies have been pursued independently of the employment goals of the country. There is a need for the restructuring of these policies—fiscal, monetary, trade-related, etc., and for combining them with an appropriate employment strategy so that they facilitate the fulfilment of the goal of providing employment as envisaged by the development process.
- Despite an improvement in management levels over the years, direct employment generation programmes, with the possible exception of MGNREGA, have not had the desired impacts in large parts of the country. Apart from the need for their restructuring, several of them also need to be more focused in the deprived regions such as the areas dominated by the tribal and backward populations, as also remote regions of the country, in order to unpack their full potential.

- The policies and measures intended to address the issue of low levels of education and skills, and their mismatch with the employment market, have not adequately handled these issues, and need to be revamped urgently. The rising aspirations of the youth have to be met and the ongoing 'youth bulge' is likely to exacerbate this challenge. The challenge pertains not only to the achievement of a major quantitative expansion in terms of the facilities for education and skill training across the country but also to the equally important task of making the latter qualitatively superior to their current levels. If it has to be able to compete globally and improve its productivity, India has to take forward its education and skill development agenda seriously under its National Skill Development Mission.

- The distorted pattern of services-led growth needs to be altered to one in which the manufacturing sector also occupies an important place. The historical experiences of both the developed countries, as also of the East and South-east Asian countries, have shown that manufacturing-led growth, backed by human resource development, can generate sustainable and productive employment opportunities, and can consequently have the potential to make a significant dent on poverty. India, therefore, has no option but to give a big push to labour-intensive manufacturing growth, which would accelerate access to employment and reduce exclusion.

- Removing the sharp dualism in the labour market and the gradual formalization of the workforce should form an important agenda of the employment strategy. Apart from removing the barriers to the growth of formal employment, both the productivity and incomes in the unorganized sector need to be enhanced to bridge the gap between the two sectors, which, in turn, would facilitate the transfer of labour from the low-productive agriculture/non-agriculture informal sector to the formal sector.

8

The Labour and Employment Agenda Today

8.1 A Balance Sheet

As the world slowly and haltingly emerges from the global economic crisis that started in 2008, the long-term consequences for the Indian economy remain unclear. At first, India weathered the storm as any other large economy, and better than most, much as it had during the Asian financial crisis of 1998-99. But today the Indian economy is more integrated into global markets for goods and capital than it was at that time, and as the global crisis persists the national impact has become more evident, with declining growth and a growing trade deficit. Not only India but other large emerging economies such as China and Brazil have also shown this vulnerability, and it is far from clear that they can return to the growth rates achieved before the crisis.

Although the Indian labour market was relatively resistant to the global downturn, it has also been relatively unresponsive to high economic growth.

Nevertheless, the adverse effects of the global crisis on the Indian labour market appear to have been modest and localized so far. It is true that these were severe in a small number of heavily export-dependent sectors such as diamond cutting and information technology. Substantial numbers of casual and temporary workers were laid off in these sectors, as well as in garments and some other sectors with strong connections to global markets. Recruitment of regular workers in those sectors came to a standstill, wages sometimes fell, and there were significant knock-on effects on the unorganized sector. But these effects were relatively small compared with the labour market as a whole (MoL&E, 2010).

Although the Indian labour market was relatively resistant to the global downturn, it has also been relatively unresponsive to high economic growth. There is a longer term concern with the pace of employment creation in the Indian economy, and with the quality of the jobs that are created. Many problems which have been highlighted in the earlier chapters of this report are delineated below.

- The Indian labour force is under-skilled. There is a small minority of highly skilled, highly productive workers, surrounded by a sea of poorly educated workers, many without even the most basic skills. Public training systems seem to be ill-adapted to private sector needs, and only reach a small proportion of workers. Most training is informal, on the job, and limited in scope.

- The growth of regular, protected jobs is slow. While the number of jobs in the organized sector is now rising, only 18 per cent of employment can be described as regular wage employment, and about 7 per cent is formal; two-thirds of the growth in regular jobs since 2004-05 has been informal.

- The corollary of the slow growth of formal jobs is that much employment is insecure. Most wage work is casual, contract work is on the rise; there is a great deal of informal self-employment which is subject to a variety of market and other insecurities, and only a small fraction of workers have adequate social security coverage.

- Indian labour markets are poorly regulated. It is true that there are a large number of laws regulating employment conditions, especially in the organized sector, but they are largely honoured in the breach. This is due to many reasons: they are poorly designed and often inapplicable; enforcement mechanisms are weak; incidence of corruption is high; and occasionally they undermine the short-term interests of both workers and employers. Trade unions are fragmented and with some honourable exceptions, primarily defend the interests of a minority of workers.

- Most employment is of low quality with low productivity. Safety standards are widely ignored, health risks are given low priority, and working hours are often excessive. This is to some extent a consequence of informality and under-regulation, but also reflects lack of training and awareness, and the priority for workers of meeting their urgent income needs regardless of the consequences. Child labour is declining but not yet eliminated, and the same is true of other forms of un-free labour.

- There is a highly unbalanced regional pattern of employment creation, which in some areas leads to vast and uncontrolled migration in search of work. In rural Bihar, for example, up to half of adult men migrate regularly for work outside the state for shorter or longer periods.

- Regional inequality is just one dimension of widening inequality in Indian labour markets in general. While real wages are rising across the board, they have clearly risen more at the top of the labour market hierarchy.

- A variety of discriminations and vulnerabilities persists and underpins the segmentation of labour markets. Women workers are particularly disadvantaged, in terms of their access to the labour market, the quality of work and wages. Home-based work, mainly undertaken by women, is often paid at extraordinarily low rates. Women are also over-represented among the more vulnerable categories of informal and casual work.

- Disadvantaged social groups are mostly concentrated in low productivity sectors such as agriculture and construction, and in low paying jobs as casual loabourers. The poverty rate amongst these social groups when compared to the all India level is disproportionately high.

But there is an important positive side to the labour market as well, and the following encouraging trends can be seen.

- Employment growth has, by and large, kept pace with labour force growth, and unemployment rates are low, except for some particularly deprived groups and for relatively better-off young people who are seeking formal jobs.

- While some part of this employment growth may be due to work-sharing at low productivity, and so the result of supply rather than demand factors, this cannot be the only or even the main factor, for real wages have been rising and poverty declining steadily.

- There is a growing middle class, which includes many better-educated and skilled workers, with rising incomes and high levels of consumption.

- There is extraordinary growth in some advanced sectors, including information technology, pharmaceuticals, automobiles, and other areas, and while direct employment creation in these sectors may be limited, there are important spillover effects which lead to job creation elsewhere, especially in services. Construction is growing particularly fast.

- There is a popular movement for both rights at work and the right to work, which has given rise to innovative and successful new policies such as the Mahatma Gandhi National Rural Employment Guarantee Act (MGNREGA).

- Persistent structural inequalities by caste and gender are increasingly being recognized and tackled by popular movements and reservation policies.

- After a long period when organized sector employment stagnated, recent data suggests that economic growth is finally leading to substantial job creation in modern industry, where employment was growing at 8 per cent per annum in the mid-2000s, and continued to grow through the economic slowdown.

- At least until 2011-12, the labour market improved through the period of crisis, with a decline in the share of casual wage work, a decrease in the wage gap between casual and regular workers and between women and men, and some increase in the share of wages in organized industry.

8.2 Emerging Research and Policy Agenda

Since the 1990s, and at least until the global crisis, the Indian economy was on a high growth path, but the figures in this report suggest that the first phase of liberalization and reform did not generate much change in the structure of the labour market. Self-employment and casual work continued to predominate and organized sector employment did not grow. The share of agriculture in employment declined, and the share of services increased, but the changes were modest. There were nevertheless substantial gains in the form of higher wages and incomes, so the benefits of growth did spread through the labour market. But the existing inequalities persisted, and in some respects were reinforced, in that the gains from growth were greater among the better-off groups than among casual workers and the self-employed, so overall inequality rose substantially.

The gains from growth were greater among the better-off groups than among casual workers and the self-employed, so overall inequality rose substantially.

The relative stability in the structural conditions is unlikely to survive if the Indian economy returns to high growth for an extended period. As we saw in Chapter 2, there is at last evidence that employment in private industry is rising and this more than offsets the continuing decline in the public sector. Consumption levels have certainly risen, notably of high-end services and consumer durables, and the construction sector has boomed as a result of both private and public expenditure. Export sectors have grown despite the downturn, and even if they do not create many jobs directly, they have indirect effects on employment through their impact on local economies. All of this generates increased demand for skills in a labour market with an abundance of low skilled labour, so wage differentials are likely to rise further. Improved communications are already facilitating movement of labour, so economic integration of labour markets is likely to increase. At the same time, past observation of labour markets in India and elsewhere suggests that new opportunities will be monopolized by particular groups that have the knowledge, resources and capabilities to take advantage of them, and existing discriminations and vulnerabilities will ensure that many are excluded.

In the remainder of this chapter, we highlight some of the questions which need to be addressed in this new economic environment. There are economic, social and institutional changes under way at present which will determine whether India achieves an egalitarian, high employment outcome in which the benefits of growth are shared, or whether the gains will be captured by a few and inequality will rise rapidly. This situation of flux gives rise to a substantial research and policy agenda.

The first item of the agenda consists of better mapping and documenting of today's principal labour and employment developments. The diverse and complex character of work and employment in India is not easy even to describe, and a better picture is required of the structure and institutions of the labour market, the nature of work and the distribution of opportunities. This report explores these issues to some extent, but existing data sources do not allow us to take more than the first step here. Economic growth is creating new employment patterns and new labour market issues, new income opportunities and new forms of exploitation, new institutions and forms of organization, new linkages between work and poverty; all these need to be better specified, measured and understood if more effective and equitable employment and labour policies are to be put in place.

The second item consists of trying to solve some major puzzles. There are many features and trends of labour and employment in India that are unexpected or difficult to explain, or are subject to contradictory explanations. Some labour market patterns and outcomes are inconsistent with expectations, others cannot be captured with existing models, yet others can only be addressed with new data or new research approaches. Many of these relationships have a direct bearing on the pattern and equity of the development path.

The third item is the policy space. What are likely to be the central labour and employment policy concerns for the next decade? What may be done to embed labour and employment objectives better within India's development path? What instruments are available to increase the employment intensity of growth? How do policies in different domains reinforce or undercut each other? What administrative and institutional structures are needed? How can the regulatory framework be reformed?

8.2.1 Documenting Major Developments

(a) The overall pattern of employment creation

The first, and most basic issue is the pace and pattern of employment creation. This often gets expressed as the number of jobs that are created. But in reality, as the analysis in Chapter 2 indicates, the total volume of employment is quite insufficient as an indicator. This is because the volume of employment tends to rise broadly in line with the growth of the labour force, simply because if there is a shortfall in direct employment creation, then there is crowding of excess labour into low productivity occupations or work sharing. The volume of employment on its own, therefore, tells us little about the employment performance of the economy. To understand the employment path properly it is necessary to have more information about the quality and content of work, and about how opportunities are distributed.

A fall in direct employment creation gives rise to crowding of excess labour in low productive occupations.

There are many dimensions which need to be measured. An obvious one is productivity and income reflected in both output and wages. Then there is the structural connection between employment relations and the production system—whether work is formal or informal, free or constrained, self-employed or wage employed, temporary or permanent. From the point of view of workers, the security of work is vital. The existing breakdown into regular and casual work is a good starting point, but that is only a part of the picture.

Beyond these dichotomies, it is important to find some ways of reflecting the nature of the work itself—its interest and intensity, the possibilities it offers for social integration or personal development, and its contribution to people's lives. This aspect of work is rarely given much attention in employment policy. For example, employment creation through the Mahatma Gandhi National Rural Employment Guarantee Scheme (MGNREGS) is generally discussed as if only the total number of days of work and the wages paid were relevant, whereas most MGNREGS work lacks intrinsic interest (it is often simple earthwork) and is physically demanding.

A better characterization of employment would make it possible to explore the connections between employment creation and other social and economic goals, and to interpret the response of employment to different external forces. For instance, the impact of globalization on employment not only comes through the direct creation of good, regular jobs in export sectors (and their distribution in sectors substituted by imports), but also through the simultaneous creation of many casual, temporary jobs in the same enterprises (easily eliminated in a downturn). Indirectly a great deal of informal work of varying quality is generated in external firms and household enterprises supplying inputs and wage goods. The overall impact of globalization on employment depends on the balance of these different effects. Similarly, the implications for employment of a development path which is dominated by the service sector, as is the case in India today, can only be adequately understood if the wide variety of employment found in this sector can be analysed and categorized based on quality, accessibility, reliability, periodicity, etc.

An important issue here is the statistical foundation for analysing employment trends. The NSSO surveys are extremely valuable but employment data has in the past been collected in detail only at five year intervals, which is too long a gap to accurately track trends in a dynamic situation. The most recent employment survey has come after only a two year gap, but this improvement may not continue, and in any case, there is a need for more frequent surveys, giving, data on major labour market outcomes (for instance, employment, wages and earnings of self-employed etc.), and covering a wider range of qualitative and regional issues. The Labour Bureau has started collecting data on employment on an annual basis, but its comprehensiveness and sample size have not been validated. The Employment Market Information (EMI) data also needs to improve in quality and coverage to give quick estimates of movements in employment in the organized sector.

(b) Migration

Labour mobility and migration need to be documented better. It is sometimes stated, on the basis of Census data, that migration flows in India are relatively limited. But this is belied by simple observation in major cities, where enormous populations of migrants are to be found working in construction, trade, and many services. Indeed, there are often enough migrants to generate xenophobic reactions, most prominently in Mumbai. These migration flows have almost certainly increased as a result of the regionally unbalanced growth of the Indian economy, but there is as yet little hard evidence on the size of the populations concerned and the implications for work and welfare. Census data do not appear to fully capture these movements, which are often short term in nature, or are not well measured.

Circulating migration gives many households a foothold in both rural and urban economies, and improved communications make it much easier to maintain this duality.

As noted in Chapters 1 and 2, there are several streams of migration, and the simple transfer of rural populations to urban areas, which dominates conventional analysis, is only one, and not necessarily the most important. Circulating migration gives many households a foothold in both rural and urban economies, and improved communications make it much easier to maintain this duality. This diversity needs to be explored further.

Better information on migration can help show whether it plays an equalizing or a dis-equalizing role, whether it supports development or acts as a source of new vulnerabilities. There is some indication that circulating migration reduces wage differentials across India, between Bihar and North-West India for instance, both in terms of raising wages in areas of origin and holding them down in areas of destination. The result may be decreasing inequality in the areas of origin and increasing inequality in the areas of destination. In Delhi for example, a large, low skilled migrant population provides low cost labour in construction, domestic service and other roles for the rising urban middle class. There is now evidence of rising wages for casual labour in Delhi, but also much anecdotal evidence of the exploitation and vulnerability of groups of migrants, and this too needs to be documented better.

(c) Wage patterns

In recent years, rising real wages, rising wage inequality and a declining wage share, have been observed (as highlighted in Chapter 4). These trends in wages reflect a variety of forces—supply of and demand for labour, public policies (minimum wages, public sector pay decisions), changing social relations in production, technology, collective bargaining, segmentation and exploitation—and the relative importance of these factors is not clear. For instance, the shift from wages to profits that has occurred in recent years may reflect a decline in the bargaining power of labour *vis-à-vis* capital, or it could reflect increasing capital intensity of production.

Wage discrimination is another key issue. Discrimination by caste, sex, ethnic origin or community is widespread, as is reported in Chapters 3 and 4. Given the importance of these cleavages across Indian labour markets, more systematic documentation is needed. In addition, wage and employment discrimination are inter-connected and should be examined together.

> Rising wages constitute one of the main mechanisms by which the benefits of growth are transferred to large sections of the population.

Tracking these patterns and trends carefully is particularly important because rising wages have been one of the main mechanisms by which the benefits of growth are transferred to large sections of the population. Groups which for one reason or another have been excluded from these mechanisms have by the same token been excluded from participation in the benefits of growth.

(d) Regional diversity

There are large regional variations in patterns of growth, employment and unemployment, which need to be documented better. India is a large and diverse country, and labour market patterns in more industrialized Western India may be entirely different from the outcomes in the eastern parts. This is widely acknowledged, but in most academic research it is addressed by presenting data disaggregated by state. However, the pattern of labour market outcomes by state is often very hard to interpret, for states are heterogeneous and vary greatly in size. It would be more helpful to identify a small number of regional labour market patterns, which can help to interpret contrasting trends in different parts of the country.

> Market forces tend to generate higher returns to investment in regions where growth is already occurring.

The importance of this issue lies in the regional concentration of the benefits of growth. Market forces tend to generate higher returns to investment in regions where growth is already occurring, so promoting polarization. It is necessary to investigate the extent of this economic polarization, and whether it also polarizes labour markets and increases income inequality. This would for instance have implications for the design of national employment policy, which should not necessarily be uniform across regions. This is an issue that is likely to take on increasing importance in the coming years, for without countervailing policies regional inequality is likely to grow further.

8.2.2 The Puzzles

Beyond better documentation of the trends, there are many puzzles in Indian labour markets, patterns and outcomes that do not appear to be consistent with conventional analysis. These need to be understood better if overall trends are to be interpreted correctly. The following are some important puzzles which merit more substantial research.

(a) Why does the Indian economy not generate more organized sector jobs?

According to some estimates, over the 20 years from the mid-1980s to the mid-2000s organized sector employment declined not only as a percentage of all employment but even in absolute terms, despite a more than respectable growth of the Indian economy as a whole. As shown in Chapter 2, since 2003 there are indications of a change in this trend, with employment growing at about one per cent per year for the eight year period of 2003-08 in organized industry but the long term trend remains a puzzle.

Various explanations can be found in the literature. A popular one is that restrictive labour laws (especially those which restrict the firing of labour) and trade union action make firms unwilling to hire labour. And it is certainly true that larger firms in India are surrounded by a complex and often counter-productive web of regulation. However, as argued in Chapters 1 and 5, it is implausible to consider this as the main cause of slow employment growth. First, the majority of labour laws are applied with great laxity, so that firms which need to lay-off labour generally have little difficulty in doing so. Second, there is widespread evidence that a more stable and better protected workforce is more productive (and large enterprises are well aware of this), so the effect of protecting jobs is by no means necessarily negative. Third, organized sector employment is mainly in the public sector, where hiring and firing reflects policy decisions rather than economic imperatives. So the lack of growth of public sector employment in recent years reflects attempts to downsize the state rather than any regulation-induced disincentive to hiring. There are similar debates around the high wage differentials between organized and unorganized sectors, and whether high minimum wages discourage hiring but the same three comments apply.

The lack of growth of public sector employment in recent years reflects attempts to downsize the state rather than any regulation-induced disincentive to hiring.

A second possible explanation lies in globalization. In many manufacturing sectors, capital-intensive production methods dominate production world-wide. Uniform production systems facilitate global decision-making and quality control, global competition is built on rising productivity and innovation and as a result, technological change is biased towards capital intensity. In such systems, the scope for increasing labour inputs is mainly confined to peripheral areas such as packaging, transport and security. This argument applies mainly to advanced consumer goods such as electronics, pharmaceuticals, automobiles and consumer durables. There are other export sectors which are highly labour-intensive, such as garments, though in these sectors international competition is intense, and their share in Indian exports has declined since the 1990s. (So there is a supplementary puzzle here: why does India not have a bigger role in the global production of labour-intensive, low-skill manufactures?)

'Jobless growth' is in reality a misnomer, for alongside every formal, organized job there may be a number of informal, regular or temporary jobs.

A third explanation may lie in the development of more complex production systems in which, in addition to the core of formal employment, there is a body of casual workers who can be hired or dismissed, as needed, through the economic cycle, and a network of external sub-contractors who are not obliged to offer the same terms and conditions of employment to their workers as the core formal employees. In such situations, 'jobless growth' is in reality a misnomer, for alongside every formal, organized job there may be a number of informal, regular or temporary jobs. However, the existing statistics do not allow us to confirm this.

These issues can only be properly addressed with new information at the enterprise level which maps out capital intensity, hiring decisions and the enterprise networks involved.

(b) Why do the frameworks of law and labour administration have so little impact on the real functioning of the labour market?

India has an extensive framework of labour regulation which goes back to colonial times. Yet there is high and persistent informality, despite economic growth. According to the National Commission on Enterprises in the Unorganized Sector, 88 per cent of workers in India were in the unorganized sector in 2004-05. The unorganized sector is broadly defined as economic activities within which most of the formal rules for employment protection do not apply.

This is a complex issue which is often subject to simplistic, ideologically-driven debates about over-regulation. In reality there are many different aspects of this question, which we have addressed in Chapter 5. The first concerns the design of regulation, and in particular whether it is well-adapted to the problem concerned. The second concerns implementation. The effectiveness of regulation depends on the structure of governance and administration, and this may be weak—if the labour inspectorate is small, for instance—and may be undermined by corruption or the lack of penalties for non-compliance. A third aspect concerns the degree of social legitimacy of the regulations concerned—safety standards may be flouted simply because they do not correspond to people's everyday behaviour. A fourth aspect concerns the extent to which private actors use the framework of regulation to buttress their demands. Thus, agricultural labourers may not receive the minimum wage, but where they are organized and aware, they may make that wage a reference point in their struggles.

To understand the effectiveness of formal regulation, it is also necessary to understand informal regulation. Each local labour market is built around informal institutions as well as formal ones, and the outcomes depend on the interaction between the two. A more sophisticated understanding of these issues is required to answer the question about the impact of regulation. The problem of India's labour market is not that it is over-regulated: it is poorly regulated. The regulation that exists is highly unbalanced, and has done little to check the growth of inequality. What is needed is a bold and imaginative rethinking of the framework of regulation so as to deliver basic rights, protection, income and security to the labour market as a whole. One idea is to move away from penalties for non-compliance towards incentives and supportive measures for compliance. The National Commission on Enterprises in the Unorganized Sector also had some good ideas. But a better understanding of the nature and impact of different forms of regulation is needed to underpin more effective public policy.

The problem of India's labour market is not that it is over-regulated but that it is poorly regulated.

(c) Why is female labour force participation not rising?

Female labour participation rates in India are low when international comparisons are drawn. The overall labour force participation rate of women today is much the same as it was 25 years ago—the most recent NSS data even suggests that it has declined.

This is, on the face of it, surprising. The rhetoric in favour of gender equality has strengthened, and there are many role models in politics and business. There are signs of incipient change in some labour markets, for instance in situations where men have migrated and women have access to labour market opportunities in their place. Educational levels of women have increased. Certain new occupations, such as work in call centres, provide increased access for women. Furthermore, rising wage levels suggest that in some areas at least the labour market is tightening, so opportunities for women's work should be increasing. Fertility rates have also dropped, implying some reduction in the competition between child care and economic activity.

Rising wage levels suggest that in some areas at least, the labour market is tightening, so opportunities for women's should be increasing.

So why does this not show up in the numbers? Those who collect household survey data are familiar with the general tendency for women's work to be underestimated compared with men's (so NSSO figures have to be treated with caution). But beyond the measurement issue, the labour market remains highly segmented, with many occupations gender-typed and women concentrated in inferior positions even when they have access. Considerable wage discrimination persists. Women are also frequently excluded from labour market opportunities which require migration. The increase in employment in urban services, and the decline in agricultural employment, has therefore probably not played out to the advantage of women. Above all, family and social attitudes to women's work have changed much more slowly than the economic environment.

Nevertheless, the lack of overall progress is surprising. This is a critical medium term issue, both from the view of equity in development, and from the point of view of the evolution of the labour market. It merits close and constant attention.

(d) Why is self-employment so persistently high?

There are good reasons to expect self-employment to decline with development. Industrial development is largely based on wage labour, and increasing population pressure on land might be expected to lead to a proletarianization of the rural workforce. Nevertheless, the data show that self-employment has declined very little overall since the early 1980s. There has been a small decline in the share of self-employment in rural areas, while in urban areas—where the informal economy remains to a large extent built on self-employment and family labour—self-employment has been quite stable as a percentage of overall employment.

Persistent self-employment is an indicator of inadequate employment creation.

Various explanations are possible. A basic one is that a large part of the economy continues to consist of small farm-based agriculture where self-employment is the natural mode of operation, and the conversion of small cultivators into casual wage workers in agriculture has been limited. A second is that self-employment can in reality be a form of work-sharing in the face of restricted employment opportunities. Under this explanation, persistent self-employment is an indicator of inadequate employment creation. Another explanation is that in the service economy, which dominates in urban areas, opportunities for self-employment are much greater than in manufacturing. A fourth explanation would root persistent self-employment in the transfer of traditional forms of rural economic organization to urban labour markets. A fifth would see much self-employment as disguised wage employment, especially in urban areas, reflecting the lower costs to employers when they are not obliged to cover the costs of social protection.

Irrespective of the reason, there are considerable implications for the extent to which economic growth in India creates decent employment opportunities. While some self-employment can be productive, in most activities there is a ceiling to productivity in the absence of wider, more capital intensive forms of economic organization. In any event, more intensive research into the nature and dynamics of urban self-employment is required, for the puzzle is greater here than in rural areas, where the intensification of agriculture on smaller and smaller plots is certainly part of the explanation.

8.2.3 The Policy Options

There is a policy agenda implicit or explicit in much of the analysis in this report. It is basically concerned with meeting the needs of the people for decent, secure work on a fair and rapid development path. Much of the policy agenda calls for action by the state, but not all of it. There is a considerable space for action by organized civil society, as can be seen from the discussion of labour institutions and social protection in Chapters 5 and 6.

This final section highlights some broader questions that policy-makers and others are likely to face over the next decade, in the light of the foregoing analysis.

Much of the policy agenda calls for action by the state, but not all of it. There is a considerable space for action by organized civil society.

(a) What instruments are available to raise the employment elasticity of growth?

There would seem to be three principal ways to increase the volume of employment in the economy. The first is through direct public action, such as MGNREGS. The second is through managing macro-economic policy in such a way as to maintain high levels of economic activity. The third is through changing the pattern of incentives and economic structures in such a way that private actors and enterprises create more jobs.

The debates on the first and second routes are well rehearsed. But it is the third which appears to offer enormous potential and yet seems most complex and difficult to achieve. Tax incentives for particular types of investment or economic activity, public sector investment in infrastructure or institutional support which promotes enterprise development, research and development which aims to open up new production methods which are more labour-intensive, training and skill systems which make labour more productive, labour codes which encourage hiring, promotion of small and medium enterprises that are known to be more labour-intensive, the list of possibilities is endless. At the same time, experience in public sector action in India and elsewhere does not suggest that such measures have in the past made much difference to the overall employment rate.

A higher employment elasticity of growth could make an important contribution to an egalitarian development path.

A higher employment elasticity of growth could make an important contribution to an egalitarian development path, and much greater attention to this area is called for. It could include the introduction of policies on an experimental basis in one or more states, the allocation of substantial resources to innovation and evaluation of its impact, and a systematic introduction of an employment criterion in development projects and activities across the board.

The points made here are, of course, not new; indeed many of them were incorporated in an exercise of the Ministry of Labour and Employment to formulate a National Employment Policy, or were treated in the recommendations of the National Commission on Enterprises in the Unorganized Sector. Such attempts to formulate a coherent overall employment policy need to be pursued.

(b) What is the correct balance between policies to raise employment and policies to raise the quality of jobs?

There is little debate in India at present on the quality of employment and yet this is the central preoccupation of workers throughout the country. The most common policy view on this question is: first let us create jobs, and we can worry about the quality of those jobs later. Implicit in this position is the idea that raising the quality of employment might be at the expense of its quantity.

Better jobs may certainly be at the cost of more jobs at the level of the individual enterprise, which survives by minimizing costs. However, this is by no means always the case—many improvements in work at the same time generate improvements in productivity. Perhaps more importantly, this equation is certainly not true at the national level, where improvements in the quality of work can be promoted across the economy as a whole, with policy measures of different types adapted to different sectors and enterprises.

In the future growth path, this issue deserves much more attention. Higher growth should not be dependent on the persistence of poor jobs. On the contrary, improvements in the quality of working lives should constitute a major development objective, and be integrated much better into the policy framework. The issue of the employment elasticity discussed above should be reformulated in this light—the goal might be better specified as raising the elasticity with respect to growth of decent employment.

Higher growth should not be dependent on the persistence of poor jobs. On the contrary, improvements in the quality of working lives should constitute a major development objective.

(c) Can social protection be designed to support transitions from informal to formal employment, or from agriculture to non-agricultural work?

Social security can have not just a protective but also a promotional or developmental role. But there is little debate in India on the developmental role of social security; it is seen as merely a well-being or rights issue. This, for instance, is the way the rural employment guarantee is conceived. But given that minimum social security needs to be ensured, can it be done in such a manner that rights and benefits can be transferred between locations and jobs? Is it possible to overcome the dualism of state-funded social protection for workers in the informal sector and employer-contributed social insurance for workers in the formal sector, which increase the barriers to formalization? Well-designed social security can facilitate economic and occupational transitions at the same time as it improves the quality of employment. Flexible social security may also make it easier for entrepreneurship and innovation to develop, by reducing the risks, and thus contribute to growth.

More attention needs to be paid to the overall issue of linking social security with desirable development transitions.

So more attention needs to be paid to the overall issue of linking social security with desirable development transitions. This is a neglected dimension of India's development pathway.

(d) How can short-term (crisis response) and long-term (developmental) policy frameworks be married in ways that preserve employment goals?

The lesson of the last two major international economic crises, both in India and elsewhere, is that the adverse impact is greatest for those who were the most vulnerable to start with—those in temporary, casual and informal work, whose jobs disappear without any compensation. On the contrary, those in relatively protected, permanent jobs are much less likely to be laid off even if the legal framework permits it. They have some entitlement to compensation if they are laid off, which imposes a cost that employers try to avoid; and employers in larger enterprises, in any case, tend to hoard labour for the economic recovery.

The implication is clear. Some form of security for informal workers is essential to limit the short-term impact of crisis. In industrialized countries, and increasingly in some middle income countries, this takes the form of unemployment insurance, but no such mechanism is on the agenda in India at the moment. It is rather the employment guarantee route (MGNREGS) which is privileged, and this is aimed at structural employment deficits rather than crisis response and so far only covers rural areas. The proposals of the National Commission on Enterprises in the Unorganized Sector for social security for unorganized sector workers provide some options, but as noted in Chapter 6, only some of its recommendations have so far been translated into law.

The long-term growth of the economy depends on the creation and participation of more secured workers.

The fundamental question here is how to connect such short-term mechanisms to provide security with longer term strategies for growth. In other words, how can the provision of security in the short term become a productive factor in the longer term? In principle this is one objective of MGNREGS, but the contribution to development of local infrastructure projects is subject to declining returns. There is a need for a better way to underpin the longer term growth of the economy through the participation in production of more secure workers.

(e) How can skills and capabilities be upgraded?

The skill profile of the workforce has a considerable impact on both the quality of work itself, and on its productivity. Inequality in skill and capability is also an important determinant of overall wage inequality. Yet this is an issue which receives relatively little academic attention. Such research tends to focus on educational and vocational qualifications rather than direct measures of capabilities, and that is reflected in our treatment of the issue in this report. Manpower and training policies suffer from a similar bias. Most attention is given to formal training which only reaches a rather small fraction of the workforce.

Resources are too heavily concentrated on the training of relatively small groups of highly skilled workers, whereas the greater need is to raise the basic skills of the bulk of the workforce.

This issue is crying out for more effective state policies. As we have seen in Chapter 7, there is a long history of public sector intervention in training, but little evidence that this is delivering the skills demanded by the private sector. Moreover, there is good reason to believe that resources are too heavily concentrated on the training of relatively small groups of highly skilled workers, whereas the greater need is to raise the basic skills of the bulk of the workforce, which are at present mainly acquired through informal apprenticeships and on the job. It would be particularly important to analyse skill needs and profiles in the most rapidly growing sectors, and in the unorganized sector, where skill deficiencies may be an important constraint on growth. In practice, most workers have little opportunity to upgrade their skills in line with new economic needs.

This is an issue which calls for re-conceptualization of the problem, away from traditional concepts of skills and qualification, and towards an approach which aims to systematically strengthen the capabilities of workers. Among other implications, this will call for re-assessment of major data sources.

(f) How to increase employment in manufacturing, including the labour-intensive segments?

India's production is disproportionately based on services, compared with both East and South-east Asian countries. And since productivity is higher in manufacturing as compared to overall productively in the country the disproportion is even greater in employment. Employment growth in manufacturing depends on both growth in demand and production, and in the level of investment. In a relatively open economy, a large domestic market does not guarantee growth in demand for domestic output, as is well illustrated by Indian imports of more than US$90 billion of electronic products. That suggests that there is a supply side problem too, which can only be resolved by growth in investment, especially in labour intensive production.

Investment depends not only on the labour market, but also on land markets and capital markets. It has recently been adversely affected by policy inconsistencies and deficiencies, including the attempt to change tax rules on a retrospective basis, the uncertainties and problems in acquisition of land, and poor infrastructure. Not only does this discourage inflows of international capital, it also leads to outflows of Indian capital to other countries, even in order to serve the large Indian market.

To achieve a greater impact on employment in manufacturing, it is necessary to address the factor market distortions that lead Indian investment to be concentrated in more skill-intensive and capital-intensive segments. Some existing policies promote greater capital-intensity, such as the high depreciation allowed by India compared to other countries. Are the high prices of land and the problems in acquiring land, which increase its effective price, promoting high-end and not low-skill, labour-intensive and low-value products? Does poor infrastructure have a greater negative impact on the production of labour-intensive, low-value products? Does the plethora of labour-related laws increase labour costs unduly? This is an area that requires a fresh look at the highest policy level.

(g) How do labour and employment goals connect with a rights-based approach?

An important dimension of the recent policy debate in India has been the development of a rights-based approach to employment, food, social protection and more generally to development. The logic behind the promotion of claimable rights is that this shifts power from the policy-maker and bureaucrat to the worker and the individual citizen.

This approach has been politically successful, both in forcing a policy agenda on the government and in arguably assisting in its electoral success in 2009. What are the implications for labour and employment goals and issues?

The right to employment has become embedded in political rhetoric through the success of MGNREGS. But employment has many dimensions. It is a means as well as an end; work and employment contribute to a diverse set of personal and societal objectives. The fundamental goal might be better expressed not just as a right to employment, but rather as the right to a life free of hunger and insecurity, in which all individuals have opportunities to participate productively in both society and economy. Whether this goal is phrased in the language of rights or the language of development, it calls for a coherent and comprehensive approach to achieving an adequate livelihood for all. The goal might be expressed as setting a social floor for all, above the poverty line, in which decent work is combined with social inclusion.

The challenge is to build a coherent framework to achieve this goal. Within this framework, policies for labour and employment do not stand on their own but need to be connected with a broader set of interventions in both economic and social spheres.

8.3 Conclusion

India's recent growth performance has been impressive. The central issues now are the sustainability of growth, and how to ensure that the benefits of growth reach the population as a whole. For both these issues, a labour and employment policy is central.

This report shows that there has been much progress, but that many challenges still persist. Structural change in the labour market has been slow, and large potential is yet to be realized. Policies to increase employment creation have to be combined with policies to enhance the quality of jobs, to improve capabilities, to overcome structural imbalances in employment opportunities, and to eliminate the many remaining sources of exploitation, vulnerability and exclusion. Inequality has been rising rapidly, and needs to be tackled if it is to prevent it from becoming a threat to growing prosperity.

The current high growth path offers real degrees of freedom in terms of resources and policy space, and some would argue that more effective labour and employment policies are just a question of political will. But a stronger knowledge base is also needed, if coherent labour and employment policies have to be developed and implemented. This Report and subsequent ones aim to help fill that gap.

References

Abraham, Vinoj (2007). "Growth and Inequality of Wages in India: Recent Trends and Patterns", *Indian Journal of Labour Economics*, 50(4): 927–41.

Acharya, Sarthi (1990). *Maharashtra Employment Guarantee Scheme: A Study of Labour Market Intervention*. New Delhi: ILO-ARTEP.

Ahn, Pong-Sul (2007). *Organizing for Decent Work in the Informal Economy: Strategies, Methods and Practices*. New Delhi: Sub-regional Office for South Asia and Geneva: Bureau for Workers" Activities.

Ahsan, A., and Carmen Pages (2009). "Are All Labor Regulations Equal? Assessing the Effects of Job Security, Labor Disputes and Contract Labour Laws in India". *http://siteresources.worldbank.org/SOCIAL PROTECTION/Resources/SP-DiscussionPapers/Labor-market-DP/0713.pdf*. Accessed 15 January 2008.

Aiyer, S. and Ashok Mody (2011). "The Demographic Dividend: Evidences from the Indian States", *IMF Working Paper 11/38*. Washington, DC: International Monetary Fund.

Anant, T.C.A. (2004). "Labour Market Reforms in India: A Review", Paper presented at the *Fifth Annual Global Development Network Conference*. New Delhi. January 28–30.

———. (2009). "Revisiting Labour Market Regulation", *The Indian Journal of Labour Economics*, 52(2): 195–202.

Anup, K. and S. Saktivel (2008). "Trends in Wages and Earnings in India: Increasing Wage Differentials in a Segmented Labour Market", *ILO Asia –Pacific Working Paper Series*. May.

Banerjee, A. and T. Piketty (2005). "Top Indian Incomes, 1922-2000", *World Bank Economic Review*, 19(1): 1–19.

Banerjee, Debdas (2008). *Labour Regulation and Industrial Development in West Bengal*. Institute for Studies in Industrial Development (ISID), European Union (EU), and International Institute for Labour Studies (IILS), New Delhi: Bookwell.

Besley, Timothy and Robin Burgess (2004). "Can Labor Regulation Hinder Economic Performance? Evidence from India", *Quarterly Journal of Economics*, CXIX: 91–133.

Bhaduri, A. (2008). "Predatory Growth: Commentary", *Economic and Political Weekly*, 43(16): 10–14.

Bhalla, G.S. (2004). *Is Growth Sans Industrialization Sustainable*. ISID Foundation Day Lecture, Institute for Studies in Industrial Development, New Delhi, India.

———. (2007). *Indian Agriculture since Independence*. New Delhi: National Book Trust.

Bhalla, S., A.K. Karan and T. Shobha (2004). "Rural Casual Labourers, Wages and Poverty: 1983 to 1999–2000", *Working Paper No. 14*. New Delhi: Chronic Poverty Research Centre, Indian Institute of Public Administration (IIPA).

Bhalla, Sheila (1992). "The Formation of Rural Labour Markets in India", in T.S. Papola and Gerry Rodgers (eds.), *Labour Institutions and Economic Development in India*. Geneva: International Institute for Labour Studies.

Bhalotra, S.R. (1998). "The Puzzle of Jobless Growth in Indian Manufacturing", *Oxford Bulletin of Economics and Statistics*, 60(1): 5–32, February.

Bhandari, Amit K. and Almas Heshmati (2006). "Wage Inequality and Job Insecurity among Permanent and Contract Workers in India: Evidence from Organized Manufacturing Industries", *IZA DP No. 2097*, *http://papers.ssrn.com/sol3/papers.cfsn?abstract_id=900362*, Accessed 13 September 2012.

Bhattacharya, Aditya (2009). "The Effects of Employment Protection Legislation on Indian Manufacturing", *Economic and Political Weekly*: 55–62, May 30.

Bhattacherjee, Debashish (1987). "Union-type Effects on Bargaining Outcomes in Indian Manufacturing", *British Journal of Industrial Relations*, 25(2): 247–466.

———. (1999). "Organized Labour and Economic Liberalization in India: Past, Present and Future", *Discussion Papers DP/105/1999*. Geneva: International Institute for Labour Studies (IILS).

Bhowmik, Sharit K. (2005). "Street Vendors in Asia: A Review", *Economic and Political Weekly*: 2256–64, May 28–June 4.

———. (2008). "Labour Organizations in the Twenty-First Century", *Indian Journal of Labour Economics*, 51(4): 958–68.

Breman, Jan (2008). *The Jan Breman Omnibus*. New Delhi: Oxford University Press.

Brofenbrenner, K. (2000). *Uneasy Terrain: Impact of Capital Mobility on Worker's Wages and Union Organizing*. A Report Submitted to the U.S. Trade Deficit Review Commission.

Cao, Hongmin (2004). "Reducing Poverty and Developing Mountainous Areas in China", in *Poverty Alleviation in Mountain Areas of China*. Kathmandu: International Centre for Integrated Mountain Development.

CBGA (2009). *How Did the UPA Spend Our Money? An Assessment of Expenditure Priorities and Resource Mobilization Efforts of the UPA Government*. New Delhi: Centre for Budget and Governance Accountability.

Chandra, Ashoka, M.K. Khanijo and R.P. Mamgain (2006). *National Employment Service in India: Perspectives on Development*. New Delhi: International Labour Organization Sub-regional Office for South Asia.

Chandrasekhar, C.P. and Jayati Ghosh (2007). "Self Employment as Opportunity or Challenges", *http://www.macroscan.com/fet/mar07/pdf/Self_employment.pdf*. Accessed 14 January 2013.

Chandrasekhar, C.P. (2008). *Revisiting the Policy Environment for Engendering Employment Intensive Growth*. Background Paper prepared for the International Labour Organization, New Delhi.

Chaudhuri, D.P. (1997). "A Policy Perspective on Child Labour in India with Pervasive Gender and Urban Bias in School Education", *Indian Journal of Labour Economics*, 40 (4), October–December.

Chavan, Pallavi and Rajshree Bedamatta (2006). "Trends in Agricultural Wages in India", *Economic and Political Weekly*, 44(38): 4041–51.

Cox, Jane (2008). "Judiciary Leaves Contract Labour in the Cold", *Combat Law:* 68–71, November–December.

———. (2012). ""With Eyes Wide Open: Recent Trends in Supreme Court Labour and Industrial Judgments", in K.R. Shyam Sundar (ed.), *Contract Labour in India: Issues and Perspectives*. New Delhi: Indian Society of Labour Economics and Daanish Publishers.

Das, Deb Kusum, Deepika Wadhva and Gunajit Kalita (2009). "The Employment Potential of Labour Intensive Industries in India"s Manufacturing", *Working Paper No.* 236. New Delhi: Indian Council for Research on International Economic Relations (ICRIER).

Das, M.B. (2003) "Ethnicity and Social Discrimination in Job Outcomes in India: Summary & Research Findings", *Mimeo*. World Bank.

Das, Subesh K. (2008). "Trade Unions in India: Union Membership and Union Identity", *Indian Journal of Labour Economics*, 51(4): 969–82.

Dash, J. (1996). "Minimum Wages Law: Agricultural Labour and Uniform Minimum Wages", *Indian Journal of Labour Economics,* 39(2).

Datt, Ruddar (2003). *Lockouts in India*. New Delhi: Indian Society of Labour Economics, Institute for Human Development and Manohar.

———. (2008). "Regional and Industrial Spread of Trade Unions in India", *Indian Journal of Labour Economics* 51(4): 993–1000.

Datta, Amrita and S.K. Mishra (2011). Glimpses of Women"s Lives in Rural Bihar: Impact of Male Migration, *The Indian Journal of Labour Economics,* 54(3): 457–77.

Datta, Amrita and Sharma, Alakh N. (2013). "Are Women Losing out on Employment in India?", *The Financial Express*, October 22.

de Swaan, Abram (1988). *In Care of the State*. Cambridge, UK: Polity Press.

Deaton, Angus (1997). *The Analysis of Household Surveys: A Microeconometric Approach to Development Policy.* Washington, DC: Johns Hopkins Press and World Bank.

Deaton, Angus and Jean Dréze (2002). "Poverty and Inequality in India: A Re-examination", *Economic and Political Weekly,* 37(36): 3729–48.

Debroy, Bibek (2005). "Issues in Labour Law Reform", in Bibek Debroy and P.D. Kaushik (eds.), *Reforming the Labour Market*. New Delhi: Academic Foundation in association with Friedrich Naumann Stiftung and Rajiv Gandhi Institute for Contemporary Studies.

Deshpande, Ashwani (2010). "Merit, Mobility and Modernism: Caste Discrimination in Contemporary Indian Labour Markets", *Indian Journal of Labour Economics,* 53(3): 433–55.

Deshpande, L.K. (1984). *Role of Trade Unions in India*, S.D. Memorial Lecture. Bombay: Tata Institute of Social Sciences (TISS).

Deshpande, Sudha, Guy Standing and Lalit Deshpande (1998). *Labour Flexibility in a Third World Metropolis.* New Delhi: Indian Society of Labour Economics and Commonwealth Publishers.

Deshpande, L.K., Alakh N Sharma, Anup K. Karan and Sandip Sarkar (2004). *Liberalization and Labour: Labour Flexibility in Indian Manufacturing*. New Delhi: Institute for Human Development.

Dev, Mahendra S. (2001). "Social Security: Performance, Issues and Policies", in S. Mahendra Dev, Piush Antony, V. Gayathri and R.P. Mamgain (eds.), *Social and Economic Security in India*. New Delhi: Institute of Human Development.

Dev, Mahendra S. and C. Ravi (2007). "Poverty and Inequality: All India and States, 1983-2005", *Economic and Political Weekly,* 42(6): 509–21.

Dhavan, Rajeev (2006). "Arguments, Protests, Strikes and Free Speech: The Career and Prospects of the Right to Strike in India", *Indian Journal of Labour Economics,* 49(1): 63–78.

Dougherty, Sean (2008). "Labour Regulation and Employment Dynamics at the State Level in India", *OECD Economics Department Working Papers No. 624. http://ideas.repec.org/p/oec/ecoaaa/624-en.html*. Accessed 20 August 2013.

Dreze, J. and Amartya Sen (1989). *Hunger and Public Action*. Oxford, UK: Oxford University Press.

Dutta Roy, S. (2002). "Job Security Regulations and Worker Turnover: A Study of Indian Manufacturing Sector", *Indian Economic Review,* 37: 141–62.

Dutta Vasudeva, Puja (2005). "Accounting for Wage Inequality in India" , *Indian Journal of Labour Economics,* 48(2): 273–95.

Epstein, G. (2000). "Threat Effects and the Impact of Capital Mobility on Wages and Public Finances: Developing a Research Agenda", *Working Paper Series No.7, http://www.umass.edu/Peri/pdfs/wp7.pdf.* Accessed 12 October 2013.

Eyraud, Francois and Catherine Saget (2005). *The Fundamentals of Minimum Wage Fixing*. Geneva: International Labour Office.

Fang, C. (2008). "Approaching a Triumphal Span: How Far is China Towards It Lewisian Turning Point?", *UN–WIDER Research Paper*.

Fallon, P. R. and R.E. B. Lucas (1993). "Job Security Regulations and the Dynamic Demand for Industrial Labour in India and Zimbabwe", *Journal of Development Economics,* 40(2): 241–75, April.

Felipe, Jesus and Rana Hasan (2006). "Labour Markets in a Globalizing World", in Felipe, Jesus and Rana Hasan (eds.), *Labor Markets in Asia: Issues and Perspectives*. New York: Palgrave Macmillan Press and Manila: Asian Development Bank.

FICCI (2013). *FICCI Survey on Inverted Duty Structure in Indian Manufacturing Sector.* New Delhi: Federation of Indian Chambers of Commerce and Industry.

Fields, G.S. (2003). "Accounting For Income Inequality and Its Changes: A New Method with Application to the Distribution of Earnings in the United States", *Research in Labor Economics,* 22: 1–38.

Gasskov, V., A. Aggarwal, A. Grover, A. Kumar and Q.L. Juneja (2003). *Industrial Training Institutes of India: The Efficiency Report*. New Delhi: International Labour Organization.

Gelb, Alan and Julia Clark (2013). "Identification for Development: The Biometrics Revolution", *Working Paper No.* 13. Centre for Global Development. Available at: *www.cgd.org*. Accessed 29 April 2013.

Ghanekar, J. (1997). "Sorry State of Agricultural Wage Data: Sources and Methods of Collection", *Economic and Political Weekly,* 32(19): 1029–36, May 10.

Ghose, Ajit K. (1994). "Employment in Organized Manufacturing in India", *Indian Journal of Labour Economics,* 37(2): 141–62, April–June.

———. (2003). *Jobs and Incomes in a Globalizing World*. Geneva: International Labour Organization.

———. (2008). "Globalization and Employment in Developing Countries", *Indian Journal of Labour Economics*, 51(4): 497–505.

———. (2012). "The Growth–Employment Interaction in a Developing Economy", *The Indian Journal of Labour Economics*, 55(1).

———. (2013). "The End of the Road for India's Services-led Growth: Resumption of Rapid GDP Expansion Requires Accelerated Growth of the Production and Export of Manufactures", *Business Standard*, October 26. Retrieved from *http://www.business-standard.com/article/opinion/ajit-k-ghose-the-end-of-the-road-for-india-s-services-led-growth-113102600719_1.html*.

———. (ed.) (2013). *Agrarian Reform in Contemporary Developing Countries: A Study Prepared for the International Labour Office within the Framework of the World Employment Programme*. London and New York: Taylor & Francis.

Ghose, Ajit, Nomaan Majid and Christopher Ernst (2008). *The Global Employment Challenge*. Geneva: International Labour Office.

GoI (2006). "Social, Economic and Educational Status of the Muslim Community in India", Report submitted by the Prime Minister"s High Level Committee. New Delhi: Government of India.

GoI-MHUPA (2008). *Annual Report 2007-08*. New Delhi: Ministry of Housing and Urban Poverty Alleviation, Government of India.

———. (2009). Annual Report 2009-10. New Delhi: Ministry of Housing and Urban Poverty Alleviation, Government of India

———. (2011). Annual Report 2011-12. New Delhi: Ministry of Housing and Urban Poverty Alleviation, Government of India

GoI-MoF (2006). *Economic Survey 2005-06*. New Delhi: Ministry of Finance, Government of India

———. (2008). *Economic Survey 2007-08*. New Delhi: Ministry of Finance, Government of India.

———. (2009). *Economic Survey 2008-09*. New Delhi: Ministry of Finance, Government of India.

———. (2010). *Economic Survey 2009-10*. New Delhi: Ministry of Finance, Government of India

———. (2012). *Economic Survey 2011-12*. New Delhi: Ministry of Finance, Government of India.

———. (2013). *Economic Survey 2012-13*. New Delhi: Ministry of Finance, Government of India.

GoI-MoL&E (2008). *Annual Report (2007–08)*. New Delhi: Ministry of Labour & Employment, Government of India.

———. (2010). *Draft National Employment Policy*. New Delhi: Ministry of Labour & Employment, Government of India.

GoI-MoMSME (2012). *Annual Report 2011-12*. New Delhi: Ministry of Micro, Small and Medium Enterprises, Government of India.

GoI-MoRD (2009). *Report of the Committee on Credit Related Issues under SGSY*. New Delhi: Ministry of Rural Development, Government of India.

———. (2012). *Annual Report 2012–11*. New Delhi: Ministry of Rural Development, Government of India.

GoI-MoSPI (2013). *Key Indicators of Employment and Unemeployment in India, 2011-2012*, NSSO 68th Round. New Delhi: Ministry of Statistics and Programme Implementation, Government of India,.

GoNCT (2013). *Delhi Human Development Report, 2013*. New Delhi: Institute for Human Development, Academic Foundation and Government of National Capital Territory.

Goldar, Bishwanath (2002). "Trade Liberalization and Employment: The Case of India", *Working Paper*. Geneva: International Labour Organization.

Goldar, Bishwanath and Suresh Chand Aggarwal (2012). "Informalization of Industrial Labour in India: Are Labour Market Rigidities and Growing Import Competition to Blame?", *Journal of Developing Economies,* 50(2): 141–69.

Gopalakrishnan, Ramapriya (2008). *Freedom of Association and Collective Bargaining in Export Processing Zones: Role of the ILO Supervisory Mechanism*. Geneva: International Labour Standards Department, International Labour Organization.

Guhan, S. (1993). "Social Security for the Poor in the Unorganized Sector: A Feasible Blueprint for India", in Kirit S. Parikh and R. Sudarshan (eds), *Human Development and Structural Adjustment*. New Delhi: Macmillan.

Gurumurthy, G. (2006). "Trade Union Power Wearing Thin – Deunionization at Textile Mills", *Business Line, http://www.thehindubusinessline.com/2004/09/28/stories/2004092801901700.htm*. Accessed 15 January 2013.

Gustafsson. B, AL Shi and T Sicular (2008). *Inequality and Public Policy in China*. New York: Cambridge University Press.

Hanlon, James, Amanda Barrientos, and Peter Hulme (2010). *Just Give Money to the Poor: The Development Revolution from the Global South*. Denver, Colorado: Kumarian Press.

Himanshu (2005). "Wages in Rural India: Sources, Trends and Comparability", *Indian Journal of Labour Economics,* 48(2): 375–406.

———. (2007). "Recent Trends in Poverty and Inequality: Some Preliminary Results", *Economic and Political Weekly,* 42(6): 497–508, February 10.

Hirway, Indira, M.R. Saluja and Bhupesh Yadav (2008). "India: Reducing Unpaid Work in the Village of Nana Kotda, Gujarat—An Economic Impact Analysis of NREGA", *The Impact of Public Employment Guarantee Strategies on Gender Equality and Pro-poor Economic Development, Research Project No. 34*. New York: The Levy Economics Institute of Bard College and UNDP.

IAMR (2005). *Evaluation of Prime Minister"s Rozgar Yojana*. New Delhi: Institute of Applied Manpower Research.

IHD (2006). *Evaluation and Impact Assessment of the National Rural Employment Guarantee Scheme in Bihar.* New Delhi: Institute for Human Development (*Mimeo*).

———. (2012). Social Protection in Urban India: Some Preliminary Findings from Delhi and Ranchi. A Study Conducted by Institute of Rural Management Anand (IRMA) and Institute for Human Development (*Mimeo*).

IIPA (2011). *Study on Assessment of Future Demand for Skill Sets in Bihar.* New Delhi: Indian Institute of Public Administration.

ILO (1997). *World Labour Report: Industrial Relations, Democracy and Social Stability.* Geneva: International Labour Organization.

———. (2001). *Social Security: A New Consensus.* Geneva: International Labour Organization.

———. (2007). *Decent Work for Sustainable Development,* Director General's Introduction to the International Labour Conference, ILC 96-2007, Report I (A). Geneva: International Labour Organization.

———. (2011). *World Social Security Report 2010–11,* Geneva: International Labour Organization.

———. (2012). *Global Employment Trends 2012.* Geneva: International Labaour Organization.

Jayadev, A., S. Motiram and U. Vakulabharanam (2007). "Patterns of Wealth Disparities in India during the Liberalization Era", *Economic and Political Weekly,* 42(38): 3853–63, September 22.

Jha, Praveen and Sakti Goldar (2008). *Labour Market Regulation and Economic Performance: A Critical Review of Arguments and Some Plausible Lessons for India.* Geneva: Employment Analysis and Research Unit, Economic and Labour Market Analysis Department, International Labour Organization.

Jhabvala, Renana (2003). "Liberalization and Women", *http://www.india-seminar.com/2003/531%20renana%20jhabvala.htm,* Accessed 3 August 2013.

John, J. (2007). "Overall Increase and Sectoral Setbacks: Lessons from Trade Union Verification 2002 Data (Provisional)", *Labour File:* 13–25, January–April.

Kanbur, Ravi (2003). "Development Economics and the Compensation Principle," *International Social Science Journal,* 55 (175): 27–35.

Kannan, K.P. (1992). "Labour Institutions and the Development Process in Kerala", in Papola, T.S. and Gerry Rodgers (eds.), *Labour Institutions and Economic Development in India,* Research Series 97. Geneva: International Institute for Labour Studies.

———. (1999). "Changing Economic Structure and Labour Institutions in India: Some Reflections on Emerging Perspectives on Organizing the Unorganized", *Indian Journal of Labour Economics,* 42(4): 753–68.

———. (2002). "The Welfare Fund Model of Social Security for Unorganized Workers: The Kerala Experience", *Indian Journal of Labour Economics,* 45(2). April-June.

———. (2006). "Social Security for Unorganized Workers: A Major National Initiative", *Economic and Political Weekly,* August 12.

———. (2007). "Social Security in a Globalizing World", *International Social Security Review,* 60(2–3). April–September.

———. (2012). "How Inclusive is Inclusive Growth in India?", *Working Paper WP 03/ 2012,* New Delhi: Institute for Human Development.

Kannan, K.P. and G. Raveendran (2008). "Growth Sans Employment: A Quarter Century of Jobless Growth in India's Organized Manufacturing", *Economic and Political Weekly,* 44(10). March 7.

Kannan, K.P., and N.V. Pillai (2007). *Social Security in India: The Long Lane Treaded and the Longer Road Ahead Towards Universalization.* Thiruvananthapuram: Centre for Development Studies.

Karan, Anup and S. Sakthivel (2008). "Trends in Wages and Earnings in India: Increasing Wage Differentials in a Segmented Labour Market", *ILO Asia-Pacific Working Paper Series.* New Delhi: Sub-regional Office for South Asia, International Labour Organization. May.

Karan, Anup K. (1997). "Minimum Wages and Its Implications in Madhya Pradesh", *Indian Journal of Labour Economics,* 41(4).

Karimullah and U. Kalpagam (2010). "Are Muslims Discriminated against in the Labour Market in India?", *Indian Journal of Labour Economics,* 53(1). January–March.

Khera, Reetika (2008). "Empower Guarantee Act", *Economic and Political Weekly,* 43: 8–10.

Krishna Murthy, R. (2006). Background Paper on *Negotiating Wage Settlements: Experiences of Innovative Managements.* A One-day Workshop. January 21. Pune.

Krishna Murthy, K. (2008). "Innovative Changes through Collective Bargaining", PPT File (*Mimeo*).

Krishnamurthy, J. and G. Raveendran (2008). "Measures of Labour Force Participation and Utilization", *Working Paper* 1. New Delhi: National Commission for Enterprises in the Unorganized Sector. January.

Kulkarni, Suchita (2002). "Competitive Pressures and Managerial Strategies: Case Study of a Composite Textile Mill in Mumbai, 1984-1999", Ph.D. thesis (Unpublished). Department of Economics, University of Mumbai.

Kundu, A. (2009). "Urbanization and Migration: An Analysis of Trends, Patterns and Policies in Asia", *Human Development Research Paper No. 16.* New York: United Nations Development Programme.

Kurien, P.H. (2000). "Labour Welfare Schemes of Kerala for Unorganized Labour", in A.S. Oberai, A. Sivananthiran and C.S. Venkata Ratnam (eds.), *Perspectives on Unorganized Labour.* South Asia Multidisciplinary Advisory Team (SAAT), International Labour Organization (ILO) and Indian Industrial Relations Association (IIRA).

Labour Bureau (2009). *Effects of Economic Slowdown on Employment in India.* Chandigarh: Ministry of Labour and Employment, Government of India.

Levy, Santiago (2008). *Good Intentions, Bad Outcomes: Social Policy, Informality and Economic Growth in Mexico.* Washington, DC: Brookings Institution.

Lindert, Peter (2004). *Growing Public: Social Spending and Economic Growth since the Eighteenth Century.* Cambridge, UK: Cambridge University Press.

Madheswaran, S. (2010). "Labour Market Discrimination in India: Methodological Developments and Empirical

Evidence", *Indian Journal of Labour Economics*, 53(3): 457–80.

Madheswaran, S. and Paul Attewell (2007). "Caste Discrimination in the Urban Indian Labour Market: Evidence from the National Sample Survey", *Economic and Political Weekly*, 42(41): 4146–54.

———. (2009). "Wage and Job Discrimination in the Urban Labour Market", in Sukhadeo Thorat and Katherine S. Newman (eds.), *Blocked by Caste: Economic Discrimination in Modern India*. New Delhi: Oxford University Press.

Mahendra Dev, S. (1995). "India"s (Maharashtra) Employment Guarantee Scheme: Lessons from Long Experience", in Joachim von Braun (eds.), *Employment for Poverty Reduction and Food Security*. Washington, DC: International Food Policy Research Institute (IFPRI).

Mahendra Dev, S. and C. Ravi (2007). "Poverty and Inequality: All India and States, 1983-2005", *Economic and Political Weekly*, February 10.

Maiti, Dibyendu (2009). "Institutions, Networks and Industrialization: Field Level Evidence of Fragmentation and Flexibility from India", *IPPG Discussion Papers, http://www.ippg.org.uk/papers/dp26.pdf*, Accessed 13 October 2013.

Mathur, Ajeet N. (1993). "The Experience of Consultation during Structural Adjustment in India (1990-92)", *International Labour Review*, 132: 331–45.

Mathur, Ashok (2007). "Economic Growth to Inclusive Growth", Keynote Paper at a *Seminar on Inclusive Growth*. Jammu University.

Mathur, Ashok and Rajendra P. Mamgain (2004). "Human Capital Stocks, Their Level of Utilization and Economic Development in India", *Indian Journal of Labour Economics*, 47(4).

Mathur, K. and N.R. Sheth (1969). *Tripartism in Labour Policy: The Indian Experience*. New Delhi: Shri Ram Centre for Industrial Relations.

Mazumdar, Dipak and Sandip Sarkar (2007). "Growth of Employment and Earnings in Tertiary Sector, 1983-2000", *Economic and Political Weekly*, 42(11): 973–81.

———. (2008). *Globalization, Labour Markets and Inequality in India*. London: Routledge.

———. (2013). *Manufacturing Enterprises in Asia – Size Structure and Economic Growth*. London: Routledge.

Mazumdar, Dipak, Sandip Sarkar and B.S. Mehta (2013). "Inequality in India", ICSSR-*IHD Programme on Globalization and Labour (mimeo)*. New Delhi: Institute for Human Development.

Mehrotra, Santosh, Ankita Gandhi and Bimal K. Sahoo (2013). "Estimating India's Skill Gap on a Realistic Basis for 2022", *Economic and Political Weekly*, 48(3): 102–11.

Mitra, Arup (2008). "The Indian Labour Market: An Overview", *ILO Asia-Pacific Working Paper Series*. New Delhi: ILO Sub-regional Office for South Asia.

MoL&E (2008). *Annual Report (2007–08)*. New Delhi: Ministry of Labour & Employment, Government of India.

———. (2010). *Draft National Employment Policy*. New Delhi: Ministry of Labour & Employment, Government of India.

———. (2010). *Report on Effect of Economic Slowdown on Employment in India (July–September, 2010)*. Chandigarh: Ministry of Labour & Employment, Government of India, Labour Bureau.

———. (2013). *Annual Report (2012–13)*. New Delhi: Ministry of Labour & Employment, Government of India.

Mukherjee, Dipa (2007). "Post Reform Trends in Wage Differentials: A Decomposition Analysis for India", *The Indian Journal of Labour Economics*, 50(4): 955–65.

Nagaraj, R. (2004). "Fall in Organized Manufacturing Employment", *Economic and Political Weekly*, 39(30).

Nam, J.L. (1991). *Income Inequality between the Sexes and the Role of the State: South Korea, 1960-1990*. Indiana University.

Narayana, D. (2010). "Review of the Rashtriya Swastha Bima Yojana", *Economic and Political Weekly*, July 17.

Nathan, Dev (2012). "Displacement and Reconstruction of Livelihoods", in Dev Nathan and Virginius Xaxa, (eds.), *Social Exclusion and Adverse Inclusion: Development and Deprivation of Adivasis in India*. New Delhi: Oxford University Press.

Nathan, Dev and Alakh N. Sharma (2013). "Cash Transfers and Social Security," in *Yojana*. New Delhi: Planning Commission, Government of India.

NCEUS (2006). *Report on Social Security for Unorganized Workers*. New Delhi: National Commission for Enterprises in the Unorganized Sector, Government of India.

———. (2007). *Conditions of Work and Livelihood in the Unorganized Sector*. New Delhi: National Commission for Enterprises in the Unorganised Sector, Government of India. August.

———. (2009). *The Challenge of Employment in India: An Informal Economy Perspective*. Main Report. Vol. 1. New Delhi: National Commission for Enterprises in the Unorganized Sector, Government of India.

———. (2009a). *Skill Formation and Employment Assurance in the Unorganized Sector*. New Delhi: National Commission for Enterprises in the Unorganized Sector, Government of India.

———. (2009b). *Social Security for the Unorganized Sector*. New Delhi: National Commission for Enterprises in the Unorganized Sector, Government of India.

NCL (1969). *The Report*. New Delhi: National Commission on Labour, Government of India.

Neetha, N. (2006). "Invisibility Continues?", *Economic and Political Weekly*, 41(32). 12–18 August.

NSSO (2013). *Status of Education and Vocational Training in India*, 66th Round, (June 2009-July 2010). Report No. 551(66/10/6). New Delhi: National Sample Survey Organization.

Pages, Carmen and Tirthankar Roy (2006). "Regulation, Enforcement and Adjudication in India Labour Markets: Historical Perspective, Recent Changes and Way Forward", Paper Presented at the Conference on *Labour and Employment Issues in India*. August 2006. New Delhi.

Panagariya, Arvind (2004). "Growth and Reforms during 1980s and 1990s", *Economic and Political Weekly*, June 19.

Panagariya, Arvind and Vishal More (2013). "Poverty by Social, Religious & Economic Groups in India and Its Largest States: 1993–94 to 2011–12", *Working Paper* No. 2013–02. USA: Program on Indian Economic Policies,

Colombia University. *http://indianeconomy.columbia.edu/sites/default/files/working_papers/working_paper_2013-02-final.pdf*. Accessed 1 November, 2013.

Pankaj, Ashok K. (2008). "The National Rural Employment Guarantee Act—Guaranteeing the Right to Livelihood", in *India Social Development Report 2008*. Council for Social Development. New Delhi: Oxford University Press.

Papola, T.S. (1992). "The Question of Unemployment", in Bimal Jalan (ed.), *The Indian Economy: Problems and Prospects*, New Delhi: Viking Penguin India.

———. (2005). "Social Exclusion and Discrimination in Hiring Practices", in Sukhadeo Thorat, Aryama and Prashant Negi (eds.), *Reservation and Private Sector: Quest for Equal Opportunity and Growth*. Jaipur: Rawat Publications.

———. (2006). "Emerging Structure of Indian Economy: Implications of Growing Inter-sectoral Imbalances", *Indian Economic Journal*, 54 (1): April–June.

———. (2007). "Employment Trends", in Kaushik Basu (ed). *The Oxford Companion to Economics in India*. New Delhi: Oxford University Press.

———. (2008). "Employment Challenge and Strategies in India", *ILO Asia-Pacific Working Paper Series*. New Delhi: Sub-regional Office for South Asia, International Labour Organization. January.

———. (2009). "Industry and Employment: Dissecting Recent Indian Experience", in H.R. Hashim, K.S. Chalapati Rao, K.V.K. Ranganathan and M.R. Murthy (eds), *Indian Industrial Development and Globalization*. New Delhi: Academic Foundation.

———. (2012). "Labour Market Segmentation in India: Role of Regulation and Reforms", Prepared for ILO as a *Country Case Study on Labour Market Segmentation for the Global Research Project on Employment and Quality of Jobs*. Geneva: International Labour Organization.

———. (2012a). "Contract Labour: An Academic Perspective", in K.R. Shyam Sundar (ed.). *Contract Labour in India: Issues and Perspectives*. New Delhi: Indian Society of Labour Economics in association with Daanish Publishers.

Papola, T.S. and Alakh N. Sharma (2003). *Employment and Poverty Reduction in India: Policy Perspectives Based on Recent ILO Studies*. Geneva: International Labour Organization,.

———. (2004). "Labour: Down and Out?", *Seminar*, May.

Papola, T.S. and P.P. Sahu (2008). *Mainstreaming Employment in Macro-economic and Sectoral Development: A Framework for Analysis and Policy*. New Delhi: International Labour Organization.

Papola, T.S. and Jesim Pais (2007). "Debate on Labour Market Reforms in India: A Case of Misplaced Focus", *Indian Journal of Labour Economics*, 50(2): 183–200.

Papola, T.S., Jesim Pais and Partha Pratim Sahu (2008). *Labour Regulation in Indian Industry: Towards a Rational and Equitable Framework*. Institute for Studies in Industrial Development (ISID), European Union (EU) and International Institute for Labour Studies (IILS). New Delhi: Bookwell.

Parthasarthy, G. (1998). "Minimum Wages in Agriculture: A Review of Indian Experiences", in Radhakrishna and Alakh N. Sharma (eds.), *Empowering Rural Labour in India: Market, State and Mobilization*, New Delhi: Institute for Human Development.

Patil, B.R. (1988). *Collective Bargaining: Perspectives and Practices*, Bangalore: Indian Institute of Management.

Pavani, P. (1985). "Indian Supreme Court and Worker-oriented Industrial Jurisprudence", *Journal of the Indian Law Institute*, 27.

Planning Commission (1956). *Second Five Year Plan 1957-62*, New Delhi: Government of India.

———. (1962). *Third Five Year Plan 1962-67*, New Delhi: Government of India.

———. (1985). *Seventh Five Year Plan 1985-90*, New Delhi: Government of India.

———. (1998). *Ninth Five Year Plan 1997-2002, Vol I*. New Delhi: Government of India.

———. (2001). *Report of Task Force on Employment Opportunities*. New Delhi: Planning Commission and Ministry of Finance, Government of India.

———. (2002). *Tenth Five Year Plan 2002-2007, Vol I.*, New Delhi: Government of India.

———. (2002a). *Tenth Five Year Plan 2000-07, Vol. I*. New Delhi: Government of India.

———. (2002b). *Report of the Special Group on Targeting Ten Million Employment Opportunities per Year*. New Delhi: Government of India,

———. (2005). *Mid-term Appraisal of Tenth Five Year Plan, 2002-07*. New Delhi: Government of India.

———. (2008). *Eleventh Five Year Plan (2007-12)*. New Delhi: Government of India.

———. (2008a). *Eleventh Five Year Plan 2007-12*. Vol. I. New Delhi: Government of India.

———. (2008b). *Eleventh Five Year Plan 2007-12*. Vol. II. New Delhi: Government of India.

———. (2008c). *Eleventh Five Year Plan 2007-12*. Vol. III. New Delhi: Government of India.

———. (2008d) *Eleventh Five Year Plan (2007-2012)*. Vol I: Inclusive Growth. New Delhi: Government of India.

———. (2008e). *Agriculture Rural Development: Industry, Services and Physical Infrastructure*. Vol III. New Delhi: Government of India.

———. (2008f). *Eleventh Five Year Plan (2007-12)*. Chapter 11. New Delhi: Government of India.

———. (2010). *Mid-Term Appraisal of Eleventh Five Year Plan*. New Delhi: Government of India.

———. (2012). *Faster, Sustainable and More Inclusive Growth: An Approach Paper to Twelfth Five Year Plan*. New Delhi: Government of India.

———. (2013). *Twelfth Five Year Plan 2012-2017*. Vol. III. New Delhi: Government of India. 40, 49.

———. (2013a). *Poverty Estimates for 2011-12*, New Delhi: Planning Commission, Government of India, 22 July.

Purushotham, P. (2008). *Micro Credit for Self Employment: Final Draft*. Hyderabad: National Institute of Rural Development (unpublished).

Radhakrishna R. (n.d.). Department of Rural Development, Ministry of Rural Development, Government of India, New Delhi, February.

Radhakrishna, R. and Shovan Ray (eds.) (2005). *Handbook of Poverty in India*. New Delhi: Oxford University Press.

Raj, K.N. (1977). "Unemployment and Structural Changes in Indian Rural Society", *Indian Journal of Labour Economics*, 11(31-33), April–June.

Rajaraman, Indira and Sanjiv Misra (2012). *Report of the Committee on Fiscal Consolidation*. New Delhi: Ministry of Finance, Government of India.

Rajeev, Meenkashi (2006). "Contract Labour Act in India: A Pragmatic View", *Working Paper* 175. Bangalore: Institute for Social and Economic Change.

Ramaswamy, E.A. (1984). *Power and Justice: The State in Industrial Relations*. New Delhi: Oxford University Press.

———. (1988). *Worker Consciousness and Trade Union Response*. New Delhi: Oxford University Press.

———. (2000). *Managing Human Resources: A Contemporary Text*. New Delhi: Oxford University Press.

———. (2006). "India: Country Report."

Rani, Uma (2008). "Impact of Changing Work Pattern on Income Inequality", *Discussion Paper 193/2008*. Geneva: International Institute of Labour Studies.

RBI (2009). *Report on Currency and Finance 2007-08*. Mumbai: Reserve Bank of India.

Reddy, D.N. (2008). *Labour Regulation, Industrial Growth and Employment: A Study of Recent Trends in Andhra Pradesh*. Labour Regulation in Indian Industry Series (General Editor: T S Papola), Volume 5. New Delhi: Institute for Studies in Industrial Development (ISID) and Bookwell.

RIS (2004). *South Asia Development and Cooperation Report 2001-02*. New Delhi: Research and Information System for Non-aligned and Other Developing Countries.

RGCC (2006). "Population Projections for India and States 2001-2026", *Report of the Technical Group on Population Projections Constituted by National Population Commission*. New Delhi: Office of the Registrar General and Census Commissioner.

RGICS (1997). *Report of the Expert Committee on Small Enterprises* (Chairman: Abid Hussain). New Delhi: Rajiv Gandhi Institute of Contemporary Studies.

Rodgers, Gerry, Amrita Datta, Janine Rodgers, Sunil K. Mishra and Alakh N. Sharma (2013). *The Challenges of Inclusive Development in Bihar*. New Delhi: Institute for Human Development.

Roy, Swadesh (2006). "Contract Workers in India", Centre for Indian Trade Unions.

RSBY (2013). *Connect Newsletter* 15, April. New Delhi: Rashtriya Swasthya Bima Yojana, Government of India.

Rudolph, Lloyd I. and Susane Hoeber Rudolph (1987). *In Pursuit of Lakshmi: The Political Economy of the Indian State*. Hyderabad: Orient Longmans Ltd.

Rustagi, Preet (2010). "Continuing Gender Stereotypes or Signs of Change: Occupational Pattern of Women Workers", *Indian Journal of Labour Economics*, 53(3): 481–500.

Rustagi, Preet, Sandip Sarkar, and Pinaki Joddar (2009). "The Gender Dimensions of Urban Poverty", *India Urban Poverty Report 2009*. Ministry of Housing and Urban Poverty Alleviation, Government of India. New Delhi: Oxford University Press.

Saget, Catherine (2006). "Wage Fixing in Informal Economy: Evidence from Brazil, India, Indonesia and South Africa", *Conditions of Work and Employment Series* 16. Geneva: International Labour Organization.

Sainath, P. (2008). "NREGA Hits Buses to Mumbai", *http://www.indiatogether.com/2008/jul/psa-mumbai:htm*. Accessed 14 September 2013.

Samant, P.N. (2004). "Change Management by Innovative Wage Settlements", *Arbiter*: 13–15, 24, December.

———. (2010). "Trends in Wage Settlements: Innovations and Ideas", *Arbiter*: 709, 714, October.

Sankaran, T.S. (2000). "Social Security in the Unorganized Sector", in A.S. Oberai, A. Sivananthiran and C.S. Venkata Ratnam (eds.), *Perspectives on Unorganized Labour*. South Asia Multidisciplinary Advisory Team (SAAT), International Labour Organization (ILO) and Indian Industrial Relations Association (IIRA).

Sarkar, Sandip and Balwant Singh Mehta (2010). "Global Production Networks and Decent Work in India"s Information Technology and IT Enabled Services Sector: Recent Experience and Trends", in Anne Posthuma and Dev Nathan (eds.), *Economic and Social Implications of Global Production Networks in India*. New Delhi: Oxford University Press.

Sen, Abhijit (1998). "Rural Labour Market and Poverty", in Radhakrishna and Alakh N. Sharma (eds.), *Empowering Rural Labour in India: Market, State and Mobilization*. New Delhi: Institute for Human Development.

Sengupta, Arjun, K.P. Kannan and G. Raveendran (2008). "India"s Common People: Who are They, How Many Are They and How do they Live?", *Economic and Political Weekly*, March 15.

Sharma, Alakh N. (2002). "Access to Employment in India: The Case of Public and Corporate Sector Jobs", *Mimeograph*, New Delhi: Institute for Human Development.

———. (2004). "Globalization Work and Social Exclusion: Emerging Global and Indian Perspective", *Kunda Datar Memorial Lecture*, Gokhale Institute of Politics and Economics, Pune, August 26-27.

———. (2006). "Flexibility, Employment and Labour Market Reforms in India", *Economic and Political Weekly*: 78–85, May 27.

———. (2013). *Experiences of National Rural Employment Guarantee Act in India and Some Aspects of Decent Work Agenda*, *Mimeograph*, New Delhi: Institute for Human Development.

Sharma, Alakh N. and V. Kalpana (2008). *Labour Regulation and Industrial Development in Uttar Pradesh: Some Recent Trends*. Institute for Studies for Industrial Development (ISID), European Union (EU) and International Institute for Labour Studies (IILS) New Delhi: Bookwell.

Sharma, Baldev (1987). "Industrial Democracy: The Indian Experience", *Indian Journal of Industrial Relations*, 22: 254–68.

Shrouti, Arvind and Nandkumar (1995). *New Economic Policy, Changing Management Strategies: Impact on Workers and Trade Unions*. New Delhi: Friedrich Ebert Stiftung (FES).

Shyam Sundar, K.R. (1999). "Official Data on Trade Unions: Some Comments", *Economic and Political Weekly*: 2839–41, October 2.

———. (2004). "The Issue of the Right to Strike" in *Four Consultations on Workers and the Right to Strike Report*. New Delhi: Indian Society of Labour Economics and Institute for Human Development.

———. (2004a). "Lockouts in India, 1961-2001", *Economic and Political Weekly*: 4377–85, September 25.

———. (2008a). *Impact of Labour Regulation on Growth, Investment, and Employment: A Study of Maharashtra*, Institute for Studies in Industrial Development (ISID), European Union (EU) and International Institute for Labour Studies (IILS). New Delhi: Bookwell.

———. (2008b). *Benchmarking Industrial Relations and Labour Market*. Hyderabad: ICFAI Press.

———. (2009). *Labour Institutions and Labour Reforms in Contemporary India, Volume I: Trade Unions and Industrial Conflict*. Hyderabad: ICFAI Press.

———. (2010a). Labour *Reforms and Decent Work in India: A Study of Labour Inspection in India*. New Delhi: Bookwell.

———. (2010b). *Industrial Conflict in India: Is the Sleeping Giant Waking Up?* New Delhi: Bookwell.

———. (2010c). "The Current State of Industrial Relations in Tamil Nadu", *ILO Asia-Pacific Working Paper Series*. New Delhi: Sub-regional Office for South Asia.

———. (2011a). "Employment Relations in India in the Post-reform Period: Positives, Challenges and Opportunities", *Indian Journal of Labour Economics* 54(1): 89–111.

———. (2011b). "Non-regular Workers in India: Social Dialogue and Organizational and Bargaining Strategies", *Working Paper* No.30, Industrial and Employment Relations Department (DIALOGUE). Geneva: International Labour Organization.

———. (2012a). "The Contract Labour in India: The Battle between Flexibility and Fairness", in K.R. Shyam Sundar (ed.). *Contract Labour in India: Issues and Perspectives*. New Delhi: Indian Society of Labour Economics and Daanish Publishers.

———. (2012b). "Industrial Conflict in India in the Post-reform Period: Battle over Hard Labour Reforms", Paper presented at the two-day *National Seminar on Globalization, Labour Market and Employment Relations in India*. July 9–10. Mumbai: Indian Society of Labour Economics and New Delhi: Institute for Human Development.

———. (2012c). *Role of Collective Bargaining in India in the Post-reform Period: A Search for Balance between Efficiency and Fairness*. Project Report submitted to ILO Sub-regional Office. New Delhi.

Silberman, Andrea and Steven Kapsos (2013). "Why is Female Labour Force Participation Declining So Sharply in India?", Paper presented at the ILO Workshop on *Women"s Labour Force Participation in India and South Asia: Have Women Benefited From an Era of Globalization and Growth?* February 14–15. New Delhi.

Singh, Gayathri (2008). "Judiciary Jettisons Working Class", *Combat Law*: 24–33, November–December.

Srivastava, Ravi (2005a). "India: Internal Migration and Its Links with Poverty and Development", in *Migration, Development and Poverty Reduction in Asia*. Geneva: International Organization for Migration.

———. (2011). "Labour Migration in India: Recent Trends, Patterns and Policy Issues", *Indian Journal of Labour Economics*, 54(3): 411–40.

———. (2013). *A Social Protection Floor for India*. A Study for the ILO and the UN System in India. PPT.

Srivastava, Ravi and S.K. Sasikumar (2005). "An Overview of Migration in India, Its Impacts and Key Issues", in Tasneem Siddiqui (ed.), *Migration and Development: Pro-poor Policy Choices*. Dhaka: The University Press. pp.157–216

Standing Committee on Labour (2007). *The Unorganized Sector Workers' Social Security Bill*. New Delhi: Government of India.

Standing, Guy (2012). *Cash Transfers: A Review of the Issues in India*. New Delhi: SEWA and UNICEF.

Sundaram, K. (2007). "Employment and Poverty in India", *Working Paper No.* 155. Centre for Development Economics, Delhi School of Economics, University of Delhi.

The Hindu (2011). "It's High Time the Subterfuge of Contract Labour System Ends: Court", *The Hindu*, September 4.

Thorat, S. (2008). "Labour Market Discrimination: Concept, Forms and Remedies in the Indian Situation", *Indian Journal of Labour Economics*, 51(1): 31–51.

Topolova, Petia (2008). "India: Is the Rising Tide Lifting All Boats", *IMF Working Paper* No. 08/54. Washington, DC: International Monetary Fund.

UNCTAD (2006). *World Investment Report*. Geneva: United Nations Conference on Trade and Development.

Unni, Jeemol (2000). "Employment Trends and Earnings in the Informal Sector", Paper presented at International Seminar on *India: Meeting the Employment Challenge, Conference on Labour and Employment Issues in India*. New Delhi. 27–29 July 2006. Organized by Institute for Human Development and supported by the World Bank.

Unni, Jeemol and G. Raveendran (2007). "Growth of Employment (1993-94 to 2004-05). Illusion of Inclusiveness", *Economic and Political Weekly* 42(3), January 20–26.

Upadhyay, S.K. (1983). *Law of Essential Services in India: A Critical Study of the Essential Services Maintenance Act, 1981*. New Delhi: Deep and Deep Publications.

Vakulabharanam, V. (2010). "Does Class Matter? Class Structure and Worsening Inequality in India", *Economic and Political Weekly*, 45(29): 67–76, July 17.

Venkata Ratnam, C.S. (2000). "Trade Unions and the Unorganized Sector", in A.S. Oberai, A. Sivananthiran and C.S. Venkata Ratnam (eds.), *Perspectives on Unorganized Labour*. South Asia Multidisciplinary Advisory Team (SAAT), International Labour Organization and Indian Industrial Relations Association (IIRA).

———. (2003). *Negotiated Change: Collective Bargaining, Liberalization and Restructuring in India*. New Delhi: Response Books.

———. (2006). *Industrial Relations*. New Delhi: Oxford University Press.

Vijayabaskar, M. (2006). "Garment Industry in India", in Gopal Joshi (ed.), *Garment Industry in South Asia: Rags or Riches? Competitiveness, Productivity and Job Quality in the Post-MFA Environment*, New Delhi: South Asia Multidisciplinary Advisory Team and International Labour Organization.

Visser, Jelle (2003). "Unions and Unionism around the World", in John T. Addison and Claus Schnabel (eds.), *International Handbook of Trade Unions*. Cheltanham: Edward Elgar.

WCSDG (2004). *A Fair Globalization: Creating Opportunities for All*. Report of the World Commission on the Social Dimension of Globalization, Geneva: International Labour Organization.

World Bank (2000). *World Development Indicators*. Washington DC.

———. (2008). *World Development Report*. Washington DC.

Statistical Appendices

1. National Income
2. Labour Force
3. Work Force
4. Unemployment
5. Quality of Employment
6. Wages and Earnings
7. Employment in Important Emerging Non-agriculture Sectors
8. Labour Institutions and Employment Relations
9. Poverty

NATIONAL INCOME

Table 1.1

Share of Gross Domestic Product by Industries (One Digit Level) at Factor Cost (At 2004-05 Prices)

Sector/Industries	*1972-73*	*1983-84*	*1993-94*	*2004-05*	*2011-12*
(1)	(2)	(3)	(4)	(5)	(6)
Agriculture and allied activities	41.1	35.5	28.4	19.0	14.1
Primary sector	41.1	35.5	28.4	19.0	14.1
Mining and quarrying	2.3	2.9	3.3	2.9	2.1
Manufacturing	13.3	14.8	14.6	15.3	15.7
Electricity, gas and water supply	1.1	1.6	2.2	2.1	1.9
Construction	7.6	6.6	6.6	7.7	7.9
Secondary sector	24.4	25.8	26.8	27.9	27.5
Trade, hotels and restaurants	10.5	11.8	12.6	16.1	16.9
Transport, storage and communication	4.0	5.6	5.5	8.4	10.6
Financing, real estate and business services	7.9	9.1	13.3	14.7	18.1
Community, social and personal services	12.1	12.2	13.5	13.8	12.8
Tertiary sector	34.5	38.7	44.8	53.0	58.4
Non-agriculture	58.9	64.5	71.6	81.0	85.9
Total	100	100	100	100	100

Source: Various Issues of National Accounts Statistics.

Table 1.2

Growth of Gross Domestic Product by Industry (At One Digit Level): 1972-73/2011-12 (At 2004-05 Prices)

Sector/Industries	*1972-73/ 1983-84*	*1983-84/ 1993-94*	*1993-94/ 2004-05*	*2004-05/ 2011-12*	*1972-73/ 1993-94*	*1993-94/ 2011-12*	*1972-73/ 2011-12*
(1)	(2)	(3)	(4)	(5)	(6)	(7)	(8)
Agriculture and allied activities	2.7	2.6	2.5	3.9	2.7	3.0	2.8
Primary sector	2.7	2.6	2.5	3.9	2.7	3.0	2.8
Mining and quarrying	6.2	6.1	5.0	3.5	6.2	4.4	5.4
Manufacturing	5.1	4.8	6.7	8.9	4.9	7.6	6.1
Electricity, gas and water supply	7.1	8.7	5.7	6.7	7.9	6.1	7.0
Construction	2.8	4.9	7.7	8.8	3.8	8.1	5.8
Secondary sector	4.7	5.2	6.7	8.2	4.9	7.3	6.0
Trade, hotels and restaurants	5.2	5.6	8.6	9.2	5.4	8.9	7.0
Transport, storage and communication	7.4	4.6	10.6	12.1	6.1	11.2	8.4
Financing, real estate and business services	5.5	8.9	7.3	11.7	7.1	9.0	8.0
Community, social and personal services	4.2	5.9	7.0	7.3	5.0	6.8	5.8
Tertiary sector	5.2	6.4	8.0	10.0	5.8	8.7	7.1
Non-agriculture	5.0	6.0	7.0	9.4	5.4	8.2	6.7
Total	4.1	4.9	6.0	8.5	4.5	7.1	5.7

Source: Various Issues of National Accounts Statistics.

2. LABOUR FORCE

Table 2.1

Labour Force Participation Rates (UPSS): 1983/2011-12 (All Ages)

Year	*Rural*			*Urban*			*Total*		
	Male	*Female*	*Person*	*Male*	*Female*	*Person*	*Male*	*Female*	*Person*
(1)	(2)	(3)	(4)	(5)	(6)	(7)	(8)	(9)	(10)
1983	55.5	34.2	45.1	54.0	15.9	35.9	55.1	30.0	42.9
1993-94	56.1	33.0	44.9	54.3	16.5	36.3	55.6	29.0	42.8
2004-05	55.5	33.3	44.6	57.0	17.8	38.2	55.9	29.4	43.0
2011-12	55.3	25.3	40.6	56.3	15.5	36.7	55.6	22.5	39.5

Note: UPSS: Usual Principal and Subsidiary Status.

Source: Employment and Unemployment Survey, various NSS quinquennial rounds.

Table 2.2

Age-specific Labour Force Participation Rate (UPSS): 1983/2011-12 (5 Years+)

Age Group (Years)	*Rural*			*Urban*			*Total*		
	Male	*Female*	*Person*	*Male*	*Female*	*Person*	*Male*	*Female*	*Person*
(1)	(2)	(3)	(4)	(5)	(6)	(7)	(8)	(9)	(10)
					1983				
5–9	2.6	2.5	2.5	0.8	0.7	0.7	2.2	2.1	2.1
10–14	25.5	24.1	24.8	12.3	7.1	9.8	22.5	20.1	21.4
15–19	69.0	46.1	58.1	49.1	17.4	34.4	63.6	38.5	51.8
20–24	92.5	49.8	70.0	83.0	21.5	54.0	89.7	42.7	65.6
25–29	97.9	56.0	76.6	97.3	24.7	62.2	97.8	48.0	72.8
30–34	98.4	59.5	78.7	98.6	27.4	66.4	98.5	52.0	75.6
35–39	98.6	62.9	81.0	98.7	30.5	66.3	98.6	55.0	77.3
40–44	98.0	62.1	80.1	97.9	31.2	67.7	98.0	55.1	77.0
45–49	97.7	60.0	78.7	97.8	30.8	66.5	97.7	53.5	75.8
50–54	95.4	54.2	75.4	94.0	27.4	62.7	95.1	48.3	72.6
55–59	91.5	48.6	69.9	83.0	23.2	54.4	89.6	43.3	66.5
60 & above	66.7	22.6	44.7	50.4	13.8	31.2	63.4	20.7	41.9
All	55.2	34.2	44.9	53.9	15.9	35.8	54.9	29.9	42.7
					1993-94				
5–9	1.2	1.4	1.3	0.5	0.5	0.5	1.0	1.2	1.1
10–14	14.0	14.1	14.1	6.9	4.6	5.8	12.3	11.7	12.0
15–19	59.8	37.1	49.5	40.4	14.1	28.4	54.5	30.8	43.8
20–24	90.2	46.9	67.9	77.1	23.0	51.1	86.5	40.7	63.3
25–29	98.0	53.0	74.6	95.9	24.8	61.0	97.4	45.9	71.0
30–34	98.9	58.7	78.6	98.3	28.3	64.7	98.7	50.9	74.9
35–39	99.1	60.9	80.9	98.8	30.5	65.6	99.0	52.5	76.7
40–44	98.9	60.6	79.8	98.4	32.1	68.7	98.7	53.4	76.8
45–49	98.4	59.4	78.9	97.6	31.8	68.0	98.1	52.9	76.2
50–54	97.0	54.2	76.3	94.6	28.7	63.8	96.4	48.3	73.4
55–59	94.2	46.7	70.2	85.6	22.7	55.1	92.1	41.3	66.6
60 & above	69.9	24.1	47.4	44.3	11.3	27.4	64.4	21.1	43.0
All	64.4	37.9	51.5	60.7	18.5	40.6	63.4	33.1	48.8

contd...

...contd...

Age Group (Years)	Rural			Urban			Total		
	Male	Female	Person	Male	Female	Person	Male	Female	Person
(1)	(2)	(3)	(4)	(5)	(6)	(7)	(8)	(9)	(10)
	2004-05								
5–9	0.3	0.3	0.3	0.3	0.3	0.3	0.3	0.3	0.3
10–14	7.0	7.5	7.2	5.3	3.5	4.4	6.7	6.5	6.6
15–19	52.9	33.1	43.7	38.1	14.4	27.3	48.8	28.1	39.3
20–24	89.1	43.5	65.6	76.9	25.0	52.6	85.4	38.5	61.9
25–29	98.2	53.0	75.0	95.7	26.1	62.6	97.4	45.8	71.5
30–34	98.8	59.3	77.6	98.7	30.8	65.1	98.8	51.9	74.2
35–39	99.1	64.2	81.5	98.4	34.0	66.8	98.9	56.1	77.5
40–44	98.5	62.7	81.1	98.3	31.7	66.5	98.5	54.1	77.0
45–49	98.2	61.6	80.9	97.6	26.9	64.3	98.0	52.1	76.3
50–54	96.3	56.2	76.9	93.9	25.9	62.1	95.6	48.1	72.9
55–59	93.1	50.9	72.1	83.2	21.8	53.3	90.5	43.5	67.2
60 & above	64.5	25.4	44.8	36.6	10.0	22.8	57.8	21.5	39.4
All	62.5	37.4	50.2	62.5	19.5	41.8	62.5	32.8	48.0
	2011-12								
5–9	0.0	0.1	0.1	0.1	0.1	0.1	0.1	0.1	0.1
10–14	2.9	3.0	3.0	3.5	0.9	2.3	3.1	2.5	2.8
15–19	33.3	16.4	25.6	25.6	8.9	18.1	31.1	14.3	23.5
20–24	78.8	29.7	54.2	66.4	19.7	43.8	74.7	26.5	50.9
25–29	96.3	36.9	65.4	95.1	25.3	60.8	95.9	33.2	63.9
30–34	99.0	43.1	69.4	98.9	25.9	62.4	99.0	37.8	67.2
35–39	99.1	48.1	72.3	99.0	28.4	63.8	99.1	42.4	69.8
40–44	98.8	48.2	74.5	98.8	27.6	64.7	98.8	42.1	71.6
45–49	98.8	48.4	75.3	97.9	24.5	63.8	98.5	41.1	71.7
50–54	96.6	44.4	71.5	94.6	21.9	58.9	96.0	37.5	67.7
55–59	93.5	39.4	66.1	86.9	17.7	53.0	91.5	33.3	62.3
60 & above	64.9	21.3	43.1	36.5	7.7	21.8	57.0	17.4	37.1
All	60.6	27.7	44.6	60.8	16.7	39.6	60.7	24.6	43.1

Source: *Employment and Unemployment Survey*, various NSS quinquennial rounds.

Table 2.3

Age-specific Labour Force Participation Rates (UPSS), 1993-94/2011-12 (5 Years+, Broad Age Groups)

Age Group (Years)	Rural			Urban			Total		
	Male	Female	Person	Male	Female	Person	Male	Female	Person
(1)	(2)	(3)	(4)	(5)	(6)	(7)	(8)	(9)	(10)
					1993-94				
5–14	7.3	7.3	7.3	3.7	2.6	3.2	6.4	6.2	6.3
15–29	80.4	45.5	63.2	68.4	20.4	45.6	77.1	39.0	58.5
30–59	98.1	57.8	78.2	96.8	29.5	65.2	97.8	50.7	74.8
15–59	89.8	52.1	71.2	83.3	25.1	55.8	88.0	45.2	67.1
60 & above	69.9	24.1	47.4	44.3	11.3	27.4	64.4	21.1	43.0
15 & above	87.7	49.0	68.6	80.1	23.8	53.3	85.6	42.7	64.6
All	64.4	37.9	51.5	60.7	18.5	40.6	63.4	33.1	48.8
					2004-05				
5–14	3.7	3.8	3.7	2.9	2.0	2.5	3.5	3.4	3.4
15–29	77.2	42.8	60.2	68.3	21.7	46.6	74.6	37.1	56.4
30–59	97.9	60.2	79.0	96.4	29.7	64.2	97.5	52.0	74.9
15–59	88.6	52.5	70.6	83.4	26.1	56.2	87.1	45.4	66.6
60 & above	64.5	25.4	44.8	36.6	10.0	22.8	57.8	21.5	39.4
15 & above	85.9	49.4	67.7	79.2	24.4	53.0	84.0	42.7	63.7
All	62.5	37.4	50.2	62.5	19.5	41.8	62.5	32.8	48.0
					2011-12				
5–14	1.6	1.6	1.6	1.9	0.5	1.3	1.7	1.3	1.5
15–29	64.9	27.1	46.4	60.7	18.1	40.5	63.6	24.4	44.6
30–59	98.1	45.7	71.9	97.1	25.3	62.1	97.8	39.6	68.9
15–59	83.5	37.8	60.9	81.0	22.2	52.7	82.7	33.1	58.3
60 & above	64.9	21.3	43.1	36.5	7.7	21.8	57.0	17.4	37.1
15 & above	81.3	35.8	58.7	76.4	20.5	49.3	79.8	31.2	55.9
All	60.6	27.7	44.6	60.8	16.7	39.6	60.7	24.6	43.1

Source: *Employment and Unemployment Survey*, various NSS quinquennial rounds.

Table 2.4

Labour Force Participation Rates in Major States (UPSS): 2011-12 (All Ages)

State	Rural			Urban			Total		
	Male	Female	Person	Male	Female	Person	Male	Female	Person
(1)	(2)	(3)	(4)	(5)	(6)	(7)	(8)	(9)	(10)
Andhra Pradesh	61.2	44.8	52.8	57.6	18.0	38.0	60.0	36.1	47.9
Assam	56.4	12.9	35.9	57.3	9.7	34.8	56.5	12.6	35.8
Bihar	48.7	5.8	28.4	44.1	5.4	26.7	48.2	5.7	28.3
Chhattisgarh	56.3	41.6	49.0	51.7	25.2	39.3	55.3	38.2	46.9
Delhi	54.4	14.6	37.1	54.8	10.9	34.9	54.8	11.1	35.0
Gujarat	60.2	27.9	44.8	60.7	13.5	38.7	60.4	22.2	42.4
Haryana	53.2	16.4	36.5	53.5	10.2	33.1	53.3	14.5	35.4
Himachal Pradesh	54.7	52.9	53.8	61.2	23.6	43.3	55.5	49.8	52.6
Jammu & Kashmir	55.9	26.3	41.5	56.3	14.5	36.2	56.0	23.6	40.3
Jharkhand	54.2	20.4	37.8	50.3	7.3	30.0	53.3	17.6	36.0
Karnataka	62.0	28.9	45.4	59.4	17.1	38.8	61.0	24.6	43.0
Kerala	58.3	25.8	41.0	56.7	22.2	38.6	57.9	24.8	40.3
Madhya Pradesh	56.4	23.9	40.7	53.3	11.9	33.4	55.6	20.8	38.8
Maharashtra	58.2	38.9	49.0	56.0	17.2	37.4	57.2	29.0	43.7
Odisha	60.6	25.1	42.7	60.3	15.8	39.5	60.5	23.8	42.2
Punjab	57.9	23.7	41.4	58.6	14.1	37.9	58.1	20.3	40.1
Rajasthan	50.0	34.9	42.7	50.7	14.4	33.6	50.1	30.1	40.5
Tamil Nadu	60.7	38.6	49.5	59.9	21.1	40.3	60.4	30.8	45.4
Uttar Pradesh	49.6	17.8	34.1	53.3	10.6	33.1	50.4	16.3	33.9
Uttarakhand	46.5	31.5	39.0	51.9	10.8	32.2	47.9	26.3	37.3
West Bengal	60.2	19.4	40.0	63.0	18.6	41.9	61.0	19.2	40.5
All India	55.3	25.3	40.6	56.3	15.5	36.7	55.6	22.5	39.5

Note: In this and other tables henceforth, major states are those which had population of more than 5 million in 2011.

Source: Employment and Unemployment Survey, various NSS quinquennial rounds.

3. WORK FORCE

Table 3.1

Work Force Participation Rates (UPSS): 1983/2011-12 (All Ages)

Year	Rural			Urban			Total		
	Male	Female	Person	Male	Female	Person	Male	Female	Person
(1)	(2)	(3)	(4)	(5)	(6)	(7)	(8)	(9)	(10)
1983	54.7	34.0	44.5	51.2	15.1	34.1	53.9	29.6	42.1
1993-94	55.3	32.8	44.4	52.1	15.5	34.7	54.5	28.6	42.0
2004-05	54.6	32.7	43.9	54.9	16.6	36.5	54.7	28.7	42.0
2011-12	54.3	24.8	39.9	54.6	14.7	35.5	54.4	21.9	38.6

Source: *Employment and Unemployment Survey*, various NSS quinquennial rounds.

Table 3.2

Age-specific Work Force Participation Rates (UPSS): 1993-94/2011-12 (5 Years+)

Age Group (Years)	Rural			Urban			Total		
	Male	Female	Person	Male	Female	Person	Male	Female	Person
(1)	(2)	(3)	(4)	(5)	(6)	(7)	(8)	(9)	(10)
					1993-94				
5–9	1.2	1.4	1.3	0.5	0.5	0.5	1.0	1.2	1.1
10–14	13.8	14.1	14.0	6.6	4.5	5.6	12.1	11.6	11.9
15–19	57.7	36.4	48.1	35.6	12.3	25.0	51.8	29.9	41.8
20–24	85.9	45.6	65.1	67.4	18.0	43.6	80.6	38.4	59.3
25–29	95.8	52.5	73.2	90.4	22.4	57.1	94.3	44.8	68.9
30–34	98.3	58.5	78.2	96.4	27.2	63.2	97.8	50.5	74.2
35–39	98.9	60.8	80.7	98.3	30.1	65.1	98.8	52.3	76.5
40–44	98.8	60.6	79.8	98.1	32.0	68.5	98.6	53.4	76.7
45–49	98.3	59.4	78.9	97.3	31.7	67.8	98.0	52.9	76.1
50–54	97.0	54.2	76.3	94.2	28.6	63.6	96.3	48.3	73.3
55–59	94.2	46.7	70.2	85.6	22.6	55.0	92.1	41.2	66.6
60 & above	69.9	24.1	47.4	44.2	11.3	27.3	64.4	21.1	42.9
All	63.5	37.6	50.9	58.2	17.3	38.8	62.1	32.5	47.8
					2004-05				
5–9	0.3	0.3	0.3	0.2	0.3	0.3	0.3	0.3	0.3
10–14	6.8	7.4	7.1	4.8	3.3	4.1	6.4	6.4	6.4
15–19	49.7	31.9	41.5	33.5	12.8	24.1	45.3	26.8	36.8
20–24	84.9	41.0	62.3	68.4	20.1	45.8	79.8	35.3	57.5
25–29	96.6	51.3	73.3	90.9	22.9	58.6	94.9	43.7	69.1
30–34	98.1	58.4	76.9	96.9	29.0	63.3	97.8	50.8	73.1
35–39	98.9	63.9	81.2	97.7	32.8	65.8	98.6	55.6	77.0
40–44	98.3	62.5	80.9	98.0	31.2	66.1	98.2	53.8	76.7
45–49	98.1	61.5	80.8	96.8	26.7	63.8	97.7	51.9	76.1
50–54	96.3	56.1	76.9	93.1	25.8	61.6	95.4	48.0	72.7
55–59	93.0	50.9	72.0	83.0	21.8	53.2	90.4	43.5	67.1
60 & above	64.4	25.3	44.8	36.6	10.0	22.8	57.7	21.5	39.3
All	61.5	36.8	49.3	60.1	18.1	40.0	61.1	32.0	46.9

contd...

...contd...

Age Group (Years)	Rural			Urban			Total		
	Male	Female	Person	Male	Female	Person	Male	Female	Person
(1)	(2)	(3)	(4)	(5)	(6)	(7)	(8)	(9)	(10)
				2011-12					
5–9	0.0	0.1	0.0	0.1	0.1	0.1	0.1	0.1	0.1
10–14	2.6	2.8	2.7	3.3	0.9	2.2	2.8	2.4	2.6
15–19	30.3	15.6	23.6	22.3	7.8	15.8	28.1	13.4	21.4
20–24	74.2	27.8	51.0	59.4	16.0	38.4	69.2	24.1	46.9
25–29	94.2	35.7	63.7	90.6	23.1	57.5	93.0	31.7	61.7
30–34	98.1	42.6	68.8	97.3	24.8	61.0	97.8	37.1	66.3
35–39	98.9	48.0	72.1	98.6	28.1	63.5	98.8	42.2	69.5
40–44	98.7	48.2	74.5	98.5	27.5	64.6	98.7	42.0	71.5
45–49	98.8	48.4	75.3	97.6	24.4	63.6	98.4	41.0	71.6
50–54	96.6	44.4	71.5	94.1	21.9	58.6	95.8	37.5	67.6
55–59	93.5	39.3	66.0	86.8	17.7	52.9	91.5	33.2	62.2
60 & above	64.9	21.3	43.1	36.5	7.7	21.8	56.9	17.4	37.0
All	59.5	27.3	43.8	59.0	15.8	38.3	59.4	24.0	42.2

Source: *Employment and Unemployment Survey*, various NSS quinquennial rounds.

Table 3.3

Age-specific Work Force Participation Rate (UPSS): 1983/2011-12 (5 Years+, Broad Age Groups)

Age Group (Years)	1983			1993-94			2004-05			2011-12		
	Male	Female	Person	Male	Female	Person	Male	Female	Person	Male	Female	Person
(1)	(2)	(3)	(4)	(5)	(6)	(7)	(8)	(9)	(10)	(11)	(12)	(13)
						Rural						
5–14	13.3	12.5	12.9	7.2	7.3	7.2	3.5	3.7	3.6	1.4	1.5	1.4
15–29	82.2	49.6	65.8	77.5	44.7	61.3	74.2	41.0	57.7	61.6	25.8	44.1
30–59	96.9	58.9	77.9	97.9	57.7	78.1	97.6	59.8	78.7	97.9	45.5	71.7
15–59	90.0	54.5	72.2	88.4	51.6	70.2	87.1	51.5	69.4	82.0	37.2	59.8
60 & above	66.6	22.6	44.7	69.9	24.1	47.4	64.4	25.3	44.8	64.9	21.3	43.1
15 & above	61.4	39.3	50.3	86.4	48.7	67.8	84.6	48.5	66.6	80.0	35.2	57.8
All	49.2	33.0	41.2	63.5	37.6	50.9	61.5	36.8	49.3	59.5	27.3	43.8
						Urban						
5–14	6.0	3.8	5.0	3.6	2.5	3.1	2.6	1.9	2.3	1.8	0.5	1.2
15–29	66.5	18.7	43.9	61.8	17.3	40.7	62.3	18.4	41.9	55.8	15.7	36.8
30–59	95.6	28.6	64.5	96.1	29.1	64.6	95.6	28.9	63.3	96.5	24.9	61.6
15–59	80.9	23.5	54.0	79.8	23.4	53.2	80.2	24.2	53.6	78.4	21.0	50.8
60 & above	50.2	13.8	31.1	44.2	11.3	27.3	36.6	10.0	22.8	36.5	7.7	21.8
15 & above	57.3	17.2	38.2	76.8	22.3	50.9	76.3	22.7	50.6	74.1	19.5	47.6
All	45.9	14.3	30.8	58.2	17.3	38.8	60.1	18.1	40.0	59.0	15.8	38.3

contd...

...contd...

Age-Group	1983			1993-94			2004-05			2011-12		
	Male	*Female*	*Person*	*Male*	*Female*	*Person*	*Male*	*Female*	*Person*	*Male*	*Female*	*Person*
(1)	(2)	(3)	(4)	(5)	(6)	(7)	(8)	(9)	(10)	(11)	(12)	(13)
							Total					
5–14	11.7	10.5	11.2	6.4	6.1	6.3	3.3	3.3	3.3	1.5	1.3	1.4
15–29	77.8	41.7	60.0	73.2	37.5	55.8	70.7	34.9	53.3	59.8	22.8	41.9
30–59	96.6	51.9	74.7	97.4	50.5	74.6	97.0	51.5	74.5	97.4	39.4	68.6
15–59	87.5	47.0	67.6	86.1	44.4	65.7	85.1	44.2	65.0	80.9	32.3	57.0
60 & above	63.3	20.7	41.9	64.4	21.1	42.9	57.7	21.5	39.3	56.9	17.4	37.0
15 & above	60.4	34.1	47.3	83.8	42.0	63.4	82.2	41.6	62.2	78.1	30.5	54.7
All	48.4	28.7	38.7	62.1	32.5	47.8	61.1	32.0	46.9	59.4	24.0	42.2

Source: *Employment and Unemployment Survey*, various NSS quinquennial rounds.

Table 3.4

Work Force Participation Rate (WFPR) by Socio-religious Groups (UPSS): 2011-12 (All Ages)

Caste/Religion	*Rural*			*Urban*			*Total*		
	Male	*Female*	*Person*	*Male*	*Female*	*Person*	*Male*	*Female*	*Person*
(1)	(2)	(3)	(4)	(5)	(6)	(7)	(8)	(9)	(10)
Scheduled Tribes (ST)	55.8	36.6	46.4	52.1	19.6	36.8	55.4	34.8	45.4
Scheduled Castes (SC)	53.9	26.2	40.4	54.6	17.3	36.4	54.0	24.2	39.5
Other Backward Classes (OBC)	54.7	25.6	40.4	55.2	16.5	36.6	54.8	23.3	39.5
Muslims	49.9	15.3	32.8	53.2	10.5	32.8	51.1	13.6	32.8
Others	56.2	21.3	39.3	55.1	13.4	35.2	55.8	17.9	37.5
All	54.3	24.8	39.9	54.6	14.7	35.5	54.4	21.9	38.6

Source: *Employment and Unemployment Survey*, NSS 2011-12 round.

Table 3.5

Share of Employment (UPSS) by Industries (At One Digit Level): 1972-73/2011-12 (All Ages)

Sector/Industry	*1972-73*	*1983*	*1993-94*	*2004-05*	*2011-12*
(1)	*(2)*	*(3)*	*(4)*	*(5)*	*(6)*
Agriculture and allied activities	73.9	68.6	64.8	58.5	48.9
Primary sector	73.9	68.6	64.8	58.5	48.9
Mining and quarrying	0.4	0.6	0.7	0.6	0.5
Manufacturing	8.9	10.6	10.5	11.7	12.8
Electricity, gas and water supply	0.2	0.3	0.4	0.3	0.4
Construction	1.8	2.3	3.1	5.6	10.6
Secondary sector	11.3	13.8	14.7	18.1	24.4
Trade, hotels and restaurants	5.1	6.3	7.4	10.2	11.4
Transport, storage and communication	1.8	2.5	2.8	3.8	4.4
Financing, real estate, business services	0.5	0.7	0.9	1.5	2.6
Community, social and personal services	7.4	8.1	9.4	7.7	8.2
Tertiary sector	14.8	17.6	20.5	23.4	26.7
Non-agricultural	26.1	31.4	35.2	41.5	51.1
Total	100	100	100	100	100

Note: Figures for the years 1972-73 are taken from Papola *et al.*

Source: Employment and Unemployment Survey, various NSS quinquennial rounds.

Table 3.6

Industry-wise Growth of Employment (UPSS): 1972-73/2011-12 (All Ages)

Sector/Industry	*Employment Growth*			
	1972-73/83	*1983/93-94*	*1993-94/2004-05*	*2004-05/2011-12*
(1)	*(2)*	*(3)*	*(4)*	*(5)*
Agriculture and allied activities	1.7	1.4	0.7	-2.0
Mining and quarrying	5.9	3.2	-0.1	-0.3
Manufacturing	4.3	2.0	3.2	1.5
Electricity, gas and water supply	7.9	5.6	-1.9	7.7
Construction	4.4	5.7	7.2	9.8
Secondary sector	4.4	2.8	4.0	4.5
Trade, hotels and restaurants	4.6	3.8	5.2	1.8
Transport, storage and communication	5.9	3.4	5.2	2.1
Financing, real estate and business services	7.4	3.6	7.2	7.8
Community, social and personal services	3.2	3.9	0.4	1.0
Tertiary sector	4.2	3.8	3.4	2.1
Non-agriculture	4.3	3.4	3.6	3.2
Total	2.4	2.0	1.8	0.4

Source: Employment and Unemployment Survey, various NSS quinquennial rounds.

Table 3.7

Industrial Structure of the Workforce (UPSS): 1983/2011-12 (All Ages)

Sector/Industry	*Rural*			*Urban*			*Total*		
	Male	*Female*	*Person*	*Male*	*Female*	*Person*	*Male*	*Female*	*Person*
(1)	(2)	(3)	(4)	(5)	(6)	(7)	(8)	(9)	(10)
					1983				
Agriculture and allied activities	77.7	87.7	81.5	10.4	31.1	14.7	62.2	81.0	68.6
Mining and quarrying	0.6	0.3	0.5	1.2	0.7	1.1	0.7	0.4	0.6
Manufacturing	7.0	6.4	6.8	26.9	26.9	26.9	11.6	8.8	10.6
Electricity, gas and water supply	0.2	0.0	0.2	1.1	0.2	0.9	0.4	0.0	0.3
Construction	2.3	0.7	1.7	5.1	3.2	4.7	2.9	1.0	2.3
Trade, hotels and restaurants	4.4	2.0	3.5	20.5	9.5	18.2	8.1	2.8	6.3
Transport, storage, communication	1.7	0.1	1.1	10.0	1.5	8.2	3.6	0.2	2.5
Other services	6.1	2.8	4.9	24.8	26.9	25.2	10.4	5.7	8.8
Total	100	100	100	100	100	100	100	100	100
					1993-94				
Agriculture, forestry and fishing	74.0	86.2	78.4	9.0	24.9	12.4	58.3	78.1	64.8
Mining and quarrying	0.7	0.4	0.6	1.3	0.6	1.2	0.9	0.4	0.7
Manufacturing	7.0	7.1	7.0	23.6	24.3	23.7	11.0	9.4	10.5
Electricity, gas and water supply	0.3	0.0	0.2	1.2	0.3	1.0	0.5	0.1	0.4
Construction	3.2	0.8	2.3	7.0	4.1	6.3	4.1	1.2	3.1
Trade, hotels and restaurants	5.5	2.1	4.3	22.0	10.1	19.5	9.5	3.1	7.4
Transport, storage and communication	2.2	0.1	1.4	9.8	1.3	8.0	4.0	0.2	2.8
Other services	7.1	3.4	5.7	26.1	34.5	27.9	11.7	7.5	10.3
Total	100	100	100	100	100	100	100	100	100
					2004-05				
Agriculture, forestry and fishing	66.5	83.3	72.7	6.1	18.1	8.8	50.8	73.9	58.5
Mining and quarrying	0.6	0.3	0.5	0.9	0.2	0.8	0.7	0.3	0.6
Manufacturing	7.9	8.4	8.1	23.5	28.2	24.6	12.0	11.2	11.7
Electricity, gas and water supply	0.2	0.0	0.2	0.8	0.2	0.7	0.4	0.0	0.3
Construction	6.8	1.5	4.9	9.2	3.8	8.0	7.5	1.8	5.6
Trade, hotels and restaurants	8.3	2.5	6.2	28.0	12.2	24.6	13.4	3.9	10.2
Transport, storage and communication	3.8	0.2	2.5	10.7	1.4	8.6	5.6	0.3	3.8
Other services	5.8	3.9	5.1	20.7	35.9	24.0	9.7	8.5	9.3
Total	100	100	100	100	100	100	100	100	100
					2011-12				
Agriculture, forestry and fishing	59.4	74.9	64.1	5.6	10.9	6.7	43.6	62.8	48.9
Mining and quarrying	0.5	0.3	0.5	0.9	0.3	0.7	0.6	0.3	0.5
Manufacturing	8.2	9.8	8.7	23.0	28.9	24.2	12.5	13.5	12.8
Electricity, gas and water supply	0.3	0.1	0.2	1.0	1.0	1.0	0.5	0.2	0.4
Construction	13.0	6.6	11.1	10.7	4.0	9.3	12.3	6.1	10.6
Trade, hotels and restaurants	8.5	3.0	6.8	27.2	13.0	24.4	14.0	4.9	11.4
Transport, storage and communication	4.2	0.1	2.9	10.2	1.1	8.4	5.9	0.3	4.4
Other services	5.9	5.2	5.7	21.4	40.9	25.3	10.4	12.0	10.9
Total	100	100	100	100	100	100	100	100	100

Source: Employment and Unemployment Survey, various NSS quinquennial rounds.

Table 3.8

Industry-wise Growth of Employment in Rural Areas (UPSS): 1993-94/2011-12

Industry	1993-94/1999-2000			1999-2000/2004-05		
	Male	*Female*	*Person*	*Male*	*Female*	*Person*
(1)	(2)	(3)	(4)	(5)	(6)	(7)
Agriculture and allied activities	0.4	0.1	0.3	0.5	2.6	1.3
Mining and quarrying	-1.9	-5.3	-2.6	2.7	4.0	2.9
Manufacturing	1.7	0.2	1.2	3.6	6.6	4.7
Electricity, gas and water supply	-1.9	-20.2	-2.6	1.0	10.0	1.1
Construction	7.0	4.6	6.8	10.8	10.9	10.8
Trade, hotels and restaurants	4.4	-0.6	3.6	6.1	8.3	6.4
Transport, storage and communication	7.2	1.9	7.2	5.6	23.5	5.9
Financing, real estate and business services	4.4	-1.4	4.0	8.3	13.2	8.6
Community, social and personal services	-1.8	1.4	-1.1	-0.1	4.7	1.2
Total	1.0	0.2	0.7	1.9	3.3	2.4
	2004-05/2011-12			1993-94/2011-12		
	Male	*Female*	*Person*	*Male*	*Female*	*Person*
Agriculture and allied activities	-0.6	-4.2	-2.0	0.02	-0.90	-0.32
Mining and quarrying	-1.3	-2.6	-1.6	-0.42	-1.74	-0.70
Manufacturing	1.5	-0.4	0.8	2.17	1.69	2.00
Electricity, gas and water supply	4.7	25.3	5.6	1.41	3.97	1.59
Construction	10.8	20.7	12.1	9.53	12.43	9.96
Trade, hotels and restaurants	1.5	-0.1	1.3	3.73	1.97	3.46
Transport, storage and communication	2.4	-6.5	2.3	4.90	3.94	4.89
Financing, real estate and business services	7.0	8.1	7.1	6.48	6.17	6.46
Community, social and personal services	0.3	1.1	0.6	-0.52	2.20	0.18
Total	1.1	-2.7	-0.2	1.26	-0.12	0.80

Source: *Employment and Unemployment Survey*, various NSS quinquennial rounds.

Table 3.9

Industry-wise Growth of Employment in Urban Areas (UPSS): 1993-94/2011-12

Industry	*1993-94/1999-2000*			*1999-2000/2004-05*		
	Male	*Female*	*Person*	*Male*	*Female*	*Person*
(1)	(2)	(3)	(4)	(5)	(6)	(7)
Agriculture and allied activities	-2.6	-4.1	-3.3	2.6	6.7	4.4
Mining and quarrying	-4.2	-7.8	-4.5	5.1	-5.9	4.3
Manufacturing	1.7	0.7	1.5	5.1	10.5	6.3
Electricity, gas and water supply	-3.7	-5.8	-3.8	2.9	6.7	3.1
Construction	6.9	3.9	6.5	4.7	1.6	4.4
Trade, hotels and restaurants	7.7	10.0	8.0	3.0	0.2	2.7
Transport, storage and communication	3.8	7.8	3.9	4.5	-0.2	4.3
Financing, real estate and business services	4.9	5.1	4.9	10.4	13.6	10.8
Community, social and personal services	-2.4	0.6	-1.5	1.8	7.3	3.7
Total	2.7	1.1	2.3	4.0	6.7	4.5
	2004-05/2011-12			*1993-94/2011-12*		
	Male	*Female*	*Person*	*Male*	*Female*	*Person*
Agriculture and allied activities	1.3	-6.0	-1.6	0.3	-2.0	-0.5
Mining and quarrying	1.6	7.4	2.0	0.6	-1.6	0.4
Manufacturing	2.2	1.4	2.0	2.8	3.6	3.0
Electricity, gas and water supply	6.6	27.0	8.8	2.1	9.5	2.9
Construction	4.7	1.8	4.4	5.4	2.4	5.1
Trade, hotels and restaurants	2.1	2.0	2.1	4.2	4.1	4.2
Transport, storage and communication	1.9	-2.2	1.7	3.2	1.6	3.2
Financing, real estate and business services	7.5	9.8	7.9	7.4	9.2	7.7
Community, social and personal services	0.9	2.1	1.3	0.0	3.0	1.0
Total	2.6	1.1	2.2	3.0	2.6	2.9

Source: *Employment and Unemployment Survey*, various NSS quinquennial rounds.

Table 3.10a

Industry-wise Employment Elasticity with Respect to Gross Domestic Product, 1972-73/2011-12

Sector/Industry	*1972-73/1983*	*1983/1993-94*	*1993-94/2004-05*	*2004-05/2011-12*
(1)	(2)	(3)	(4)	(5)
Agriculture and allied activities	0.46	0.49	0.26	-0.42
Primary sector	0.46	0.49	0.26	-0.42
Mining and quarrying	0.86	0.53	-0.02	-0.07
Manufacturing	0.78	0.41	0.47	0.13
Electricity, gas and water supply	1.00	0.64	-0.32	1.17
Construction	1.44	1.16	0.94	1.15
Secondary sector	0.87	0.53	0.59	0.48
Trade, hotels and restaurants	0.81	0.67	0.61	0.16
Transport, storage and communication	0.91	0.56	0.49	0.13
Financing, real estate and business services	1.25	0.39	0.99	0.59
Community, social and personal services	0.71	0.67	0.06	0.12
Tertiary sector	0.77	0.57	0.43	0.17
All non-agricultural	0.81	0.55	0.48	0.28
Total	0.52	0.41	0.29	0.04

Source: Estimates are based on various rounds of NSS data on Employment and Unemployment and National Account Statistics, CSO, Government of India.

Table 3.10b

Level of per Worker Gross Output (in ₹) (at 2004-05 Prices): 1993-94/2011-12

Sector/Industry	*1993-94*	*1999-2000*	*2004-05*	*2011-12*
(1)	(2)	(3)	(4)	(5)
Agriculture and allied activities	18,156	21,786	21,949	32,955
Primary sector	18,156	21,786	21,949	32,955
Mining and quarrying	182,150	303,957	322,377	419,564
Manufacturing	55,902	78,714	80,728	132,563
Electricity, gas and water supply	238,636	436,474	479,733	453,501
Construction	84,939	83,467	87,870	82,714
Secondary sector	72,930	94,412	96,340	123,603
Trade, hotels and restaurants	67,594	80,547	95,989	157,337
Transport, storage and communication	77,595	103,764	135,130	261,240
Financing, real estate and business services	554,335	682,789	558,244	720,816
Community, social and personal services	57,301	97,936	109,565	166,900
Tertiary sector	86,812	121,396	138,716	233,808
All non-agricultural	81,045	110,400	120,445	181,874
Total	40,827	56,819	64,967	111,083

Source: Estimates are based on various rounds of NSS data on Employment and Unemployment and National Account Statistics, CSO, Government of India.

Table 3.11

Workers by Employment Status (UPSS): 1983/2011-12 (All Ages)

Status	Rural			Urban			Total		
	Male	Female	Person	Male	Female	Person	Male	Female	Person
(1)	(2)	(3)	(4)	(5)	(6)	(7)	(8)	(9)	(10)
					1983				
Self-employed	60.8	62	61.2	40.9	45.8	42	56.2	60.1	57.5
Regular wage/salaried	9.8	2.7	7.2	43.6	25.7	39.9	17.7	5.4	13.5
Casual labour	29.4	35.3	31.6	15.4	28.4	18.2	26.2	34.5	29.0
All	100	100	100	100	100	100	100	100	100
					1993-94				
Self-employed	57.7	58.6	58	41.7	44.8	42.3	53.7	56.8	54.7
Regular wage/salaried	8.5	2.7	6.4	42	29.2	39.4	16.7	6.2	13.2
Casual labour	33.8	38.7	35.6	16.3	26.1	18.3	29.6	37.0	32.0
All	100	100	100	100	100	100	100	100	100
					2004-05				
Self-employed	58.1	63.7	60.2	44.8	47.7	45.4	54.7	61.4	56.9
Regular wage/salaried	9.0	3.7	7.1	40.6	35.6	39.5	17.2	8.3	14.3
Casual labour	32.9	32.6	32.8	14.6	16.7	15	28.1	30.3	28.9
All	100	100	100	100	100	100	100	100	100
					2011-12				
Self-employed	54.5	59.3	55.9	41.7	42.8	41.9	50.7	56.1	52.2
Regular wage/salaried	10.0	5.6	8.7	43.4	42.8	43.3	19.8	12.7	17.9
Casual labour	35.5	35.1	60.1	14.9	14.3	26.7	29.4	31.2	29.9
All	100	100	100	100	100	100	100	100	100

Source: *Employment and Unemployment Survey*, various NSS quinquennial rounds.

Table 3.12

Educational Profile of Workers (UPSS): 1993-94/2011-12 (5 Years+)

Education Level	Rural			Urban			Total		
	Male	Female	Person	Male	Female	Person	Male	Female	Person
(1)	(2)	(3)	(4)	(5)	(6)	(7)	(8)	(9)	(10)
					1993-94				
Not literate	45.6	79.2	57.7	19.9	50.0	26.3	39.4	75.3	51.2
Below primary	13.9	6.9	11.4	10.8	8.9	10.4	13.1	7.2	11.2
Primary and middle	27.5	11.2	21.7	31.4	18.9	28.7	28.5	12.2	23.1
Secondary and higher secondary	10.5	2.4	7.6	23.8	12.0	21.3	13.7	3.6	10.4
Graduate and above	2.5	0.4	1.7	14.1	10.2	13.3	5.3	1.7	4.1
Total	100	100	100	100	100	100	100	100	100
					2004-05				
Not literate	36.9	67.7	48.2	15.2	39.0	20.4	31.3	63.5	42.0
Below primary	10.5	7.2	9.3	6.9	6.8	6.9	9.6	7.1	8.8
Primary and middle	34.2	18.9	28.6	33.4	24.4	31.5	34.0	19.7	29.2
Secondary and higher secondary	13.7	4.9	10.5	24.0	12.2	21.4	16.4	5.9	12.9
Diploma and certificate	1.0	0.5	0.8	3.6	3.3	3.6	1.7	0.9	1.4
Graduate and above	3.8	0.9	2.7	16.8	14.3	16.2	7.1	2.8	5.7
Total	100	100	100	100	100	100	100	100	100
					2011-12				
Not literate	28.4	56.5	37.0	11.7	28.8	15.1	23.5	51.3	31.2
Below primary	12.3	9.7	11.5	7.2	8.0	7.4	10.8	9.4	10.4
Primary and middle	33.9	22.9	30.5	28.8	23.2	27.7	32.4	22.9	29.8
Secondary and higher secondary	19.4	8.4	16.0	27.3	16.1	25.0	21.7	9.8	18.4
Diploma and certificate	1.1	0.5	0.9	2.9	2.3	2.8	1.6	0.8	1.4
Graduate and above	4.9	2.0	4.0	22.1	21.6	22.0	10.0	5.7	8.8
Total	100	100	100	100	100	100	100	100	100

Note: Secondary and Higher secondary include diploma and certificate for 1993-94.

Source: Employment and Unemployment Survey, various NSS quinquennial rounds.

Table 3.13

Educational Profile of Workers (UPS): 1993-94/2011-12 (5 Years+)

Education Level	*Rural*			*Urban*			*Total*		
	Male	*Female*	*Person*	*Male*	*Female*	*Person*	*Male*	*Female*	*Person*
(1)	*(2)*	*(3)*	*(4)*	*(5)*	*(6)*	*(7)*	*(8)*	*(9)*	*(10)*
					1993-94				
Not literate	46.5	80.8	56.5	20.1	49.6	25.3	40.1	76.3	49.7
Below primary level	13.9	6.8	11.8	10.9	8.7	10.5	13.2	7.1	11.6
Primary and middle level	27.1	9.9	22.1	31.4	16.9	28.8	28.1	10.9	23.6
Secondary and higher secondary level	10.0	2.0	7.7	23.6	12.6	21.6	13.3	3.6	10.7
Graduate and above	2.4	0.4	1.8	14.1	12.2	13.8	5.3	2.1	4.4
Total	100	100	100	100	100	100	100	100	100
					2004-05				
Not literate	37.5	69.3	47.1	15.3	39.5	19.8	31.7	64.6	40.8
Below primary level	10.6	7.3	9.6	7.0	6.9	7.0	9.6	7.2	9.0
Primary and middle level	34.0	17.5	29.0	33.5	22.3	31.4	33.9	18.3	29.6
Secondary and higher secondary level	13.3	4.4	10.6	23.8	11.6	21.5	16.0	5.6	13.1
Diploma and certificate level	1.0	0.5	0.8	3.6	3.5	3.6	1.6	1.0	1.5
Graduate and above	3.7	1.0	2.9	16.8	16.1	16.7	7.1	3.4	6.1
Total	100	100	100	100	100	100	100	100	100
					2011-12				
Not literate	28.7	57.3	35.6	11.8	27.9	14.7	23.8	50.8	29.8
Below primary level	12.4	10.1	11.8	7.2	7.8	7.3	10.9	9.6	10.6
Primary and middle level	34.0	21.5	31.0	28.9	22.1	27.7	32.5	21.7	30.1
Secondary and higher secondary level	18.9	8.2	16.4	27.1	15.8	25.1	21.3	9.9	18.8
Diploma and certificate level	1.1	0.6	1.0	2.9	2.5	2.8	1.6	1.0	1.5
Graduate and above	4.9	2.3	4.3	22.1	23.8	22.4	10.0	7.1	9.3
Total	100	100	100	100	100	100	100	100	100

Note: Secondary and higher secondary levels include diploma and certificate for 1993-94.

Source: *Employment and Unemployment Survey*, various NSS quinquennial rounds.

Table 3.14

Employment Growth (UPSS) in Major States: 2004-05 to 2011-12 (All Ages)

State	*Rural*			*Urban*			*Total*		
	Male	*Female*	*Person*	*Male*	*Female*	*Person*	*Male*	*Female*	*Person*
(1)	(2)	(3)	(4)	(5)	(6)	(7)	(8)	(9)	(10)
Andhra Pradesh	0.0	-0.9	-0.4	2.9	-0.7	2.0	0.9	-0.9	0.2
Assam	1.1	-6.0	-0.5	1.9	0.1	1.6	1.2	-5.5	-0.2
Bihar	2.1	-10.9	0.1	1.9	-2.3	1.5	2.1	-10.3	0.2
Chhattisgarh	1.4	0.3	1.0	2.5	8.0	4.0	1.7	1.2	1.5
Delhi	-8.6	8.6	-6.6	2.0	5.1	2.4	1.6	5.2	2.1
Gujarat	1.0	-5.1	-1.2	3.7	1.3	3.3	2.2	-3.7	0.4
Haryana	0.8	-8.2	-1.8	3.7	-0.6	3.0	1.7	-6.8	-0.4
Himachal Pradesh	0.8	1.7	1.2	0.7	0.1	0.5	0.8	1.6	1.2
Jammu & Kashmir	1.8	1.0	1.6	3.4	3.8	3.4	2.2	1.4	2.0
Jharkhand	1.7	-4.7	-0.3	2.9	-6.7	1.4	2.0	-4.9	0.0
Karnataka	0.5	-5.8	-1.8	2.8	1.3	2.4	1.3	-4.3	-0.5
Kerala	-2.9	-4.9	-3.5	6.8	6.2	6.6	0.9	-0.9	0.4
Madhya Pradesh	2.1	-4.3	-0.1	2.1	-1.8	1.4	2.1	-3.9	0.3
Maharashtra	1.3	-1.9	-0.1	1.7	0.3	1.4	1.5	-1.4	0.5
Odisha	1.3	-2.7	0.0	4.3	3.3	4.1	1.7	-2.2	0.5
Punjab	1.1	-3.7	-0.4	2.1	2.7	2.2	1.5	-2.3	0.5
Rajasthan	1.3	-0.5	0.6	2.0	-1.0	1.3	1.5	-0.6	0.7
Tamil Nadu	0.6	-2.2	-0.6	2.2	-0.1	1.6	1.3	-1.5	0.3
Uttar Pradesh	1.5	-2.7	0.3	2.1	0.6	1.9	1.6	-2.2	0.6
Uttarakhand	-1.0	-3.5	-2.1	3.0	-1.8	2.2	0.3	-3.4	-1.1
West Bengal	1.0	1.6	1.2	2.6	4.6	3.0	1.5	2.5	1.7
All India	1.1	-2.8	-0.2	2.5	1.1	2.3	1.5	-2.0	0.4

Source: Calculated from *Employment and Unemployment Survey*, NSS, 2004-05 and 2011-12 rounds.

4. UNEMPLOYMENT

Table 4.1

Unemployment Rates by Various Concepts: 1983/2011-12 (All Ages)

Year	Rural			Urban			Total		
	Male	Female	Person	Male	Female	Person	Male	Female	Person
(1)	(2)	(3)	(4)	(5)	(6)	(7)	(8)	(9)	(10)
					UPS				
1983	2.1	1.4	1.9	5.9	6.9	6.1	3.0	2.2	2.8
1993-94	2.0	1.3	1.8	5.4	8.3	5.2	5.6	2.4	2.6
2004-05	2.1	3.1	2.5	4.4	9.1	5.3	2.7	4.1	3.2
2011-12	2.1	2.9	2.3	3.2	6.6	3.8	2.4	3.7	2.7
					UPSS				
1983	1.4	0.7	1.1	5.1	4.9	5.0	2.3	1.2	1.9
1993-94	1.4	0.9	1.2	4.1	6.1	4.5	2.1	1.5	1.9
2004-05	1.6	1.8	1.7	3.8	6.9	4.5	2.2	2.6	2.3
2011-12	1.7	1.7	1.7	3.0	5.2	3.4	2.1	2.4	2.2
					CWS				
1983	3.7	4.3	3.9	6.7	7.5	6.8	4.4	4.7	4.5
1993-94	3.0	3.0	3.0	5.2	8.4	5.8	3.5	3.8	3.6
2004-05	3.8	4.2	3.9	7.5	11.6	6.0	4.2	5.0	4.5
2011-12	3.3	3.5	3.4	3.8	6.7	4.4	3.5	4.2	3.7
					CDS				
1983	7.5	9.0	8.0	9.2	11.0	9.5	8.0	9.3	8.3
1993-94	5.6	5.6	5.6	6.7	10.5	7.4	5.9	6.3	6.0
2004-05	8.0	8.7	8.2	7.5	11.6	8.3	7.8	9.2	8.3
2011-12	5.5	6.2	5.7	4.9	8.0	5.5	5.3	6.6	5.6

Note: UPS-Usual Principal Status; UPSS-Usual Principal and Subsidiary Status; CWS-Current Weekly Status; CDS-Current Daily Status.

Source: Employment and Unemployment Survey, various NSS quinquennial rounds.

Table 4.2

Unemployment Rates (CDS) across Broad Age Groups: 1993-94/2011-12 (All Ages)

Year	Rural			Urban			Total		
	Male	Female	Person	Male	Female	Person	Male	Female	Person
(1)	(2)	(3)	(4)	(5)	(6)	(7)	(8)	(9)	(10)
					1993-94				
15-24	9.7	8.2	9.3	16.7	24.7	18.2	11.4	10.8	11.2
25-34	6.4	5.8	6.3	6.8	11.5	7.6	6.5	6.7	6.6
35 & above	3.3	4.1	3.5	2.1	3.4	2.4	3.0	4.0	3.3
Total	5.6	5.6	5.6	6.7	10.5	7.4	5.9	6.3	6.0
					2004-05				
15-24	13.8	13.9	13.8	16.7	23.5	18.1	14.5	15.7	14.8
25-34	8.0	9.5	8.5	7.3	14.3	8.6	7.8	10.4	8.5
35 & above	5.4	6.3	5.7	3.5	5.2	3.8	4.9	6.1	5.3
Total	8.0	8.7	8.2	7.5	11.6	8.3	7.8	9.2	8.3
					2011-12				
15-24	12.1	12.3	12.2	14.8	21.5	16.2	12.9	14.7	13.3
25-34	5.7	6.7	5.9	4.9	9.2	5.7	5.4	7.4	5.9
35 & above	3.3	4.2	3.5	1.9	2.3	1.9	2.9	3.8	3.1
Total	5.5	6.2	5.7	4.9	8.0	5.5	5.3	6.6	5.6

Source: *Employment and Unemployment Survey*, various NSS quinquennial rounds.

Table 4.3

Unemployment Rates by Location (UPSS) for Major States: 2011-12 (All Ages)

State	*Rural*			*Urban*			*Total*		
	Male	*Female*	*Person*	*Male*	*Female*	*Person*	*Male*	*Female*	*Person*
(1)	(2)	(3)	(4)	(5)	(6)	(7)	(8)	(9)	(10)
Andhra Pradesh	1.7	0.5	1.2	3.9	5.4	4.3	2.4	1.3	2.0
Assam	4.3	5.7	4.5	5.4	7.0	5.6	4.4	5.8	4.6
Bihar	2.7	8.2	3.2	4.5	16.5	5.6	2.9	8.9	3.4
Chhattisgarh	1.1	0.3	0.8	4.1	4.7	4.3	1.7	0.9	1.4
Delhi	9.4	0.0	7.8	3.3	4.6	3.5	3.8	4.2	3.8
Gujarat	0.4	0.2	0.3	0.6	1.7	0.8	0.5	0.6	0.5
Haryana	2.6	1.7	2.4	4.0	5.0	4.2	3.0	2.4	2.9
Himachal Pradesh	1.1	0.8	1.0	1.9	9.9	4.0	1.2	1.3	1.3
Jammu & Kashmir	2.2	3.0	2.5	4.1	19.0	7.0	2.7	5.3	3.4
Jharkhand	1.8	2.8	2.1	4.6	8.9	5.1	2.4	3.4	2.6
Karnataka	1.2	0.4	0.9	2.4	4.4	2.9	1.6	1.4	1.6
Kerala	3.1	14.2	6.8	2.7	13.9	6.1	3.0	14.1	6.6
Madhya Pradesh	0.6	0.0	0.4	2.4	3.5	2.6	1.0	0.5	0.9
Maharashtra	0.9	0.3	0.7	1.8	3.8	2.3	1.3	1.2	1.3
Odisha	2.3	2.0	2.2	3.9	2.0	3.5	2.5	2.0	2.4
Punjab	2.2	1.3	1.9	2.6	3.6	2.8	2.3	1.9	2.2
Rajasthan	0.9	0.4	0.7	3.2	2.5	3.1	1.4	0.7	1.2
Tamil Nadu	2.1	1.9	2.0	2.1	4.5	2.7	2.1	2.7	2.3
Uttarakhand	2.7	2.1	2.5	2.5	20.0	5.3	2.7	3.9	3.1
Uttar Pradesh	1.0	0.7	0.9	4.2	3.7	4.1	1.8	1.1	1.6
West Bengal	2.8	2.4	2.7	4.3	6.4	4.8	3.2	3.4	3.3
All India	1.7	1.7	1.7	3.0	5.2	3.4	2.1	2.4	2.2

Source: *Employment and Unemployment Survey*, NSS, 2011-12 round.

Table 4.4

Youth Unemployment Rates (UPSS) by Major States: 2011-12 (15-29 Years)

State	*Rural*			*Urban*			*Total*		
	Male	*Female*	*Person*	*Male*	*Female*	*Person*	*Male*	*Female*	*Person*
(1)	(2)	(3)	(4)	(5)	(6)	(7)	(8)	(9)	(10)
Andhra Pradesh	5.2	1.6	3.6	11.2	13.7	11.7	7.3	3.7	5.9
Assam	14.8	14.1	14.6	18.6	17.8	18.5	15.2	14.4	15.0
Bihar	8.1	20.5	9.3	11.5	43.6	14.8	8.4	23.1	9.8
Chhattisgarh	3.8	0.3	2.3	10.3	12.4	11.0	5.2	2.4	4.1
Delhi	26.1	0.0	21.1	10.1	11.1	10.3	11.5	10.0	11.3
Gujarat	1.0	0.5	0.9	1.6	4.9	2.1	1.3	1.6	1.3
Haryana	6.8	5.9	6.6	11.2	17.3	12.0	8.0	8.5	8.1
Himachal Pradesh	4.2	3.1	3.6	3.0	21.4	7.2	3.9	4.1	4.0
Jammu & Kashmir	6.9	7.4	7.1	12.2	35.3	18.8	8.1	12.2	9.5
Jharkhand	5.2	9.5	6.2	13.6	24.1	15.3	6.7	11.2	7.7
Karnataka	2.7	1.8	2.4	6.7	11.9	7.9	4.1	5.0	4.4
Kerala	9.7	47.4	21.6	8.4	37.1	17.9	9.4	44.5	20.6
Madhya Pradesh	1.7	0.0	1.2	7.3	10.6	7.9	3.0	1.3	2.6
Maharashtra	2.7	1.3	2.3	4.9	8.4	5.7	3.7	3.9	3.8
Odisha	6.2	5.6	6.0	10.3	4.9	9.2	6.8	5.6	6.5
Punjab	6.5	4.1	5.8	5.7	5.6	5.7	6.2	4.5	5.8
Rajasthan	2.4	1.0	1.9	7.1	6.5	7.0	3.6	1.6	2.9
Tamil Nadu	7.6	6.4	7.2	6.6	13.9	8.7	7.2	9.0	7.8
Uttar Pradesh	2.6	1.7	2.4	10.6	8.6	10.3	4.6	3.1	4.3
Uttarakhand	13.0	7.7	10.5	5.5	27.5	9.4	10.1	10.3	10.2
West Bengal	7.7	6.0	7.2	11.7	17.7	13.1	8.8	8.8	8.8
All India	5.0	4.8	4.9	8.1	13.1	9.2	5.9	6.6	6.1

Source: Employment and Unemployment Survey, NSS, 2011-12 round.

Table 4.5

Youth Unemployment Rates (UPS) by Major States: 2011-12 (15-29 Years)

State	*Rural*			*Urban*			*Total*		
	Male	*Female*	*Person*	*Male*	*Female*	*Person*	*Male*	*Female*	*Person*
(1)	(2)	(3)	(4)	(5)	(6)	(7)	(8)	(9)	(10)
Andhra Pradesh	5.5	2.8	4.4	11.4	14.7	12.1	7.6	5.1	6.7
Assam	15.3	20.1	16.1	19.2	19.5	19.2	15.7	20.1	16.4
Bihar	8.8	30.3	10.3	14.2	53.1	17.8	9.4	33.5	11.1
Chhattisgarh	6.0	0.4	4.0	13.7	20.1	15.6	7.8	3.9	6.4
Delhi	26.1	0.0	21.1	10.5	12.1	10.8	11.9	10.8	11.7
Gujarat	1.6	0.7	1.4	1.8	6.0	2.4	1.7	2.2	1.8
Haryana	6.8	14.6	7.4	11.2	20.1	12.3	8.1	16.7	8.8
Himachal Pradesh	6.3	6.0	6.2	3.5	24.2	7.7	5.8	7.1	6.4
Jammu & Kashmir	9.4	29.3	12.2	14.0	44.9	21.7	10.5	35.4	14.6
Jharkhand	5.6	19.9	7.5	14.9	27.6	16.7	7.2	21.3	9.1
Karnataka	3.0	1.9	2.7	8.4	13.4	9.5	4.9	5.8	5.1
Kerala	11.7	58.6	25.9	9.4	44.8	20.9	11.1	54.7	24.5
Madhya Pradesh	1.8	0.0	1.4	7.5	13.6	8.3	3.1	1.7	2.8
Maharashtra	3.1	2.0	2.8	5.2	9.1	6.1	4.0	5.0	4.2
Odisha	7.5	10.0	8.0	10.6	6.2	9.9	8.0	9.5	8.3
Punjab	6.9	17.8	7.8	6.1	6.9	6.2	6.6	11.7	7.1
Rajasthan	3.4	1.7	2.9	7.5	9.0	7.7	4.5	2.6	4.0
Tamil Nadu	8.0	8.2	8.1	7.3	15.2	9.4	7.7	10.9	8.7
Uttar Pradesh	4.8	5.4	4.8	11.3	11.4	11.3	6.4	7.6	6.5
Uttarakhand	16.5	15.2	16.0	5.8	44.2	10.7	12.3	18.9	14.3
West Bengal	10.0	12.1	10.4	14.4	23.2	16.2	11.2	15.7	12.0
All India	6.1	7.8	6.5	8.9	15.6	10.2	6.9	10.0	7.6

Source: *Employment and Unemployment Survey*, NSS, 2011-12 round.

Table 4.6

Unemployment Rates of Educated Youth (Secondary and Above) (UPSS) for Major States, 2004-05 (15-29 Years)

State	*Rural*			*Urban*			*Total*		
	Male	*Female*	*Person*	*Male*	*Female*	*Person*	*Male*	*Female*	*Person*
(1)	(2)	(3)	(4)	(5)	(6)	(7)	(8)	(9)	(10)
Andhra Pradesh	9.2	7.5	8.8	17.6	25.9	19.3	12.4	13.3	12.6
Assam	22.8	38.0	25.8	29.6	25.3	28.6	24.0	35.2	26.3
Bihar	10.6	12.3	10.6	31.7	71.9	33.4	14.1	24.6	14.5
Chhattisgarh	5.0	17.8	7.0	17.5	18.5	17.7	8.4	17.9	9.9
Delhi	9.6	0.0	8.5	17.7	21.0	18.1	17.0	19.4	17.3
Gujarat	3.4	3.1	3.3	3.9	18.3	6.0	3.7	7.9	4.5
Haryana	12.9	9.0	12.0	11.1	30.0	14.9	12.3	14.7	12.9
Himachal Pradesh	6.9	7.9	7.4	6.2	37.2	15.9	6.8	9.8	8.2
Jammu & Kashmir	10.9	10.2	10.8	20.1	51.0	28.2	13.3	21.0	15.2
Jharkhand	9.9	2.5	8.8	29.5	26.7	29.2	16.4	9.3	15.4
Karnataka	4.1	15.4	6.9	7.4	25.2	11.9	5.7	20.3	9.4
Kerala	19.4	60.2	39.9	17.0	65.9	39.9	18.7	61.8	39.9
Madhya Pradesh	4.3	1.5	3.9	12.2	13.1	12.4	7.9	7.8	7.9
Maharashtra	6.0	3.6	5.3	11.3	12.4	11.6	8.4	7.5	8.2
Odisha	19.2	55.3	28.3	41.5	54.4	45.8	23.8	55.1	32.2
Punjab	15.0	28.4	19.8	10.7	34.7	17.9	13.4	30.3	19.1
Rajasthan	8.8	5.7	8.4	8.5	18.0	9.7	8.7	9.4	8.8
Tamil Nadu	8.7	15.7	11.3	11.3	23.5	14.6	10.1	19.1	13.0
Uttar Pradesh	2.6	2.7	2.6	10.0	24.1	12.0	4.7	10.5	5.3
Uttarakhand	9.5	4.2	7.2	13.8	22.4	16.2	11.0	8.0	9.8
West Bengal	16.2	51.7	21.8	18.1	22.0	19.2	17.0	32.5	20.5
All India	9.1	20.7	11.9	13.3	27.0	16.5	10.8	23.0	13.7

Source: *Employment and Unemployment Survey*, NSS, 2004-05 round.

Table 4.7

Unemployment Rates of Educated Youth (Secondary and Above) (UPSS) for Major States, 2011-12 (15-29 Years)

State	Rural			Urban			Total		
	Male	Female	Person	Male	Female	Person	Male	Female	Person
(1)	(2)	(3)	(4)	(5)	(6)	(7)	(8)	(9)	(10)
Andhra Pradesh	9.1	6.6	8.3	17.0	24.1	18.4	12.8	12.1	12.6
Assam	26.9	40.3	29.2	27.8	24.7	27.1	27.0	37.5	28.9
Bihar	9.2	54.2	12.0	15.1	58.1	20.6	10.1	55.3	13.4
Chhattisgarh	10.4	2.3	8.2	11.3	18.6	13.5	10.6	8.0	9.9
Delhi	30.8	0.0	23.0	10.6	13.0	11.2	12.8	11.6	12.5
Gujarat	3.0	0.0	2.6	2.6	2.4	2.6	2.8	1.5	2.6
Haryana	8.7	12.2	9.3	13.6	16.0	14.0	10.2	13.3	10.7
Himachal Pradesh	6.0	4.3	5.1	3.9	20.3	8.6	5.6	5.5	5.6
Jammu & Kashmir	8.9	14.9	10.6	19.6	49.6	29.3	11.8	26.0	15.9
Jharkhand	8.8	39.6	15.7	16.1	39.9	20.1	11.1	39.7	17.0
Karnataka	5.0	5.7	5.2	8.4	15.5	10.4	6.5	11.3	7.6
Kerala	15.0	52.0	29.5	13.9	42.5	26.2	14.7	49.1	28.5
Madhya Pradesh	4.0	0.0	3.6	12.0	25.2	14.1	6.6	11.6	7.2
Maharashtra	4.5	4.6	4.5	4.7	13.2	6.8	4.6	9.3	5.7
Odisha	13.5	29.5	16.3	12.6	12.2	12.6	13.3	25.7	15.4
Punjab	10.5	9.2	10.1	7.6	6.6	7.4	9.1	8.2	8.8
Rajasthan	5.1	9.8	6.1	8.9	21.3	10.7	6.5	12.9	7.7
Tamil Nadu	12.4	13.1	12.7	8.7	19.1	11.6	10.4	16.2	12.1
Uttar Pradesh	3.6	3.4	3.6	23.8	23.6	23.7	9.1	10.0	9.2
Uttarakhand	17.3	16.7	17.0	11.9	33.0	17.6	15.5	19.9	17.2
West Bengal	10.8	27.4	14.5	17.2	23.4	19.0	13.3	25.5	16.3
All India	8.2	15.5	9.8	11.6	20.0	13.5	9.5	17.4	11.3

Source: Employment and Unemployment Survey, NSS, 2011-12 round.

Table 4.8

Unemployment Rates of Educated Youth (Secondary and Above) (UPS) for Major States, 2004-05 (15-29 Years)

State	Rural			Urban			Total		
	Male	Female	Person	Male	Female	Person	Male	Female	Person
(1)	(2)	(3)	(4)	(5)	(6)	(7)	(8)	(9)	(10)
Andhra Pradesh	11.5	10.8	11.3	18.3	26.7	20.1	14.1	16.1	14.6
Assam	31.1	54.1	35.1	32.8	43.3	35.1	31.4	51.5	35.1
Bihar	12.5	15.0	12.6	33.3	74.1	35.1	16.1	29.0	16.6
Chhattisgarh	7.5	22.1	9.5	21.7	24.9	22.1	11.5	22.8	13.0
Delhi	9.6	0.0	9.2	17.9	27.1	19.1	17.2	26.4	18.3
Gujarat	6.1	4.9	5.9	5.9	23.4	8.2	6.0	12.1	7.0
Haryana	16.0	26.3	17.2	12.7	40.9	17.3	15.0	32.1	17.2
Himachal Pradesh	20.0	24.4	22.0	7.4	44.8	18.1	18.2	25.8	21.6
Jammu & Kashmir	15.8	27.6	17.6	21.9	56.3	30.9	17.4	39.4	21.5
Jharkhand	10.9	3.4	9.9	31.4	31.2	31.4	17.6	10.9	16.8
Karnataka	7.1	19.2	10.0	9.1	27.2	13.5	8.1	23.3	11.7
Kerala	28.1	70.1	49.1	28.0	74.9	49.8	28.1	71.5	49.3
Madhya Pradesh	4.7	1.9	4.4	13.5	14.2	13.6	8.7	9.1	8.7
Maharashtra	9.7	5.4	8.7	14.3	17.3	15.0	11.9	10.9	11.7
Odisha	22.4	64.6	32.1	42.8	55.7	47.0	26.7	61.9	35.6
Punjab	16.0	64.9	26.0	11.0	41.3	19.5	14.1	53.7	23.4
Rajasthan	9.6	13.8	9.9	9.1	22.8	10.5	9.5	17.7	10.1
Tamil Nadu	10.8	20.6	14.3	12.7	25.8	16.2	11.8	22.8	15.3
Uttar Pradesh	4.8	6.5	4.9	10.9	39.6	14.1	6.6	21.7	7.8
Uttarakhand	16.3	7.3	13.2	14.2	29.5	17.7	15.5	13.0	14.7
West Bengal	21.8	73.0	29.4	23.2	38.1	26.8	22.4	52.0	28.1
All India	12.4	30.5	16.1	15.4	33.4	19.2	13.6	31.7	17.3

Source: *Employment and Unemployment Survey*, NSS, 2004-05 round.

Table 4.9

Unemployment Rates of Educated Youth (Secondary and Above) (UPS) for Major States, 2011-12 (15-29 Years)

State	Rural			Urban			Total		
	Male	Female	Person	Male	Female	Person	Male	Female	Person
(1)	(2)	(3)	(4)	(5)	(6)	(7)	(8)	(9)	(10)
Andhra Pradesh	10.0	10.2	10.0	17.3	25.7	18.9	13.4	15.4	13.9
Assam	28.4	60.2	32.7	27.9	26.0	27.5	28.3	52.9	32.0
Bihar	11.0	58.4	14.0	20.7	61.6	26.2	12.5	59.4	16.1
Chhattisgarh	15.5	2.9	12.5	18.7	36.4	23.8	16.5	15.2	16.2
Delhi	30.8	0.0	23.0	11.2	13.9	11.9	13.4	12.3	13.1
Gujarat	4.9	0.0	4.5	3.0	2.6	2.9	3.9	1.8	3.6
Haryana	8.8	32.4	10.4	13.6	17.7	14.2	10.3	25.0	11.7
Himachal Pradesh	9.6	8.9	9.2	4.7	21.9	9.4	8.6	10.0	9.3
Jammu & Kashmir	14.4	42.1	18.3	22.7	53.0	32.3	16.9	48.1	23.3
Jharkhand	10.2	60.4	18.7	16.9	42.5	21.1	12.4	54.7	19.5
Karnataka	5.1	5.8	5.2	9.9	17.6	12.0	7.3	12.5	8.5
Kerala	18.2	63.5	35.8	15.9	49.4	30.2	17.6	59.3	34.2
Madhya Pradesh	4.2	0.0	3.9	12.6	27.1	14.9	7.0	13.9	7.7
Maharashtra	5.2	6.3	5.4	5.0	14.1	7.2	5.1	11.0	6.4
Odisha	17.8	51.4	21.4	12.7	12.5	12.7	16.5	38.9	19.2
Punjab	11.6	27.3	13.6	8.5	7.8	8.3	10.1	15.0	10.9
Rajasthan	8.2	16.7	9.5	9.0	27.2	11.1	8.5	20.1	10.1
Tamil Nadu	13.1	14.8	13.6	9.7	20.3	12.5	11.3	17.7	13.0
Uttar Pradesh	8.7	8.4	8.6	25.7	26.3	25.8	13.6	17.7	14.0
Uttarakhand	25.0	29.5	26.8	13.0	50.7	21.1	20.7	33.4	25.1
West Bengal	17.6	49.0	22.8	22.8	30.7	24.9	19.7	39.1	23.7
All India	10.7	23.6	13.0	12.8	22.6	14.9	11.5	23.1	13.8

Source: *Employment and Unemployment Survey*, NSS, 2011-12 round.

5. QUALITY OF EMPLOYMENT

Table 5.1

Industry-wise Employment in Organized Public and Private Sectors (in '000): 1991/2011

Industry	*Public Sector*				*Private Sector*				*Total*			
	1991	2000	2005	2011	1991	2000	2005	2011	1991	2000	2005	2011
(1)	(2)	(3)	(4)	(5)	(6)	(7)	(8)	(9)	(10)	(11)	(12)	(13)
Agriculture and allied activities	556	514	496	477	891	904	983	918	1,447	1,418	1,479	1,395
Mining and quarrying	999	924	1,014	1,090	100	81	79	132	1,099	1,005	1,093	1,222
Manufacturing	1,852	1,531	1,130	1,016	4,480	5,085	4,489	5,397	6,332	6,616	5,619	6,413
Electricity, gas and water supply	905	946	860	831	40	41	49	70	945	987	909	901
Construction	1,149	1,092	911	847	73	57	49	102	1,222	1,149	960	949
Trade, hotels and restaurants	150	163	184	170	300	330	375	546	450	493	559	716
Transport, storage and communication	3,026	3,077	2,751	2,384	53	70	85	189	3,079	3,147	2,836	2,573
Finance, insurance, real estate etc.	1,194	1,296	1,408	1,361	254	358	523	1,718	1,448	1,654	1,931	3,079
Community, social and personal services	9,227	9,771	9,252	9,095	1,480	1,723	1,820	2,350	10,707	11,494	11,072	11,445
All	19,058	19,314	18,006	17,271	7,671	8,649	8,452	11,422	26,729	27,963	26,458	28,693

Source: Government of India, Ministry of Labour and Employment, Directorate General of Employment and Training, New Delhi.

Table 5.2

Industry-wise Shares of Employment in Organized Public and Private Sectors: 1991/2011

Industry	*Public Sector*				*Private Sector*				*Total*			
	1991	2000	2005	2011	1991	2000	2005	2011	1991	2000	2005	2011
(1)	(2)	(3)	(4)	(5)	(6)	(7)	(8)	(9)	(10)	(11)	(12)	(13)
Agriculture and allied activities	2.9	2.7	2.8	2.8	11.6	10.5	11.6	8.0	5.4	5.1	5.6	4.9
Mining and quarrying	5.2	4.8	5.6	6.3	1.3	0.9	0.9	1.2	4.1	3.6	4.1	4.3
Manufacturing	9.7	7.9	6.3	5.9	58.4	58.8	53.1	47.3	23.7	23.7	21.2	22.4
Electricity, gas and water supply	4.7	4.9	4.8	4.8	0.5	0.5	0.6	0.6	3.5	3.5	3.4	3.1
Construction	6.0	5.7	5.1	4.9	1.0	0.7	0.6	0.9	4.6	4.1	3.6	3.3
Trade, hotels and restaurants	0.8	0.8	1.0	1.0	3.9	3.8	4.4	4.8	1.7	1.8	2.1	2.5
Transport, storage and communication	15.9	15.9	15.3	13.8	0.7	0.8	1.0	1.7	11.5	11.3	10.7	9.0
Finance, insurance, real estate etc.	6.3	6.7	7.8	7.9	3.3	4.1	6.2	15.0	5.4	5.9	7.3	10.7
Community, social and personal services	48.4	50.6	51.4	52.7	19.3	19.9	21.5	20.6	40.1	41.1	41.8	39.9
All	100	100	100	100	100	100	100	100	100	100	100	100

Source: Government of India, Ministry of Labour and Employment, Directorate General of Employment and Training, New Delhi.

Table 5.3

Industry-wise Annual Growth Rate of Employment in Organized Public and Private Sectors: 1991/2011

Industry	*Public Sector*				*Private Sector*				*Total*			
	1991-2000	*2000-2005*	*2000-2011*	*1991-2011*	*1991-2000*	*2000-2005*	*2000-2011*	*1991-2011*	*1991-2000*	*2000-2005*	*2000-2011*	*1991-2011*
(1)	(2)	(3)	(4)	(5)	(6)	(7)	(8)	(9)	(10)	(11)	(12)	(13)
Agriculture and allied activities	-0.87	-0.71	-0.68	-0.76	0.16	1.69	0.14	0.15	-0.22	0.85	-0.15	-0.18
Mining and quarrying	-0.86	1.88	1.51	0.44	-2.31	-0.50	4.54	1.40	-0.99	1.69	1.79	0.53
Manufacturing	-2.09	-5.89	-3.66	-2.96	1.42	-2.46	0.54	0.94	0.49	-3.21	-0.28	0.06
Electricity, gas and water supply	0.49	-1.89	-1.17	-0.43	0.27	3.63	4.98	2.84	0.48	-1.63	-0.83	-0.24
Construction	-0.56	-3.56	-2.28	-1.51	-2.71	-2.98	5.43	1.69	-0.68	-3.53	-1.72	-1.26
Trade, hotels and restaurants	0.93	2.45	0.38	0.63	1.06	2.59	4.68	3.04	1.02	2.54	3.45	2.35
Transport, storage and communication	0.19	-2.21	-2.29	-1.19	3.14	3.96	9.45	6.56	0.24	-2.06	-1.81	-0.89
Finance, insurance, real estate etc.	0.91	1.67	0.45	0.66	3.89	7.88	15.32	10.03	1.49	3.15	5.81	3.84
Community, social and personal services	0.64	-1.09	-0.65	-0.07	1.70	1.10	2.86	2.34	0.79	-0.75	-0.04	0.33
All	0.15	-1.39	-1.01	-0.49	1.34	-0.46	2.56	2.01	0.50	-1.10	0.23	0.36

Source: Calculated from Government of India, Ministry of Labour and Employment, Directorate General of Employment and Training, New Delhi.

Table 5.4

Contractual Status of Wage/Salaried Workers Outside Agriculture by Type of Enterprise, 2004-05/2011-12

Type of Enterprise	*No Written Contract*	*Contract for 1 Year or Less*	*Contract for 1 Year to 3 Years*	*Contract for More Than 3 Years*	*Total (Incl. Non-reporting)*
(1)	(2)	(3)	(4)	(5)	(6)
			2004-05		
Proprietary and partnership	93.1	1.0	0.9	3.9	100
Government sector	26.7	2.1	1.6	69.2	100
Public limited	58.0	3.4	3.7	34.4	100
Cooperative	46.8	3.3	6.9	42.7	100
Others	91.0	1.1	0.3	4.8	100
Total (Incl. Non-reporting)	73.2	1.6	1.4	21.9	100
			2011-12		
Proprietary and partnership	94.0	1.8	0.9	2.8	100
Government sector	33.2	4.9	1.8	51.1	100
Public limited	64.2	5.8	5.0	24.5	100
Cooperative	61.1	4.3	4.2	30.0	100
Others	92.9	1.1	0.7	1.8	100
Total (Incl. Non-reporting)	75.3	2.9	1.6	16.5	100

Note: Salaried workers include regular wage workers and casual workers

Source: *Employment and Unemployment Survey*, NSS, 2004-05 and 2011-12 rounds.

Table 5.5

Percentage of Contract Workers in Organized Manufacturing Sector by Major States: 2004-05/2011-12

State	2004-05		2011-12	
	Total No. of Workers (in '000)	*% of Contract Workers*	*Total No. of Workers (in '000)*	*% of Contract Workers*
(1)	(2)	(3)	(4)	(5)
Andhra Pradesh	784	49.9	1040	48.1
Assam	101	14.1	141	19.7
Bihar	51	50.7	91	64.3
Chhattisgarh	78	35.3	77	75.2
Delhi	81	5.4	79	12.6
Gujarat	607	33.7	992	36.1
Haryana	269	41.5	427	46.6
Himachal Pradesh	34	18.8	120	26.4
Jammu & Kashmir	25	28.7	44	48.3
Jharkhand	117	13.2	128	23.2
Karnataka	431	13.0	609	21.1
Kerala	274	7.6	328	16.3
Madhya Pradesh	164	26.1	232	33.1
Maharashtra	815	28.0	1203	40.5
Odisha	117	37.4	229	48.0
Punjab	310	27.1	485	28.5
Rajasthan	208	33.1	338	36.3
Tamil Nadu	1047	13.4	1593	19.9
Uttar Pradesh	453	28.7	626	36.4
Uttarakhand	35	29.4	234	50.2
West Bengal	418	15.2	514	30.4
All India	6599	26.5	9902	33.9

Source: Annual Survey of Industries (ASI) Volumes, 2004-05 and 2011-12, Volume I, Ministry of Statistics and Programme Implementation, Central Statistical Organization, Government of India.

Table 5.6

Percentage Share of Non-farm, Regular and Regular Formal Workers (UPSS), Major States, 2004-05 and 2011-12

State	*Non-farm*				*Regular*				*Regular Formal*			
	2004-05		2011-12		2004-05		2011-12		2004-05		2011-12	
	%	*Rank*	%	*Rank*	%	*Rank*	%	*Rank*	%	*R*	%	*R*
(1)	(2)	(3)	(4)	(5)	(6)	(7)	(8)	(9)	(10)	(11)	(12)	(13)
Andhra Pradesh	40.6	10	47.1	15	13.0	13	17.9	11	4.4	15	6.0	12
Assam	31.5	18	44.0	17	12.1	14	14.2	14	5.4	13	6.0	14
Bihar	26.6	20	37.6	20	4.2	21	5.8	21	1.7	21	2.3	21
Chhattisgarh	22.3	21	27.2	21	8.4	20	9.7	20	3.8	19	2.9	20
Delhi	99.3	1	99.8	1	61.0	1	62.9	1	21.4	1	26.5	1
Gujarat	41.8	9	51.2	8	17.3	7	24.7	5	6.9	10	6.8	11
Haryana	47.9	6	56.7	7	20.2	5	23.9	6	8.1	5	11.5	2
Himachal Pradesh	35.4	16	41.6	18	13.9	10	18.2	10	8.5	4	8.6	8
Jammu & Kashmir	46.7	7	57.5	6	16.5	8	20.5	9	9.4	2	10.8	4
Jharkhand	37.6	13	49.6	12	8.5	19	10.2	19	4.6	14	5.6	15
Karnataka	36.7	14	50.1	11	13.1	12	22.5	7	6.2	11	11.0	3
Kerala	63.9	2	74.5	2	19.2	6	22.5	7	7.7	7	7.9	9
Madhya Pradesh	30.6	19	41.0	19	10.7	15	11.3	16	4.1	17	5.2	16
Maharashtra	44.3	8	50.9	10	20.7	4	26.5	3	8.5	3	10.3	5
Odisha	36.7	14	44.3	16	8.7	18	10.6	17	4.2	16	4.7	17
Punjab	50.1	5	63.6	4	21.7	2	27.5	2	7.4	8	7.5	10
Rajasthan	38.3	12	49.6	12	10.6	16	13.0	15	3.9	18	4.2	18
Tamil Nadu	53.6	3	64.8	3	21.6	3	25.5	4	7.8	6	9.7	6
Uttar Pradesh	38.5	11	47.6	14	9.7	17	10.6	17	3.2	20	3.3	19
Uttarakhand	33.9	17	51.0	9	13.6	11	17.5	12	7.1	9	8.9	7
West Bengal	52.5	4	60.8	5	15.1	9	16.8	13	6.0	12	6.0	13
All India	41.5		51.1		14.3		17.9		5.6		6.8	

Source: Calculated from *Employment and Unemployment Survey*, NSS, 2004-05, 2011-12 rounds.

Table 5.7

Percentage Distribution of Regular Formal Workers, ASI Workers, and Population across States, 2011-12

State	*Regular Formal*	*Organized Manufacturing Workers (ASI)*	*Population*
(1)	(2)	(3)	(4)
Andhra Pradesh	7.9	10.3	7.3
Assam	1.9	1.3	2.4
Bihar	2.0	0.8	8.3
Chhattisgarh	1.1	1.4	2.1
Delhi	4.0	1.0	1.2
Gujarat	5.6	10.2	5.1
Haryana	3.4	4.3	2.2
Himachal Pradesh	1.0	1.2	0.6
Jammu & Kashmir	1.4	0.4	0.9
Jharkhand	1.8	1.5	2.5
Karnataka	9.0	6.2	5.1
Kerala	3.3	3.0	2.9
Madhya Pradesh	4.5	2.5	5.9
Maharashtra	16.1	13.4	9.5
Odisha	2.6	2.2	3.5
Punjab	2.6	4.8	2.4
Rajasthan	3.5	3.4	5.5
Tamil Nadu	10.0	15.3	6.1
Uttar Pradesh	7.0	6.4	16.6
Uttarakhand	1.0	2.3	0.9
West Bengal	6.9	5.0	7.7
Other States	3.5	3.2	1.5
All India	100	100	100

Sources: *Employment and Unemployment Survey*, NSS, 2011-12 round and Annual Survey of Industries, Volume-I, Ministry of Statistics and Programme Implementation, Central Statistical Organization, Government of India.

6. WAGES AND EARNINGS (15-59 YEARS)

Table 6.1a

Daily Average Wage Rates of Regular Workers in Major States, 2004-05

(in ₹ at 2011-12 prices)

State	Rural			Urban			Total		
	Male	Female	Person	Male	Female	Person	Male	Female	Person
(1)	(2)	(3)	(4)	(5)	(6)	(7)	(8)	(9)	(10)
Andhra Pradesh	191	103	169	318	230	299	264	169	241
Assam	261	133	230	435	263	405	313	164	282
Bihar	317	175	299	433	364	430	368	229	354
Chhattisgarh	221	144	209	313	120	282	276	128	252
Delhi	281	344	283	432	438	432	424	444	426
Gujarat	239	194	234	301	193	289	283	194	271
Haryana	430	184	414	271	285	273	354	253	343
Himachal Pradesh	371	274	349	513	395	491	396	294	375
Jammu & Kashmir	326	202	317	451	341	437	371	276	363
Jharkhand	324	184	301	501	249	465	424	216	392
Karnataka	229	124	203	397	268	369	352	224	322
Kerala	295	211	263	351	298	331	312	238	283
Madhya Pradesh	185	56	158	320	183	294	269	132	241
Maharashtra	279	193	266	383	311	367	356	292	343
Odisha	252	169	241	369	251	346	297	211	283
Punjab	302	221	292	345	393	353	324	340	327
Rajasthan	266	157	254	320	266	313	296	225	287
Tamil Nadu	221	133	196	332	195	296	297	174	264
Uttar Pradesh	221	180	216	308	256	303	268	222	262
Uttarakhand	349	243	337	371	238	345	359	241	340
West Bengal	259	95	216	345	226	322	313	165	282
All India	261	153	241	353	266	336	317	224	299

Source: *Employment and Unemployment Survey*, NSS, 2004-05 round.

Table 6.1b

Daily Average Wage Rates of Regular Workers in Major States, 2011-12

(in ₹ at 2011-12 prices)

State	Rural			Urban			Total		
	Male	Female	Person	Male	Female	Person	Male	Female	Person
(1)	(2)	(3)	(4)	(5)	(6)	(7)	(8)	(9)	(10)
Andhra Pradesh	250	224	246	423	257	395	365	246	346
Assam	344	181	303	615	562	607	423	250	384
Bihar	452	188	413	418	380	415	440	239	414
Chhattisgarh	260	164	239	362	269	337	324	236	303
Delhi	530	378	500	567	695	589	564	662	581
Gujarat	266	180	254	328	281	322	313	253	306
Haryana	397	366	396	784	631	754	605	588	603
Himachal Pradesh	435	254	398	427	307	398	433	272	398
Jammu & Kashmir	459	231	433	513	501	510	480	381	465
Jharkhand	521	295	483	575	395	553	557	354	529
Karnataka	231	142	209	525	387	490	414	300	386
Kerala	371	239	318	488	405	458	421	303	376
Madhya Pradesh	269	109	244	455	327	434	392	256	370
Maharashtra	366	304	357	510	375	482	477	364	456
Odisha	244	223	241	456	288	431	337	253	324
Punjab	302	161	285	351	397	360	330	328	330
Rajasthan	327	175	304	416	413	415	378	305	367
Tamil Nadu	291	197	267	409	287	378	370	256	341
Uttar Pradesh	298	174	279	492	393	481	410	278	392
Uttarakhand	458	394	450	447	441	446	453	420	448
West Bengal	301	135	260	452	344	428	396	260	365
All India	320	203	298	463	369	445	412	310	392

Source: Employment and Unemployment Survey, NSS, 2011-12 round.

Table 6.2a

Daily Average Wage Rates of Casual Workers in Major States, 2004-05

(in ₹ at 2011-12 prices)

State	Rural			Urban			Total		
	Male	Female	Person	Male	Female	Person	Male	Female	Person
(1)	(2)	(3)	(4)	(5)	(6)	(7)	(8)	(9)	(10)
Andhra Pradesh	90	56	76	113	66	101	92	55	76
Assam	113	97	108	129	89	120	111	95	107
Bihar	83	70	81	96	127	103	83	72	79
Chhattisgarh	68	52	63	84	57	71	69	53	62
Delhi	–	–	–	151	94	143	151	95	143
Gujarat	94	77	88	143	78	120	97	76	90
Haryana	139	108	131	141	85	131	136	104	128
Himachal Pradesh	160	113	157	122	110	118	151	111	146
Jammu & Kashmir	178	95	173	186	139	184	178	100	172
Jharkhand	94	70	88	104	96	103	93	72	88
Karnataka	90	56	76	143	80	129	97	56	81
Kerala	241	121	214	238	129	223	238	120	213
Madhya Pradesh	74	56	68	92	73	87	76	56	69
Maharashtra	85	50	70	136	71	118	95	53	77
Odisha	77	54	70	96	59	87	76	53	69
Punjab	137	99	133	146	82	141	136	97	132
Rajasthan	113	94	110	118	84	113	113	92	107
Tamil Nadu	126	65	101	146	84	131	128	65	104
Uttar Pradesh	95	74	92	111	70	106	97	72	92
Uttarakhand	124	99	119	122	106	120	121	99	118
West Bengal	90	72	88	113	61	106	92	70	88
All India	101	63	88	132	78	120	104	63	92

Note: - stands for not available.

Source: Employment and Unemployment Survey, NSS, 2004-05 round.

Table 6.2b

Daily Average Wage Rates of Casual Workers in Major States, 2011-12

(in ₹ at 2011-12 prices)

State	Rural			Urban			Total		
	Male	Female	Person	Male	Female	Person	Male	Female	Person
(1)	(2)	(3)	(4)	(5)	(6)	(7)	(8)	(9)	(10)
Andhra Pradesh	163	110	138	195	123	178	168	111	143
Assam	144	106	138	158	106	154	145	106	139
Bihar	131	93	128	158	167	159	132	95	129
Chhattisgarh	91	81	87	122	93	112	96	83	91
Delhi	-	-	-	265	93	254	265	93	253
Gujarat	116	105	113	161	99	148	123	104	117
Haryana	204	160	198	206	155	203	204	159	199
Himachal Pradesh	173	122	163	173	123	168	173	122	164
Jammu & Kashmir	210	222	211	215	181	210	211	207	210
Jharkhand	139	80	133	161	95	154	141	82	136
Karnataka	165	99	143	192	102	174	170	99	148
Kerala	352	169	309	343	166	315	350	168	310
Madhya Pradesh	109	99	107	133	104	130	113	100	110
Maharashtra	136	94	118	173	103	155	142	95	123
Odisha	126	92	119	139	94	131	127	92	120
Punjab	203	163	199	203	85	192	203	153	198
Rajasthan	164	117	153	181	134	174	167	118	156
Tamil Nadu	194	103	156	230	127	210	204	106	168
Uttar Pradesh	135	95	131	147	112	144	137	97	132
Uttarakhand	177	127	171	173	145	171	177	128	171
West Bengal	127	108	124	139	101	133	128	107	125
All India	150	105	138	185	115	173	155	106	143

Note: - stands for not available.

Source: Employment and Unemployment Survey, NSS, 2011-12 round.

Table 6.3

Percentage Share of Casual Workers not Getting Minimum Wages in Major States, 2009-10

State	Rural						Urban		
	Farm			Non-Farm			Non-Farm		
	Male	Female	Person	Male	Female	Person	Male	Female	Person
(1)	(2)	(3)	(4)	(5)	(6)	(7)	(8)	(9)	(10)
Andhra Pradesh	92	95	93	15	48	25	27	67	36
Assam	61	90	71	55	71	57	68	100	70
Bihar	66	77	70	57	37	57	54	84	56
Chhattisgarh	85	94	87	39	56	47	71	83	74
Gujarat	82	99	89	37	73	43	71	96	77
Haryana	50	80	57	24	48	26	58	95	62
Himachal Pradesh	12	58	23	5	5	5	31	22	28
Jammu & Kashmir	22	0	22	8	13	8	27	22	26
Jharkhand	61	90	74	31	73	35	80	83	80
Karnataka	100	82	94	17	64	27	49	91	58
Kerala	97	97	97	9	53	18	10	56	18
Madhya Pradesh	83	100	89	61	89	67	85	89	86
Maharashtra	93	88	91	45	67	48	61	92	65
Odisha	71	88	76	51	78	55	35	55	39
Punjab	15	79	44	16	53	19	43	94	47
Rajasthan	61	86	64	11	55	20	67	?	67
Tamil Nadu	98	99	99	19	69	34	30	80	39
Uttar Pradesh	61	100	66	32	40	33	19	61	23
Uttarakhand	32	75	54	8	44	11	36	100	39
West Bengal	71	88	73	52	94	61	44	83	56
All India	66	87	73	32	65	37	49	82	54

Source: Calculated from *Labour Bureau*, Ministry of Labour, Government of India, 2010 and *Employment and Unemployment Survey*, NSS, 2009-10 round.

7. EMPLOYMENT IN IMPORTANT EMERGING NON-AGRICULTURE SECTORS (UPSS Workers)

Table 7.1

Top 30 Non-agriculture Sectors in Terms of Net Additional Employment between 2004-05 and 2009-10

Broad Industry	*Industry at 4 Digit*	*Net Additional Employment during 2004-05 to 2009-10 (in '000)*	*Share in Total Employment (2009-10)*	*Annual Growth of Employment (2004-05 to 2009-10)*	*Distribution of Employment across Status of Employment (2009-10)*			*Weekly Earning (in ₹) (2009-10)*		*Sector Share (means) (2009-10)*	
					Self Employment	*Regular*	*Casual*	*Regular*	*Casual*	*Rural*	*Urban*
(1)	(2)	(3)	(4)	(5)	(6)	(7)	(8)	(9)	(10)	(11)	(12)
Manufacturing	Manufacture of electric motors, generators, and transformers	403	0.3	24.9	26	68	6	1941	896	29	71
	Manufacture of other transport equipment	323	0.2	84.9	43	44	13	995	655	38	62
	Manufacture of furniture	301	0.8	3.9	60	20	21	1503	1042	55	45
	Manufacture of ferro alloys	287	0.4	7.7	3	78	19	2938	747	28	72
	Manufacture of wearing apparel, except fur apparel	231	3.5	0.6	72	20	7	1072	679	41	59
	Manufacture of other food products	229	0.3	9.3	42	41	17	1050	646	34	66
	Manufacture of structural metal products	198	0.5	4.4	26	44	30	1252	791	41	59
Construction	Building of complete constructions or parts thereof; civil engineering	17,403	18.4	11.8	10	4	86	2048	718	73	27
	Building completion	675	0.9	8.1	25	5	69	1344	997	44	56
	Building installation	176	0.6	3.1	39	31	30	1823	951	37	63
Wholesale and retail trade	Retail sale of food, beverages and tobacco in specialized stores	2,390	8.6	2.7	90	7	3	886	681	52	48
	Retail sale of textiles, clothing, footwear and leather goods	663	2	3.3	68	29	3	992	696	27	73
	Retail sale of household appliances, articles and equipment	353	0.9	3.8	72	25	3	1184	823	25	75
	Retail sale of pharmaceutical and medical goods, cosmetic and toilet articles	289	0.7	4	72	25	3	929	710	43	57
	Wholesale of construction materials, hardware, plumbing and heating equipment and supplies	175	0.2	9.3	56	27	17	1337	879	25	75
Hotel and restaurant	Hotels; camping sites and other provision of short-stay accommodation	248	0.3	9.1	25	61	14	1385	695	33	67

contd...

...contd...

Broad Industry	Industry at 4 Digit	Net Additional Employment during 2004-05 to 2009-10 (in '000)	Share in Total Employment (2009-10)	Annual Growth of Employment (2004-05 to 2009-10)	Distribution of Employment across Status of Employment (2009-10)			Weekly Earning (in ₹) (2009-10)		Sector Share (means) (2009-10)	
					Self Employment	Regular	Casual	Regular	Casual	Rural	Urban
(1)	(2)	(3)	(4)	(5)	(6)	(7)	(8)	(9)	(10)	(11)	(12)
Transport	Other non-scheduled passenger land transport	1,569	3.8	4.2	63	25	12	1136	826	50	50
	Freight transport by road	634	3.1	1.9	35	32	33	1162	756	58	42
	Cargo handling	200	0.1	22.4	19	42	39	2603	624	32	68
Financial intermediation	Other monetary intermediation	289	0.7	4.1	2	96	3	3968	587	23	77
Insurance	Life insurance	338	0.4	10.8	49	49	2	3993	1208	28	72
Real estate	Real estate activities on a fee or contract basis	257	0.2	24.6	87	11	2	1798	1067	14	86
Computer related activities	Software publishing	628	0.5	16.9	3	96	0	5522	1444	3	97
	Data processing	191	0.1	30.8	3	96	1	2304	1034	8	92
Public admin.	General (overall) public service activities	561	2.9	1.9	0	98	2	3199	793	32	68
	Public order and safety activities	361	0.7	5.7	0	98	2	3150	1240	35	65
Education	Primary up to higher secondary education	671	5	1.3	12	86	1	2408	438	48	52
	Higher education	216	0.6	3.6	1	98	1	4002	804	22	78
Other community service	Sewage and refuse disposal, sanitation, and similar activities	182	0.3	7.5	20	61	19	998	493	22	78
	Hair dressing and other beauty treatment	175	1.1	1.5	87	9	4	3300	534	63	37

Source: Calculated from *Employment and Unemployment Survey*, NSS, 2004-05 and 2009-10 rounds.

Table 7.2

Top 30 Non-agriculture Sectors in Terms of Higher Employment Growth between 2004-05 and 2009-10

Broad Industry	*Industry at 4 Digit*	*Growth (CAGR) (2005-10)*	*Share in Total Employment (2009-10)*	*Net Additional Employment in '000 (2005-10)*	*Status of Employment (2009-10)*			*Weekly Earning (in ₹) (2009-10)*		*Sector Share (2009-10)*	
					Self Employment	*Regular*	*Casual*	*Regular*	*Casual*	*Rural*	*Urban*
(1)	(2)	(3)	(4)	(5)	(6)	(7)	(8)	(9)	(10)	(11)	(12)
Mining	Mining of iron ores	47	0.09	166	2	83	16	1616	713	72	28
	Extraction of salt.	39.4	0.07	127	37	0	63		893	83	17
	Mining of non-ferrous metal ores, except uranium and thorium ores	27.5	0.05	81	2	66	32	2386	873	57	43
	Extraction and agglomeration of peat	21	0	2	0	64	36	3854	834	100	0
Manufacturing	Manufacture of other transport equipment	84.9	0.15	323	43	44	13	995	655	38	62
	Manufacture of steam generators, except central heating hot water boilers	53.3	0.01	18	2	98		751		22	78
	Manufacture of machine-tools	31.8	0.08	140	23	60	17	1297	739	24	76
	Manufacture of malt liquors and malt	28.4	0.05	75	11	75	14	1302	489	76	24
	Manufacture of electric motors, generators and transformers	24.9	0.27	403	26	68	6	1941	896	29	71
	Manufacture of veneer sheets; manufacture of plywood, lamin board, particle board and other panels and boards	22.6	0.08	120	48	32	20	942	667	42	58
	Manufacture of lifting and handling equipment	21.5	0.02	30	17	83		2263		6	94
	Manufacture of sports goods	20.4	0.02	27	30	70		1116			100
	Service activities related to printing	18.2	0.09	111	48	39	14	1504	964	20	80
	Processing of nuclear fuel	16.6	0	5	12	88		2150	679	0	100
Transport	Cargo handling	22.4	0.14	200	19	42	39	2603	624	32	68
	Transport via pipelines	21.7	0.01	17	1	94	5	990	357	98	2
	Other supporting transport activities	17.3	0.06	78	21	68	11	7669	735	12	88
	Activities of travel agencies and tour operators; tourist assistance activities	16.1	0.1	120	21	72	7	1755	1335	10	90
Financial intermediation	Security dealing activities	16.4	0.08	99	38	62		2951		5	95

contd...

...contd...

Broad Industry	Industry at 4 Digit	Growth (CAGR) (2005-10)	Share in Total Employment (2009-10)	Net Additional Employment in '000 (2005-10)	Status of Employment (2009-10)			Weekly Earning (in ₹) (2009-10)		Sector Share (2009-10)	
					Self Employment	Regular	Casual	Regular	Casual	Rural	Urban
(1)	(2)	(3)	(4)	(5)	(6)	(7)	(8)	(9)	(10)	(11)	(12)
Insurance	Activities auxiliary to insurance and pension funding	22.6	0.06	83	85	15		4764		30	70
Real estate	Real estate activities on a fee or contract basis	24.6	0.17	257	87	11	2	1798	1067	14	86
Renting	Renting of other machinery and equipment	53.5	0.01	29	95	5		1869		25	75
Computer-related activities	Computer hardware consultancy	54.2	0.09	173	17	83		3117		0	100
	Data processing	30.8	0.12	191	3	96	1	2304	1034	8	92
	Maintenance and repair of office, accounting and computing machinery	26.3	0.06	95	40	59	1	2122	500	19	81
	Software publishing	16.9	0.52	628	3	96	0	5522	1444	3	97
Other business activities	Labour recruitment and provision of personnel	27.1	0.05	71	46	54		2399		5	95
	Architectural and engineering activities and related technical consultancy	17	0.06	77	55	45		1649		15	85
Public administration	Compulsory social security activities	18	0.07	85	0	98	2	2322	656	48	52
	Activities of trade unions	53.8	0	6	24	23	53		720	0	100

Source: Calculated from *Employment and Unemployment Survey*, NSS, 2004-05 and 2009-10 rounds.

Table 7.3

Top 30 Non-agriculture Sectors in Terms of Net Decline in Employment between 2004-05 and 2009-10

Broad Industry	*Industry at 4 Digit*	*Growth (CAGR) (2005-10)*	*Share in Total Employment (2009-10)*	*Net Decrease in Employment in '000 (2005-10)*	*Status of Employment (2009-10)*			*Weekly Earning (in ₹) (2009-10)*		*Sector Share (2009-10)*	
					Self Employment	*Regular*	*Casual*	*Regular*	*Casual*	*Rural*	*Urban*
(1)	(2)	(3)	(4)	(5)	(6)	(7)	(8)	(9)	(10)	(11)	(12)
Manufacturing	Preparation and spinning of textile fibre including weaving of textiles	-2.8	3.6	-1231	53	30	17	952	536	39	61
	Manufacturing of wooden containers	-13.7	0.3	-691	96	1	3	1286	631	87	13
	Manufacture of other products of wood, manufacture of articles of cork, straw, and plaiting materials	-6.9	0.5	-519	90	3	7	1050	555	78	22
	Manufacture of tobacco products	-2.2	1.9	-490	77	3	20	830	273	73	27
	Manufacture of builders' carpentry and joinery	-6.3	0.6	-486	64	8	28	795	884	68	32
	Manufacture of grain mill products	-4.5	0.7	-426	62	21	17	838	679	66	34
	Manufacture of other chemical products	-13.7	0.1	-323	27	55	18	2390	390	55	45
	Manufacture of jewellery and related articles	-2.9	0.8	-274	40	38	23	1372	868	30	70
	Manufacture of non-structural non-refractory ceramic ware	-7.3	0.3	-270	87	11	2	768	864	60	40
	Manufacture of footwear	-7.9	0.2	-268	45	41	14	998	629	25	75
	Manufacture of other fabricated metal products	-6.7	0.2	-213	21	61	19	1391	654	22	78
	Tanning and dressing of leather	-19.8	0	-211	8	76	16	1040	493	6	94
	Cutting, shaping, and finishing of stone	-8.2	0.2	-208	21	12	66	1039	623	78	22
	Embroidery work, *zari* work, and making of ornamental trimmings by hand	-1.8	0.9	-193	72	17	12	1239	481	45	55
	Manufacture of cutlery, hand tools and general hardware	-5.3	0.3	-183	60	31	9	770	713	53	47
	Other manufacturing, stationery articles, umbrellas, candles, and other decorative items	-3.4	0.4	-175	76	17	8	715	632	24	76
	Manufacture of knitted and crocheted fabrics and articles	-6.5	0.2	-135	13	62	25	922	501	17	83
	Manufacture of pulp, paper and paper board	-9.5	0.1	-126	8	81	10	1856	686	39	61

contd...

...contd...

Broad Industry	Industry at 4 Digit	Growth (CAGR) (2005-10)	Share in Total Employment (2009-10)	Net Decrease in Employment in '000 (2005-10)	Status of Employment (2009-10)			Weekly Earning (in ₹) (2009-10)		Sector Share (2009-10)	
					Self Employment	Regular	Casual	Regular	Casual	Rural	Urban
(1)	(2)	(3)	(4)	(5)	(6)	(7)	(8)	(9)	(10)	(11)	(12)
	Dressing and dyeing of fur; manufacture of articles of fur	-20.3	0	-118	45	38	17	822	877	2	98
	Manufacture of carpet and rugs other than by hand	-2.5	0.3	-101	42	31	27	980	486	46	54
Wholesale and retail trade	Other non-store retail sale, lottery ticket and non store retail sale	-6.6	0.4	-348	94	4	2	1254	731	37	63
	Other retail sale in specialized stores	-2.2	1.3	-337	78	18	4	1177	832	31	69
	Retail sale in non-specialized stores with food, beverages or tobacco predominating	-3	0.8	-310	89	9	2	744	725	55	45
	Wholesale on a fee or contract basis	-6.9	0.3	-278	73	12	15	1551	739	26	74
	Retail sale via stalls and markets	-9.4	0.1	-132	93	3	4	817	772	45	55
	Other wholesale, lottery ticket, e-commerce, etc.	-20.6	0	-120	62	20	18	1940	618	18	82
Transport	Other scheduled passenger land transport	-6.2	0.4	-370	13	74	13	2002	948	47	53
Tele-communication	National post activities	-8.5	0.1	-176	6	94	0	2660	1500	53	47
Community service	Washing and (dry-) cleaning of textile and fur products	-6.4	0.7	-600	96	2	2	1048	680	63	37
Private HH activities	Activities of private households as employers of domestic staff	-4.4	1.7	-974	0	68	32	678	483	32	68

Source: *Employment and Unemployment Survey*, NSS, 2004-05 and 2009-10 round.

8. LABOUR INSTITUTIONS AND EMPLOYMENT RELATIONS

Table 8.1

Trade Unions in India, 1991-2010

Year	Number of Registered Trade Unions	Number of Trade Unions Submitting Returns	Membership (of col. 3) (000s)	Employment in Organized Sector (000s)	Average Size of Trade Union	Year-on-Year Change (in col. 2) (%)	D.U. 1 (%)
(1)	(2)	(3)	(4)	(5)	(6)	(7)	(8)
1991	53,535	8,418	6,100	26,733	725	-	22.82
1992	55,680	9,165	5,746	27,056	627	4.01	21.24
1993	55,784	6,806	3,134	27,177	460	0.19	11.53
1994	56,872	6,277	4,094	27,355	652	1.95	14.96
1995	57,952	8,162	6,538	27,525	801	1.90	23.75
1996	58,988	7,242	5,601	27,941	773	1.79	20.05
1997	60,660	8,872	7,409	28,245	835	2.83	26.23
1998	61,992	7,403	7,249	28,166	979	2.20	25.74
1999	64,817	8,152	6,407	28,113	786	4.56	22.79
2000	66,056	7,253	5,420	27,960	747	1.91	19.38
2001	66,624	6,531	5,873	27,789	900	0.86	21.13
2002	68,544	7,812	6,973	27,206	893	2.88	25.63
2003	74,649	7,258	6,277	27,001	865	8.91	23.25
2004	74,403	5,242	3,397	26,443	648	-0.33	12.85
2005	78,465	8,317	8,719	26,459	1,048	5.46	32.95
2006	88,440	8,471	8,960	26,993	1,058	12.71	33.19
2007	95,783	7,408	7,877	27,276	1,063	8.30	28.87
2008	84,642	9,709	9,573	27,549	986	11.63	34.75
2009*	22,284	3,861	6,480	28,172	1,678	**	23.00
2010*	18,602	2,937	5,097	28,708	1,735	**	17.75

Notes: 1. Trade unions include unless specified otherwise in this and subsequent tables refer to workers' and employers' organizations.

2. Average size is membership per union submitting returns

3. DU – degree of unionization; DU 1 – Union membership (reported) as a percentage of employment in the organized sector;

4. Women union membership constituted on an average 17.55 per cent during 1991-2004; its share ranged from 9.69 per cent in 1991 to 26.83 per cent in 2001.

* - The low numbers are due to poor receipt of annual returns on trade unions from the states and union territories, see,

** - Due to the provisional and incomplete nature of data for (2) the rates of change are not calculated for these two years

Sources: 1. Indian Labour Year Book (various issues), Trade Unions, 2008, Labour Bureau, Shimla.

2. *http://labourbureau.nic.in/Trade_Unions_In_India_2010.pdf*, accessed 11 August 2013.

Table 8.2

Proportion of Registered Trade Unions Submitting Returns (Response Rate), 1974-2008

Period	*Total Number of Estimated Registered Trade Unions*	*Total Number of Trade Unions Submitting Returns*	*Response Rate (%)*
(1)	(2)	(3)	(4)
1974-1980	221,544	62,085	28.02
1984-1990	339,309	64,010	18.86
1991-93	221,871	30,666	13.82
1995-98	239,592	31,679	13.22
1999-2004	415,093	42,248	10.18
2005-2008	347,330	33,905	9.76
1991-2008	1223,886	138,498	11.32

Note: Trade unions include both workers' and employers' organizations.
Source: Indian Labour Year Book (various issues), Trade Unions, 2008, Labour Bureau, Shimla.

Table 8.3

Work Stoppages, Strikes and Lockouts in India, 1991-2006 (WI and WDL) (in 000')

Year	*Work Stoppages*			*Strikes*			*Lockouts*		
	Number	*WI*	*WDL*	*Number*	*WI*	*WDL*	*Number*	*WI*	*WDL*
(1)	(2)	(3)	(4)	(5)	(6)	(7)	(8)	(9)	(10)
1991	1,810	1,342	26,428	1,278	872	12,428	532	470	14,000
1992	1,714	1,252	31,259	1,011	767	15,132	703	485	16,127
1993	1,393	954	20,301	914	672	5,615	479	282	14,686
1994	1,201	846	20,938	808	626	6,606	393	220	14,332
1995	1,066	990	16,290	732	683	5,720	334	307	10,570
1996	1,166	939	20,285	763	609	7,818	403	331	12,467
1997	1,305	981	16,971	793	637	6,295	512	344	10,676
1998	1,097	1,289	22,062	665	801	9,349	432	488	12,713
1999	927	1,311	26,787	540	1,099	10,625	387	211	16,162
2000	771	1,418	28,763	426	1,044	11,959	345	374	16,804
2001	674	688	23,767	372	489	5,563	302	199	18,204
2002	579	1,079	26,586	295	900	9,665	284	179	16,921
2003	552	1,816	30,256	255	1,011	3,206	297	805	27,050
2004	477	2,072	23,866	236	1,903	4,829	241	169	19,038
2005	456	2,914	29,665	227	2,723	10,801	229	191	18,864
2006	430	1,810	20,324	243	1,712	5,318	187	98	15,006
2007	389	725	27,167	210	606	15,056	179	118	12,111
2008	421	1,579	17,434	240	1,514	6,955	181	66	10,479
2009	351	1,626	17,434	205	1,544	4,247	185	82	1,626
2010	371	1074	23,131	199	990-	13,151	172	85	9,980

Note: WI: Workers involved; WDL: Work days lost.
Source: *Indian Labour Year Book* and *Indian Labour Statistics*, Labour Bureau, Shimla (various issues).

Table 8.4

Work Stoppage Proneness of Selected States in India, 1997-99 and 2005-2007

States	1997-99		2005-2007	
	WDL/N	Rank	WDL/N	Rank
(1)	(2)	(3)	(4)	(5)
Andhra Pradesh	1408	2	608	4
Bihar	237	12	124	11
Chhattisgarh	-	-	40	17
Gujarat	495	7	102	13
Haryana	832	5	480	5
Himachal Pradesh	-	-	53	16
Karnataka	323	9	151	8
Kerala	996	4	1172	2
Madhya Pradesh	138	13	63	15
Maharashtra	283	11	173	7
Odisha	95	14	124	10
Punjab	345	8	77	14
Rajasthan	793	6	1166	3
Tamil Nadu	1010	3	370	6
Uttar Pradesh	317	10	104	12
Uttarakhand	-	-	139	9
West Bengal	3878	1	7922	1
All India	780	-	946	-

Note: The average work days lost (WDL/N) for 1997-99 for each state was standardized by employment in the organized sector for 1998-99 for the respective states and the same for 2005-07 by the employment figure for 2002.

Source: Directorate General of Employment and Training (DGE&T), Ministry of Labour and Employment, Government of India.

Table 8.5

Factory Inspections in Selected States, 2006-2009

(in number)

States/UTs	*2006*		*2007*		*2008*		*2009*	
	Registered	*Inspected*	*Registered*	*Inspected*	*Registered*	*Inspected*	*Registered*	*Inspected*
	(1)	*(2)*	*(3)*	*(4)*	*(5)*	*(6)*	*(7)*	*(8)*
Andhra Pradesh	39,563	7,527	40,766	7,211	30,054	6,356	43,175	4,975
Assam	3,280	665	3,490	483	1,946	776	3,946	655
Bihar	-	-	6,443	2,893	6,668	2,047	7,000	2,411
Gujarat	30,604	14,769	--	--	--	--	--	--
Haryana	9,642	2,453	9,959	2,552	9,978	1,550	10,378	1,482
Jharkhand	10,399	5,593	10,641	3,336	6,496	1,539	--	--
Karnataka	11,049	-	11,592	--	11,782	--	--	--
Kerala	18,179	13,945	--	--	--	--	--	--
Madhya Pradesh	12,690	2,554	13,147	2,721	9,061	2,721	--	--
Maharashtra	36,271	--	36,221	--	--	--	40,969	0
Meghalaya	112	35	115	50	125	16	130	16
Odisha	3,047	2,335	3,110	2,365	2,345	2,186	3,192	1,926
Punjab	16,258	2,564	16,726	--	17,007	2,200	17,618	680
Rajasthan	10,552	6,443	10,837	--	11,253	5,993	11,600	5,619
Tamil Nadu	38,976	32,498	--	--	--	--	--	--
Tripura	1,555	1,055	1,477	1,013	1,547	1,026	1,626	1,313
Uttar Pradesh	--	--	--	--	13,129	--	--	--
Uttarakhand	--	--	--	--	1,486	190	2,410	190
West Bengal	--	--	14,044	--	14,209	--	--	--
India	243,309	92,261	179,787	22,845	137,808	26,732	152,747	19,585

Note: -- data not available.

Source: Statistics of Factories, various years, Labour Bureau, Government of India.

Table 8.6

Industrial Injuries and Deaths in Factories, Mines, and Ports and Docks, 1991-2009

Year	*Number of Fatal Injuries per 1000 Workers Employed in Factories (Incidence Rate)*	*Death Rate per 1000 Persons Employed in Mines*	*Serious Injury Rate per 1000 Persons Employed in Mines*
(1)	(2)	(3)	(4)
1991	0.18	0.31	1.49
1992	0.19	0.33	1.52
1993	0.18	0.31	1.58
1994	0.20	0.44	1.39
1995	0.20	0.40	1.48
1996	0.20	0.31	1.40
1997	0.19	0.34	1.44
1998	0.16	0.31	1.21
1999	0.06	0.32	1.37
2000	0.22	0.31	1.41
2001	0.19	0.37	1.55
2002	0.16	0.28	1.50
2003	0.11	0.31	1.35
2004	0.08	0.29	2.10
2005	0.09	0.30	2.24
2006	0.13	0.38	1.80
2007	0.10	0.26	1.92
2008	0.06	0.31	1.51
2009	0.10	0.24	1.37

Source: Indian Labour Statistics (various issues), Labour Bureau, Government of India.

9. POVERTY

Table 9.1

Percentage of Persons below Poverty Line in Major States, 2011-12

State	*Percentage of Persons below Poverty Line*		
	Rural	*Urban*	*Total*
(1)	(2)	(3)	(4)
Andhra Pradesh	11.0	5.8	9.2
Assam	33.9	20.5	32.0
Bihar	34.1	31.2	33.7
Chhattisgarh	44.6	24.8	39.9
Delhi	12.9	9.8	9.9
Gujarat	21.5	10.1	16.6
Haryana	11.6	10.3	11.2
Himachal Pradesh	8.5	4.3	8.1
Jammu & Kashmir	11.5	7.2	10.4
Jharkhand	40.8	24.8	37.0
Karnataka	24.5	15.3	20.9
Kerala	9.1	5.0	7.1
Madhya Pradesh	35.7	21.0	31.7
Maharashtra	24.2	9.1	17.4
Odisha	35.7	17.3	32.6
Punjab	7.7	9.2	8.3
Rajasthan	16.1	10.7	14.7
Tamil Nadu	15.8	6.5	11.3
Uttar Pradesh	30.4	26.1	29.4
Uttarakhand	11.6	10.5	11.3
West Bengal	22.5	14.7	20.0
All India	25.7	13.7	21.92

Source: Planning Commission, Government of India, 2013.

Table 9.2

Poverty in Major States Using US$ Two PPP Value, 2011-12

	Rural	*Urban*	*Total*
(1)	(2)	(3)	(4)
Andhra Pradesh	46.4	18.2	37.1
Assam	81.0	33.9	76.1
Bihar	85.4	58.0	82.7
Chhattisgarh	87.4	53.5	80.2
Delhi	21.7	13.7	14.4
Goa	16.3	9.7	12.9
Gujarat	57.5	17.1	41.1
Haryana	26.6	13.6	22.6
Himachal Pradesh	39.8	11.4	36.7
Jammu & Kashmir	43.9	24.4	39.5
Jharkhand	89.1	42.7	79.5
Karnataka	62.5	24.2	48.6
Kerala	27.7	18.9	25.4
Madhya Pradesh	80.5	47.3	72.0
Maharashtra	55.2	15.5	37.1
Orissa	88.1	45.7	81.7
Punjab	22.6	15.0	19.9
Rajasthan	51.0	24.7	44.8
Tamil Nadu	49.7	22.0	37.3
Uttar Pradesh	80.6	52.2	74.5
Uttarakhand	52.4	26.1	45.7
West Bengal	73.0	31.4	61.9
India	66.8	28.0	55.7

Notes: (i) Purchasing power parity conversion factor is the number of units of a country's currency required to buy the same amount of goods and services in the domestic market as a US dollar would buy in the United States. The ratio of PPP conversion factor to market exchange rate is the result obtained by dividing the PPP conversion factor by the market exchange rate. The ratio also referred to as the national price level, makes it possible to compare the cost of the bundle of goods that make up Gross Domestic Product (GDP) across countries. It tells how many dollars are needed to buy a dollar's worth of goods in the country as compared to the United States. In case of India, this ratio is 0.4 for 2005 to 2013. Using this ratio, 1 dollar PPP value turned out to be
₹ 16 (40*0.4) and ₹ 22 (55*0.4) for the year 2004-05 and 2011-12 respectively. For calculating poverty at US$ 2 PPP from Monthly Per Capita Consumption Expenditure (MPCE) available at unit records of National Sample Surveys, hence monthly PPP dollar value of ₹ 1320 for 2011-12 and ₹ 960 for 2004-05 is used.

(ii) Data from World Bank, International Comparison Program Database, World Development Indicators and Consumer Expenditure Survey, NSS, 2011-12 round have been used for calculation..

Table 9.3

Proportion of Poor across Household Status of Employment, 1993-94/2011-12

Sector	*Household Employment Status*	1993-94	2004-05	2011-12	2011-12*
(1)	(2)	(3)	(4)	(5)	(6)
Rural	Self-employed in non-agriculture	44.0	36.3	19.3	61.5
	Self-employed in agriculture	41.8	33.2	16.8	65.5
	Regular workers	-	-	7.6	39.3
	Casual labour in agriculture	70.3	63.1	31.6	82.1
	Casual labour in non-agriculture	57.0	48.6	27.8	75.7
	Others	26.5	21.8	17.4#	52.9
Urban	Self-employed	34.2	27.5	15.3	31.6
	Regular workers	20.6	15.3	7.4	16.0
	Casual	64.5	58.8	33.0	57.8
	Others	24.1	15.9	8.4	16.4

Notes: # combines regular and others.
*using PPP US$2 and other estimates are as per Tendulkar Poverty Line.

Source: Calculated from *Consumer Expenditure Survey*, various NSS quinquennial rounds. For $2 PPP calculation, same criteria as in Table 9.2.